Jessie Ball duPont

Jessie Ball duPont

Richard Greening Hewlett

University Press of Florida
Gainesville · Tallahassee · Tampa · Boca Raton
Pensacola · Orlando · Miami · Jacksonville

Unless otherwise noted, all illustrations reproduced courtesy of the Jessie Ball duPont Collection at Washington and Lee University, Lexington, Virginia.

University Press of Florida is the scholarly publishing agency for the State University System of Florida, comprised of Florida A & M University, Florida Atlantic University, Florida International University, Florida State University, University of Central Florida, University of Florida, University of North Florida, University of South Florida, University of West Florida.

University Press of Florida, 15 Northwest 15th Street, Gainesville, FL 32611

Library of Congress Cataloging in Publication Data may be found on the last printed page of the book.

Contents

Illustrations

Acknowledgments

I am grateful to the trustees of the Jessie Ball duPont Religious, Charitable, and Educational Fund, not only for giving me the opportunity to write this book but also for their personal interest and enthusiastic support through months of research and writing. I owe special thanks to George D. Penick, Jr., former executive director of the fund, who first called me and who made all the facilities and his excellent staff available to me. Both Jo Ann P. Bennett, executive secretary of the fund, and Helene Evans promptly responded to dozens of requests for guidance and information about Mrs. duPont's personal files. Ronald V. Gallo, now executive director of the fund, acquainted me with current issues in foundation management.

Perhaps the person most critical to the success of this project was Hazel O. Williams, who served for more than twenty years as Mrs. duPont's personal secretary and then as secretary to the executors of her estate and executive secretary and trustee of the fund. Sometimes persons in her position feel the need to protect the untarnished image of the "boss"; Hazel Williams, to the contrary, took a personal interest in seeing that I had an unvarnished image of Mrs. duPont, and she was always ready to provide information on points large and small that were recorded only in her memory.

She was especially helpful in tracking down the few relatives and close friends of Mrs. duPont who were still living. In every case the persons I interviewed made our discussions enjoyable as well as profitable. I am most grateful to all of the interviewees, whose names appear in the essay on sources.

The enormous research effort required by the magnitude of Mrs. duPont's personal files and the broad range of related subjects could not have been completed on schedule without the help of research historians at History Associates, Incorporated. Margaret C. Rung, now a doctoral candidate in history at the Johns Hopkins University, prepared the inventory of Mrs. duPont's files in Jacksonville and, under my direction, made the primary selection of documents for the manuscript. She also assisted me in identifying topics for further study, prepared several annotated literature surveys, and read several drafts for interpretation and accuracy. Susan Burnam, Eileen Pingitore, and Ann Deines of History Associates performed a variety of tasks such as searching record groups at the National Archives, chasing down scores of secondary sources at the Library of Congress, and checking source notes.

Brian Hart at the Texas Women's University in Denton, Texas, and Mary Hoogterp at the University of California, San Diego, applied their expert knowledge of local history in providing background for sections in chapter 1 on Jessie Ball's early life.

Jacob C. Belin, chairman of the board and chief executive officer of the St. Joe Paper Company, graciously gave me access to the files of Edward Ball in company records. Thomas P. Ferry, administrator of the Alfred I. duPont Institute in Wilmington, arranged my visits to Nemours. Ruth C. Linton, then curator at the mansion house, assisted me with research in her files as did Virginia Habich in the records of the Institute. I thank them all for their assistance.

Our most memorable experience was our visit on a blustery winter day in March 1987 to Ball's Neck, where Jessie Ball was born and spent much of her childhood. Despite the weather, her cousin Robert Carter Ball showed us the local haunts and gave us an insight into life in the Northern Neck that we could never have acquired in any other way. I am grateful to him for his hospitality and expert knowledge.

For background on Florida history I am indebted to Mary Ann Cleveland in the Florida Room of the Florida State Library in Tallahassee; David Coles, archivist at the Florida State Archives; and Burton Altman at the Mildred and Claude Pepper Library at Florida State University. Elizabeth Alexander, director of the Florida Historical Collections at the University of Florida in Gainesville, led me to several valuable manuscript collections and secondary sources on Florida history.

Charles T. Akre, who helped write Mrs. duPont's will and who served as co-counsel of the estate, graciously consented to review and sharpen my account of the handling of Mrs. duPont's affairs after her death. John Edie, general counsel of the Council on Foundations, read sections on the

Tax Reform Act of 1969 for technical accuracy. Their suggestions greatly improved the accuracy of those sections.

Finally I wish to thank Philip L. Cantelon, Ruth Dudgeon, and Dian O. Belanger, my colleagues and senior historians at History Associates, who read the entire manuscript and offered valuable comments and suggestions. To them, as to all the others mentioned above, I owe a great debt of gratitude. The remaining errors and shortcomings in this book are solely my responsibility.

Preface

*B*orn into one of the oldest families in tidewater Virginia in 1884, Jessie Ball as a child experienced the genteel but impoverished life-style shared by many families that struggled to survive in the South in the aftermath of the Civil War. Her parents provided her with enough education to qualify for a teaching certificate, and about 1902 she began a successful teaching career, first in her native Virginia and later in public elementary schools in San Diego, California. Even in these early years she exhibited a determination to make her mark as a woman in pursuits usually reserved in her generation for men.

There was also a romantic side to the attractive Miss Jessie Ball. As a teenager she met Alfred I. duPont, the man who later would become the center of her life. Twenty years her elder and married, Alfred brought the young country girl visions of a life she could hardly imagine. What for Jessie began as a secret infatuation blossomed almost twenty years later, after the death of Alfred's second wife, into passionate love and marriage in 1921.

The marriage catapulted Jessie overnight from the life of a middle-class schoolteacher into a world of elegance and luxury that few Americans other than her husband could have offered. She easily assumed her new role and gave her husband the love, support, and inspiration he needed to escape from the past and to plan for the future. The sixteen years of their marriage were an idyllic romance.

The rest of her life centered around the duPont estates in Delaware and Florida. In Florida she, Alfred, and her brother Edward Ball invested millions in timberland, real estate, banks, and commercial property. By the time of Alfred's death in 1935, they had erected a financial empire that virtually dominated the economy of the state.

As Alfred grew more feeble and deaf in his last years, Jessie became his constant companion and business advisor. After his death, she assumed executive positions in the banking business, paper company, and investment company that were part of the duPont empire in Florida. With Edward in charge of day-to-day operations, brother and sister over the next three decades continued by wise investment and skillful financial management to multiply the assets of the estate that Alfred had entrusted to them.

During these same years Mrs. duPont amassed her own fortune with assets that her husband had given her in the early years of their marriage and on the income from his estate. By the time of her death in 1970, Mrs. duPont's own estate totaled almost $50 million.

Money was important to Mrs. duPont, but the focus of her later life was philanthropy. After Alfred's death she carried out his wishes to establish a hospital for crippled children and to support his personal charities. She also devoted her time and energy to her own charitable and philanthropic activities. Much of it was conventional charity: annuities to relatives and close friends and hundreds of small cash gifts to the needy. But she also gave scores of college scholarships each year to students from low-income families, large endowments to private universities, and hundreds of grants to hospitals, community centers, churches, and historic preservation projects. From the time of her marriage in 1921 until her death in 1970, Mrs. duPont gave more than $100 million to charitable, religious, and educational institutions, mostly in the southeastern United States. Her will provided for a perpetual trust, the Jessie Ball duPont Religious, Charitable and Educational Fund, to carry on her philanthropic work after her death.

Officials of the fund in Jacksonville, Florida, first approached me in May 1986 about writing this book. A new executive director and a new generation of trustees had just taken over the administration of the fund. None of them had known Mrs. duPont personally, and they had only a general understanding of how she came to devise the specific instructions incorporated in her will for the guidance of her trustees. The primary purpose of the new trustees in commissioning a biography, then, was a practical one: they wanted to know and understand Mrs. duPont and why she organized her philanthropic activities in the way that she did. They also expected the biography to serve an educational purpose, both for institutions receiving grants from the fund and for the general public. The trustees were not, however, looking for a dry statistical analysis of Mrs.

duPont's philanthropies; rather they wanted a full-scale portrait that would reveal her character and personality.

Neither the executive director nor the trustees had any fixed notions about the specific content of the book or about any predetermined theme or emphasis. They wanted an honest, straightforward study that would describe Mrs. duPont's private and professional life. I was given full access to all of the documents in the collection, and I was free to determine the character, approach, and emphasis of the book.

Mrs. duPont's personal papers consist of 325 linear feet of documents, all quite reasonably organized and including carbons of virtually every one of the thousands of letters she dictated each year from 1927 until about 1965. Her papers reveal not only details of her personal life but also her involvement in many issues of her day, including public education, the role of independent colleges, professional opportunities for women, democratic ideals and individualism, racial integration, and the application of religious and moral principles to the social and economic problems that she feared were undermining Western civilization.

This extraordinary documentary collection made it possible to determine not only the patterns of Mrs. duPont's charitable giving but also the motivations that influenced her actions. In this respect this book can serve as a detailed case study that will be of interest to scholars in the newly emerging field of the history of philanthropy.

A similar opportunity was available in the field of women's history. Although historians have been producing a burgeoning literature in this area, most of this work has focused on women who lived in the Northeast in the nineteenth century or earlier. The papers made it possible to describe in some detail the household and domestic life-style of a wealthy southern woman in the middle years of the twentieth century.

No issue caused Mrs. duPont more anxiety than did the federal government's efforts to impose racial integration in public schools and colleges. As a Virginia conservative she espoused the separate but equal principle that dominated educational policy in the South until the U.S. Supreme Court's landmark decision in *Brown* v. *Board of Education* in 1954. How she addressed the civil rights issue and how she joined forces with other like-minded southern leaders, especially in the Episcopal church, in opposing school integration is a major theme in this book.

It is perhaps presumptuous, if not foolhardy, for a Yankee male whose great-grandfather was a sergeant in the Union army during the Civil War to write the biography of a southern lady who inherited and lived by the precepts as well as the prejudices of the Old South. It is possible that my background and experience have made it difficult at times for me to comprehend and describe what it meant to be a southerner, a woman, and a female professional in the first half of the twentieth century. At least my credentials should relieve readers of the suspicion that I have tried to write an apology for Mrs. duPont's convictions and actions. I hope at the same time that I have recorded her life with charity and understanding. Although some of her persuasions, especially on racial segregation, seem strangely archaic and unacceptable today, she remains a distinctive and significant figure in the history of the South.

A Picturesque Romance

*T*he wedding made newspaper headlines on January 22, 1921. "Million-aire Dupont Weds in L. A.," announced one West Coast newspaper. "Alfred I. Dupont, aged 56, powder magnate of Wilmington, Del., and reputed to be worth $100,000,000, and Miss Jessie Dew Ball, aged 36, a beautiful society woman of Hollywood, were married in Los Angeles today." The Reverend Baker P. Lee performed the ceremony in his home with only a few close friends and members of the family attending. The paper noted that the bride was a member of "one of the most prominent families in Virginia. Her father was the late Capt. Thomas Ball, a relative of Col. William Ball, grandfather of George Washington." The bride had lived in Los Angeles only a short time. It was the third marriage for the bridegroom, who, the press reported, had lost one wife by death and had divorced the other. It was, the *Los Angeles Examiner* observed, "a picturesque romance of national interest."[1]

The San Diego *Union* came nearer the truth the next day when it reported that Miss Ball "was one of the most popular school teachers in San Diego." Having moved to San Diego with her family twelve years earlier, Miss Ball and her sister, Isabel, had obtained teaching positions, and for some years Jessie had been vice-principal of the Washington Elementary School. After the death of her father in 1917, the paper reported, Jessie had moved into the U. S. Grant Hotel in San Diego, where she had lived until "last fall, when she became engaged to Mr. DuPont."[2]

That Jessie and her sister were schoolteachers suggested that the Ball family, if socially prominent in Virginia, was hardly wealthy in California. That circumstance gave the story a Cinderella quality that did not fit the overblown, snobbish reports in the Los Angeles press, which found added spice in the revelation that the Reverend Mr. Lee had performed the marriage after the Episcopal bishop of Los Angeles had declined to marry the couple because Mr. duPont's divorce had not been in accordance with canon law. The propriety of Mr. Lee's action had become a heated subject of debate among the clergy at the annual convention of the diocese the following week.[3]

None of these stories, including the erroneous one that duPont was going to marry Hollywood star Pauline Frederick, could begin to capture the extraordinary nature of the "picturesque romance."[4] It was true that Jessie was the descendant of one of the oldest families in Virginia. Like many of those who came to the New World in the seventeenth century, the Balls had settled on the shores of Chesapeake Bay, on the long peninsula called the Northern Neck between the Potomac and the Rappahannock. And if genealogists counted back seven generations, they would find in a collateral line Mary Ball, the mother of George Washington.[5]

Over the generations since 1650 some Balls had acquired large plantations and lived in mansions, but the extent of these holdings ebbed and flowed with the tides of fortune through the several lines of the Ball clan. One property in the Ball family since 1675 was Bayview plantation fronting on Chesapeake Bay on a spit of land called Ball's Neck between Dividing Creek and Mill Creek, south of the Great Wicomico River. There Jessie's father, Thomas, had been born in 1836, had grown up, gone to William and Mary College, and studied law. When the Civil War broke out, young Thomas had no trouble obtaining a lieutenant's commission in the Army of Northern Virginia. Promoted to the rank of captain when he raised his own company, Ball fought in more than a dozen battles during the war, was wounded, taken prisoner, and spent eight months in a military prison at Point Lookout before he was exchanged shortly before the end of hostilities.[6]

Like many dedicated officers of the Confederate army, Captain Ball was in poor health and disillusioned when he returned to the family plantation in 1865. His father had died in 1849, but his mother still lived at Bayview. With no taste for farming, Ball soon gave up the idea of rebuilding the run-down plantation and decided to seek his fortune on the Texas frontier. In 1869 he put out his shingle in the dusty town of Weatherford, just west of Fort Worth. Three years later he moved north to Jacksboro, where he first made his mark as a court-appointed attorney for two Indians charged with murder in connection with a raid on a wagon train in North Texas. Although Ball lost the case, a Dallas paper reported that "his speeches were at some points most eloquent and displayed not only a thorough knowledge of the Indian character" but also skill as a lawyer.[7] One historian has observed that the affair was of national interest because it established a legal precedent for prosecuting Indians for raids on the western frontier.[8]

Ball seemed to prosper on his newfound reputation. Within a few years he had acquired a section of land, several town lots, some jewelry, and "a gold-headed cane."[9] A conservative Democrat, he rode the wave of the Redeemers in 1876 and was elected for one term as state senator, an office that won him political and legal connections throughout Texas. Two years later he married Lalla Gresham, a sister of Walter Gresham, a prominent Galveston lawyer.[10]

The Greshams, like the Balls, were an old Virginia family. Lalla's father, Edward Gresham, a farmer and onetime Baptist minister, was educated at William and Mary. His Woodlawn plantation of two thousand acres of farmland and a large forest in King and Queen County south of the Rappahannock had a complement of a hundred slaves before the war. Years later Lalla wrote down her reminiscences of plantation life during the war. It was a romantic, nostalgic tale of homespun dresses, an adored Mammy, a loving family, and faithful slaves. "When their masters and sons were away in defense of home and firesides, these dear old colored people stayed and took care of the family, worked the plantation and saw that they needed nothing that their love and care could provide," Lalla wrote. "I believe any one of these slaves would have laid down his life for his master or any member of his master's family."[11]

By the end of the 1870s the golden days of Woodlawn were long past. Lalla's father had died, and her mother had moved in with her married daughter. With the family home gone, Lalla, then twenty-two, went to Texas, where her brothers were carving out a new life on the frontier. There she met the forty-two-year-old Thomas Ball and married him.[12]

Ball took his young bride to live in Jacksboro and there their first child, also named Thomas, was born in 1879. With something of a statewide reputation, Ball was able to extend his law practice beyond Jacks County. When Oran M. Roberts, an elderly ex-Confederate colonel, was elected governor in 1878, Ball was appointed assistant attorney general of the state, a position that kept him on the road for weeks at a time. Life was hard on the notoriously low salaries paid to state officials. After leaving home once again in September 1880, Ball wrote to Lalla: "This morning was the hardest time in my life & nothing but the consideration for you & the boy ever induced me to leave you."[13]

When Governor Roberts refused to accept a third term in 1882, Ball's days in Texas were numbered. During his years of public service his law practice had withered, and he was more than ready to take his family back to Virginia. Although Ball had adapted to a new South that nurtured a growing class of professionals, his roots lay in the Old South with its longstanding traditions of gentility and honor. In fact, he had returned to Virginia in the summer of 1881 and had purchased at auction a 190-acre farm that had once belonged to his great uncle, Joseph Ball. Cressfield, as the Balls had always called it, lay just a stone's throw across a small inlet south of his father's home at Bayview, where his older brother Warner now lived.[14]

Surrounded by family and old friends, the Balls found Virginia living more congenial than life on the dusty Texas frontier. As for many Southerners whose lives had been shattered by the upheavals of the Civil War and Reconstruction, ties to ancestral lands and traditions provided some stability in a rapidly changing, even chaotic world. Southern planters were steeped in the values assigned to place, tradition, hierarchy, and family. They adopted "a romanticism of fixed institutions, timelessness, and changelessness" and fostered "a culture of personal relationships, other-directedness, [and] community validation." Although waning, a code of honor still pervaded their society. Honor reinforced their loyalty to family, their adherence to a hierarchy of leaders and subordinates, and their belief that people should be evaluated on the basis of such biological qualities as race, gender, age, and bloodlines. But the Balls, particularly their children, also represented a growing class-consciousness that was replacing honor as the cultural code. This awareness, based on inextricable links between wealth, occupation, and social standing, would eventually become especially important to one of the Ball children.[15]

Captain Ball settled down to a local law practice, and seven children followed young Thomas in quick succession before the end of the decade. Jessie Dew Ball, the third child, was born January 20, 1884, at Cressfield. At that time her older sister, Isabel, was just two years old. Elsie was

Thomas Ball (1836–1917), Jessie Ball's father, was a promising Virginia lawyer before the Civil War.

born two years later, and Edward, the youngest, in 1888. Three children died in infancy. The three girls, close together in age, shared a common childhood. With their two cousins, Rebecca and Floride Harding, and Placidia Hudnall, who lived nearby, the Ball sisters enjoyed a close and warm relationship that was to endure the separations and vicissitudes of a lifetime. It was easy to run down the road to the head of the creek and over to Bayview to sample Grandmother Ball's good cooking or to spend the night with Cousin Minnie Edwards. It was not much farther to the Hardings' or the Hudnalls' for an occasional card game.[16]

Ball's Neck was almost as isolated from the rest of the state and nation in the 1880s as it had been in the seventeenth century. The broad rivers to the north and south made the Northern Neck a veritable island, except for the dirt roads that stretched almost fifty miles to the railroad and the turnpike from Fredericksburg to Washington. The best transportation was still by the steamboats that plied Chesapeake Bay from Baltimore to Norfolk, with stops at villages on the deep-water rivers and creeks along the Virginia and Maryland shores. Jessie recalled being snowbound for ten days at Cressfield when she was a girl and finally riding bareback on a horse to reach neighboring farms.[17] Her world enclosed, Jessie knew little of the urban, industrialized nation of the late nineteenth century. Not until she left Virginia would she appreciate the relative homogeneity and tight community focus of the rural South or see how rapidly values and behavior were changing in a new social order.

For the Ball children the horizons of daily life were a few miles from home. They went to the two-room Shiloh schoolhouse, which was almost in sight of Cressfield on a dirt road that stretched north and south along the heads of the inlets from the bay. To the south the road curved eastward on a narrow finger of land to Harding's Landing, where steamboats could navigate the narrow waters of Dividing Creek. Clearly visible across the creek was Ditchley, built by Kendall Lee in the middle of the eighteenth century and acquired by another branch of the Ball family in 1790. To the north the road passed the old mansions at Cloverdale and Gascony and wound on to the Hudnalls' Magnolia on a bluff overlooking Mill Creek.[18]

Religion often proved an integrating force in the rural southern community of that time. Few immigrants settled in the South, leaving the region overwhelmingly Protestant, though fragmented by denominations. Denominations reflected the social cleavages ingrained in

Shiloh school, Ball's Neck, Virginia, as it looks today. Jessie and her siblings attended this school a short distance from their home at Cressfield.

communities as blacks and whites worshipped separately. Even on the isolated Northern Neck, churches dotted the landscape.

One of Jessie's earliest recollections was attending Sunday school at the Morattico Baptist Church, on the main road north from Kilmarnock, where her mother was a member. The teachers knew their Bible and gave the young girl a foundation in the Scriptures on which she relied for the rest of her life. Jessie's mother was the churchgoer in the family. Her father, although a religious man in his outlook on life, had little use for "man-made creeds" and most preachers. As did many Southerners schooled in antebellum social mores, Ball's sense of identity was steeped less in religion than in the intricate web built by a code of honor. He still adhered to once-predominant notions of honor rooted more in stoicism than in Christianity. He especially deplored the camp meetings, which he said went on all summer as they did in other parts of the South at that time. To Ball's mind they were nothing but "money-getting gather-ings." "The working of salvation into avarice seems a perversion of the teachings of Christ, but it may be right," he concluded. Unlike many of their contemporaries, the Balls, including Lalla, did not seem to display any interest in the evangelical revivals overtaking the region. It is likely that the first Balls who came to America were Cavaliers, an assumption supported by the fact that some of the Balls were Roman Catholics. Many Virginia Balls in the eighteenth century had been prominent Anglicans, but Captain Ball had no ties to either the Roman Catholic or the Episcopal church.[19]

The idyllic, cozy world of little Jessie Ball was not without its troubles. By 1891 Virginia and the South were already feeling the pangs of economic depression that would hit the rest of the nation two years later. Virginia banks refused to release deposits unless customers gave sixty days' notice, and the last solvent railroad on the South Atlantic seaboard was about to fail in Virginia.[20]

For Thomas Ball the depression spelled disaster. With five children under the age of twelve, he struggled with a law practice that did not support his family. In desperation he decided to seek a federal position. His chances as a Democrat were not promising under Benjamin Harrison's Republican administration, but he could call on Texas's two Democratic senators for endorsements. In May 1892 he wrote the assistant attorney general in Washington to suggest that, given his Texas experience, he could save the government "a vast sum of money" if he were retained to investigate claims filed against the government for Indian depredations on the frontier.[21]

Within two weeks Ball was appointed a U.S. Special Attorney and set out by train for Texas with his wife and children. For Jessie, a girl of eight, it was an extraordinary adventure to leave the familiar surround-ings of the Northern Neck, to witness the magnificent scenery as the train rolled around Lookout Mountain in Tennessee, and to find a warm welcome with her Gresham relatives in Galveston. While Tom Ball moved about the state taking depositions from claimants, Lalla set up housekeeping in Austin and put the children in school.[22]

Hard times were not over. Ball suffered a heart ailment during the fall of 1892, forcing him to return with the family to Baltimore for treatment and then to Cressfield for convalescence. In the course of events Jessie picked up one semester of schooling in Austin and another in Baltimore. In January 1893 Captain Ball was on the road again, this time to California, leaving his family in Virginia. In July he was summoned home from San Francisco when the house at Cressfield burned to the ground. After moving the family into a smaller house on adjacent property, Ball set off in the fall of 1893 for Texas.[23]

Thomas Ball's fortunes continued to decline with the national economy. Federal funds for investigating depredation claims began to run low in 1894, and he was forced to accept a reduced salary of seven dollars per day plus expenses. Threatened with termination early in 1895, Ball offered to lobby the Congress for funds personally. Not only was his proposal rejected by the new Grover Cleveland administration but he was also summarily dismissed. To make matters worse, Ball pressed for the reasons behind his dismissal and was informed that the Justice Department did not think he had been sufficiently diligent "in searching for testimony for the government after testimony for the claimants had been taken."[24]

This curt dismissal seems to have hurt Ball psychologically as well as financially. He was so disillusioned by his treatment at the hands of the Cleveland administration that he joined the Republican party, much to the consternation of his family. His self-confidence shaken and his health failing, Ball no longer looked to the future with great expectations. Back in the Northern Neck, he dabbled at his law practice but apparently did not take it seriously. He was no doubt pleased when Jessie showed an interest in his business and professional concerns. He was more than willing to accept her offer to ride about the county to pay his bills and collect his legal fees.[25] For a girl in rural Virginia at the turn of the century, Jessie showed an extraordinary degree of initiative.

Now in her middle teens, Jessie reveled in these tasks her father no longer cared to face. Not only could she help her father, whom she respected and adored, but she also found herself in what must have seemed the busy, fascinating world of merchants and lawyers. Jessie was beginning to draw new boundaries for herself. She began to explore the frontiers beyond domestic life, frontiers that were beginning to open for women. She found that the new culture emerging at the end of the century offered her far more than the fading Victorian notions of womanhood ever could. Despite the confines of her rural surroundings, she seemed determined to create her own definition of womanhood that would reflect her upbringing as a product of southern gentility and her awareness that women could succeed at intellectual and business activities as well as men. Her brand of feminism was an implicit acknowledgement that people could be judged on qualities other than gender.

Money was scarce in the Northern Neck, but the old families of Virginia managed to maintain some semblance of the cultural and social amenities of southern life before the war. Captain Ball, however, complained that "the awful parties every night are making paupers of the entire country and wrecking the physical system. Before the war when people were rich, one party a winter was satisfactory, two were wonderful, now 20 & more are thought nothing." But Lalla discounted the good-natured grumblings of her husband and encouraged her daughters to join the social whirl. Last year's party dresses were sold to provide some funds for new fashions. She urged the girls to keep up with their music lessons and to learn to play euchre, a fashionable card game.[26]

Decades later Jessie recalled going to her first dance, at Cloverdale. She was just thirteen, the youngest girl at the party, and it was a thrill she never forgot. Lalla gloried in her daughters' popularity and saw to it that the meager family resources provided fashionable frocks ahead of other expenditures. Jessie remembered these days as a continuing run of parties and dances at West End, Paradise, Kilmarnock, and Lancaster Court House. At Christmas she and her sisters spent weeks preparing for the stately Holly Ball, which included a grand march and the coronation of the holly queen. The annual event had been started by Jessie's mother, whom Jessie later called "one of the best sports and one of the most Bohemian natures I have ever known."[27]

The social whirl that all three Ball sisters enjoyed was evidence that they were attractive to young men. Jessie, now approaching maturity, was of medium height, about five feet four inches, but her excellent posture made her seem taller. Slender and agile, she could easily perform the newest dance steps, and her light brown hair, fair complexion, and deep-set gray eyes probably bewitched more than a few of her partners at parties around the county.

For the Ball and Harding girls in their teens at the turn of the century, romance and fantasy filled the air, especially when the larger world that lay beyond the shores of Ball's Neck intruded upon their lives. The young recruits marching off to fight the Spanish in 1898 sparked images of local boys fighting for honor and glory in strange tropical lands. For the girls the dances and parties provided relationships with men, new opportunities for friendship besides the bonds among women traditional in the previous century. Jessie, who seemed to prefer the company of men, took advantage of this new heterosocial structure.[28]

The Ball family, probably at Hurstville, Ball's Neck, Virginia, about 1900. *Left to right:* Thomas, Isabel, Jessie, Cousin Warner Ball, Lalla Gresham Ball, Elsie, Captain Thomas Ball, Edward.

The following autumn another intrusion stirred the lives of the Balls and the Hardings. Three men in a hunting party arrived by steamboat at Harding's Landing and began looking for lodgings. Fannie Ball Harding, the widow of a Confederate veteran with five children to support, was more than happy to put them up. Hunters were nothing unusual at Ball's Neck, but there was something special about this group. Mrs. Harding and her family soon learned that their guests were Alfred Irénée duPont, his brother Maurice, and Frank Mathewson, a friend and one of Alfred's employees at the DuPont Powder Company in Wilmington, Delaware.

The three men soon met the Balls, who lived only a short distance up the dirt road from the landing. Alfred was a man of striking appearance and bearing in his middle thirties. He was a member of one of America's most distinguished families and a man of great wealth, but his personality showed no signs of pomposity or conceit. Quite the contrary, he seemed completely at ease with these unpretentious, impoverished, but genteel families of Ball's Neck.

Alfred quickly warmed to Captain Ball, who could spend hours on end telling stories about the old days in Virginia, where Alfred's mother had been born. And it was not just the stories but the way that the captain told them with a flair for the colorful if exaggerated turns of phrase that delighted his daughters. But Alfred did not overlook the younger set. He had two daughters of his own, the older just three years younger than Jessie. The ten Ball and Harding cousins enjoyed his friendly banter and joking. Although twenty years older than Jessie, he had not lost his taste for adolescent humor or his enthusiasm for spirited dancing to fiddle, accordion, and banjo.[29]

By the time Alfred left the Neck for home that fall, he had cemented friendships of a kind that he did not often find in Wilmington. In the course of his stay Mrs. Harding had told him of the misfortunes of many of her neighbors. Before Christmas he sent her a check and asked her to use her judgment in distributing the money to people in need. The checks continued to arrive every Christmas for years thereafter. Alfred's visits to Ball's Neck proved to be at least annual affairs, and the two families scurried about with joyful preparations when they received short notice that Mr. duPont was about to arrive.[30]

Alfred's visits gave the Ball children a momentary glimpse of life far beyond the Northern Neck, and that in itself had some educational value. The captain and his wife, however, knew there was more to life than good connections and social graces. A sound education, even for the girls, was worth some sacrifice. Lalla Ball had supplemented their elementary education with McGuffey's readers and other books; the girls were among the few students selected for secondary courses. There was no high school in Northumberland County at that time; selected students simply took advanced courses in the same rural schoolhouses where they had received their elementary training. The Ball family's meager

Alfred Iréné duPont, about the time he first met Jessie in 1899.

resources, however, precluded a college education for the girls. Whatever funds were available would go for the elder son's education at William and Mary. Then Tom would be expected to work his own way through law school.

Virtually the only occupation open to country girls in Virginia at the turn of the century was elementary school teaching, but a teaching certificate required some further education. In most parts of the country, girls could qualify to teach by taking a county supervisor's examination or by attending a normal school. High school graduation was not required. About the time of Jessie's birth, Virginia had established the State Female Normal School (now Longwood College) in Farmville, Virginia, and had made provisions for more than a hundred scholarships each year. The superintendent of schools in each county was entitled to select three or four girls to attend the normal school. The girls had to be at least sixteen and able, as at the leading normal schools of the time, "to stand a good examination" in the six areas required by law: writing,

A party at Ball's Neck about 1904. The three women all in white are (*standing*) Elsie and (*seated, left to right*) Isabel and Jessie.

arithmetic, English grammar, reading, spelling, and geography. The state paid all tuition and fees but charged the students for board, which cost $12 per month.[31]

Somehow the Balls were able to scrape together the $24 that were needed each month to keep Isabel and Jessie at Farmville for the school year of 1900–1901. The curriculum included nothing on teaching techniques but was broadly based in the liberal arts: English, arithmetic, U.S. history, geography, drawing, and music during the first semester; with algebra and Latin replacing arithmetic and history in the second semester. Jessie and Isabel were by no means at the top of the class, but they both made a respectable showing, certainly good enough to pass comfortably.[32]

At Farmville Jessie roomed with her sister Isabel and Rebecca Harding. Years later she reminded one of her former teachers that she was a rather "fresh student." "You will remember we were in quite a bit of trouble. . . . Our main offense was that we did not know that deference was due the older girls, as we had not been in school for two years and had done nothing but dance. . . . I was one of the two younger students in the school, aged fifteen. They let me in because my Sister and I had always been classed together."[33]

In 1901 Captain Ball sent all three of his daughters to a female academy in Wytheville, Virginia, more than three hundred miles from home in the southwestern part of the state. Despite Wytheville's distance and expense, its status as a summer normal institute may have convinced the Balls of its worth. Until the mid-1880s summer normal institutes were the only source of teacher training in Virginia. The academy had a small staff of trained teachers who offered courses in English, Latin, French, music, and art. The principal of the academy was Mrs. Thomas R. Dew, whose deceased husband, a minister, had been a distant cousin of Lalla Ball.[34]

At Wytheville the girls were isolated in the mountains for the entire school year. The separation at Christmas time was especially difficult, and the parents tried to cheer their daughters with long chatty letters. The week before Christmas the captain wrote to "My Little Mice: Will these rodents remind me of you at times, because they can get away with so many little things in such an artless way, that, their little doings are at times quite attractive."[35] Soon after the new year he indulged his daughters in a bit of creative writing that revealed his love of language and his fond memories of California:

Today is cold & bright, the sun shines nice, but still it is a land of ice. The chilly winds turn the nose first red, then pale, white as the snow we trod. This makes me sigh for the land of perenial [*sic*] flowers, tho' no frozen oysters are there to cool the fevered palate, but the figs grow there & no blizard [*sic*] brings numbness to the evening walkers. It makes me think of the palms of the morning land, where the emerald dew drops shine & glitter, refracting all the tints of the sleeted groves.[36]

These playful digressions in her father's letters seemed to enchant Jessie. Like many Southern parents, Ball frequently displayed his deep ties to family. The love Jessie felt for her father continued to echo throughout her life in the importance she attached to family and in her unflagging loyalty to her siblings. Years later she wrote: "Dad was a rare combination of a brilliant mind, with the dreamer of the poet, a philosopher, an historian and an able lawyer."[37] She loved the turn of phrase that transformed mundane words into colorful images charged with sentiment, romance, and the sense of the exotic. This same kind of rhetoric would creep into her own most personal letters and into the lines she would write at moments of nocturnal solitude throughout her life.

With the completion of the years at Farmville and Wytheville, Jessie and Isabel were eligible for elementary school certificates. Under the new system of certification just established in Virginia, applicants who completed the first year of the standard normal school course were issued an elementary certificate good for five years. Teachers could obtain a professional certificate good for seven years by graduating from the normal school or by passing a written examination. The examination, which the Ball sisters may have taken, included questions on government, general history, English, American literature, geography, algebra, pedagogy, and school law.[38]

The next step was to find positions in the country schools of the Northern Neck. Salaries were low, averaging less than $27 per month at the time, but teachers were accorded respect and status in the community. Teaching was an especially attractive profession for women, who were now rapidly replacing men as teachers in elementary schools; by 1910 about 80 percent of these teachers would be women. The young women were usually welcomed as boarders in comfortable homes near their schools, an arrangement that most of them considered attractive for social as well as financial reasons. Jessie later stated that she taught in Lancaster County, which was close to home, but that probably indicated that she did not always teach at the Shiloh school, where she and her siblings had gone as children.[39]

The decision of the Ball girls to go into teaching was perfectly natural for those times. In fact, their family background was in many ways typical of young women who chose teaching careers in the nineteenth century. Profiles recently compiled on several thousand young women in New England are similar to the background of the Ball sisters. They were often the daughters of clergymen or other professionals. They lived on farms and went into teaching for economic reasons. Many came from homes of genteel poverty.[40]

In the late nineteenth century women were entering the paid work force in increasing numbers, and single women, even in the best southern families, might be expected to earn a living. The image of the antebellum lady—the gracious, devoted, delicate, submissive wife and mother— gave way to new models of womanhood. By the end of the century American women might aspire to the "vigorous femininity" fostered by the newly popular women's colleges as they would later aspire to the image of the independent flapper of the 1920s. This process echoed the emergence of what one scholar has called a "certain kind of seriousness of purpose beyond the domestic and religious spheres" with "a degree of personal aspiration" that precluded frivolity.[41]

When Jessie Ball received her teaching certificate in 1902 she was eighteen, no longer a girl but a young woman. Like other women beginning teaching careers, she was prepared to accept the burden of contributing to the family income. But she was also taking a more adult view of the men in her life, and particularly of her relationship with Alfred duPont. In earlier years she had accepted Alfred as a sort of uncle who indulged the Ball and Harding children in hilarious games such as "Button, button, who's got the button?" Now, in 1902, she saw Alfred more as a Prince Charming. Years later she recalled his visit over the Fourth of July that year, when she walked in the moonlight with him. She was wearing "a white organdie [*sic*] dress with that black galume" (probably *galloon,* an ornamental braid trim) that she and Rebecca had bought in Norfolk.[42] Quite likely she, her sisters, and the Harding girls were all infatuated with this witty, charming man of the world who

Playing cards at Ball's Neck, about 1904. *Left to right:* Rebecca Harding, Jessie, Isabel, two gentlemen, and Elsie.

showered on them so much attention. Alfred may have been oblivious to such sentiment in the girls; at least he chose to overlook it. Because his handwriting was almost undecipherable, he dictated to his secretary his occasional letters to Jessie and the other girls; the tone was always lighthearted, teasing, but carefully proper. In December 1903 he wrote to Jessie: "Did we not have a fine time the night of the dance? I'll never forgive you for preferring the orchestra to me. I always knew I danced poorly, but never had it rubbed in like that. However, my revenge will come some day."[43]

Mr. duPont's business ventures also intrigued young Jessie. More than half a century later she recalled his visit in 1903, when she, her father, and Mr. duPont stood by the well at the Ball farm as he recounted the momentous events that had taken place in the DuPont Powder Company. He explained how the elder duPonts had lost their nerve when his cousin Eugene duPont, president of the company, had died in January 1902. Unwilling to take the responsibilities of leadership themselves, the elders had decided to sell out to competitors. Alfred, although a stockholder and director, had concentrated his attention on powder production at the Hagley Yards and had taken little interest in the larger affairs of the company. Alfred almost never attended board meetings, but the decision to sell the company had shocked him into uncharacteristic action. He had refused to accept this ignominious decision and had informed the elders that he was determined to buy the company himself. Within a matter of days, Alfred had convinced his first cousins, T. Coleman duPont and Pierre S. duPont, to join him in a proposal to buy the company with $12 million in thirty-year bonds and $3.36 million in stock, which went to the old stockholders and the estate of Eugene duPont. Alfred ended up with 24,600 shares of stock worth $2.46 million. Coleman became president of the new company; Pierre, treasurer; and Alfred, vice-president and general manager for the production of powder in all the company's plants.[44]

Alfred probably did not convey to the captain and his daughter all the details of the financial transaction or of the complicated relationships within the family that gave Coleman the presidency and the largest share of the stock, but Captain Ball heard enough to warn Alfred that he had made a mistake in giving away control of the company. Jessie was obviously fascinated with this insight into the affairs of a large corporate enterprise. She was already looking far beyond the horizons of Ball's Neck, and Alfred duPont was the kind of man who could show her the way out. As she wrote many years later: "The [Harding] boys were all attractive, good looking and talented, but they lacked the force to get out from a locality and mingle with the world, thereby developing initiative and success."[45]

If the pursuit of success no longer motivated Captain Ball, he had passed on a taste for it to his children. Tom was by now a young man in his mid-twenties and apparently very much like his father at that age. He had assumed the responsibilities of the eldest son and had followed his father's footsteps to William and Mary. With money borrowed from Mr. duPont, he had worked his way through law school at Washington and Lee University and was on the lookout for business opportunities wherever he might find them. Eddie, the younger son, was a round-faced little fellow who had been badly spoiled by his parents and his older sisters. Having learned how to wheedle his own way, Eddie had dropped out of elementary school against his parents' wishes to pursue a variety of money-making activities such as flushing game for hunters, protecting his father's crab pots in Chesapeake Bay, and finding black walnut logs in the woods. Before Christmas in 1901 Captain Ball had written of his younger son's business ventures: "He has gone in[to] the Holly bus[iness], has shipped north, & has running cedar to ship today. So the little fellow is right industrious in his way."[46]

By 1904 it was apparent to Jessie, Isabel, and their brother Tom that there would be no end to the life of genteel poverty that they were enduring unless they left the Northern Neck. By teaching school and taking on odd jobs that his legal training brought him, Tom had saved enough money by spring to make the break. On April 29, he packed his bags and set off to seek his fortune in California. No doubt his father's stories of his adventures on the West Coast a decade earlier had sparked Tom's interest in the Golden State. He was not disappointed. In contrast to the stable, unchanging, deeply rooted, and backward-looking life of Ball's Neck, California was vibrant, full of activity and opportunity, with all eyes on the future. Tom soon found a job to his liking as a traveling salesman for a law book publisher. Not only did the job pay well, but it also gave the young Virginian the opportunity to travel up and down the West Coast from San Diego to Seattle. He wrote Jessie glowing letters describing his "nomadic life," his new friends in Seattle, Berkeley, and Pasadena, and the little extravagances that he was now able to afford, such as collecting souvenir spoons from the California missions. He could pay some of the family's bills and send an overcoat that could be cut down for his brother, Eddie. He added a note in pencil to one of his letters: "Don't tell Mother & Father about my collecting habits. They might think I am crazy but I am not."[47]

Tom also supplied Jessie with bits of intelligence that he had picked up about school systems in California. He knew the superintendents of schools in several cities in southern California, and he assured his sister that he could find her any number of teaching positions if she had a professional teaching certificate. Even without one, he thought she could easily pass the examination for an elementary school teacher. The opportunities were good if she should decide to come.

Jessie probably needed no further convincing that a move to California would be in her best interests, but there were reasons to hesitate. At least until Tom was well established, she would have to share the burden of supporting her family, and that she could not do without a steady income. In any case, the declining health of both her mother and her father made it impossible to think of leaving them alone in Virginia. Furthermore, she had her own social and family ties in the Northern Neck. Among her acquaintances she had developed a close relationship with Charles Hardwicke, a charming Englishman who was studying medicine at the University of Maryland in Baltimore. Like Alfred duPont, Hardwicke was a colorful man of the world, well educated and well read, and ten years older than Jessie. By 1906 their romance had become serious enough to prompt Tom to warn his sister that he found Englishmen on the whole "cold and indifferent" and not good prospects for husbands of American women.[48]

By this time Alfred duPont had drifted out of Jessie's world, except for an occasional chatty letter more about the Balls and Hardings than about his own life. He had come to the Neck in November 1904 on a hunting trip but did not see Jessie. Within a few hours of his arrival at Hardings, he had suffered a serious injury when one of his partners on the opposite side of a hedgerow fired a shot that hit Alfred in the left eye. Rushed to a hospital in Philadelphia, he lay critically ill for weeks, eventually lost the eye, and spent the rest of the year and the winter of 1905 recuperating in Florida.[49]

His recovery was certainly delayed by the final collapse of his marriage after years of turmoil and heartbreak. He had married Bessie Gardner in January 1887. The daughter of a distinguished linguist at Yale, Bessie was an attractive, sophisticated woman who had a lively interest in the arts, literature, and world affairs. The early years of their marriage, blessed by the birth of two daughters, Madeleine and Bessie, had been happy ones, but by the end of the century the relationship had begun to fall apart. Alfred was absorbed for weeks on end in engineering and production problems at the Brandywine powder mills. During the Spanish-American War he worked all hours of the day and night to meet production quotas imposed by the government. Bessie in the meantime had a gathered a coterie of her own friends, a smart set that responded to her cultural and intellectual interests but that excluded Alfred. To make matters worse, Alfred was growing deaf as the result of a boyhood swimming accident, and Bessie tended to equate Alfred's difficulties in maintaining a conversation with dullness. Joseph Wall, Alfred's biographer, has written that he was "ignored, or worse, ridiculed by his wife, embarrassed in front of guests, isolated by his own increasing deafness and by her increasingly sharp denigration."[50]

Alfred rejoiced in the reconciliations with Bessie that resulted in the birth of a son, Alfred Victor II, in 1900, and Victorine, a third daughter, in 1903, but these interludes of happiness ended when Bessie left for Europe with the children in the summer of 1904. When Alfred was lying gravely ill in a Philadelphia hospital following his hunting accident, Bessie came home with the children unannounced and stood for a few moments at a distance in his room, showing no sign of sympathy or concern. Her cold reaction spelled the final doom, and Alfred spent six months in 1905 in seclusion in South Dakota to establish residence for a divorce, which was finally granted in December 1906.

It was this domestic nightmare and the constant frustrations with the company brought about by Eugene duPont's ineffective management at the turn of the century that made Ball's Neck the comforting haven of innocent and honest friendship that Alfred came to treasure. The Hardings and the Balls had detected the shadow in Alfred's life without knowing what it was.[51]

Alfred saw Jessie one more time, in 1906, before they set off on separate paths that took them literally to opposite ends of the continent. By that time Alfred was already hopelessly in love with Alicia Bradford Maddox, the beautiful, intelligent, and vivacious daughter of Edward Green Bradford and Eleuthera duPont, Alfred's second cousin. The high-spirited young woman had been a trial to her father since childhood, and he had vehemently opposed her engagement in 1897 to George Amory Maddox, the charming but unpromising son of an old Maryland family. All but disowned by her father, Alicia had accepted the aid and comfort of her older cousin, Alfred, who admired her wit, sharp mind, and independent spirit as much as he disliked her father's cold, censorious manner. When Maddox could not find a job with the stature and income needed to marry a duPont, Alicia had appealed to Alfred, who against his better judgment gave the young man a senior position in the DuPont Company.

Judge Bradford had hoped that the long engagement would lead his wayward daughter to give up Maddox and find a better match, preferably beyond the reaches of Wilmington society where she could no longer disgrace the family. The judge was therefore outraged in 1902 when Alfred made the marriage to Maddox possible and settled the newlyweds in a home in Wilmington. Bradford was convinced that Alfred had arranged the marriage only to hide an illicit relationship with

Alicia. Although the judge was able to convince most of the duPont clan that his suspicions were true, Alicia saw Alfred only as her protector and advisor.[52]

The malicious rumors spread by Judge Bradford gained credence in 1905, when Alfred decided finally to divorce Bessie, and Alicia, forced at last to accept reports of Maddox's repeated infidelities, undertook to divorce him. Scorned by both her own family and most of the duPonts, Alicia turned to Alfred, who for years had offered her sympathy, support, and avuncular advice. When Alfred first proposed marriage, she did not take the idea seriously. She admired him and was deeply devoted to him, but she had already lost the one love of her life. This confession did not deter Alfred. He was determined to marry Alicia despite her frank reservations. They were married in New York in May 1907, and Alfred set out to build a new life for himself and his bride.[53]

Jessie's decision to move to California was probably related to Alfred's remarriage. Although she never let slip the slightest hint of her true feelings to Alfred or even to her sisters, Jessie had fallen deeply in love with him. At the time of his divorce from Bessie in 1906 she may well have indulged in the fantasy that Alfred would now recognize where his true love lay, but his remarriage dashed these hopes, it seemed, forever. Perhaps this terrible disappointment inspired her to copy or write the following lines of verse:

> So I will say goodby dear;
> Tho' it breaks, yes breaks my heart;
> There is nothing else to do dear;
> Since you say that we must part.
> Part, to meet as strangers only
> In this world so cold and dark.
> O' it will seem sad and lonely,
> Without you here sweetheart.
> Why should fate decreed [sic] to sever?
> Hearts which were so fond and true,
> Hearts which naught could part, no never;
> Except those fatal words from you
> Must I bow in meek submission
> To a fate which seals my doom?
> Yes, for you make the decision
> And inflict the smarting wound.[54]

Before the end of 1907 Tom, Isabel, and Jessie had completed the arrangements to move their parents to California. No doubt on Tom's recommendation they had decided on San Diego, then, as Jessie remembered it, a sleepy community of retired people. The mild climate, the quiet life, and moderate living expenses made it an ideal location for the Ball family. Jessie, who was then living and teaching in Lively, Virginia, remained behind to finish out the school year in 1908. To clear the way for a teaching position in San Diego, she had finally obtained a professional certificate from the Commonwealth of Virginia; but as her father pointed out to her in a letter, her certificate was only for seven years, and California would accept an out-of-state certificate only if it were for the life of the individual.[55]

Jessie left for California on September 1, 1908. Tom met her in Los Angeles and took her to San Diego for a joyous reunion with the family on September 13. The family had a modest but comfortable home on Colonial Avenue in City Heights. With no permanent position, Jessie started as a substitute teacher in Florence Elementary School while she obtained a San Diego teaching certificate. The following year she had a full-time position at the Middletown School, where she remained until 1915.[56]

With her sister Isabel, who was now teaching at Lincoln School, Jessie soon found new friends and quickly became a part of the social life of San Diego. One of her earliest and closest friends was Winifred Eldred, a fellow teacher at Middletown. The two young women shared ideas not only on teaching but also on a wide variety of subjects. Jessie enjoyed Winifred's liberal and flexible outlook on life, which seemed quite refreshing to a conservative Virginian. Winifred at the time was taken with socialist writers and tried to interest Jessie in political affairs. Politics was something new to Jessie because women in California at that time had the vote while those in Virginia did not. In their spare time, the two women read serious books and compared notes. At one point they read through the great Russian novels. Jessie later reminisced with Winifred: "I was very fond of Dostoevsky, but Tolstoy was my favorite, I think, even more than Turgenev."[57]

A lovely young woman with both charm and grace, Jessie turned the heads of men at social affairs in San Diego just as she had done on the Northern Neck. Her dance programs for the Christmas balls that first year, 1908, were always full. For the next several years her name and Isabel's often appeared in the society columns of the San Diego *Union*. In December

1910, Jessie was among two hundred guests at a reception at the "bungalow home" of John Vance Cheney, who entertained the group by reading his poetry while an ensemble played music he had written.

In July 1911, she and her sister attended a dinner party for eight guests, including their friend Maude Ervay Fagan, at the home of E. Bartlett Webster. The next afternoon they were "entertained delightfully" at a social for two young friends. "The afternoon was enjoyably passed with music and conversation and dainty refreshments were served."[58]

Both Jessie and Isabel joined the local chapter of the Daughters of the American Revolution and were among six hostesses at a DAR reception in February 1912, but Jessie's name appeared less frequently in the following years. As a teacher she could hardly be active in women's events on weekday afternoons during the school year, and much to Isabel's disgust showed little interest in the San Diego Woman's Club or the Wednesday Club. Women's clubs, flourishing since the last years of the nineteenth century, had not yet turned their attention to social causes and for the most part concentrated on garden parties and similar social events. Jessie was quickly bored by the idle chatter of society matrons and preferred to devote her time to more profitable pursuits. By 1915 she had

Jessie and Isabel Ball on vacation about 1911.

The Ball family at San Diego, about 1915. *Left to right:* Isabel, Jessie, father Thomas Ball, and mother Lalla Gresham Ball.

accumulated a modest savings, which she carefully invested in real estate, mostly small residential lots. She also preferred the company of older men, men of the business and intellectual world who were interested in talking about matters of substance. Years later she wrote to Isabel: "Certainly my method of life and associations, if you will remember even back in San Diego days were not in accord with yours, namely, I should go to more teas . . . and not associate as much with older men as I did or older people—that it wasn't good for me."[59]

In June 1916 Isabel married N. Addison Baker, a Unitarian minister from New England who had a church in southern California. Soon thereafter the Bakers moved to Seattle, where Addison had been called to a new church. After her sister left San Diego, Jessie felt less inhibited about pursuing the sort of social life she preferred. Her disdain for social events in the afternoon did not extend to the evenings or weekends. She took lessons to learn the latest dance steps and loved formal dances at the Hotel del Coronado. Sociable but always proper, she turned a cold shoulder to one young man in her group of friends who asserted his independence by refusing to wear formal attire for a Coronado party. There were convivial house parties with her friends on the beach at La Jolla and pleasant evenings with army officers who were stationed at Lakeside. Fifty years later Rebecca Harding Adams still remembered the big outdoor picnic given by Colonel Frick and the other officers and the dinner dance that May evening at the inn. "I even remember the dresses that we wore and how pretty you looked in a green silk gown embroidered in water lilies."[60]

Jessie enjoyed warm friendships but apparently no serious romances. Most of the men she found particularly interesting were much older than she, and some of them were married. She continued to carry on a correspondence with Charles Hardwicke, who was studying medicine on the East Coast. Over the years Hardwicke had fallen in love with her, but she thought of him only as a dear friend. When Hardwicke, a British subject, was called home for military service at the beginning of World War I, he asked her to marry him. Perhaps as much out of kindness as affection Jessie agreed to consider the possibility after the war if neither of them found anyone else in the meantime.[61]

Jessie Ball was approaching a crossroads in her life. Some years later she observed: "Early I realized that love and knowledge were the only things of value—one being (I thought) forever denied me, I concentrated all my forces and efforts on the other." She had indeed become a popular and successful teacher. In 1915 she had won a coveted teaching position in the newly built Washington Elementary School. The following year the superintendent of schools noted that "her ability as an instructor and disciplinarian has been recognized by our department in promoting her to

Jessie Ball stands with the pupils in her eighth-grade class at Washington School in San Diego, June 1916. She is second from the left in the back row. The bearded man half-hidden at the back is her close friend and colleague Pete W. Ross.

the Vice-principalship of one of our large buildings. She is a bright, attractive young woman." At Washington, with its more than six hundred students, she had found a congenial group of teachers and formed personal friendships with Pete W. Ross, the principal, and his wife. Jessie had joined the growing ranks of women school officers. Although women had been readily accepted as elementary teachers, their suitability for administrative positions had long been a subject of debate. An increase in female school administrators occurred only after 1900, most notably in the western states.[62]

Love, the other "value" of life, was quite another thing. It had been denied her, not because she lacked suitors like Charles Hardwicke, but because her secret passion for Alfred duPont seemed impossible to fulfill. In her secret dream world she had written him "hundreds" of letters declaring her eternal love and devotion to him, her "Precious Angel," only to destroy them lest they fall into the hands of others. She loved to go out on the rocks on the ocean side of Coronado Island during storms and dream of fantasy lands as the wind, rain, and surf swirled about her. On starlit nights with the silver rays of the new moon shimmering on the sea, she probably recalled a similar magical evening with Alfred on the shores of the Chesapeake more than a decade earlier. The mystery and ethereal beauty of the night helped her to escape the harsh realities of everyday life.[63]

In addition to her disappointments in love, Jessie faced tragedy in her family. Her father died in the spring of 1917 and her mother, already suffering from a slight stroke, was devastated by her husband's loss. Jessie took her mother to live with Isabel and her husband near Seattle and then went on alone to explore Alaska. Such an expedition was almost unheard-of for an unescorted woman at that time. Even more unusual was her enterprise in searching out the most influential men in any social gathering and making their acquaintance. On the ship to Alaska she succeeded in meeting the assistant to the secretary of the interior and the governor of Alaska. Before leaving Alaska, she seriously considered accepting a teaching position there. No doubt she concluded in the end that she could not afford to give up her professional accomplishments and friends in San Diego.[64]

After her father's death Jessie had taken rooms in the U. S. Grant Hotel in downtown San Diego. Living in the center of a thriving city that had more than doubled its population in the decade she had lived there, she took a lively interest in local business opportunities. She had borrowed money to buy residential lots in East San Diego and was carefully paying off the loan month by month. By this time her brother Tom had established a prosperous law practice in Los Angeles. Her younger brother, Eddie, was doing well as Tom's replacement as a law book salesman and had joined her in real estate ventures. If teaching rather than love and marriage was to be Jessie's future, she could hardly do better than her situation in San Diego.[65]

In addition to her fantasy letters to Alfred duPont, Jessie maintained a friendly but quite proper correspondence with him. Like the fantasy letters, few of those she actually sent have survived, but these few indicate the nature and frequency of the correspondence. Alfred appears to have written to both Jessie and Rebecca Harding several times each year, usually after receiving a letter from them. Early in 1918 he teased Rebecca: "I think your resolution not to bother to get engaged but to get married first and engaged later is all right. Most girls only get engaged in order to make the other girls jealous, but after all surprises are more fashionable just at the present time, so I am daily expecting a letter informing me that you have been married for a year. . . . You know I have to keep a sharp eye open in order to prevent surprises being sprung on me by such festive ladies as you and Floride and Miss Jessie Ball."[66]

In December Alfred wrote Jessie to apologize for his "lack of civility" in not responding sooner to her letter of September 30. He had been preoccupied by his venture into Delaware politics and his concern about the presidential election. A page later he lapsed into the sort of banter he had written to Rebecca: "I am much pleased to know that you do not approve of cooking and housekeeping in the abstract as being silly occupations. This will prevent you from contracting a silly marriage, which is always a thankless occupation, though I imagine now that the war is practically over the Macedonian threat will again appear on the horizon and you will have to steel your heart against the numerous attempts which will be made to change your views on cooking and housekeeping."[67] The "Macedonian threat" was probably Charles Hardwicke, who had spent much of the war in Greece. Perhaps by this time Hardwicke had informed Jessie of his decision to marry a woman he had met in Europe.

Evidently Jessie had written Alfred something about her dream world, although not in the passionate tone of her fantasy letters. In reflecting on her September letter he wrote:

> Unfortunately, our lives are so desperately material, unless we give up entirely to the al frescoed dream you so vividly depict, that one rapidly becomes unfitted for thinking of or dealing in anything which appeals to the better side of one's nature. I used to enjoy a moonlit night as you do, but now they are a nuisance, as they keep me awake and I am constantly consigning the moon to a place that is more spacious than cool and where one cannot keep ice cream over-night.

Two typewritten pages later he added:

> I am surprised to learn that you are apparently unable to live even for a short time without a sweetheart, even if it be only a make-believe one. I suppose, however, that safety lies in numbers, but I should imagine they would prove to be an awful nuisance. If I were sufficiently attractive to warrant ladies' endeavoring to hold my hands at every opportunity, I should certainly consult a dermatologist in order to secure peace and comfort. Take my advice and leave your "Papier maché company" alone.

By the time Alfred wrote Jessie again in May 1919, she had written to him twice, this time, he noted, on her "bestest" stationery. "I have evidently been lifted from the class with whom you usually correspond on hotel paper to the higher plane of your selected friend." Again he apologized for dictating his letters and having them typed. He mentioned a photograph of himself that he had sent her earlier, "taken in 1913 or 1914, which was my last effort at self-perpetuation. In any event, I think it much better to let you remember me as you must on the banks of Dividing Creek in 1906, which I believe was the last time we met. My life has not been what is usually termed in fiction as 'A bed of roses,' and Papa Time with his usual sense of humor has not added to my stock of beauty, which at its best would hardly have been considered in business terms a quick asset."[68]

In an earlier letter Jessie had mentioned that she might go to New York after school closed in June, and Alfred had urged her to let him know so that they could meet. There is no record of what Jessie Ball did in the summer of 1919, but from a letter that she wrote to Alfred on October 8,

Family and friends in San Diego about 1920. Jessie's mother is in the white blouse in the center of the back row. Her lifelong friend Billy Martin is at the far right in the back row. Isabel Ball is in the white dress at the center of the picture sitting next to her brother Tom.

it is difficult to believe that their friendship could have suddenly blossomed into a passionate romance through infrequent letters exchanged over a distance of three thousand miles. The October letter reveals that Jessie had let Alfred into her fantasy world, and he had entered it willingly if not with some reservations. For Jessie the new relationship was not so novel. She had now merely to mail the same sort of letters that she had written to her fantasy lover. Her letter of October 8 was full of endearments and deep concern that she might be adding to the troubles he already faced. In her passion she had forgotten his instructions to write to him only once a week, on Sundays, so that he would know when to expect her letters and thus make certain that they were not intercepted.[69]

Jessie already knew something of Alfred's financial misfortunes. In the newspapers she had followed the shameful court proceedings of *duPont* v. *duPont,* in which Alfred had sued his cousin Pierre for using the company's credit secretly to buy up cousin Coleman duPont's large block of stock in the company. Alfred had won the case but had lost the battle when the remaining stockholders voted their shares to support Pierre and thus forced Alfred out of the company. She also knew of the financial disaster he faced in the failure of the Nemours Trading Company, which he had established in New York during the war. Alfred had spurned the suggestion that he seek bankruptcy protection and was determined to use all of his fortune, if necessary, to pay off the debt. Whether this would be possible he did not yet know.[70]

During the spring she had detected a deeper, more personal anguish in Alfred. In none of his letters over the years had he written a sentence about his life with Alicia, and he had refused to discuss the subject. His troubled mind and physical exhaustion seemed to heighten her love. "God forbid that I should ever be a burden in any sense—it is enough that others have been that have crushed you and forbidden your life—you one of the few capable of life in all its fullness. I wish, Dearest, I knew something of the conditions under which you exist—it is hard to make deductions from just a hint now and then. You can't tell me?"[71]

Two days later she was frantic that she had received no letter that week. She wrote Alfred:

> Why am I so desperately weak and dependent on your words, your love, *you*. Oh, Dearest Heart, it is as if a whirlwind of fire were raging through my blood. It is glorious, but it is terrific and a consuming flame. Do you feel that way? Does your fiery (I know you are) nature blaze and burn you till you feel a helpless, buffeted, beaten thing before it? I know what I should do; but I haven't the courage to do it, though my plans were to have "done it" in June.
>
> This has been an ideal day & I could but think that had you have been here—we would have wandered by the waters, found a cosy nook where we might have rested in quiet contemplation of the beauties of nature, with but few thoughts to molest us. This evening is a fitting close for such a day. Now as I look over the broad expanse before me all inundated by that caressing radiance drowned in the langorous [*sic*] charm of a moonlit night—I am more convinced than ever that such a night was never meant for sleep—never—? I love you Sweet Heart, and want you—come for a little while, that would be better than nothing. God—you see I am daft and wretchedly homesick for you.[72]

Alfred could no longer resist such appeals and made plans to go to California immediately after the Christmas holidays. His purpose ostensibly was to visit the Ball family, and perhaps to add credibility to that claim, he took Alicia's daughter, known in the family as little Alicia, with him on the train. Jessie, who had been in Los Angeles with her family for her mother's funeral, arrived in San Diego just in time to meet Alfred's train. Somehow she missed him at the station and, shrewdly guessing that his first impulse would be to send a telegram home, she found him at the telegraph office. He had sent little Alicia and his valet, Thomas Horncastle, on ahead to catch the ferry to Coronado. Jessie had but a few words with him before she returned to her rooms at the Grant Hotel. A few minutes after arriving there, little Alicia telephoned to tell her that on arriving at their hotel, Alfred had received a telegram that his wife had just died of a heart attack in Charleston, South Carolina, on her way to Florida. He and little Alicia were returning immediately to Wilmington.[73]

When Alfred arrived in Wilmington he found a warm, endearing, and compassionate letter from Jessie waiting for him. She, more than any of the scores of others who wrote to him in those weeks, seemed to comprehend the depth and dimensions of his grief. Overcome with emotion, he sent her a long handwritten letter.

Dearest Little Jessie:

I wonder if you can possibly estimate what your letter meant to me today—for it came this morning, just when everything is at its worst & I am nearly crazy with what seems to me, my empty life. I made a statement to my wife some time ago, apropos of my unending solicitude for her welfare and happiness to the effect that, in my opinion the bond of misery was far stronger than any bond wrought by happiness—and so it has proven to be. I have worked by day and by night without ceasing for her, as I should, and though my efforts were not successful my mind has centered on one object and my body strove for but one goal. Now she has gone and while she is happy at last and at rest in paradise, I find myself alone and without any reason for existence.[74]

Racked by grief and despairing of his business affairs, Alfred spent the winter in Florida with little Alicia. In February he wrote to his daughter Madeleine in Germany extolling his late wife's courage and virtues. "Her

Jessie Ball in San Diego about 1920.

loss makes a void in my life which nothing can replace and leaves only a desire to live alone with the past and its memories as the one solace."[75]

By spring, however, Jessie Ball had given him a new outlook on life and new hope. Taking a six-month leave from her teaching position in San Diego, she went to New York late in March 1920, where Alfred arranged rooms for her at the Belmont Hotel. On April 5, the day after Easter, she made her first visit to Nemours, the magnificent mansion that Alfred had built for Alicia. Started in 1909, the mansion had been designed by a firm of distinguished New York architects in classic eighteenth-century French style, which Alicia admired. Although Alfred modified the architect's design to give it something of the flavor of an ante-bellum southern mansion, the seventy-seven-room edifice with its 1,500 acres of land was the grandest and most costly home in the Mid-Atlantic states. The house, with its formal gardens and colonnade of trees stretching northward to a splendid belvedere, was much closer in style to Versailles than to the unadorned, utilitarian homes of the other duPonts living in the Brandywine valley.[76]

Jessie quickly became a part of Alfred's life, and his spirits soared accordingly. She could spend weekends at Nemours when her younger married sister, Elsie, could come up from Virginia to act as chaperon. When Alfred was in New York City Jessie stayed at the Belmont and could see him every day. In May Alfred took Jessie and Elsie with some of his family to his fishing retreat at Cherry Island in the Little Choptank River near Cambridge, Maryland. Cherry Island, which Alfred had purchased in 1893 with his cousin Charles I. duPont, provided an idyllic springtime setting for a woman in love. When Alfred returned to his business affairs in New York, Jessie stayed on at the island with Alfred's brother Maurice and his wife and the Francis I. duPonts, the only relatives who were on speaking terms with Alfred. As the boat carrying Alfred moved out of the river into the bay, Jessie poured out on paper her eternal love and devotion. "Our love, my Precious Angel, is wealth sufficient—and will give to you the happiness that your wealth in $'s $'s [sic] failed to give; so what if you should lose them, right here on this little island we still would have the wealth that would make Morgan and Rockefellow [sic] look like paupers."[77]

In June Alfred invited all the Hardings and Balls living in the East to a grand reunion. Meeting at Nemours, Mrs. Harding and her two daughters joined Jessie, Elsie, and Alfred as they took the bay steamer to

Ball's Neck. Jessie stayed on through the rest of June to visit the haunts of her childhood and to call on relatives whom she had not seen since she left the Neck in 1908. In her daily letters to Alfred she confessed her regret that she had decided to return. To visit her old aunts whom she would probably never see again was more than she could bear. "I am too raw, I shouldn't have made this trip, too many memories return with it. This is the land once the pride of my people, though now owned by riff-raff—I can't help it, there lingers around something,—I know not what but I know how my Father loved it."[78]

Alfred managed to write or wire Jessie almost every day while she was in Virginia. He teased her about some photographs she had given him. The contrast, he noted, between the ones taken the previous summer and those taken two years earlier was remarkable. "The latter ones have much sweeter eyes with much more in them. It only emphasizes what I have said. That your real love for me is of recent creation." He added: "I simply must be on the go each moment to keep you from my thoughts if such be possible."[79]

To most of the family who saw Jessie and Alfred during their visit to Ball's Neck the reunion had an unspoken but obvious significance: the couple intended to be married as soon as social conventions of the time would allow. Everyone teased Jessie about Alfred, but only Jessie's Aunt Ella Haile in Tappahannock actually spoke of marriage, and she was obviously pleased because Alfred had completely charmed her. Jessie was impatient with the "camouflage" that convention demanded, but she took comfort in knowing that the days preceding the fulfillment of her dream were numbered.[80]

There was, however, the long summer and fall before the full year since Alicia's death would pass. Jessie's teaching career now seemed years behind her, and there was no thought of returning to San Diego before the wedding. Instead, Jessie stayed as close to Alfred as she dared—at Nemours when suitable guests could be present to satisfy convention, otherwise at the Belmont in New York. She spent Christmas with the duPont family at Nemours. She and Alfred did not leave for San Diego until a few days before the wedding.

On January 22, 1921, just two days more than a year since Alicia's death, Alfred and Jessie stood before Baker Lee in his Los Angeles study and took the vows of matrimony. On that bright, cold Saturday morning, one of the coldest in the memory of local residents, Jessie Ball realized the dreams of her "kittenhood" days, as she always referred to them. Her romance with Alfred duPont had indeed been "picturesque," but it was much more than that. She was convinced that fate or destiny had somehow brought them together again after a decade of separation. She was determined to make a success of her new life, which she knew would be filled with uncertainties as well as happiness.

The Fruits of Compassion

*N*either Alfred duPont nor Jessie Ball told any of their friends of their intentions before their marriage in Los Angeles. Jessie had spent most of the year in the East and had not seen most of her San Diego friends before the wedding. It was no wonder that, in their congratulatory letters to her, Jessie's former associates at Washington School found it difficult to think of her as Mrs. duPont. Was it possible that the charming, unpretentious young teacher who had shared their daily routines had suddenly become a woman of extraordinary wealth and social stature?[1]

It took Pete Ross, the principal at Washington School, three letters before he could address her as "Mrs. duPont" rather than as "Miss Ball," but he rejoiced in her good fortune. He reminded her that she was "not an ordinary young lady. You were not born, nor has your training and development been for becoming a 'mere wife,' to be mayhaps a social leader in some of the vagarious 'social sets' of a little city like this. . . . But now, as wife of Mr. Alfred Dupont, what widened fields of opportune usefulness are yours!"[2]

During her long stay in the East in 1920 Jessie had learned something of the challenge that would face her in her new role. It was true that she would now be living on a scale completely different from that of her past life. There was the magnificent estate at Nemours, the mansion lavishly decorated with works of art, acres of gardens, a small army of gardeners, and a household staff of eleven. As a wedding present Alfred had given her jewelry and a tan sports car, custom built with a Don Legh body on a Cadillac chassis.[3] To her own modest investments, Alfred would no doubt in time add generous funds that she could manage on her own account. No

Jessie Ball at the time of her marriage to Alfred duPont, January 1921.

longer tied to her teaching position, she would be able to travel and pursue her interests unimpeded by the restrictions of her earlier life.

The new Mrs. duPont, however, was equally aware of the hazards she faced. Nemours was indeed a splendid palace, but it had been built for Alicia and reflected her tastes and interests in every detail. Her presence still haunted the house as if her spirit were confined by the stone wall topped with shattered glass bottles that Alfred had ordered built around the estate. The wall served not only as a physical barrier designed to exclude most of the duPonts and members of Wilmington society but also as a psychological screen that might deflect the venomous insults heaped upon him and his second wife. But in time it seemed that the wall not only kept the unwanted out but also confined Alfred and Alicia to a prison of their own making. Even Alicia had found Nemours depressing in the last years of her life and had spent more of her time in Paris or at the new home that Alfred had built for her on Long Island.[4]

Alicia's spirit was also clearly evident in the children she left behind. Her daughter by George Maddox, Alicia, was now seventeen, only twenty years younger than Jessie. Inheriting her mother's high style of extravagant living and independent spirit, young Alicia had already become something of a problem for her stepfather. Far from mature in Alfred's and Jessie's opinion, Alicia had fallen in love with and was determined to marry a Rhodes scholar whom she had met in England. A student with a working-class background, the young man hardly seemed a likely partner for a girl with Alicia's expectations.

Even more complicated was the status of Adelaide Camille Denise duPont, the infant war orphan whom Alicia had brought home unannounced from Paris in 1916. Denise was now a sweet child going on six, but she did not fit easily into the new household at Nemours. In the year since Alicia's death Denise had seen little of her foster father and even less of Jessie Ball. The new Mrs. duPont clearly intended to be a mother to the child, but that relationship was yet to be established when the couple returned to Nemours in March 1921.[5]

Jessie at once threw herself into a frenzy of activity in her new home. Like the spring, she was a ray of sunshine and a breath of fresh air in the long-dark and empty rooms of Nemours. The stuffy duPonts and Wilmington matrons who had snubbed Alicia with such relish could hardly have the same effect on Jessie. She did not know them and was too caught up in her own life to care. Instead she threw open the doors of Nemours to her extended family, the Balls, the Hardings, and the Greshams, and to the few duPonts with whom Alfred was still on speaking terms.

Alfred was delighted with his bride's enthusiasm and energy after the clouded, frustrating years with Alicia. He wrote a friend: "Jessie and I are safely installed at Nemours. She is busy getting the house in shape for Spring and Summer, while I endeavor to dig up a little bread and butter for our daily nourishment. She is the most delectable companion possible and improves so rapidly each day as to make one embarrassed in the effort to describe her many virtues." Alfred explained his wife's failure to write

Nemours, the mansion built by Alfred duPont in Wilmington in 1909 and Jessie Ball duPont's new home after her marriage. Courtesy of the Nemours Mansion and Gardens, Wilmington, Delaware.

to old friends: she was valiantly attempting to answer in her own hand the scores of congratulatory letters that had flooded in after the wedding. He noted with some amusement that she had refused to dictate her letters to Mary Brereton, his secretary, on the grounds that typewritten letters looked too impersonal.[6]

Alfred's reference to "bread and butter" was an attempt to make light of the precarious financial position in which he found himself. Refusing to declare bankruptcy, he had decided early in 1920 to liquidate the Nemours Trading Company and to attempt to pay off its debts from his personal fortune. Although $7 million had been paid off by the spring of 1920, undetermined claims or damage suits might run to $5 million or more. There was also a $4 million loan from J. P. Morgan & Company that carried what Alfred considered an extortionate interest rate of 9 percent. Finally, the federal government had billed Alfred for more than $1.5 million in additional tax on his 1915 income. Because he had always been careful about paying his taxes, the bill was totally unexpected and therefore devastating. The government's case rested upon alleged profits realized by DuPont stockholders when Pierre reorganized the company as part of his effort to obtain Coleman's stock. Alfred insisted that he had not earned one penny in the stock split. His attorneys had appealed the government's ruling, but the chances for a favorable decision seemed slight.[7]

At the time of their marriage Alfred had told Jessie that he might well lose everything he had except the seven-room hunting and fishing lodge at Cherry Island, a fate that she probably could have accepted more easily than he. The fact was, however, that neither of them expected to retire in genteel poverty to Cherry Island—Alfred, because he would have held on to Nemours until everything else was gone; Jessie, because she could not believe that such a vast fortune could so quickly be dissipated. By selling some of the inventories from the trading company at cut-rate prices, Alfred was able to reduce the principal on the Morgan loan by $500,000 and the interest rate to 7 percent. A plan to sell 25,000 shares of DuPont stock would have paid off the Morgan debt, but the market for the stock dried up and an unfavorable ruling by the U.S. Supreme Court on the tax appeal brought by a small DuPont stockholder dashed Alfred's hopes in November. After a gala New Year's Eve party the duPonts prepared for the inevitable by shutting down Nemours except for one bedroom suite and taking their meals at the DuPont Hotel in Wilmington.[8] Alicia was studying in Europe and Cousin Minnie Edwards was taking care of Denise at her home in the Northern Neck.

It was probably at this time that Jessie began spending some of her days at her husband's office in downtown Wilmington in the Delaware Trust Building, which he owned. There she learned the various office routines established by Mary Brereton and immersed herself in the details of her husband's financial predicament. In February 1922 the government rejected Alfred's claim of abatement of the additional assessment on his 1915 taxes, and he set about finding a way of selling his assets: first his Liberty bonds; then his holdings in the Delaware Trust Company; next, the Long Island estate he had built for Alicia; and finally in May, as a last resort, 20,000 shares of his DuPont stock. All these sales brought him close to $5 million in cash, which he could use to pay the 1915 tax bill and other troublesome debts. Freed at last from the worst of the financial threat, Alfred and Jessie sailed for England to attend little Alicia's wedding. It was Jessie's first trip abroad, the fulfillment of one more dream made possible by her marriage.

Alfred had been serious when he talked of financial ruin, and Jessie told herself that she was willing to accept whatever fate brought her. Neither of them, however, was able to go beyond the token economies that they had instituted at Nemours early in 1922. Alfred was soon talking of building a new yacht to replace the aging and ill-named *Alicia*. Jessie thought it important to maintain a wardrobe suitable for the wife of Alfred duPont and, like most brides, redecorated her husband's home to satisfy her own tastes. Her interest in fashions was more a matter of social propriety than of keeping abreast of the latest styles. By the standards of many American households, Jessie's expenditures in times of financial difficulties would have seemed extravagant, but for a woman of her new status they were not unreasonable. By comparison with Alicia's life-style, they were modest indeed.

In establishing herself as the new Mrs. duPont, Jessie sought to give Alfred the kind of life his earlier marriages had failed to provide. She now had what she had dreamed of all her life, and she was determined to do everything possible to make her marriage a success. She was also motivated by a passionate devotion to her husband. In setting the tone of domestic life at Nemours, she tried to strike a happy balance between the economies imposed by Alfred's financial straits and Alicia's extravagant life-style. The redecorating at Nemours, the family parties, and her own wardrobe were all planned to give Alfred's life a new tone without, on the one hand, skimping too much on the life-style to which he was accustomed, or, on the other hand, pressing expenditures beyond prudent limits.

Jessie's efforts to bring Alfred out of the chilly isolation of Nemours would not have succeeded without the presence of her own family and friends. Alfred cheerfully welcomed the old gang who reminded him of his happy days in the Northern Neck. The Balls had a mutual affection for Alfred and could hardly have failed to appreciate the opulent life-style that Jessie and her husband maintained at Nemours.

Reestablishing Alfred's relationships with his own family, however, was a much more difficult task that required sensibility, patience, and finesse on Jessie's part. The years of feuding within the duPont clan had cut off Alfred from his immediate family, both of his own generation and of the next. Of his four brothers and sisters, who had banded together in defiance of the duPont elders after their parents died in 1877, only Maurice and Marguerite were part of Alfred's life in 1921. Having secretly married a young woman who worked in a hotel in Ireland in 1889, Maurice had suffered the same ostracism from the family that Alfred experienced after his marriage to Alicia; unlike Alfred, Maurice had declined to face up to the family in Wilmington and had retired quietly to North Carolina. Perhaps sharing a similar fate drew the two brothers together, and Maurice's wife, Margery, despite the newspaper descriptions of her at the time of their marriage as an "Irish bar maid," proved herself a woman of character who quickly earned Jessie's admiration and affection.[9]

Two of the five orphans had died before the turn of the century, and Alfred seldom saw his only surviving sister, Marguerite, although they continued to correspond regularly. Fully as independent and strong willed as her brother, Marguerite Lee lived as a spartan widow in Washington, D.C., where she spent most of her own money and huge annual sums from her brother on charitable and church projects. She had nothing but contempt for the extravagance and conceit of Alfred's second wife and had refused ever to set foot within the walls of Nemours.

After Alfred and "The Brid" (as he affectionately called her) returned from Europe in the summer of 1923, Jessie suggested to her husband that he invite Marguerite to visit them. Now that Alicia was gone, it was just possible that Marguerite would relent in her quarantine of Nemours.

Alfred welcomed the idea and besieged his sister with photographs of Nemours and glowing descriptions of Jessie. Marguerite resisted until Christmas, when she finally came to Nemours to join in a family celebration. Alfred later wrote: "Her coming was entirely due to Jessie's sweetness. Being a duPont and therefore ornery, like myself, which a lady terms firmness, I had no effect on her. But of course no one can refuse Jessie anything."[10]

Brother and sister were quickly reunited, and Marguerite's two sons, their wives, and their children became part of the Nemours family. Within a few years Marguerite decided that Jessie, like Alicia before her, was diverting too much of Alfred's money away from her pet projects in Washington, and the relationship between the two women cooled. Jessie realized, however, that Marguerite was one who would never be satisfied with the way Alfred ran his life, and she did her best to keep channels open to her sister-in-law.[11]

Incredibly, the task of bringing Alfred's own children back into the fold was much more difficult than the reunion with Marguerite had been. Alfred's consuming hatred for his first wife had become an obsession that had spilled over into his relationship with his own children. Of the four, only Madeleine had turned against her mother in the harrowing disintegration of the family in 1904. Now thirty-six, married for a second time, and living with her three sons in Munich, Madeleine had maintained a sporadic correspondence with her father. Bessie, the eldest daughter, had stayed with her mother. In 1917 Bessie had married Reginald S. Huidekoper, a cousin of one of Alfred's old friends and hunting companions, by 1923 a successful lawyer living in Washington. That summer one of Alfred's old associates confided to Jessie that Bessie (or Bep as her father had called her) was visiting her mother in Wilmington and told Jessie that little Bep had always been close to Alfred's heart. Jessie soon arranged a meeting in Alfred's office in the Delaware Trust Building for Bep, her husband, and their two small children. Alfred was overjoyed at the sight of his grandchildren, but his conversation with his daughter was strained, especially when she discovered that Alfred did not even know that his son, Alfred Victor, had served in the marines during the war.[12]

Both Alfred Victor and his younger sister, Victorine, had been too young at the time of the divorce in 1906 to make any choice between their parents. After Alfred had evicted his first wife and children from the family home and had it demolished to the last stone, Bessie Gardner duPont had moved to a roomy, unpretentious house in Wilmington. There the children heard no word spoken of their father, but they learned to recognize his car on Wilmington streets, and Victorine as a girl had even walked beside him for several blocks without his having any idea who she was. In 1922, fifteen years after he had last seen his son, Alfred identified him in the program for an amateur theatrical in Wilmington. In 1925 Jessie had pointed out Victorine at an adjoining table in the grill room at the DuPont Hotel, but Alfred had made no effort to approach her.

Despite Jessie's promptings, Alfred made no further overtures to his children until the summer of 1926, when he suddenly hit upon the idea of giving them something of his fortune while they were young enough to enjoy it. Jessie at once supported the idea, and Alfred arranged to give each of the four children two thousand shares of DuPont debenture stocks, which would have an annual income of $12,000. In accepting the gifts, the children were asked to sign statements that they would not contest their father's will. All signed, and all wrote warm and appreciative letters to their father.[13]

Victorine took the initiative for the final reconciliation. She was engaged to Elbert Dent, a Princeton man and navy pilot during the war, who was starting a law practice in Philadelphia. Victorine's compulsion to show off her fiancé to her father led her to write him of her engagement and to ask him for permission to call. When Jessie learned that Alfred Victor and his wife Marcella were visiting Wilmington, she arranged for the two couples to come to Nemours on April 27, 1927. The meeting was strained at first, but Jessie in her own charming and cordial way knew how to get things warmed up. Soon everyone relaxed, and what Alfred expected to be fifteen minutes of formal introductions became an evening of pleasant conversation.[14]

The April meeting was the beginning of correspondence between Alfred and his children and occasional visits to Nemours. Jessie rejoiced in the reconciliation that had taken all of six years. Christmas 1927 was the first that Alfred celebrated with his children in almost a quarter-century. After the guests had left, Jessie could not wait to write the good news to Madeleine, the only member of the family who had not been present:

> I thought of you many, many times on that Day, and wished that you could have been with the happy throng, then the family would

have been complete; as Bessie and Mr. Huidekoper and her four babies arrived on Christmas Eve about noon, then Victorine and her husband, Elbert Dent, and Alfred and his wife, Marcella, came for Dinner on Christmas Day. Really wanted to have them for the night, but there wasn't space, as Cazenove Lee, his wife and three children, my sister, Belle, and her two children, and my sister, Elsie, and her one were all with us, and as it was a day given over to the youngsters I couldn't think of pushing them out.

It is the first time I have had a chance to get acquainted at all with Bessie and Mr. Huidekoper, though they have been at the house quite a number of times, but just for calls, when other callers were in. I found Bessie very sweet and charming, with a very gracious and genuine manner, and so was Mr. Huidekoper. . . . Victorine and Elbert were with us on a house party some time ago and Victorine seemed more than anxious to hear some news of you. . . . I forgot to tell you also that your Aunt Marguerite was also with us, and she, too, seemed to enjoy Bessie and her family as well as the other nieces and nephews, being the first time, I believe, that she had seen them in years.[15]

Children were the center of attention at Nemours on holidays and during the summer months. In 1925 Jessie had her sister Isabel's children at Nemours for the entire summer. John and Jessie Gresham Baker were just a few years younger than Denise, and the three children with their dogs and other pets had the run of the estate. Daily life, however, was not all play. Jessie had a governess for the children that summer, and they were "in school" from nine until twelve-thirty each day. She explained to an old California friend: "I really feel that this is necessary on account of none of the private schools running more than seven months and most of them only about six, so that it is impossible for a child to get a fundamental education in that length of time." The following summer Jessie herself took over teaching the three children. "Jessie Gresham was only three years old when I started with her," she recalled, but she recognized "the indelible imprints made on the child through the first seven years of its life, and I am rather convinced that if the foundation is faulty through those years it is almost impossible to put a superstructure on it. Besides a little child is a great pleasure to everyone."[16]

Alfred also shared Jessie's love of children. For years he had taken scores of underprivileged Wilmington children on swimming outings

Mrs. duPont with the "pirates" on vacation at Cherry Island, Maryland about 1925. *Standing left to right:* Mrs. duPont's nephew John Baker and niece Jessie Gresham Baker; her foster daughter, Denise duPont. *Seated left to right:* Alfred's great-niece and great-nephews Vandegrift Lee, Marga Lee, and Richard Henry Lee.

several times each summer. For his own extended family there were weeks on the beach every summer at Atlantic City, but the most memorable of all the excursions for the children were the happy days at Cherry Island. Denise never forgot the ride over the dirt roads from Cambridge, Maryland, in the "basket" car, a big open Rolls-Royce with wicker panels on its sides. Local residents recognized it as the duPont car, a mark of notoriety that caused Denise to slide down on the floorboards in embarrassment. The summer of 1925 found Marguerite's grandchildren, Francis I. duPont's children, a collection of Jessie's young relations, and Denise all at the Cherry Island lodge. The highlight of the occasion was an excursion aboard the *Nenemoosha* on Chesapeake Bay, during which Alfred told pirate stories and ran up the Jolly Roger while the children played at being swashbuckling freebooters.[17]

There were glorious family celebrations on the Fourth of July with magnificent displays of fireworks that only an old black-powder man like Alfred could assemble. In 1925 the guests included Marguerite and her family, Jessie's sisters and children, several friends of Jessie and her sisters, and Henry Dew, a distant cousin who had lived with his aunt at Wytheville when the Ball sisters were in school there. Henry was now an engineer working for Union Carbide in New York and frequently came down to Nemours for parties. As Jessie wrote to her brother, "There are several more I would like to have asked, but have no vacant 'bunks.' " Alfred's version was somewhat different: "We have had quite a peaceful week at Nemours but the delectable Brid is getting ready to start one of her Social Hells, beginning this afternoon and probably lasting until after the Fourth. Ed and I are trying to look happy and patient but these words poorly describe what our real feelings are!"[18]

In these early years at Nemours Jessie disdained the idea of having a housekeeper to manage the domestic staff. As the new mistress of Nemours, she wanted to supervise the staff herself. That meant decisions on guest accommodations, staff assignments, and menus for meals for twenty or more, two or three times a day. Jessie, however, drew the line at cooking.

> If there is anything I do loathe and despise on the face of the universe it is cooking. . . . I do not mind the work in a house at all. I rather enjoying [*sic*] fixing up a room so it is pretty and attractive, and that has a more or less degree of permanence. Not so with the kitchen; you work yourself to death, preparing a meal, to see it all vanish in half an hour, and in the course of two hours it is all to be done over again. . . . [A]s my father very naively remarked once to one of my would-be beaus in the presence of his doting mother, "As to Jess, she will starve you to death and then grin at you."[19]

In addition to her domestic duties as mistress of Nemours, Jessie was maintaining a burgeoning correspondence with family members and friends. By 1925 she had overcome her inhibitions about having personal letters typewritten and had adopted her husband's practice of dictating virtually every letter she sent. Now it was possible to send off dozens of letters every day, and Miss Brereton even made carbon copies, carefully preserved in the same kind of filing system that Alfred used for his outgoing letters: they were filed alphabetically by addressee, and a new file was started at the beginning of each calendar year.

In the late 1920s Jessie's most frequent correspondents were members of her family, especially her brother Tom in California and Denise, who was in private school in Baltimore, where she lived with her Aunt Elsie Ball Wright and Cousin Judith Bland Dew in a house Jessie had bought. Her correspondence with Ed was infrequent and usually on business matters. On those rare occasions when the duPonts were separated, even for a few days, Jessie wrote her husband long letters almost as passionate as those she penned before her marriage. In June 1927, she went to California to care for Tom, who had been seriously injured in a car accident. She wrote:

> I must not think it now, as it is impossible to leave Tom in his present condition—but oh! the raptuous [*sic*] joy when we are together once again—no partings again; certainly not of such duration. Sweetheart, it does not seem exactly right that one individual should be for another, life and the whole world—so you are to me. Have always thought that love was the sole compensation for life—a love from God's most perfect being, You,—has made of earth a place for me which Heaven must pale beside. Your letter is so precious and sweet that tears come to my eyes as I read it o'er and o'er—the longing that aches to pain to be together again. [20]

Her personal letters contained the usual chitchat about family and friends, but birthday greetings usually included a check. During the early years of her marriage, Jessie followed the prescript that charity begins at home. With Alfred's encouragement she showered gifts, usually of cash, on her many Ball and Gresham relatives, duPont children, and close friends. Most of the checks were not large but they reflected Jessie's personal knowledge of the recipients' needs and her sensitivity to them. During April 1926, for example, her checks for charities and schools totaled little more than $500, while her gifts to family and friends were more than $2,500. Many of these people received monthly checks, which in some cases were their only source of support. Her Christmas list in 1927 included 40 persons, with checks ranging from $50 to $300. [21]

As her private fortune grew, Mrs. duPont recognized the need to provide for its disposition in the event of her death. In 1927 she executed a will that was to remain in effect for seven years. Perhaps as a precaution against unnecessary complications, all copies of the 1927 will were later destroyed, but its contents can almost certainly be determined from the

Jessie Ball duPont, a few years after her marriage in 1921.

existing codicil. The 1927 will appears to have been little more than long lists of gifts or annuities for members of her family (including distant "cousins"), friends, and employees.[22]

Outside her family and circle of friends Mrs. duPont was responding to an increasing number of requests for financial help from the indigent, sick, and infirm in the Northern Neck. In her correspondence she did not state explicitly what motivated her to devote a substantial portion of her time to charity, but her actions were consistent with the practices of wealthy people of her time.

Acts of charity, as Warren Weaver and others have pointed out, stemmed directly from the Christian tradition of caring for the poor and afflicted among one's neighbors. Christians understood Jesus to have said that the poor would always be present in this world and that helping them would therefore be an endless responsibility of his followers. Because these acts of charity were usually directed to people the donor knew, they were usually secret to protect the dignity of the recipient. Secrecy also followed Jesus's admonition that in giving, the right hand should not know what the left hand is doing.[23] Certainly young Jessie Ball must have learned these principles in the Christian home in which she was raised, just as they had been part of Alfred's life.

There was, however, in the early years of the twentieth century another conception of giving that among the wealthy was rapidly replacing acts of personal charity. Philanthropy antedated the Christian practice of charity and was intended, in the Greek city-state, not to alleviate the miseries of individuals but to promote the welfare of society as a whole. In the passing centuries of the Christian epoch, this original meaning of philanthropy had been blurred, and during most of the nineteenth century in the United States, the words *charity* and *philanthropy* were used interchangeably. But with the rise of industrial capitalism and the amassing of huge personal fortunes, a distinction between the two began to emerge. Edward Grubb, writing an article on philanthropy in 1917 in the *Encyclopedia of Religion and Ethics,* saw philanthropy as "charity grown up; i.e., the impulse to help the needy, which may be but a casual and superficial emotion, develops in some minds into a settled disposition and a steady life effort. The typical philanthropist is a prosperous person who gives up a large share of his life to the work of improving the lot of his fellow creatures." Philanthropy,

Grubb suggested, was "the outcome of the charitable impulse, when disciplined by reflective thought, in a strongly individualized society."[24]

In the decade in which Grubb was writing, American giving was growing at a phenomenal rate. In 1892 charitable and philanthropic giving nationally totaled $29 million; by 1902, $85 million; and by 1905, $135 million. What is more, much of this generosity was in the form that Robert Bremmer has called "scientific philanthropy." That is, instead of giving money haphazardly and with little thought of its impact, large donors were beginning to plan their gifts. Charity reformers and civic leaders in the 1870s believed that "the charitable impulse was being disciplined, the head was triumphing over the heart, the 'machinery of benevolence' was coming to be understood and usefully operated, and 'philanthropology,' the study of the scientific principles of philanthropy, would soon be as well organized as any other branch of learning."[25]

It would be foolish to claim that Alfred or Jessie Ball duPont were philanthropists in the 1920s. Alfred's chaotic business career and the wild fluctuations of his personal fortune left little time or incentive for the kind of planned giving that the word *philanthropy* was coming to denote. For Jessie the possession of great wealth and the responsibilities it entailed were problems she had not encountered before 1921. All of her giving during these years could properly be termed charity, but there was one aspect of her effort that suggested elements of scientific philanthropy: She did not dole out gifts casually to those who appealed for help. Rather she insisted on evaluating each case to determine the true need and the probable impact on the recipient.

As her charitable activities grew in scope and complexity, Mrs. duPont could not hope to manage them alone. Fortunately in 1926 she was able to obtain the services of Mary G. Shaw as her personal secretary. In her late twenties, Mary Shaw had been born and raised in a solid Irish-Catholic family in Baltimore. She had graduated from the University of Delaware and had two brothers in Wilmington—one a physician, the other an adventuresome business man. Mary Shaw was just the sort of assistant Mrs. duPont needed. She was well educated, a skilled secretary, deadly serious about her work, and a good judge of people.[26]

Although Miss Shaw was able to handle the correspondence and accounts, neither she nor Mrs. duPont could investigate the plight of everyone who wrote to her. By the spring of 1927 Mrs. duPont was relying on H. J. Edmonds, a physician in Kilmarnock, Virginia, to examine claimants and determine their financial situation. As she wrote to Edmonds in April 1928: "I know a great many of them are totally unworthy in every respect. Having been raised in that part of the country, I realize that while there are very few wealthy people there is almost no dire poverty such as is known in the cities. There are a great many people of a certain class who think they are too good to go to work at the only line of work they are capable of doing, namely, laboring work or domestics; and the sooner they realize they are not above this work the better for them."[27]

In the face of true need, however, Mrs. duPont was quick to respond. In 1927 she arranged through Dr. Edmonds to send a child from Remo, Virginia, to Richmond for an operation to correct a cleft lip. She funded an operation for a young black woman who had never been able to walk except on all fours; she was delighted to know that some time after the operation the woman was able to walk without crutches. She readily provided funds to support sanitarium treatment for four black youths suffering from tuberculosis. There were small amounts in 1928 for dozens of causes: to help alleviate the debt of a black congregation, to help start a public library, to pay off the debts of a deceased black physician who had spent much of his career on charity cases, and to provide winter clothes and shoes for a destitute child.[28]

By the late 1920s Mrs. duPont's contributions for scholarships occupied far more of her time than did her private charities. As early as 1923 she was financing the college education of students who lived in the Northern Neck. As people in the region learned of her generosity, the number of applications soared, and administration of the scholarships required more attention than either she or Miss Shaw could give to it.

Evaluating the applicants was difficult enough, but Mrs. duPont had no intention of doling out money to worthy candidates as a reward for their academic records in high school. She wanted to make certain that scholarships went only to students who were in financial need and that their records in college justified continued support. Virtually all of her scholarships at this time went to students in Virginia institutions.

To assist her, Mrs. duPont called upon a few persons whose judgment she could trust. One of her earliest advisors was Julian A. C. Chandler. A graduate of the College of William and Mary with a doctorate in history from Johns Hopkins, Chandler had taught in several city colleges and had been superintendent of public schools in Richmond before returning to William and Mary as president in 1919. His academic experience gave him a practical approach to education that appealed to Mrs. duPont. He was conscientious about reporting the grades of each scholarship student and did not hesitate to recommend cutting off support to students with poor academic records. Chandler not only selected and evaluated students but also administered the funds that Mrs. duPont provided for tuition, room, and board.[29]

Frederick D. Goodwin, rector of several rural Episcopal churches in and around Warsaw, Virginia, selected promising students from that part of the Northern Neck. Mrs. duPont had known him when she was a schoolgirl in Farmville and trusted his judgment. She also knew that he was something more than the average country pastor. A graduate of William and Mary, he had earned a master's degree before going to the Virginia Theological Seminary in Alexandria. Following his ordination, Goodwin had returned to the Northern Neck and had become a specialist in rural ministry. He interrupted his assistance to Mrs. duPont for two years beginning in 1924, when he went to New York as secretary for rural work on the National Council of the Episcopal Church. Each year Goodwin typed long reports to Mrs. duPont on each prospective and continuing scholar. His evaluations were fair, realistic, and thorough. As a result, Mrs. duPont almost always accepted his recommendations and sent him lump-sum checks to cover the expenses of all the students selected.[30]

A third advisor was Ethel Markham Tignor, who lived in Northumberland County not far from Mrs. duPont's birthplace. Mrs. Tignor, a native New Englander, probably had a college education and some professional experience as a teacher. Her assignment was to find worthy students in the tidewater counties surrounding Mrs. duPont's birthplace.[31]

In May 1928 Mrs. duPont wrote to Mrs. Tignor: "It is always a pleasure to help some worthy boy or girl to acquire the tools with which to make a living and enjoy life, but it is getting exceedingly difficult for me to sift out the ones that really can go further in an educational sense and haven't the means to so do, and those who have the means but just want someone else to pay the expenses other than the family, and the latter seldom are good students or worth while at all."[32]

Thus education was a tool that an enterprising youth needed to achieve material success and happiness. Education held the key to one's future; it separated the achiever from the masses of untrained, unthinking people who were content to lead a humdrum existence. She wrote to her nephew: "If you are going to take any position in life or hold the position to which we were born, it is only through education that people rise in life and that is quite right. That is why so many of the servant class of a former generation are in the foremost ranks to-day. Their parents realized that an education was essential to them, and that is why quite a number of our aristocratic families have gone down to servants, thinking that their name was all that they needed."[33]

But education was also a scarce commodity; resources for education should not be wasted on frivolous activities like athletics. Even such studies as literature and the fine arts should give way to practical courses, which were the tools for success. Mrs. duPont wrote to one student: "It is perfectly all right to take your art work on the side, if possible, but bear in mind, young man, that the greatest artists of the world to-day are scarcely making a living."[34]

Knowing full well that the needs for educational support were endless, Mrs. duPont tried to make sure that every dollar was well spent. Each year she carefully reviewed the evaluations by her advisors and often responded with comments of her own. In June 1928 she disapproved Chandler's proposal to continue support for two students for a half-semester to see if their grades would improve. "I am going to change this. I am not going to return them at all." As for another student, "It is just what one more or less expects where the child has to make no sacrifice and no sacrifice is made on the part of the parents. I shall certainly follow your suggestions and not return her to school." In the same letter she cut off aid to two students whose parents were "good prosperous citizens and fully capable of educating their children."[35]

In only one instance during the 1920s did Mrs. duPont contribute directly to the general fund of a college: a grant of $10,000 to Hollins College, on the condition that the college raise all but that amount of its goal of $650,000.[36] All of her other contributions went through the institutions to scholarships. Mrs. duPont's expenditures for scholarships during the school year 1928–29 are summarized in table 2-1.[37] The dollar amounts seem minuscule by modern standards, but a scholarship of $250 or $300 in the late 1920s could send one student to college for a year. Even with this modest scholarship program, Mrs. duPont was making it possible for more than fifty students to earn a college degree.

TABLE 2-1 Student Scholarships, 1928–29

Recipient	Number of scholarships	Amount ($)
F. D. Goodwin	13	3,350
J. A. C. Chandler	12	3,787
State Teachers College, Fredericksburg	6	1,725
State Teachers College, Harrisonburg	3	850
Virginia Polytechnic Inst.	4	1,300
Individual students	15	6,940
Total	53	17,952[a]

a. $162,000 in current dollars.

Mrs. duPont's tight-fisted policy on scholarships, however, was more than just a matter of husbanding her funds. She was convinced that keeping her students under financial pressures weeded out the weak and motivated the strong. She expected students to work to support their education when they were not in college. In one case she refused to finance a boy who had been out of school for three years because he had not earned any money in the meantime for his education. "[E]vidently while he is perfectly willing to accept it if some one will hand it out to him on a silver platter, he is not willing to work for it. This to you may sound a little harsh, but I have had so much experience with the boys and girls whom I send to schools, seldom have I found one who has any appreciation of an education if I pay the full board and tuition. For this reason, another year I shall adopt a different system with all of them, paying only a portion of their board and tuition."[38]

There were other restrictions. Mrs. duPont provided no support for high school pupils on the grounds that local high schools were by this time good enough to qualify them for college. For college students she would not provide support for more than three years. "After that time they should be in a position to meet all of their own expenses, even if they have to stay out of college a year while they make money enough to return the following year." The same reasoning applied to postgraduate and professional studies: graduate students should be able to support themselves and not deprive younger students who needed help.[39]

In some respects Mrs. duPont's scholarship program was in the mainstream of American philanthropy, which since the Civil War had provided large sums for higher education. And, like many philanthropists, she was measuring the need and systematically budgeting her resources. In other respects, her giving was typical of the charitable motivations of earlier Americans. Her focus on the individual and her insistence that education should have a practical more than a cultural value were both very much in the American tradition.[40]

More than anything else, however, Mrs. duPont's attitudes on education reflected her own experience as a student and teacher. She expected her scholarship students to work for an education just as she had done, and she saw her own success as a product of the self-discipline that her education had required. Furthermore, her own education was grounded in the fundamentals of knowledge and the practical skills she needed to become a teacher. She was determined to impart these same values to her students. In fact, she never stopped thinking like a teacher. She wrote to a former San Diego colleague in 1926: "I never pass a school to-day but that there is some of that desire to get out and go in and try my hand at it."[41]

It was Jessie Ball the teacher as much as Mrs. duPont who sternly lectured her charges on grammar, usage, and penmanship. To one young man she wrote: "I would suggest that you try to develop a dignified bearing, a courteous and respectful manner as well as order and neatness, and place emphasis on composition and diction in your letter-writing. Slang will help no one to succeed in the business or professional world, as it is used to conceal a pauperized vocabulary."[42]

She was hardest of all on Denise, who was at this time attending a private school in Baltimore. She accepted the probability that her adopted daughter would never be an outstanding student, but she was determined to improve the girl's penmanship, composition, and accuracy. In November 1928, when Denise was thirteen, Mrs. duPont sent her a book of letters to be copied in longhand. "Spend forty-five minutes Saturday or Friday evening, it matters not to me, copying these letters, and the same length of time on Sunday copying some one of the psalms, as the biblical spelling and wording is a little different from what you are accustomed to. It will teach you concentration. I shall mark these papers with a red or blue pencil, and return them to you every week. For each mistake I shall take off three points."[43]

As one would expect, Mrs. duPont took a special interest in young women who wished to go into teaching. Of the few professions open to women in her youth, teaching still appeared to her to be a high calling.

She warned her advisors, however, that only the brightest girls should go into teaching. Nor would she support the practice of sending girls from low-income families to normal school for two years and then having them begin teaching. Unless a girl could go on to college after normal school, Mrs. duPont thought she should go to business school where she could "be prepared to make a good living, . . . then [if] she does not succeed her employer will be the only sufferer and not the poor little helpless children."[44]

This note of compassion expressed a feeling deep in Jessie duPont's personality. It had quickened her love for Alfred in the final years of his troubled marriage to Alicia. Compassion sparked her efforts to build a new life for her husband at Nemours. It led her to seek out his children and his sister Marguerite to bring about a reconciliation after decades of estrangement. It was the source of her generosity in showering her relatives and friends with gifts. It motivated her charities among the unfortunate in the Northern Neck. It lay at the heart of her love for children and her devotion to education. Even the harsh terms of her scholarships reflected a deep concern for young men and women who, without her help, would never have had an education commensurate with their abilities.

The fruits of her compassion were impressive even during the first few years of her marriage. Yet these first efforts in philanthropy would pale in comparison with those she would make in the future.

3

A Partner in Business

*U*nlike most women of her class, Jessie Ball duPont was not limited to the domestic sphere in building a solid base for her marriage. She had professional skills and experience that enabled her to support her husband in his business enterprises. Once Alfred had put behind him his career with the DuPont Company and the Nemours Trading Company fiasco, he needed some new business venture to occupy his time and recoup his fortune. Jessie knew that her marriage could be threatened as much by her husband's lack of purpose as by a colorless domestic life.

Alfred, however, was not completely idle. Dozens of ideas came unsolicited by mail, occasionally from Jessie's brother Tom in California. Alfred found good reasons for rejecting most of these, but he was intrigued by one proposal that Jessie brought to his attention. Will Harding, one of Jessie's distant cousins in the Northern Neck, had come up with the design of a tomato-peeling machine. Alfred loved to tinker with mechanical gadgets, and the tomato peeler could give him something to do as well as provide a livelihood for one of Jessie's many relatives. Alfred needed little encouragement from Jessie and was soon convinced that the device, with suitable modifications, could revolutionize the harvesting of tomatoes.[1]

Alfred had the knowledge and experience required to turn a raw invention into a marketable product, but both he and Jessie knew that he could not give the project the kind of attention that would ensure effective marketing and avoid the kind of troubles that had plagued the Nemours Trading Company. She proposed that Alfred bring her brother Ed from the West Coast to handle that part of the business. Alfred remembered Ed as the enterprising little fellow who had scouted with him on hunting parties on the Northern Neck; he had not seen Ed since he served as best man at their wedding in 1921, and Ed, unlike his older brother, Tom, was not given to letter writing. The younger brother, however, had continued to demonstrate unusual skills as a salesman. He had been involved in a variety of small business ventures in California before taking over his brother Tom's position as a traveling salesman for a law-book publishing company. Returning to California in 1919 after a stint in the army, Ed had joined the biggest furniture company on the West Coast as a salesman. Within fifteen months Ed and two partners had taken over the office-furniture division on a profit-sharing basis and were making $1,500 a month. Alfred could offer him only $5,000 a year, but Ed was willing to give the tomato peeler a try. He later recalled: "I was involved in an interesting business, and had made some success in it, but it was becoming obvious to me that there was little further advancement

Edward Ball, the successful businessman in 1922, about to become the financial manager of Alfred duPont's fortune.

opportunity for me in that field. And, besides, my sister wanted me to do it. I told Mr. duPont I would come to work for him for one year."[2]

The tomato peeler proved a mechanical success but a business failure. Ed learned in that first season in 1923 that tomato harvesting was a decentralized operation inappropriate for mass production. Advising Alfred to write off his investment in the enterprise, Ed prepared to return to California. Jessie's sister Elsie looked upon her brother's role in the tomato-peeler adventure with a jaundiced eye. Ed was too coarse, too much of a money grubber for her taste. She thought Ed was exploiting poor Alfred's naive generosity and that Jessie was playing the same game. Elsie believed that Alfred for years really had preferred her to Jessie, but that her sister with unseemly haste had connived to grab Alfred when Alicia died. Now, in Elsie's opinion, Jessie was trying to isolate Alfred from other influences so that she and Ed could protect their own selfish interests. Such considerations were not beyond Jessie or Ed, but Jessie's motivation probably rested more in her love and concern for her husband than in personal gain. Perhaps, as Elsie claimed, Ed had never believed in the tomato peeler but had cynically used it to get a job with Alfred. When the time and the tomatoes were ripe, according to Elsie, Ed dumped the peeler and Will Harding at the same time.[3]

Alfred, however, was not nearly so helpless as Elsie liked to believe. He admired the way Ed took hold of the project and would not think of letting him return to California. Alfred asked Ed to look into the construction of his new yacht, the *Nenemoosha,* and the finances of his real estate holdings in Wilmington. Quickly converting losses into profits, Ed turned next to Alfred's remaining debts from the Nemours Trading Company debacle. With no experience in banking, Ed went to New York and in a few hours obtained a bank loan at 4 percent to replace the Morgan loan at 7 percent. The White Shoe Company in Boston was still holding a $1.5 million claim against the defunct trading company, and Alfred was prepared to pay it off to rid himself of it once and for all. Before he could do that, Ed went to Boston and in a series of hard negotiating sessions with a team of veteran lawyers, came away with a settlement for $490,000. Ed's notable success brought an offer of $10,000 a year from Alfred if he would stay in the East; two years later Alfred raised Ed's salary to $25,000.[4]

Ed Ball was not only worth the money, but he was the kind of man Alfred had long been seeking. In October 1924 he wrote to Tom Ball:

"Ed is surely a nice boy, the most livable human being, next to the Brid, that I know. Being a Ball, he is naturally a gentleman and excuse me from living with anybody less. He is a little pig-headed—another Ball feature (also a duPont feature, I being the exception)—so it is necessary to bat him over the head with a club once in a while; but he has a well-balanced cabeza and is a fine, loyal, hard worker, as tenacious as a bull dog on a tramp's pants—all qualities appealing most strongly to me."[5]

The new life of joy and genuine affection that Jessie brought to Nemours as its mistress was only one source of the enormous gratitude that Alfred felt for his wife. Her quick mind, sound judgment, and natural ability in financial affairs proved invaluable in Alfred's later years. Ed Ball was a trusted subordinate and loyal brother-in-law; Jessie was his adored wife, business partner, and confidante. Ed accorded his older sister the same deference that he reserved for "Mr. duPont," and her decision on any matter was law with him. As his deafness became more severe, Alfred relied on his wife to follow the nuances of business discussions, and he sought her opinion on major decisions. In 1923 or 1924, when her brother Tom was visiting, Jessie and Alfred took him to Cherry Island. On chairs out on the lawn near the water tower, Alfred described in detail the vicissitudes of his first marriage and the bitter dispute with his cousins. As Jessie recalled it, "Later he talked to Tom about his confidence in my business ability and also about Eddie's. The only doubts he had about me were that I might be inclined to be too generous and give away everything I had. To tell you the truth, . . . I sometimes wish I had. I believe no one knows the valuelessness of money as such than do I. Great wealth if taken as a trust as it should be taken makes one a galley slave, and if it is not so accepted it should be taken from them."[6]

For the Balls, family ties had stretched westward from Virginia to Texas and California, but marriage gave Jessie a new orientation, one that extended south from Wilmington to Virginia and on to Florida. In the 1870s Jacksonville and the broad St. Johns River beyond the small city had been a popular winter resort for the wealthy. As a boy, Alfred had been impressed by his mother's glowing accounts of her annual visits there. After the turn of the century Alfred had taken to going to Florida every year after Christmas to escape the worst of the winters in Wilmington.

In 1923 Alfred took Jessie to Miami, where they stayed for several weeks at the old and sedate Royal Palm Hotel. A land boom was then sweeping Miami, a phenomenon that both Jessie and Ed had experienced in San Diego. Partly to try her hand at investments and partly to distract Alfred from his interest in a million-dollar estate at Coconut Grove, Jessie invested $33,000 of her own money in some strips of sand on Miami Beach. The following year the couple set off by ship for the Bahamas in late January, returned to Miami for a few weeks, then went on to Jacksonville, where Alfred's old yacht, the *Alicia,* was awaiting them. After the crowds of tourists and speculators in Miami, the duPonts found life more to their liking on the quiet waters of the St. Johns. Large areas along the river above the busy waterfront at Jacksonville were undeveloped, and a winter home in these peaceful and spacious surroundings seemed a better possibility than Jessie's lots at Miami Beach.[7]

Reasons other than climate, however, were drawing the duPonts to Florida. In 1923, after rescuing the investment of the DuPont Company in General Motors, Pierre S. duPont had returned to Wilmington and accepted the post of state tax commissioner. When one of Pierre's deputies came by to see Alfred's books relating to his taxable property in Delaware, Alfred bridled at the possibility that his cousin might be prying into his private affairs. He ordered Ed Ball to find an attorney to set up three corporations under Florida law, to which he intended to transfer title of all of his Delaware properties except Nemours. Ed, in his typical fashion, concealed the duPont connection until he had obtained the services of an unsuspecting Florida law firm at a bargain rate.[8]

In November 1924 a new incentive for moving to Florida appeared when voters in the state approved a constitutional amendment prohibiting inheritance or income taxes, much to the delight of business interests and promoters.[9] None of Alfred's correspondence ever mentions this new advantage, perhaps because the voters removed the restriction a few years later when the great land boom of the 1920s collapsed. At the time, however, the measure must have reinforced the decision to move to Florida, in Ed's mind, if not in Alfred's.

The choice of Jacksonville as the duPonts' new headquarters made good business sense in other ways. During winter visits to Florida before 1920, Alfred must have noted the startling transformation of the sleepy town into a thriving, modern urban center. In 1900, with less than 30,000 inhabitants, more than half of whom were black, Jacksonville was the largest city in the state. Except for Tampa on the west coast, there was hardly a community south of Jacksonville that could honestly qualify as a city. Miami had been little more than a fishing village, cut off from the rest of the state by rivers, swamp lands, and sand dunes until Henry M. Flagler pushed his Florida East Coast Railroad into the town and opened the posh Royal Palm Hotel there in 1896.

Jacksonville, at the head of the peninsula in the east coast corridor, held a strategic position as the gateway to the state, which in the next quarter-century would enjoy incredible growth and development. The future looked bright in 1900, but a disastrous fire the following spring destroyed most of the downtown area, including all of the local government buildings, banks, office blocks, warehouses, schools, shops, and churches. More than two thousand buildings covering 140 blocks and valued at $15 million went up in smoke. Half the tax base disappeared and 10,000 people were homeless.[10]

This disaster, however, opened the way for rebuilding the city. Within weeks crews cleared the rubble and civic leaders laid ambitious plans that would see a modern city rise on the ruins of the old. Prompt construction of new structures marked the beginning of a building boom that lasted through the decade and into the twenties. By 1910 Jacksonville boasted its first skyscrapers: the six-story Dyal-Upchurch Building, the ten-story Bisbee Building, and the Atlantic National Bank Building on Forsyth Street. The new Seminole Hotel, city hall, courthouse, library, YMCA, and a number of new churches set the tone for a sparkling, up-to-date downtown. Suburban growth also mushroomed in Riverside and Ortega to the southwest for more prosperous families; in Murray Hill, Lackawanna, and Grand Park to the west for blue-collar workers; in College Park, Northside Park, and Highland Heights to the northwest along King's Road for black families. To the north, Springfield, the city's best residential area in earlier decades, expanded beyond the city line to Twenty-first Street, and by the end of the decade to Panama Park. Similar expansion occurred to the northeast and east, all the way to Talleyrand Avenue. The St. Johns River, still unbridged, hampered development to the south. A modern streetcar line tied the suburbs to the city's center.[11]

Rapid economic development accompanied the building boom. Deepening the St. Johns channel to the ocean made possible a five-fold increase in maritime shipping within two years as the export of fertilizers, lumber, and naval stores opened the city to world trade. Equally important was the rapid expansion of railroads, terminals, and warehouses that tied North Florida to the sea. In 1902 the Atlantic Coast Line joined the Seaboard Air Line and Henry Flagler's Florida East Coast Railroad in building terminals in Jacksonville, to be joined later in the decade by a subsidiary of Southern Railways. The port and rail facilities stimulated the wholesale industry, and Jacksonville soon became a major distribution center for meat, liquor, groceries, drugs, hardware, dry goods, electrical supplies, and machinery.[12]

Rapid growth and prosperity gave Jacksonville cultural advantages rare in other Florida communities at that time. New theaters brought vaudeville and minstrel shows, and later motion pictures, to the city. Much of the social life, all rigidly segregated, still centered around the city's sixty-four black churches, fifty white churches, and two synagogues, but amusement parks, racetracks, professional baseball, and college football provided new diversions.

The building boom brought with it modern water and sewer systems, which, together with new sanitation standards and medical facilities, eliminated the epidemics of yellow fever, smallpox, and typhoid that had recurred in earlier decades. Civic groups, led by the Jacksonville Woman's Club, raised private funds and later obtained tax dollars to support the city's hospitals and health care systems. The woman's club and the board of trade also took the lead in efforts to improve the city's substandard public school system. With the help of new bonding authority in 1912 to increase school budgets and strong leadership from a capable young school superintendent, there was some progress in expanding the curriculum and constructing fireproof school buildings. Many of these improvements, however, were overtaken by the heavy influx of war contracts and war workers in 1917 and 1918.[13]

By the time Alfred and Jessie visited Jacksonville in 1923 the city had grown to more than 100,000 persons. The downtown area had been completely rebuilt. The new George Washington Hotel had just opened and an even more elegant hostelry, the Carling, was under construction. The residential suburbs to the southwest and west were growing rapidly as the building boom continued unabated. Completion of the first bridge across the St. Johns in 1921 had sparked the explosive growth of South Jacksonville and had opened the way for large homes and estates along the river further south on San Jose Boulevard. Bank deposits were at an all-time high. A new municipal water system, a second bridge across the St. Johns, a new city hall, court-house, fire stations in the suburbs, and the purchase of additional park land were all in the planning stage.[14] Jacksonville was a thriving metropolis, prosperous, and full of optimism. What could be a more promising home for the duPonts' Florida enterprise?

Once Ed Ball had incorporated the St. Johns River Development Company and the Brandywine Hundred Realty Company he set out to find ways to invest duPont assets in Florida. First he proposed in April 1925 to trade Alfred's old yacht, the *Alicia,* for some property in Jacksonville. A few weeks later he was off on a three-hundred-mile expedition to the Florida Panhandle to look for properties not yet touched by the land boom in the southern part of the state. Ed's sturdy six-cylinder Chevrolet served him well as he made his way over the desolate and almost deserted terrain. He later recalled, "There was not a foot of paved road in north Florida west of Lake City, except seven miles of nine-foot brick pavement just east of Milton. If two automobiles met, both cars had to get their wheels off the brick road and, if they got back on it was by helping each other."[15]

Before the Civil War, the Panhandle counties, just south of the Georgia line, had provided some of the best cotton-growing areas in the region. But after the war the large plantations had given way to sharecropping. The lack of rail service killed efforts to produce vegetables for northern markets. Some of the plantations became pecan orchards or hunting preserves for wealthy Yankees, and much of the remaining land had been exploited for its virgin timber. The decline of the lumber and cotton economy had left disintegrating towns, a few dirt roads, a declining population, and thousands of acres of land at bargain prices.[16]

On a peninsula between St. Andrews Bay and the Gulf of Mexico near Panama City Ed found an offer he could not forego. He wired Alfred: "HAVE THIRTEEN THOUSAND ACRES ABOUT TEN MILES WATER FRONT OFFERED FIFTEEN PER ACRE THINK GOOD BUY." Alfred agreed. He wired Ed that he and another speculator could take as much of the deal as they wanted; Alfred and Jessie would pick up the rest "in proportion two to one."[17] Jessie was clearly to be a full-fledged business partner in Florida. She had demonstrated her ability in real estate investment earlier in the year when she sold her Miami Beach lots for $160,000. Neither Alfred nor Jessie nor

Ed was inclined to gamble. They had seen land booms before and knew that sooner or later the bubble would break. Caution was the word, but in the summer of 1925 as prices soared in Miami, the trio were obviously buying land in the Panhandle for quick profit and not for long-term development. Ed was back in West Florida in June, closing deals on more land. By this time Alfred had $165,000 in the venture; Jessie, $85,000; and Ed, $2,800.[18]

When Ed returned to Jacksonville in early September, he wired Alfred: "THIS TOWN IS JAMMED AND EVERY TRAIN COMES IN PACKED EVERY ONE LOOKING FOR REAL ESTATE STOP LEAVING NOW FOR PANAMA CITY." The higher the boom went, however, the more Alfred worried. He wanted to set up a corporation to buy the property by selling stock and thus avoid personal liability. He was troubled by persistent predictions in the press that the boom was about to collapse. "While I think the whole matter is an attempt to discourage emigration to Florida, which seems to be seriously affecting the other Southern states, I do think that very careful consideration should be given to the subject of just how long we should hang on to our mud." Ed replied by return mail: "I am leaving Saturday afternoon for Florida and anticipate selling enough of our mud while there to get all of your money back. Once we are in velvet, we do not need to worry about when the boom will blow up."[19]

As it happened, the boom fizzled rather than exploded early in 1926, doing little damage to duPont holdings, which Alfred, Jessie, and Ed had carefully protected. In fact Ed was able to spend $800,000 to buy more than 66,000 acres of land stretching along the coast west of Panama City and north toward the Georgia line. The duPonts closed Nemours early that fall and took rooms at the Mason Hotel in Jacksonville. From an office in the Barnett National Bank Building, they organized Almours Securities, Incorporated, a real estate and investment company with assets of $34 million.[20]

The duPonts found Jacksonville not only a good place to do business but also a pleasant community in which to live. With a population of barely one hundred thousand in 1926, the city was still small enough to be friendly and to have a sense of civic pride. At the same time it was big enough to have some of the refinements of life. Bankers and other business leaders made up the social elite centered around the Ortega and Riverside areas and the Florida Country Club. In 1927 Jacksonville became the first city in the South to broadcast an opera program, and the more sophisticated residents brought symphony orchestras and other cultural attractions to the city.

The year 1926 established a new record for residential housing construction in Jacksonville. One of the most ambitious developments was the San Jose area six miles south of the city center on the east bank of the river. Riding the Florida land boom, developers built a grand hotel, a clubhouse, and thirty-one villas along the riverfront before the bubble collapsed. When plans to build an even larger hotel on a seventy-four-acre tract had to be abandoned, Ed Ball took advantage of the situation to acquire the site for the duPonts' Jacksonville home. Alfred engaged Harold Saxelby of the Jacksonville architectural firm of Marsh Saxelby to design the mansion in the Spanish-Mediterranean style of the San Jose Estates, but he took a personal hand in the details. He designed the formal gardens that stretched from the mansion down to the river and made drawings for the fountains, which were adorned with frogs, alligators, and pelicans. Construction started in the spring of 1926 under the watchful eye of Ed Ball and was completed early in 1927.[21]

Nestled within a grove of huge live oaks and hickories covered with Spanish moss, the mansion had a superb vista of the river, which was more than two miles wide at that point. Alfred had docks and a splendid boathouse built on the river to accommodate the *Nenemoosha;* a shallow-draft house-boat, the *Gadfly;* and a noisy speedboat, the *Hellcat.* The house was small by comparison with Nemours, but it had more the atmosphere of a home than did the museumlike Wilmington estate. Jessie could make the new estate her own home in a way that she never could at Nemours. Perhaps to reflect her stewardship, the duPonts named it Epping Forest, after the Northern Neck homestead once inhabited by Mary Ball Washington, which in turn took its name from the Balls' ancestral home in England.[22]

The end of the Florida land boom in the spring of 1926 had a profound influence on the state and in turn on the course of the duPonts' investment plans. For the state the collapse was devastating. Land speculators were wiped out overnight and the thousands of Northerners who had flocked into Florida during the winter left in the spring. Natural disaster followed financial ruin when a mid-September hurricane destroyed $100 million worth of property, killed 327 people, injured more than 6,000, and left 43,000 homeless.[23] William T. Edwards, who had grown up on the Northern Neck and married Jessie's childhood friend Placidia Hudnall,

Epping Forest, the winter home of the duPonts on the St. Johns River, Jacksonville.

had come to Florida at Alfred's request to work with Ed Ball. Of the 1926 disaster Edwards recalled: "Anything [about] Florida brought forth a sneering burst of ridicule all over the nation. From its place in the minds of millions, as a land of promise, in a miraculously short time, it became the thing to be avoided, to be shunned, to be afraid of, and to be blamed for more defalcations and failures of trust than could ever before have been imagined."[24]

In Edwards's view, Alfred duPont stood among the financial and material ruins of Florida as the only national figure of wealth "who had

The gardens at Epping Forest, designed by Alfred duPont.

the vision, the will and the courage, to make large investments and herculean efforts to assist the people back to the path of prosperity." Edwards vividly remembered a conversation with Alfred duPont and Ed Ball after dinner one evening in the fall of 1927 at Epping Forest. Alfred announced that "we are now in Florida to live and work. We expect to spend the balance of our days here." With ample financial resources, the duPonts' purpose would be not to make more money for themselves but to help Florida grow and develop.[25]

There is no reason to believe that either Alfred or Jessie saw their future role in Florida in any less altruistic terms. They were both by nature sensitive to the needs of others, and Alfred had often demonstrated in his political and civic activities in Delaware his personal concern for the public welfare. For Ed Ball, however, the duPonts' altruism was more a means than an end. It provided a justification for amassing more millions, and it is fair to say that Alfred did not discourage his agent's enthusiasm for making money. Also, there was no better time to buy land in Florida at bargain prices. In 1927 Ball was off again to Panama City, where he succeeded in purchasing an additional 13,000 acres in Bay County.[26]

That same spring Ball spent several arduous weeks at the state capital, Tallahassee, lobbying the senate highway committee to approve appropriation bills that would support the construction of a gulf coastal highway and a series of bridges from Panama City to Tallahassee. Once the state bills were passed, Ball and Edwards set out to encourage the counties through which the road would pass to sell bonds to support the project. Edwards's role was to bid up the bonds at the county auctions so that they would bring a fair price to the counties. He saw the project as a civic achievement on the part of Mr. duPont, whose leadership was acknowledged when he was elected president of the Gulf Coast Highway Association. Not even Edwards, however, could deny that the road would open for development the thousands of acres of land that Ball had purchased along the right of way. The dual character of Alfred's motives was clear in a letter that Ball wrote him telling his boss of his successful lobbying efforts: "Following your suggestion that we pick up any good bargains on the main thoroughfares in Jacksonville, I have contracted for several lots that I think are genuine bargains. I will bring a blueprint or map of Jacksonville and show you the exact location of these lots, when I come North."[27]

A few weeks later Ball reported that "we succeeded in putting through most of our road and bridge bills." Encouraged by this success, he was now trying to promote two new bridges across the St. Johns in Jacksonville. He was confident that the bridges would stimulate real estate on both sides of the river.[28]

Alfred also directed Ed Ball to investigate the banking situation in Jacksonville. After the collapse of the land boom in the spring of 1926, scores of Florida banks failed, and others tottered on the brink of disaster during the summer months, when the weaker banks had a hard time staying alive even under the best conditions. The magnitude of duPont assets being transferred to Florida dictated the need for a sound banking institution, preferably one in which Alfred had some control. Now that his fortunes were to be tied to the economy of the state, he also recognized the importance of keeping a few safe banks in the Jacksonville area if the state was to recover from the 1926 disaster. He asked Ball to begin buying up small blocks of stock in the three largest Jacksonville banks.

This unobtrusive move into the banking business gave both men an opportunity to determine which bank might best serve their needs. Early in 1927 Ball reported that the Florida National Bank, the smallest of the three, was definitely the weakest, but its stock was not closely held and was easier to buy. Another advantage was that Florida National was not dominated by a single strong personality as were the other two. Ball kept on buying up Florida National stock until the duPonts had potential control by late 1927. He then obtained a seat on the board, but Alfred chose not to show his hand until the spring of 1929, when he stepped in to abort a proposed merger that he believed would shake public confidence in Jacksonville's banks.[29]

With the new home at Epping Forest furnished and operating in the winter of 1927, the Florida base was now complete. For Jessie, it meant maintaining two homes and two offices. Although the two residences were seldom open at the same time, both demanded her attention throughout the year. After Thanksgiving and again early in May she would for many years stage the semiannual migration between Wilmington and Jacksonville. There were always the matters of determining which members of the household staff would make the transition and of finding replacements for those left behind. Jessie herself decided what provisions and supplies would be needed to stock each home at the beginning of its season.

During the late 1920s the duPonts kept Epping Forest open until late April, when they returned by train to Wilmington. In May there were usually short trips to Cherry Island either by car or on the *Nenemoosha* and a few days in New York shopping for spring and summer fashions. As Jessie wrote to her friend Inga Orner in 1925: "It is very essential that I get somewhere or I will be picked up off the streets by the ragman, or else stuffed in an ash can, as my wardrobe is decidedly at a low ebb."[30]

The summers brought trips to Europe or extended cruises on the *Nenemoosha* up the East Coast to Long Island Sound or New England, outings with the children at Cherry Island or on the beach at Atlantic City. In August Nemours was closed for two or three weeks for staff vacations. Thanksgiving and Christmas were occasions for family

The yacht *Nenemoosha,* built for Alfred duPont in 1922 and donated to the U.S. government in World War II.

The dining salon in the *Nenemoosha* in the 1920s.

reunions at Nemours, and soon after Christmas the southern migration
to Epping Forest began again. Whether they were at Nemours or Epping
Forest, the duPonts had a steady stream of visitors, almost always family
or very close friends, who stayed for a weekend or a few days. In Florida
there were often short excursions by car to Miami or Palm Beach; in
Delaware, frequent trips by train to Washington, Baltimore, or New
York. Mrs. duPont was a familiar figure at the Wilmington railroad
station. Her Christmas gift list in 1928 included fifteen employees at the
station.[31]

Managing two large homes with all the social commitments that they
involved would have been more than enough to occupy most society
matrons of the day, but domestic responsibilities were not the most
demanding part of Jessie's life. While in Wilmington or Jacksonville, she
spent most of her weekdays in her downtown offices rather than at

home—in Jacksonville at Almours Securities in the Barnett Bank Building; in Wilmington in room 803 of the Delaware Trust Building.

The greatest volume of her correspondence related to her business, charitable, and educational interests. During these years Ed Ball usually addressed his letters, almost always on business matters, to Mr. duPont and seldom wrote directly to his sister. After Alfred transferred his financial records and assets to Jacksonville, James G. Bright with several other Almours employees handled Jessie's business accounts and taxes. For her Florida correspondence, she relied on Irene Walsh, who served as an executive secretary for both Alfred duPont and Ed Ball. A competent and experienced manager, Mrs. Walsh had come up through the clerical ranks of the banking business and could be relied on for some business judgments as well as for preparing correspondence.

Even after the move to Florida Mrs. duPont continued to use the offices in Wilmington as her own base of operations. There she managed her personal affairs, including her investment, charitable, and educational activities. One reason for this decision was that she had come to rely more and more on her Wilmington secretary, Mary G. Shaw, to handle her affairs. What Mrs. duPont particularly admired in Miss Shaw was her interest in business affairs and her willingness to learn the ways of the corporate world. In 1928 Mrs. duPont began advising Miss Shaw on making her own investments in the stock market, and Miss Shaw in turn was soon following the market and reporting tips to her boss. It soon became apparent that the young woman had good business sense and was not reluctant to take the initiative in making decisions on all sorts of personal and financial matters during the extended periods when Mrs. duPont was not in Wilmington.[32]

Despite her many responsibilities and interests, Jessie's first thoughts and concerns were always for Alfred. She doted on him when they were together and wrote to him daily when they were separated. She constantly worried about his health and tried to arrange their lives to include periods of rest and relaxation aboard the *Nenemoosha* or at a resort hotel. Although Alfred was only sixty-five, he did suffer from heart trouble, and he tired easily. Of equal concern to Jessie was the continuing deterioration of his hearing. By the late 1920s he was almost totally deaf and could no longer hear with the various types of amplifiers that Jessie

The master stateroom in the *Nenemoosha* in the 1920s.

had found for him. He had never been able to learn lipreading, and most people communicated with him with written notes. In these circumstances Jessie often served as his ears, particularly in business discussions. But, unlike Alfred's first two wives, she did not accept his deafness and never gave up in her attempts to find a cure.[33]

Having exhausted the resources and ideas of hearing experts in America, Jessie set off for Europe with Alfred in the summer of 1928 and again in 1929 in search of a physician who could restore Alfred's hearing. Their greatest hopes lay in Dr. Isadore Muller, who operated a hearing clinic in Carlsbad, Czechoslovakia. Jessie never described the treatment in detail, but it seemed to consist of some kind of ear therapy plus a large measure of rest and relaxation. Jessie was convinced that nervous tension impaired Alfred's hearing as much as anything else, and the peace and solitude of the Carlsbad resort seemed to improve it. After the 1928 visit she gave Muller $20,000 for his clinic. While in Europe, they were able to spend some time with Alfred's daughter Madeleine and her sons in

Munich, and there was also a reunion with Madeleine and Alfred Victor and his wife in 1929.[34]

In the spring of 1929, when more than eighty Florida banks had closed in the aftermath of the collapse of the land boom, Alfred duPont had been forced to show his hand and take control of the Florida National Bank. The bank itself was on solid ground, but even rumors of weakness could threaten a bank's existence at that time. Despite the precarious financial situation in Florida, Jessie insisted that they not delay their trip to Europe and another session with Dr. Muller. They had every confidence that Ed Ball could handle the situation while they were abroad, and in fact Alfred left his brother-in-law instructions to proceed with the acquisition of banks in other parts of the state. Furthermore, Alfred and Jessie had given Ed general power of attorney over the holdings of Almours Securities, worth at that time as much as $150 million. This resource Ed used to stave off a run on Florida National in July 1929.[35]

Alfred and Jessie reached home barely two weeks before the stock market crashed on October 29, 1929. Thanks to Ed's foresight, their losses were heavy only on paper and not disastrous. Convinced that the market was greatly inflated, Ed had been steadily selling stocks during the summer for the account of Almours Securities. As a result, when the smoke cleared in November, neither Alfred nor Almours was heavily in debt, and there were sizable assets to meet the demands of the future. In fact, Almours Securities was in good enough shape that Ed could proceed with the acquisition of banks in Lakeland and Bartow.

Of much greater concern to Alfred in the autumn of 1929 was Jessie's string of illnesses. After their return from Europe she found it difficult to resume her usual vigorous schedule of activities. The annual departure for Florida was delayed for several weeks while Jessie recuperated in a Baltimore hospital from a urinary infection. Alfred hoped that a winter of rest in Florida would restore her vitality, but on January 20, 1930, she collapsed. Alfred rushed her by train back to Baltimore, and for weeks her life hung in the balance. Diagnosis proved difficult, her doctors finally deciding that she was suffering from ulcers. Surgery proved the analysis correct, but Jessie almost died in the operating room. Both Alfred and Ed Ball were at her side for a month until she passed through the most critical period. Her sister Elsie, who lived in Baltimore, arranged daily visits to the hospital by members of the Ball family, and by early March Miss Shaw began regular trips to Baltimore to read correspondence and take dictation.[36]

Jessie took great comfort in all the love and affection showered upon her by her family. She was especially touched by Alfred's devoted attention. She wrote one of her cousins from the hospital: "He is an eternal joy and I do feel so bad and apologetic for having caused him so much worry with this spree of mine, but he has been as sweet and patient as it is humanly possible for a mortal to be throughout it all, though he says he couldn't have gone through it but for Elsie, who was a tower of strength to all."[37]

That Alfred had been close to despair was all too evident. One night walking home from the hospital with Elsie at the worst of the crisis, he was almost overcome with grief. He told his sister-in-law: "The one eventuality in life I am not prepared for is that Jessie should go before me." He called her illness "really the worst blow that I have ever received for many reasons, but principally for the fact that it's the only thing I never anticipated could possibly happen."[38]

There followed a long recuperation at Epping Forest during the spring of 1930. By the first of May Jessie seemed to be gaining some of her old fighting spirit. She wrote to her friend Billy Martin:

> My orders are to take it easy, not to go in crowds, and not to do very much in a social way. These orders, as you know, are not hard for me to carry out, but there is one that was given me, namely, to rest for two hours every afternoon and have breakfast in bed, which I find impossible to abide by. Why anybody likes to eat in bed in a disorderly room is beyond my comprehension. It would take the appetite away from a starving Bengalese tiger. Then if one is to lie down for an hour before dressing for dinner, I would like to know when one is to accomplish anything or even shake hands with the passing crowd to wish them Good [*sic*] speed.[39]

Her critical illness in 1930 marked a turning point in Jessie's life. Surviving her first serious illness and then only by a thread, she light-heartedly attributed her recovery to her Ball heritage. The experience, however, did put her future into new perspective. She was now forty-six years old, no longer the exuberant young teacher who had set off for California in 1908, but a middle-aged woman who had found her place in life.

Her brush with death also marked the end of the transition that Jessie Ball had begun nine years earlier in her determination to establish herself as Mrs. duPont. She had given Alfred in her brother Ed a loyal lieutenant with unusual talents in business administration and finance. She had demonstrated her own considerable ability in financial matters and had become her husband's trusted business partner as well as his lover, nurse, and pal.

In the process, she had taken upon herself the attributes that Wilmington society would expect to find in the wife of a distinguished member of the duPont family. At the same time, however, she had maintained her integrity. Two decades later she wrote to a young friend who had also married into a distinguished family:

> The more important families are, the more inclined they are to dictate, so to speak, to all the incoming members of the family, or rather that was true of the duPonts. . . . They ran up with a new customer, a new type when I came along. However, I never had an unpleasant moment or word with any, I am thankful to say. Yet I wouldn't yield my independence and A. I. wouldn't have had me do it for the world. He knew the characteristics of the family—and it wasn't just this generation—that superiority complex, which he dubbed ignorance, that feeling [that] they had a corner on all the aristocracy in the United States and that all who came into the family should bend their knee, so to speak, in obeisance every time the name duPont was pronounced.[40]

Since 1921 she had won the respect, and in some cases, the affection of members of the family. She had acquired bearing, reserve, and poise along with her natural warmth and intelligence that left no doubt in anyone who knew her that she had met the family challenge. Traces of the bright, fresh country girl who had grown up on the shores of the Chesapeake would never entirely disappear from her personality, but only her closest friends could find the girl in the lady who was now Mrs. duPont.

The Great Depression

In the years since her marriage Jessie Ball duPont had been steadily building the assets in her personal account. By the end of 1927 her assets, almost entirely in securities, totaled more than $4.5 million ($42 million in current dollars). Her only liabilities were brokers' accounts for stocks she was buying on margin and as yet unpaid-for shares in the land companies that her brother Edward had set up in the Florida panhandle. These liabilities, coming to almost $700,000, looked formidable on paper, but by careful management, Mrs. duPont had always been able to meet these obligations. Her annual income in 1927 had been slightly less than $500,000, and she had tailored her expenditures to leave a balance of only $16,000 at the end of the year. About 75 percent of her expenditures of $480,000 had gone for regular monthly gifts to family and friends, about $18,000 for charity, $25,000 for scholarships, $10,000 for taxes, and $113,000 for personal use.[1]

As long as financial conditions were stable, she could put to work in investments virtually every dollar over and above her expenditures. Her annual salary of $50,000 as vice-president of Almours Securities, regular annual gifts from her husband, and increasing returns from her securities assured her a reliable and growing income highly unusual for a woman of her day. *Fortune* magazine noted in a 1935 series on women in business that, even in the boom year of 1929, "there were only some ten or twelve thousand women in the entire country, out of a thousand times that number commonly employed, who earned $5,000 or more." In September 1929, just before the stock market crashed, Mrs. duPont's assets were approaching $6 million ($54 million in current dollars), largely as a result of a $1 million gift from Alfred earlier that year. During the same year,

TABLE 4-1 Assets, Jessie Ball duPont, 1926–35 (in $ thousands)

	1926	1927	1928	1929	1930	1931	1932	1933	1934	1935
Assets										
Investments	3,752	4,577	4,650	5,739	5,392	5,296	4,909	5,013	5,076	5,088
Real estate	192	16	16	17	17	17	17	17	18	17
Cash	200	67	37	36	16	12	48	25	37	116
Accounts receivable	1	1	1					41	50	62
Total assets	4,145	4,661	4,704	5,792	5,423	5,325	4,974	5,096	5,181	5,283
Liabilities										
Brokers	208	505	574	629	97	156	207	568	489	477
Bank loan					500	493	337	303	293	293
Florida		185	185	184	42					
Almours					88	101	101		58	48
Personal loans						2	25		2	
Total liabilities	208	690	759	813	727	752	670	871	842	818
Capital account										
Previous balance	2,975	3,905	3,970	3,945	4,789	4,696	4,573	4,303	4,223	4,465
Excess income	50	16	(135)	4	(143)	(175)	(320)	(11)	17	
Gifts, AIP	912	50	110	1,029	50	56	50	54	74	
Adjustment	(32)					(3)		(113)		
Year-end balance	3,905	3,970	3,945	4,978	4,696	4,573	4,303	4,223	4,314	4,465

however, her liabilities had grown to $813,000, and her margin over expenditures was a mere $4,000 (see table 4-1).[2]

As the full effects of the depression took hold in 1930, Mrs. duPont began retrenching. She paid for most of her stock in the Florida land companies and cleaned up her brokerage accounts with a bank loan at favorable interest rates. But even after a gift of $50,000 from Alfred, she could not keep her expenditures for the year from exceeding income by $143,000. This annual deficit grew to $320,000 in 1932. Although her net assets continued to be close to $4 million through 1935, the annual deficits that continued through these years were her overriding concern. Try as she might, she was unable for four years to pay off her debts without going into principal, and this solution was for her out of the question.[3] Under these circumstances she felt compelled to impose financial restraints on her activities even when her assets continued to be in the millions. She wrote to a distant cousin who was destitute, with illness in his family: "I am enclosing herewith check for Fifty Dollars ($50.00). . . . I regret I can send no more, but you know what the economic condition is throughout the land. Those living on the farm or by the water are truly fortunate, as they can raise enough to eat, but think of the poor and unemployed in the cities, who have no means of getting anything and who must depend entirely on charity. It is up to all who have money to give every possible dollar to these people."[4]

Despite her own sense of financial stringency, Mrs. duPont could not turn away the scores of indigent people who were struggling for existence in the Northern Neck. She had Miss Shaw send $10 to one woman who wrote: "My heart aches because I have to write this letter to you but this is the only hope I have. I have got only 6 lb. of flour in the house and I haven't got 25 cents to buy anything with if I was to get it on credit. I see no sight of paying for it. . . . I don't see how or what I am going to do, so please Madam, do lighten my heart by sending me a few pennies to get something to eat."[5]

In addition to responding to direct appeals for cash, Mrs. duPont supported several medical projects in the Northern Neck. Late in 1930 Dr. Thomas Wheeldon of Richmond opened an orthopedic clinic for children in Kilmarnock. After checking with H. J. Edmonds, a physician in Kilmarnock, she agreed to provide funds for the clinic and also for individuals who needed surgery. One case that she found especially touching was that of a ten-year-old boy who had lost a leg in a hunting accident and had fashioned an artificial leg out of a stick and a baking powder can. Helping such people, however, was not just a humanitarian act; it was also a contribution to society. She wrote Edmonds: "[O]ne so often sees the grown-up cripples, who are derelicts of Society, when, if given the proper treatment in childhood, would have been made useful members of it."[6] Her concern for crippled children no doubt stemmed from Alfred's long-time concern about childhood afflictions and marked an early expression of her own interest, which would become a dominant element in her later life.

Mrs. duPont's careful and deliberate management of her charitable efforts was in sharp contrast to the reversion to alms giving that dominated U.S. philanthropy during the first two years of the depression. In the large metropolitan areas business men, religious leaders, and society matrons hastily opened soup kitchens and breadlines for the unemployed. In New York City, it was rumored, "society woman, . . . admiring the bread line run by Mrs. X, 'Lady Bountiful of the Bowery,' said to a social worker: 'Please find out what it costs. I'd love to have one.' "[7] Many of the beneficiaries of Mrs. duPont's charity must have thought of her as Lady Bountiful, but the image of a shallow socialite indulging in the latest fad certainly did not apply to her thoughtful, caring, and quiet work.

One of the most difficult decisions was cutting back on the college scholarship program, but this became inevitable in the summer of 1931. Miss Shaw informed the college advisors that the scholarship budget would be cut by 50 percent and that no new students would be considered. Ethel Tignor turned from applications for scholarships to charity cases in the Northern Neck. Frederick Goodwin, who continued to appraise applicants for Mrs. duPont even after he was elected bishop coadjutor of Virginia, reevaluated his recommendations to come in under the new ceiling of $2,000 for all of his scholarships. President Chandler at William and Mary did likewise, and Mrs. duPont carefully matched the recommendations against the students' academic records in order to weed out the weakest. Cutbacks in state funds at William and Mary in the spring of 1934 forced Chandler to reduce all faculty salaries 10 percent and to consider dropping ten professors. In response to an appeal for $30,000 to retain the ten professors, Mrs. duPont was unable to pledge more than $500. As for cuts in salaries, she thought they were essential, "and I am sure that all of the professors realize that, as living expenses have been greatly reduced."[8]

For the 1932–33 school year the scholarship budget had dropped to $9,775 ($115,000 in current dollars), or less than half of what it had been four years earlier. The recipients were limited to eleven colleges, all in Virginia, with two-thirds of the total going to William and Mary and the Virginia Polytechnic Institute. The following year for the first time applicants were required to respond to a list of questions. They were designed to reveal the financial situation and educational background of the applicant's family, the college selected by the student, and the course of study to be pursued. The questions reflected Mrs. duPont's continuing concern that her limited funds go only to truly needy students with a reasonable educational background, that they not "waste" money on expensive colleges, and that they take "practical" courses that would help them make a living.[9]

Even with the cutbacks, the scholarship program was proving effective. The selection process imposed during the depression ensured that a greater percentage of students would complete college, and some of the better students were beginning to show up at the top of their graduating classes. Two students whom Bishop Goodwin recommended from Warsaw, Virginia, received good commendations upon graduation: W. Thomas Rice from VPI and Blake T. Newton, Jr., from William and Mary. Both were to enjoy distinguished careers in the business world. Two young women, Lucille Hurst and Ada Kelley, who also graduated from William and Mary in 1934, were the first of Mrs. duPont's students to be elected to Phi Beta Kappa.[10]

The depression was a national and world phenomenon as well as a local disaster, and Mrs. duPont studied the larger picture. She wrote Alfred's daughter Madeleine in Germany that conditions were much worse in America than they were in Europe. She noted the large number of suicides among prominent men in the United States. Even more regrettable was the danger of communism. "Communism flourishes in times of distress like this. There is no time for Communism during prosperity."[11]

"What we need now and really have always needed," she wrote to Margery duPont, "is . . . that our 'mass populace' come down to earth and realize that it is the responsibility of each man and woman in America to-day to do his part day by day; to make and keep our country prosperous and sane and not to play up our criminals on front pages each morning." America had been on a "prosperity jag" for a decade and now the "fiddler's bill" had to be paid. The only bright side that Mrs. duPont saw in the depression was the reestablishment of the American home. The family home, in her opinion, was "a permanent factor, and there can be no cultural civilization without it." She was pleased to learn that the nightclubs in New York were almost empty and that parents were no longer giving their sons "$25.00 to $40.00 to spend in one evening, lads that should have been home playing tiddlie-winks or checkers." The Roaring Twenties were over and good riddance![12]

Putting her convictions into practice, Mrs. duPont effected some modest economies at home. Her personal expenses dropped substantially in the early 1930s, and she cut staff salaries at Epping Forest 15 percent in April 1932. But the constant stream of houseguests at both Nemours and Epping Forest did not slacken. In addition, she took an extensive trip to Europe in the fall of 1931 and spent the winter of 1932 in Egypt with Alfred.[13]

During the summer months in the early 1930s Mrs. duPont's social life centered around Nemours with frequent trips to Virginia. Through Alfred she had become a good friend of Secretary of War Patrick J. Hurley and his wife, Ruth. Both the Hurleys were active in the stock market and frequently exchanged market tips with Mrs. duPont. A highlight of the 1932 social season was the dinner party that the Hurleys gave at their estate near Leesburg, Virginia, for President and Mrs. Hoover. The duPonts had entertained the Hurleys for a week at Epping Forest and then left Alfred's youngest daughter, Victorine Dent, and her husband, Elbert, there as houseguests while they took the train north for the presidential dinner.

For the occasion Mrs. duPont went to the unusual lengths of having her fingers "butchered," her term for a manicure; her fingers were so sore that she had trouble dressing for dinner. She and Alfred had cocktails with the Huidekopers and then rushed to the Hurleys' estate, to arrive only minutes before the president. Jessie was pleased that Ruth had used pink, her favorite color, for the tablecloth, decorations, and her own gown. She wrote to Denise: "There were twenty-six at the dinner, all intelligent, good looking, clean-cut men and women. Father was put between the two youngest there, and he had a royal good time.

Incidentally he gave the girls a good time, as you know he can do. He did tease them pretty much." The next day Mrs. duPont went to tea at the White House, "just a small affair with twenty or thirty guests. As a rule, I don't enjoy teas, but I did enjoy this one." The following evening the Huidekopers were dinner guests at Nemours and Jessie's sister Elsie, now married to Gen. Albert J. Bowley, arrived from Honolulu. From Wilmington it was back to Jacksonville by train to catch up with new houseguests at Epping Forest.[14]

Although Mrs. duPont's life revolved around Nemours and Epping Forest, she was never far from her Virginia roots in the early 1930s. There were still many cousins living in the Northern Neck. Whenever she was in that part of the state, she stopped at Bayview to see the Balls or in Tappahannock to stay with Aunt Ella Haile, whom both she and Alfred adored. Tappahannock was a convenient stopping place for the *Nenemoosha* during the semiannual migrations between Wilmington and

Ditchley, built by Kendall Lee on Dividing Creek in the Northern Neck and purchased by Mrs. duPont in 1932.

Jacksonville. The ties of family and tradition continued to draw her back to the land of her birth.

For years Mrs. duPont had wanted a home in the Northern Neck, a quiet place where she could relax in the familiar surroundings of her childhood. At one time she had thought of rebuilding the family homestead at Cressfield, but that idea seemed impractical because she spent little time in the area. In 1930 she learned that it might be possible to purchase Ditchley, the old Ball-Lee homestead across Dividing Creek from Harding's Landing. Although the house had been built by Kendall Lee, it had been in the Ball family for more than a century. Taken with the idea of buying the property and restoring the house, she asked her old friend Joseph W. Chinn in Warsaw, Virginia, to investigate. Judge Chinn found that the house was sound though in need of some repair. There was still enough property around the house to provide some privacy, although the location of the public road and the fish factory on the point posed some problems. The road could be relocated, and Mrs. duPont decided to purchase the fish factory to avoid "that brand of sachet" and to provide a dock for the *Nenemoosha*.[15]

Well versed in the precautions that duPonts always took in buying property, she asked Judge Chinn to approach the owner without revealing her interest. She thought the asking price of $25,000 was too high and finally settled on $18,000. At Ed Ball's suggestion, she did not put the house in her name but set up a separate corporation as owner. In 1934 she arranged with a contractor in Kilmarnock to have the house renovated and a kitchen wing added. She wrote to her cousin Wilmot Ball: "You will be glad to hear that the work at 'Ditchley' is progressing nicely. After it is completed and furnished, . . . I want you and your children to go down there for a week and stay. Am eager to have as many members of my family enjoy 'Ditchley' after the work is completed as possible."[16] The former Jessie Ball had now fulfilled a lifelong dream, to reestablish the Ball family in an ancestral home on the shores of the Chesapeake.

An opportunity for new ties to Virginia and the Northern Neck came in 1929 in an invitation to help restore Stratford, the birthplace of Robert E. Lee on the banks of the Potomac. Stratford, like Ditchley, was decaying and vulnerable to destruction. The idea of acquiring the property and restoring the mansion had originated with May Field Lanier, whose husband, Charles, had been the son of Sidney Lanier, the revered southern poet. Young southern women like May Field and Jessie Ball had learned to venerate Lee as the saintly champion of the southern cause.

Mrs. Lanier had a personal bond to General Lee through her father-in-law, who had delivered a eulogy in Macon, Georgia, at the time of the general's death. Lanier had judged Lee "greater than any antique deity. All the gods of Greece are dead; but Lee has only now begun to live. . . . [T]here is not a heart beating about this board, wherein he does not sit, shining with immortal radiance and encompassed with the purest loyalties that human hearts can offer."[17]

The poet's celebrated statement convinced Mrs. Lanier that the sacred shrine at Stratford had to be preserved. With no funds and no knowledge of how to go about such an enterprise, she welcomed the offer of assistance from Ethel Armes, an archivist and professional writer who had worked on the restoration of George Washington's home at Mount Vernon. On Miss Armes's advice, Mrs. Lanier decided to organize the Stratford project on the Mount Vernon model, which was to recruit a prominent and preferably wealthy woman in each state to serve as state director.[18]

Mrs. Lanier launched her campaign for state directors in the summer of 1929. Mrs. duPont was in Europe at the time and after her return did not get around to responding to Mrs. Lanier's letter before she was taken ill and hospitalized during the fall. When she did reply in December, she suggested that seeking funds in the wake of the stock market crash might not be wise, and furthermore fund-raising campaigns didn't do well during the winter. "I have always found people much more optimistic and generous in warm weather. This may sound a little odd, but there is a definite psychology about it, or rather such has been my experience."[19]

Mrs. duPont's serious illness in the winter of 1930 precluded any immediate role for her in creating the Robert E. Lee Memorial Foundation, but she was pleased to learn that Mrs. Lanier's efforts had been surprisingly successful. In April Mrs. Lanier reported that she had directors in twenty-one states and had pledges for $80,000 of the $157,000 purchase price. Reflecting the social structure of the time, the national advisory board consisted entirely of prominent men, including Governor Franklin D. Roosevelt of New York, Senators Harry F. Byrd and Carter Glass of Virginia, and Gen. R. A. Sneed, commander in chief

The gardens at Nemours, opened to the public for the first time in 1932, to raise funds for Stratford. Courtesy of the Nemours Mansion and Gardens, Wilmington, Delaware.

of the United Confederate Veterans. The active officers and all the state directors were women.[20]

Mrs. duPont saw the ruins of Stratford for the first time in many years in October 1930, when she and her husband took the *Nenemoosha* up the Potomac to the site. They were both much impressed by the majesty of the old mansion and saw great possibilities for its development. From that time on they were major contributors to the project.[21]

In the summer of 1932 Mrs. duPont made plans to open the gardens at Nemours for the first time as a fund-raiser for Stratford. Mr. duPont, with his son Alfred Victor and his architectural partner, had just completed the sunken garden at Nemours, in the area between the Terrace Colonnade and the Temple of Love. More than twenty Stratford directors and contributors joined the duPonts for dinner at Nemours on September 17. The garden tours on the following two days were a great success as the public and many duPonts flocked to see for the first time what was inside the walls of the estate. The affair raised more than five thousand dollars for Stratford, and the compliments of the visitors were gratifying. The consensus, Mrs. duPont observed, was that "there is nothing lovelier in Europe. All were very much surprised at the beauty and were impressed with the fitness and the poetry of it all, and to think that one brain [Alfred's] had conceived and executed this monumental art."[22]

A month later Mrs. duPont was at Stratford for the annual board meeting. "They are progressing very well at Stratford," she wrote her brother Tom. "The Board is composed of a splendid group of women, very cultured and refined and ardent admirers of General Lee. They are doing good work, and when once the depression has been relegated to the past, think we will have no trouble collecting funds to restore the place to its former pristine glory."[23]

A second opening of the gardens in the spring of 1933 raised another $1,700, and more contributions were coming in. The directors had been working together long enough to become close friends, and they looked forward to their annual meetings at Stratford. Because there was no suitable lodging near the plantation, the "Stratties," as they now called themselves, decided to build cabins at their own expense near the mansion house. The cabins were completed for the meetings that October. "My log cabin was ready for occupancy or rather my half of a log cabin. . . . Thought having much older cabin-mates I was going to have a most restful time and make up on the sleep that I had lost, but

Jessie's brother Tom Ball in his law office in Los Angeles in 1929.

don't think so. Those dear ladies talked with me until two o'clock in the morning every morning. Consequently I looked like a ghost when the nine days were up."[24]

Each cabin had a small central room with a pot-bellied stove and four cell-like bedrooms, each with a cot, a mirror, and a Stratford-made dressing table. "Miss Jessie," as her companions called her, decorated her cabin with all sorts of stuffed and ceramic owls, and the Delaware cabin thus came to be called the Owl's Roost. When the work day was over, ladies would gather in the Owl's Roost to tell stories far into the night. One of the favorites was a skit by Jessie and Mrs. Granville Valentine of Richmond. They took the parts of two black washerwomen meeting on the street in a friendly conversation which soon degenerated into a hilarious quarrel, "with Miss Jessie and Mrs. Valentine dancing and bouncing around the cabin like a pair of fighting chickens. These two elegant and dignified ladies brought peals of laughter at every performance."[25]

The Stratford gatherings became for Jessie a psychological and emotional relief from the self-discipline that she imposed on herself in maintaining her role as Mrs. duPont. In the forests of rural Virginia, she could once again for a few days express something of the character of the carefree, exuberant young woman who had been Jessie Ball. It was more than coincidence that the Stratford gatherings were the only occasions on which she enjoyed the company of women to the exclusion of men. Close friendships, a way of life for middle-class women in the nineteenth century, were nurtured by such organizations as well as by women's colleges in the twentieth.[26] Mrs. duPont had never been more than a nominal member of the Daughters of the American Revolution or the Daughters of the Confederacy. In the 1920s she had made token contributions to the National Woman's Party and to support equal rights legislation in 1929 and 1933, but she did not see greater political power for women as crucial. In 1934 she wrote to an Austrian friend: "Personally I do not believe that women in control would be any different from men in control, therefore, I am willing for men to keep the control of the world. It would indeed be a joy if they would recognize the mental calibre of women, but I suppose just as two races have never lived in a country on a fifty-fifty basis, it would be equally as impossible for the two sexes. Egotism makes one want to be in the ascendancy."[27]

Some years earlier she had written to her old friend Winifred Stephenson on the role of upper-class women in American society:

> I agree with you that it would be well worth while and we would have a far more livable society if every mother could have worth-while employment . . . when the children are at school; as it would keep her intellectually alert and in contact with the world. . . . The sad part of the average woman's life . . . is that she does not have this; of course, I mean the intelligent class. While her children are growing up, she has a definite object and certainly, the most worth while one in life. . . . When the children leave for boarding school, the mother's work is practically finished. Here she is, . . . at her mental height, left without a definite object; to drift; kill time. . . . She quite naturally either drifts into a butterfly's life or seeks amusement away from that of her home and husband.[28]

Mrs. duPont's views on women reflected her tendency to apply class distinctions in judging people. She saw the working class as the largest group of white Americans. With limited education and abilities, most people in the working class, in her opinion, were generally satisfied with their station in life and were not upwardly mobile. They worked with their hands more than with their minds. Occasionally working-class parents aspired to see their children move up the class ladder, but they often underestimated the difficulties involved. Mrs. duPont wrote to one of her advisors: "The boy comes from the laboring classes and I feel that we have already injured this boy by keeping him in a private school where he is associated with boys, who in all probability will not be called upon to make their living with their hands, therefore, I could not conscientiously contribute further towards [his] education."[29]

It was possible for individuals to move out of the working class, Mrs. duPont believed, if they had enough intellectual ability and the determination to strive against the odds. Many of her scholarship students, like Tom Rice and Ada Kelley, were evidence of that. It was somewhat easier, though still difficult in her opinion, for young people who came from families with no financial resources to make the grade if the family had some educational background. Her own experience had convinced her of that, and it was this conviction that inspired her giving to students and colleges.

Those who succeeded in acquiring a college education were admitted to a vast new world of professional opportunity. No longer confined by the limitations of the working class, successful students could move up the social ladder as far as their ability and perseverance would take them. The very best could reach the top of the upper class, reserved for men of exceptional ability and vision, such as Alfred I. duPont, J. P. Morgan, or Herbert Hoover.

With some limitations, Mrs. duPont added another factor into her formula for success. She believed that inherited characteristics and abilities made a difference. Coming from a good family had biological as well as cultural advantages. She assumed that people coming from pure Anglo-Saxon stock with many generations of accomplished forebears behind them had a distinct advantage over others, but breeding alone did not assure success. As she warned a wayward nephew, young men from "good" families could end up as "servants" if they did not apply themselves and obtain a good education. Conversely men from the lower classes could rise to the top despite their humble origins. Thus it seems that, in Mrs. duPont's view, breeding was a factor in determining one's potential, but it was not a controlling factor. It was possible for a family to improve its position over several generations if there were people in each generation who made the most of their opportunities.[30]

The tinges of racism in this interpretation of social mobility were certainly not uncommon among white Americans, north and south, in the 1930s. But for Mrs. duPont and other southerners of her time, these attitudes were only part of a much more pervasive mentality that concerned the foundation of southern society: the role of blacks in a white culture. So deeply ingrained were white attitudes toward blacks that the existing relationship between the races was taken by many white southerners as given, fixed for all time, without the possibility of alternatives or changes. Wilbur J. Cash, a perceptive journalist of Mrs. duPont's generation, deplored in his classic book, *The Mind of the South,* the violence and degrading treatment heaped upon blacks in the South, but at the same time he seemed to accept as unchangeable the almost universal conviction in the region that blacks were by nature substantially inferior to white people. The conviction, Cash claimed, had its origins in the plantation system, which "introduced distinctions of wealth and rank among the men in the old backcountry" and caused poor whites to introduce "that other vastly ego-warming and ego-expanding distinction between the white man and the black. Robbing him and degrading him in so many ways, it yet, by singular irony, had simultaneously elevated this common white to a position comparable to that of, say, the Doric knight of ancient Sparta."[31]

This "proto-Dorian convention," Cash claimed, continued to explain the dynamics of race relations in the South. It also explained the exalted position assigned to the southern white woman in the southern white mind. She was seen, Cash wrote, as the perpetuator of white racial superiority and established "her enormous remoteness from the males of the inferior group, to the absolute taboo on any sexual approach to her by the Negro." The abolition of slavery had removed the "rigid fixity of the black at the bottom of the scale, in throwing open to him at least the legal opportunity to advance, had inevitably opened up to the mind of every Southerner a vista at the end of which stood the overthrow of this taboo."[32]

It is not likely that Mrs. duPont ever read Cash's book, but she did not have to. It reflected as few books have the prevailing mentality within a social group at the time it was written. As historian Joel Williamson has put it, the book was in itself an artifact of its age. "Cash's book could have been written only by a totally native Southerner who came of age in the 1920s and ripened in the 1930s. Certainly never since and probably never before, with the possible exception of the months surrounding the Civil War, had the South come so close to generating what was, in truth, a single mind."[33]

Although, as Cash claimed, southerners in the 1930s were of one mind on the question of white supremacy, they did not all approach it with the same mentality. The liberals, who had carried some weight in the 1880s, believed that blacks, if given the opportunity, could eventually achieve some measure of equality. At the opposite extreme were the radicals, a powerful group until about 1915, who saw the freed black falling rapidly into a natural state of savagery and bestiality. The third mentality, which prevailed in Virginia in the time of Wilbur Cash and Jessie duPont, was represented by the conservatives. Conservatism, Williamson has written, "always began, proceeded, and ended upon the assumption of Negro inferiority. The Negro problem for Conservatives was simply a matter of defining the nature and the degree of Negro inferiority and of accommodating society thereto. It looked quite literally to the conservation of the Negro. It sought to save him by defining and fixing his place in American society. *Place* was the vital word in the vocabulary of Conservatism, and it applied to whites as well as to blacks."[34]

It was not surprising that Jessie Ball duPont was a good example of the conservative mentality. She had grown up in Virginia during the very years that Cash's "mind of the South" was developing, and Virginia was the center of the conservative mentality in the South. That blacks were inferior she had no doubt, but she believed they should be protected in their innocence. During a visit to Miami in 1926 Jessie had written: "I was glad to see the development on the island, which is quite tropical and with the little darkeys' shacks all freshly whitewashed, it was a lovely picture. How anyone would want to disturb those poor creatures in their native happiness by trying to cram a little learning, which they are not capable of receiving, down their throats, is beyond my comprehension."[35]

The following year she had wanted to visit Bayview to take a photograph of an old black couple "looking from behind the cabin just as [they] did so many years ago and with any number of little pickaninnies around it. I regret the passing of these old darkies, for they were a very lovable type, but the new 'crap' as 'Uncle' Wash termed them are the most obnoxious creatures on the face of the universe, I believe, but it is all the white man's fault."[36]

Jessie was expressing the same sort of romantic, nostalgic view of

blacks that her mother had recalled a generation earlier in her reminiscences of the old Gresham plantation. Both expressions reflected the
conservative mentality, the desire to protect an inferior race from the
disruptions of modern life. "Of course, I will do anything possible to help
the negroes better their condition," she wrote in 1930. "They certainly
should all be taught to read and write and to do a little figuring in order
to protect themselves. Beyond this, as a mass, they cannot take an
education, as you and I both know." She admitted, however, that "I have
a very kindly feeling towards some of the 'darkies' in the Northern
Neck."[37]

In the five years from 1926 through 1930 she had softened her opinion
of the intellectual inferiority of blacks; she now conceded them some
capacity for education. She was adamant, however, on the need to
protect the "purity" of the white race. In November 1932, after seeing a
Broadway musical she wrote: "This was the most nauseating, revolting
and vulgar show I have ever seen. Due to the mixture of whites with
negroes on the stage in the chorus, we left early in the evening. Cannot
understand people willing to put themselves on a social equality with
negroes."[38] As Williamson noted, "place" was all-important in the
conservative mentality.

It is more than coincidence that Mrs. duPont's views on race reflected
the conservative mentality at the very time that her ties with the Virginia
establishment were strengthening. Meetings at Stratford opened up
possibilities for new friendships with upper-class women in Richmond,
and her contributions to the Stratford project attracted the attention of
prominent Virginians, including Governor John Garland Pollard. For
several years she had carried on an occasional correspondence with
Pollard, who insisted on calling her Cousin Jessie. She granted him the
relationship although she admitted to others that she never knew how
they were related, except that his family had come from King and Queen
County, where her Gresham grandparents had lived. Jessie had become
better acquainted with Pollard in the summer of 1931, when the governor
invited the duPonts to attend the unveiling of a bust of President John
Tyler in the old Hall of Delegates in Richmond.

Mrs. duPont was captivated by the address by Claude G. Bowers,
who used the occasion to give his audience a summary of his study of the
Reconstruction period, recently published in his book *The Tragic Era*. "It
is quite a time," she wrote her brother Tom. "To think that a damnable

set of curs like those 'Carpet Baggers' could have ridden roughshod over a cultural people, as they did, trying, (and succeeding in most instances), to put the negroes (slaves of the year before) in official positions over their masters, exciting them to the torch, to every line of violence. . . . If the South in her defeat had been permitted to work out her own salvation, many of the tragic situations of to-day would never have existed, and a great deal of the mixture of negroes and whites would have been avoided."[39]

Cousin Garland was unsuccessful in convincing Cousin Jessie to endow a professorial chair at William and Mary in honor of William Dew, her most illustrious ancestor after Mary Ball Washington, but he found her enthusiastic about supporting the new Virginia Museum of Fine Arts in Richmond. She pledged $25,000, the second largest amount pledged for construction of the museum, and supported Pollard in his efforts to prevent other large donors from overriding the architect's decisions on design. When the general assembly accepted the project, Mrs. duPont was appointed to the board of directors, on which she would serve for three decades.[40]

Winters in Florida during the early 1930s brought Jessie duPont face to face with the task her brother Edward had undertaken—to expand duPont business interests in the state. The Great Depression had left Florida's economy in shambles, but the cautious investment policies pursued by Alfred and Ed had made the duPont enterprises a beacon of hope in a sea of troubles. Not only had the Florida National Bank remained sound during the lean years of 1930 and 1931, but Ed Ball was able to take advantage of the situation to extend the chain of duPont banks. Weakened banks tottering on the edge of collapse were easier to acquire than strong ones, provided anyone had the money with which to buy them, and Ball seemed to have both cash and credit. In March 1930 he bought up the North Orlando State Bank; in May, the Daytona Bank and Trust Company. When all but one of the banks in St. Petersburg failed, Mr. duPont obtained a charter to open a new bank in that city. A year later he agreed to liquidate and take over the Third National Bank in Miami. Thus in eighteen months the Florida National Bank Group had grown from one bank in Jacksonville to a chain of seven.[41]

During these same years Alfred duPont continued to acquire real estate in Florida cities and to add to Almours' holdings of land in the Florida

Panhandle. Early in 1931 William T. Edwards began to explore the possibility of acquiring five small companies in the shabby fishing village of Port St. Joe. These companies owned a small railroad, the local telephone company, almost 200,000 acres of good pine land, the town, and a good site for a paper plant. Within a year Edwards had obtained options on all the securities of the five companies with the anticipation that they might be purchased when the depression eased. In the meantime he scouted out promising but solid companies that might invest in the project while he searched for a plant design that would turn the pulp from southern pine into newsprint.[42]

When Jessie was in Florida, she followed the development of these business ventures from her office on the fourteenth floor of the Barnett Bank building. Her office was next to her husband's, where she could quickly join him to provide him with "ears" for business conferences. Although Ed Ball always obtained Alfred's approval on major policy issues, he knew that the boss was increasingly consulting Jessie on such matters. Technically, Jessie was vice-president of Almours and a member of the board; in fact, she did not follow daily operations. Ed Ball ran Almours, but he was careful to defer to his sister when she chose to express an opinion. She kept a close eye, for Alfred and herself, on the investment portfolio and its adjustment to changing economic conditions during the depression.

To a lesser degree, Jessie shared her husband's concern about the proper use of federal authority and resources in restoring the national economy. While Alfred privately fumed over the inaction of the Hoover administration in 1931 and 1932, Jessie looked forward to Hoover's reelection as a guarantee of stability for the future. Stability and security of place were still important for a Virginia conservative. In 1930 she even expressed some admiration for Benito Mussolini. He was, she thought, a "God-send to the Italians." In 1934 she wrote, "It is strange that in all of the chaos of the last fifteen years, Mussolini is the only man of any vast ability and leadership that has been produced. I don't say this especially as an ardent admirer of Mussolini because he has shown this ability—either we like him or we don't like him. Wish that the United States might have produced one as able as he is."[43]

Neither she nor Alfred, however, looked upon Roosevelt's election as a disaster. On March 3, 1933, the day before Roosevelt's inauguration, the couple stayed all day in their Jacksonville offices in order to be in constant touch with Ed Ball as he worked to keep panicky depositors from cleaning out their banks. The new president's prompt decision to close the banks saved the Florida National Group along with the banking structure of the nation.[44]

For Jessie the change of administration brought the need to establish new social ties in Washington. In February 1933 she had gone to Washington to enjoy with the Hurleys the last social events of the Hoover administration. There was a musical at the White House, a luncheon with Secretary of War and Mrs. Hurley at Fort Myer, "eight dinners in Washington, all beautifully appointed affairs, the largest being the one at Count and Countess Szechenyi's; he is the Hungarian Minister. . . . When I was at the White House, I was the only outsider, as it was given for the Diplomats and the Cabinet."[45]

Soon after the inauguration, Mrs. duPont set about establishing new contacts in Washington—with the Democrats back in power, not a difficult task for a Virginian. She was most anxious to win the friendship of George H. Dern, who had replaced Hurley as secretary of war. For that she could rely on "Cousin" J. Garland Pollard, whom Roosevelt had appointed to head the Veterans' Administration. Pollard arranged an interview for her with the secretary in May 1933, and she made plans to entertain the Derns at Nemours during the summer. That accomplished, she invited two of the Derns's children to a house party at Epping Forest in the spring of 1934. On the strength of that relationship, she wrote to the secretary in April to thank him for arranging to have her sister Elsie's husband, General Bowley, transferred back to the States from Hawaii. Having General Bowley closer to home, Mrs. duPont believed, gave him "a better chance for a Washington appointment this fall." Her ultimate purpose was to secure for her brother-in-law appointment as army chief of staff, a petition that Cousin Garland carried personally to the president. Neither request, however, damaged Jessie's friendship with either the Pollards or the Derns. In fact, by the spring of 1935 the Derns had become her close friends.[46]

The spring of 1933 also brought the marriage of Jessie's brother Edward to Ruth Latham Price in a private ceremony in Washington, D.C. Ed had met Ruth in 1930, when Jessie was in the hospital in Baltimore. He had told Alfred that he intended to marry her, but he did not let the duPonts know the June wedding date until a week before the event. Jessie found her new sister-in-law "an exceedingly pretty girl about my height, . . . Has very lovely golden hair, very dark blue eyes, and carries her head and shoulders well." At last her bachelor brother was married, and she hoped that Ruth would give him a home of domestic bliss, something he had never enjoyed.[47]

As Alfred duPont approached the age of seventy, Jessie worried more and more about the state of his health. At Ed's wedding in June he had choked while laughing with his mouth full of whiskey and had suffered a seizure. He seemed to tire more easily than in earlier years and was subject to colds. She tried constantly to protect him from "nervous tension," as she put it, which she believed damaged his hearing and depleted him physically. The trip to Egypt in the winter of 1932 had indeed been a delightful vacation, but to Jessie it was also a way to get her husband away from cold weather and the nagging pressures of business. She was immensely pleased by his energy and high spirits when they returned to Epping Forest in March with Mummy, the little mongrel that they had picked up on the streets of Cairo.[48]

Once home, however, both Alfred and Jessie soon fell back into the old routines, and she resumed her role of trying to protect him from annoyances and unnecessary fatigue. Alfred was consumed that autumn with the West Florida project. He authorized Ed Ball to purchase an additional 145,000 acres of land in Bay and Gulf counties, which brought their total holdings to almost a half-million acres in the coastal areas south of Tallahassee. Early in 1934 Alfred set aside $1.5 million for large-scale improvements in and around Port St. Joe. He was planning to dredge a harbor for oceangoing ships, rebuild the Apalachicola Northern Railroad, and improve the telephone and telegraph system. His greatest dream was to turn the ramshackle fishing village of Port St. Joe into a model community for low-income families. The paper mill he intended to build would provide employment for the impoverished people of the area. They would then be able to purchase the modest homes that Alfred expected to build on the tree-lined avenues. He included schools, a playground, and a park in his plans for the new company town. Now that he had decided, at Ed Ball's insistence, to build the mill to produce kraft paper rather than newsprint, he could proceed with the engineering design of the first unit of the mill, which would cost $5 million.[49]

At Christmastime at Nemours in 1933 Alfred seemed so tired and run-down that Jessie was determined to get him away from the office for a rest. They left for Epping Forest as soon as the Christmas crowd had departed. Once in Florida, Alfred came down with a bad cold and other complications. Early in February Jessie arranged a leisurely trip on the *Gadfly* up the St. Johns River and on to Miami. On the way Alfred suffered chest pains, which were diagnosed in Miami as a coronary attack. They returned immediately to Jacksonville by train, and the doctors ordered Alfred to bed for two weeks. He seemed to recover quickly, and by the end of the month was coming downstairs for lunch and would sometimes spend the afternoon on the terrace. Jessie had dinner with him upstairs in her boudoir while Ed Ball and his wife or other members of the family entertained dinner guests.[50]

Jessie, in her usual fashion, played down Alfred's illness in letters to her family. She even thought of not telling her brother Tom about the attack, then decided she should because he might get a garbled version of the event. Alfred, however, was not improving after the initial stages of recovery from the heart attack. He had little energy and occasional bad days with a low fever. In fact, Alfred had spent most of two months in bed. Eventually his doctors decided the trouble was abscessed teeth. Six teeth were removed in a painful operation before the ménage started

Jessie, Alfred, and Mrs. Patrick Hurley on the *Nenemoosha* about 1934.

north in May. Jessie arranged to take the train to Wilmington, North Carolina, where they boarded the *Nenemoosha* for an easy and relaxing cruise to Delaware. Alfred chose not to attend Denise's graduation from boarding school in June, preferring to make plans for two more lakes at Nemours and to tinker with machinery.[51]

It was already clear to all concerned, including Alfred and Jessie, that he would never fully recover from the February attack. Before they had left Florida in May, Alfred had arranged for Jessie to replace him on the board of the Florida National Bank. Although she had dealt with many banks over the years, she knew little about bank management. Addison Baker, her brother-in-law who now worked for Ed Ball as a banker in the Florida National Group, took on the task of giving her a short course on the subject. By the autumn of 1934 Jessie had taken over most of her husband's correspondence, but although she sometimes made decisions, she informed him of them later.[52]

Jessie took Alfred to Florida early that year, and for the first time they spent Christmas at Epping Forest. Denise and Elizabeth Ball, one of Jessie's young relatives, came down for the holidays. To keep them entertained and out of Alfred's way, Jessie organized a round of parties, including a seated dinner for two hundred youngsters at the Timuquana Country Club.[53]

The parties for Denise were among the few occasions when the duPonts entered the social circles of Jacksonville. Although they were listed in the social register, they, like most winter residents, were never in Jacksonville long enough to adjust their schedules to the social calendar of the city. Furthermore, Jessie's lifelong aversion to daytime women's activities prevented her from taking any active part in the Jacksonville Woman's Club, which held a central position in the social and civic life of the city. Epping Forest was the scene of many dinner parties, but the guests were limited mostly to a few business associates, vacationing family members, and old friends from the North. As Alfred's health failed, even this close circle of guests shrank.[54]

In January Jessie tried to get away with Alfred on the yacht whenever possible, as she worried increasingly about his health. She wrote her sister Elsie, "We returned yesterday after a lovely two days on the water. A. I. needs two months rest, however. We hope to get off again on Monday to join the yacht at Daytona, and shall proceed at once slowly down the inland water-way. We shall be alone; so shall get an absolute rest. Have never seen A. I. quite so tired nor so nervous. This is not for publication, needless to say."[55]

Alfred had long since resigned himself to the idea that his life was nearing its end. He was satisfied with the financial condition of Almours Securities and of the banks. Plans for the Port St. Joe project were far enough along that he was confident they could be completed. Most of all, he was now convinced that he could fulfill his dream of leaving most of his estate to a charitable foundation, which he planned to establish at Nemours. Three years later, in 1937, Jessie wrote to her old friend Will Edwards a recollection of a conversation that they had shared with Alfred in the sunken garden at Nemours in the autumn of 1934: "Mr. duPont talked at length about his plans for Nemours, about the love and lack of love that had been accorded him by his family over the years, about his affection for my family, making the statement that he had had more love for my family in the few short years we had been together than he had ever had in all of his life from all of his own family. I think this time he spoke of his affection for EB as he called Eddie, and said he would like to have had a son like him."[56]

Alfred was still uncertain, however, about his will, and in January 1935 asked his Jacksonville attorneys to write a new one. His most recent will, signed in November 1932, was the product of a decade of discussions with Jessie about the disposition of his fortune, which even in the lean years of the depression totaled more than $40 million. He had always intended to make reasonable bequests to members of his family and those loyal people who had worked for him over the years, but he wanted the bulk of his estate to be used for the relief of human suffering. In this intention, Jessie fully concurred. As Alfred's wife she had used the funds he had entrusted to her to build her own fortune and then to complement in her own way Alfred's sometimes astounding charitable acts. Alfred had followed the biblical admonition never to let the left hand know what the right was doing. He was known to stuff $100 bills into the pockets of destitute young mothers whom he encountered on the streets with their children. For several years, until the State of Delaware established an old-age pension plan, Alfred personally supported every pensioner in the state.[57]

Alfred's way of giving was a fine example of classical charity. Jessie's giving during the first decade of her marriage was less flamboyant and spontaneous. In that sense it took on some of the aspects of philanthropy.

She knew exactly where her charity was going, what purpose it served, and how worthy the recipients were. Alfred never bothered to keep lists of his gifts; Jessie made sure that Miss Shaw kept an accurate record of every gift to support her claims for tax deductions. Their methods were different; their intentions, the same.

Alfred's 1932 will granted five thousand shares of Almours stock to each of his children and one thousand each to Jessie's sisters and brother Tom. Ed Ball was to receive five thousand shares, but this amount was to be in lieu of any compensation that he might receive as an executor of the will or as trustee of the estate. Every employee at Almours, Nemours, Epping Forest, or on the *Nenemoosha* was to receive one thousand dollars. To Jessie Alfred left all the contents of Nemours, his personal possessions, and the title to the estate at Epping Forest.[58]

The remainder of Alfred's property was to be held in trust, to be administered by four trustees: the Florida National Bank of Jacksonville, his wife, Jessie, her brother Ed, and John F. Lanigan, a personal friend. The trustees were to "take possession and . . . have entire management and control of the corpus of my estate." From the income of the estate the trustees were directed to pay annuities to Denise and some of Alfred's nieces and nephews. The remainder of the annual income was to go to Jessie in quarterly payments. At some time not specified in the will, the trustees were to set up a charitable corporation called the Nemours Foundation, to which the trustees were to transfer the land, mansion house, and other buildings at Nemours. The principal of his estate would remain in the hands of the trustees, but the net income was to be used to maintain Nemours "as a charitable institution for the care and treatment of crippled children, but not of incurables, or the care of old men or old women, and particularly old couples, first consideration, in each instance, being given to beneficiaries who are residents of Delaware."[59]

The mansion house at Nemours was not to be used for housing or as a hospital, but for "the reception of visitors and their entertainment" and for administrative purposes. Maintenance of the mansion and gardens was to have priority over all other uses of either income or principal of the estate. Nor was more than $1 million of principal to be used for the construction or equipping of buildings. Additional funds for these purposes would have to come from income or from bequests by others. The will also provided that after Alfred's death, Jessie could ask the trustees to establish the foundation under the same terms and conditions.[60]

On March 4, 1933, the day before President Roosevelt declared the bank holiday, Alfred signed a codicil to the will he had executed just three months earlier. With the Jacksonville bank and perhaps his whole Florida enterprise facing an uncertain future, he did not want to leave Jessie with merely the residue from the income of his estate after all other annuities had been paid. In "deliberate consideration of world conditions" and impressed that he had not protected his wife "against possible eventualities," he provided Jessie with an annuity of $200,000 ($2.3 million in current dollars), which was to be paid before any of the other annuities provided for in his will.[61]

By January 1935 many things had changed in Alfred duPont's life. His death and the creation of his life dream, the Nemours Foundation, no longer seemed in the distant future. He believed the day would soon come when Jessie and the other trustees would face the responsibilities imposed upon them by his will. He also knew that Jessie had every intention of carrying out his wishes, and that she would want to create the foundation as soon as possible after his death. Thus it seemed reasonable to write a new will that would require establishment of the foundation soon after his death. Another consideration was that economic conditions had vastly improved during the twenty-one months since he had signed the codicil to his will. The size of his estate had grown proportionately. His accountants estimated that his estate totaled between $55 million and $65 million.[62] He regretted having to impose a burden of that size on his wife, and he wanted to lighten the load as much as possible.

Alfred was fully prepared in January 1935 to have a new will drafted, and it seems likely that Jessie supported the idea, not just because it would carry out Alfred's wishes but also because it would automatically set in motion the process of establishing the foundation. She would not have to seek agreement with the other trustees on the date when the process was to begin. Raymond F. Knight, Alfred's Florida attorney, however, saw an overriding obstacle. Under a new Florida law, a charitable bequest was held invalid if it was executed less than six months before the death of the testator. Alfred did not expect to live that long, so the idea of a new will was out. Instead, he added a second codicil to his 1932 will, which made a few changes in his list of annuities and named his daughter Bessie's husband, Reginald S. Huidekoper, to replace John F. Lanigan as trustee. Alfred made clear in the second codicil, however, that he was "making thereby such changes only as will not by any chance jeopardize the interest which the proposed 'The Nemours Foundation' will receive" under the 1932 will.[63]

What the second codicil did not state, however, was that Alfred did sign another document on the same day, this one a conditional instrument that would become effective only if he lived for six months, or until July 15, 1935. The conditional instrument carried out the intent of the proposed new will. It stated that "immediately upon my death my Executors or Trustees shall cause to be incorporated a corporation for charitable purposes, to be designated and known as 'The Nemours Foundation.' " The rest of the paragraph establishing the foundation was identical to the 1932 will except that the words "Executors or" were inserted wherever the word "Trustees" appeared in the original. Because the conditional instrument required immediate transfer of the mansion house and property of Nemours to the foundation, the document provided that Jessie would have the right to lease the mansion and live there if she wished. The conditional instrument also provided that the net income of the estate would go directly to the foundation rather than to Jessie, but it also increased Jessie's annuity from $200,000 to $450,000. This change relieved her of the responsibility for determining how much of the annual net income should go to the foundation.[64]

The device of a conditional will was legal but tricky. The existence of two wills could always prove troublesome in settling estates. Even when every reasonable precaution had been taken, there was always a possibility of a legal complication that could thwart the intentions of the deceased. Alfred, however, was so determined to protect his dream that he was willing to take the chance. The best way to avoid future trouble was to keep the existence of the conditional will a secret. For that reason, it was never referred to in any of the documents related to Alfred's estate.[65]

Despite the frail state of his health, Alfred remained active and cheerful during the winter of 1935. In February he and Jessie had taken the train to Richmond to attend the wedding of Elsie Bowley's son, Thomas Ball Wright. After the wedding, Jessie had arranged a large dinner party for the newlyweds, and was pleased that the Pollards, the Derns, and Ruth Hurley could attend. Back in Jacksonville, Jessie made plans for a family reunion at Miami Beach. To make things easier for Alfred she made reservations for them to stay at the Roney Plaza Hotel, while the rest of the family were given rooms at the Pancoast.[66]

Alfred granted the newspapers an interview in which he was able to make some astute remarks about the policies of the Roosevelt administration, but in the photographs in the *Miami Herald* he looked tired and gaunt. On one occasion he suggested to Elsie Bowley that she take Jessie to Europe that summer. When Elsie asked why he didn't plan to take her, Alfred replied, "I shan't be here." He left Miami Beach a few days before the rest of the family to attend to business affairs in Jacksonville.[67]

Early in April Jessie lured him away from his desk for a restful trip up the St. Johns River on the *Gadfly,* but Alfred was soon back in his old routine. After a particularly hard day on Wednesday, April 24, he suffered a severe heart attack. A heart specialist was summoned from Philadelphia. Alfred's condition was serious, but with rest and quiet his doctors thought he might recover. On Saturday, Jessie wired Elsie that Alfred's heart action was much improved and his lungs were clearing; there was "NO IMMEDIATE CAUSE FOR ALARM." On Sunday evening, however, while the family was having dinner, Alfred suffered another attack and died early Monday morning, April 29.[68]

Frank A. Juhan, the Episcopal bishop of Florida, conducted a private service in Jacksonville. A friend in St. Petersburg arranged a private railroad car to take the body and the funeral party north to Wilmington. There the body was moved directly to Nemours, where the bishop of Delaware and the boys' choir from the Cathedral of St. John the Divine in New York City participated in the service with most of the family present.[69]

A half-century later Alfred duPont Dent was quoted in *Forbes* magazine as claiming that Jessie and Ed Ball poisoned his grandfather to prevent the conditional instrument from coming into effect. The presumed motive for murder was that in the conditional instrument of January 1935, Alfred's estate would go directly to the Nemours Foundation and "Jessie's income was cut sharply and Ed Ball's scope as controller of the vast fortune would be severely limited."[70] In fact, had the conditional will come into effect, Jessie's annuity would have more than doubled. It was true, however, that in time Jessie's annual income from Alfred's estate would exceed by twenty times the $450,000 annuity that she would have received under the conditional instrument, but in the depths of the depression in 1935, the enormous growth of the estate could hardly have been imagined. Neither is it clear from the terms of the conditional instrument how Ed Ball's control of the estate would have been reduced if the new will had come into effect. Furthermore, the murder claim was based not on any evidence but only on the suspicions of Ruth Ball Morrell, who had divorced Ed in 1949 after a long and bitter lawsuit.[71] Her hatred for her former husband could well have aroused other suspicions besides suspicions of murder.

The most convincing argument against the murder claim is Jessie's correspondence with Alfred over a period of twenty years before his death and with others for the rest of her life thereafter. That he was the love of her life, in fact the very center of her life, is beyond question. In scores of letters over the next three decades both Jessie and Ed continued to invoke their pledge of loyalty to the memory of Alfred in carrying out his wishes, even to the extent of putting his interests before those of his survivors.

When Jessie returned to Epping Forest after Alfred's funeral, she finally had time to write to her brother Tom:

> There is nothing I can say in the greatest sorrow that can befall mortal. The path ahead seems absolutely black. Everyone has been sweet, lovely and as sympathetic as human hearts could be. Suppose that helps some, but it is hard to realize that we will never again feel the warm response of that handclasp, of the cheek against cheek, nor know the great love of his incomparable heart. Of course, to have been pal, sweetheart and wife to a man like A. I. for a little over fourteen years I realize is a blessing that is seldom given to woman. It is this very realization that makes the parting unbearable.[72]

Out of the dark shadows of death would come a new purpose that would give meaning to her life: she would carry the great responsibilities that Alfred had entrusted to her.

True to Every Trust

Given the state of Alfred's health during the spring of 1935, Jessie had delayed any plans for opening the mansion at Nemours. After Alfred's death James Finnie and the winter caretaker force removed the dustcovers and arranged the furniture on the first floor for the funeral, but there was no time for the complicated logistics of moving north for the summer. Besides, Alfred's attorneys and all his business records were in Jacksonville. So after the funeral Jessie sent Denise back to college and returned to Jacksonville with her two sisters, Elsie and Belle. Her brother Ed and his wife, Ruth, were also near at hand.

At Jessie's request, Alfred's family was quickly on the scene. His son, Alfred Victor, had returned to Florida with Jessie—"a dear, sweet young man," who was a comfort to her. Alfred Victor's sister, Victorine Dent, came down later in the week, to be followed by his sister Bessie Huidekoper and her husband, Reginald, whom Alfred had named as an executor of his will. Alfred's daughter Madeleine was still living in Germany and could not be present, but Jessie wanted Alfred's children there for the reading of the will on May 14. She wrote to her brother Tom: "I realize that it is not necessary, yet I deem it a wise and fair measure, as they should be the first ones to know the disposition of his property."[1]

The next day she wrote Tom: "We are busy trying to get the essential things done. It is pretty hard to have spirit enough to do anything. Reginald, Eddie, the Florida National Bank and I are the Executors and Trustees for A.I.'s estate. A good deal of the preliminary work has to be done, which will hold me here until early June, I am afraid. . . . Reginald is down at the office now working over some of the papers, etc., just perfunctory work." As an outsider Huidekoper knew nothing of Alfred's plans or his business, and, as an attorney, he was eager to begin the process of settling the estate. "He is very nice and we are giving him all the assistance possible. The whole office is at his disposal for information, all of which I think he appreciates very much."[2]

Because Alfred had not lived for six months after signing the last codicil to his will, the conditional instrument of January 15, 1935, would never be probated, and his 1932 will with the amending codicils would govern the disposition of his estate. From the net income of the estate, Jessie would receive an annuity of $200,000, to be followed by annuities and gifts to other persons specified in the will. Then Jessie would receive the remainder of the net income, which she could use for her own purposes or for funding the Nemours Foundation.

From the day of Alfred's death there was never any question in her mind that she would fund the foundation as soon as possible. "I know that A. I. wanted his work to go on," she wrote to Tom, "and he depended a vast deal on me with Eddie to carry it on; so some God-given power I suppose under A. I.'s direction will lead us on later." A few months later she wrote: "I recognize that we can take no chances, as we must carry out A. I.'s wishes, and that is that the income of his Estate shall be saved that crippled children may benefit thereby and 'Nemours' be perpetuated."[3] In a long and touching letter to William duPont, one of Alfred's closest cousins, she observed: "From babyhood he [Alfred] fulfilled every trust that was ever imposed on him. 'Nemours' is a monument to that trust, its inception being a remark his Father made to him as a little child. That is why on his resting place is the short sentence: 'True To Every Trust.' "[4] That principle would guide Jessie Ball duPont for the rest of her life.

It would be months, even years, however, before Mrs. duPont would be able to realize the full expression of her commitment. The vast network of Alfred's holdings in Almours Securities, the Florida National Banks, the timberlands, railroad, telephone company, and beach property in the Florida Panhandle, real estate in Delaware and across Florida in addition to his DuPont stock and other investments, would take months to sort out and appraise. Once that task was complete, there would be the thorny problems of negotiating a settlement of estate and income taxes with the state of Florida and the federal government. In the months following

Alfred's death, virtually all of his property was tied up in the hands of his attorneys. Jessie understood that she could not take the *Nenemoosha* north in the spring of 1935 because ownership had not yet been transferred to her from the estate.

Fortunately Jessie could have every confidence in the ability and loyalty of Henry P. Adair of the firm of Knight, Adair, Cooper, and Osborne, which had for a decade provided legal services for the duPont enterprises in Florida. Reginald Huidekoper, a capable and energetic attorney, was on hand to represent the family, and he quickly came to appreciate Adair's ability and integrity. And from California her brother Tom could draw on his legal experience to give Jessie personal advice. He suggested that, before the estate was finally settled, the executors should consult an able tax counsel, perhaps the firm of Miller & Chevalier in Washington, D.C. Jessie heartily agreed: "I realize that the firm of Miller and Chevalier is one of the best firms in the country. Personally, and I am not speaking as an Executrix, I think it would be well to submit it to several firms; as one might see a point of law whereby the inheritance taxes and income taxes could be reduced."[5]

During the summer and fall of 1935 Mrs. duPont made frequent quick trips to Jacksonville to handle estate and business matters. She felt an obligation to represent Alfred as a board member of the Florida National Bank and took an active interest in the bank's affairs. She had also replaced him as president of Almours Securities, a position that required her to be in frequent touch with her brother Ed and the Jacksonville office. The assets of the company were close to $56 million at that time and were invested in a variety of enterprises that required skillful management and policy direction.[6]

The largest question facing Almours in 1936 was how to organize and use the enormous assets that the company held in the Florida Panhandle. The goal was to carry out Alfred's plan to use the tens of thousands of acres of pine timber as feed for the paper mill to be built at Port St. Joe, which he envisioned as a model community. It was a grand scheme that Alfred had hoped would revitalize the economy of West Florida. Before his death, however, he had not decided how to proceed. It was now up to Jessie, Ed Ball, and Will Edwards to decide how to finance and build the mill. The plan that evolved in 1936 was to form a partnership with the Mead Corporation, a large Ohio paper company. The $6-million plant was to be financed with $1 million in cash each from Almours and Mead, the rest to be raised with mortgage bonds or bank loans. Edwards spent most of the year analyzing the financial aspects of the proposal. He demonstrated to Jessie's satisfaction that bank loans would be preferable to bonds. He also found solid reasons for believing that the paper mill would make a handsome profit and furthermore would enhance the value of Almours' holdings in land, the railroad, and the telephone company. Huidekoper, as an executor and trustee, had a legitimate interest in the enterprise and sometimes served as devil's advocate as Jessie and Ed pondered decisions. There were risks involved, but Edwards could cite some conservative assumptions in the plan as well. In January 1937 a press release from Almours announced that the St. Joe Paper Company had awarded $20 million in contracts as the first step in constructing the mill.[7] Under the agreement, the Mead Company would design, build, and operate the mill; Almours would supply the land and the timber for pulp.

The paper mill represented an important part, but only a part, of Alfred's plan for Port St. Joe. The press release announced that half the $20 million would be used to build a "model town" at Port St. Joe. Will Edwards had not forgotten the weeks of effort that Alfred had put into planning a model community for the dilapidated Gulf Coast town. He had assured representatives of the Mead Company that Almours Securities intended to carry out the plan by building homes, parks, and community facilities along the lines of Mr. duPont's design. But when nothing happened on housing construction during the summer of 1937, Mead officials warned Ed Ball that without comfortable housing the mill at Port St. Joe could never be a profitable operation. Ball admitted that Edwards had expressed hopes that Almours would build at least part of the community, but he reminded his associates that he himself had since made it clear on several occasions that Almours was not going into the housing business. The housing issue was but another example of the tension between Edwards, who was determined to carry out Alfred's wishes, and Ball, who always put hard considerations of profitability ahead of amenities.

It was Jessie's role to work out a compromise. Her sympathies lay with Edwards's position, but she was not about to overrule her brother on financial matters. She even considered having some model homes built at her personal expense. The compromise, worked out in a meeting that Jessie called in Washington, was that Almours would finance some of the community facilities from the sale of residential lots in the town and offer discounts of 25 percent on purchases if the buyer started construction immediately and continued the work until the house was built. In August Ed Ball reported that lot sales were going well. When Edwards arrived in Port St. Joe in October, he found that several contractors were willing to begin construction on a comprehensive scale as soon as he could obtain approval of a mortgage insurance plan from the Federal Housing Administration. With construction of the mill and dredging of the harbor now in progress, it seemed that Alfred duPont's dream for rebuilding West Florida was on its way to realization.[8]

Business affairs in Florida preoccupied Mrs. duPont in 1935 and 1936, but she had not forgotten her first commitment to Alfred, to build a hospital for crippled children at Nemours. In January 1936 Adair and Bright looked into the legal and tax ramifications of setting up a corporation to carry out the terms of Mr. duPont's will. After consulting with attorneys in New York, Adair drafted a charter and deed of assignment for the corporation, to be called the Nemours Foundation. The charter, signed on February 25, 1936, provided that Mrs. duPont would serve as president, Huidekoper as vice-president, and Edward Ball as secretary-treasurer. The deed of assignment enabled Mrs. duPont to transfer one million dollars from her husband's estate to construct the hospital and to release the land on which the hospital was to be built. In the deed Mrs. duPont also granted 2 percent of the residuary income from the estate for operation and maintenance of the hospital. The deed stated that she intended to increase the percentage substantially after the hospital was built, and she later increased the figure to 12 percent.[9]

A children's hospital was not a project that could be undertaken hastily; it was not something that could be found in a mail-order catalog. In September 1936 Mrs. duPont had discussed the project with Huidekoper, who suggested that the first step should be "to select two or more topnotch children's specialists and surgeons who shall be paid a substantial salary commensurate with their work and take their advice . . . after visiting as many of such institutions as we are able to."[10]

In December she wrote to Baker Lee, the clergyman who had presided at her marriage to Alfred:

[T]he affairs of the estate have taken a great deal of my time, and I have gone back and forth to Florida a great many times. I went down to Florida last Thursday, and returned on Sunday, but I accomplished a good deal while there. Then to Baltimore yesterday, where the doctors took me through two hospitals, which took up the entire day. Three hours in the morning were spent at the Maryland University Hospital, which is a new one, and considered by many of the medical fraternity, to be a very efficiently built building. Then three hours in the afternoon were spent with Dr. George Bennett at the Crippled Children's hospital. The day was one that was most beneficial.

In a few minutes I am off to New York, hoping to return to-morrow evening. Christmas is near, and I am planning to move my household on the sixteenth to Florida, and so it goes. Denise was anxious to be down there for Christmas. I would rather spend it on a train.[11]

Soon after the holidays Mrs. duPont was back on the trains as she traversed the Atlantic Coast to interview doctors who could provide advice on the hospital. She knew that the interviews would take careful planning if they were to produce any information of substance. Although the duPont name would mean something to most physicians, it would not assure her their serious attention. She long remembered her appointment with Dr. Robert B. Osgood, one of the nation's leading orthopedic surgeons. With her usual persistence, Miss Shaw had arranged an appointment one January morning in his office in Boston. Miss Shaw was warned that the doctor was very busy and would have only a few minutes free at nine o'clock on a Monday morning in February. Mrs. duPont arrived in Boston the night before and the next morning nervously paced the sidewalk outside the doctor's office on Marlborough Street until the precise time of the interview. She was received with a formal courtesy suggesting that Dr. Osgood considered her just another wealthy woman who wanted advice about some unimportant matter. When, however, he heard her plans for the foundation and discovered that she was already quite well informed on the subject, he became so interested that the conversation continued for most of the morning. The meeting was the beginning of a long and rewarding friendship.[12]

By the first of March 1937, Mrs. duPont had captured the interest of eight prominent physicians, whom she had invited to Epping Forest with their wives for a meeting to discuss her plans for the foundation and the hospital. In addition to Dr. Osgood the group included three men from Baltimore: Dewitt B. Casler, who served as Mrs. duPont's surgeon during her serious illness in 1929; George E. Bennett, whom she had met at the Children's Hospital in Baltimore; and Thomas R. Brown, who had taught at Johns Hopkins and now practiced general medicine at three Baltimore hospitals. Others included Philip D. Wilson, a graduate of Harvard Medical School, now an orthopedic surgeon and director of surgery at the Hospital for Ruptured and Crippled in New York City, and Michael Hoke, also an orthopedic surgeon, who had a large practice in Atlanta. Rounding out the board were two old friends from Richmond, William Tate Graham and Beverly R. Tucker, the latter a neuropsychiatrist who was a professor of nervous and mental diseases at the Medical College of Virginia and ran the Tucker Sanatorium in Richmond. The distinction of the group was evidence of Mrs. duPont's resourcefulness and persistence in organizing the foundation.

The meeting of the eight doctors at Epping Forest in March 1937 was for Mrs. duPont a high point of the winter season. To accommodate the doctors and two of their wives, Mrs. duPont asked four of her guests to take sleeping quarters on the *Gadfly,* which had been moved into the yacht basin at the foot of the garden. "Our meetings were all on the quarter deck of the 'Gadfly,' therefore, there were no interruptions by telephones, passing servants or others."

On the first day the executors of the estate, Henry Adair, and the doctors discussed Alfred duPont's hopes and intentions for Nemours. The next day the doctors met alone as an advisory committee to map out a plan for the institute, which they agreed to present to the executors in Baltimore a month later. Jessie wrote long letters to Elsie and Tom describing the meeting. "Have never been with quite so interesting a group of men, I believe. . . . You don't know what it has meant to me that we have such competent leaders."[13]

There is no record of the April meeting, but the advisory board did meet at Nemours in June 1937. Mrs. duPont was thrilled by the interest and enthusiasm of the members who, she believed, would bring Alfred's dream "to its fullest fruition with all of the ideals that its Founder had planned for it." The board thought the trustees of the estate should move ahead at once with design and construction of the hospital, and they urged the trustees to select a young orthopedic surgeon to head the institute. Early selection of the director would enable him to have a prominent role in designing the hospital at Nemours. Mrs. duPont wrote to a friend: "On their recommendation the Trustees elected Dr. Shands of Duke University as the medical director for a period of five years. He is a Virginian. His father is an orthopaedic surgeon in Washington. His mother was a Miss Eppes from City Point, Virginia. . . . He is young, only about thirty-eight or thirty-nine years of age, has a wife and I believe one little child. Am delighted that he is such a congenial fellow, as naturally I will see a great deal of him."[14]

Mrs. duPont had never heard of him, but Alfred R. Shands, Jr., was indeed a rising star in his profession. A graduate of the University of Virginia, he had specialized in orthopedic surgery at Johns Hopkins and taught orthopedics at The George Washington University in Washington, D.C. In 1930 he had moved to Durham, North Carolina, where he helped to organize the Duke University Medical School. By 1937 he was head of the orthopedic department and had written the *Handbook of Orthopedic Surgery,* which was to be a standard text in the field for the next thirty-five years. Shands, however, was more than a good physician and surgeon; he was a seasoned administrator. Equally important, his congeniality and soft Virginia accent made his relationship with Mrs. duPont comfortable from the start.

Also on the advice of the advisory board, the trustees selected the architectural firm of Crisp and Edmondson to design the hospital in association with the firm of Messena and duPont, the latter being Alfred Victor, Alfred I. duPont's son. Shands himself knew little about hospital design, so in the spring of 1937 he set off with his wife, Polly, to visit more than a hundred orthopedic hospitals, especially those treating crippled children, in both the United States and Europe.

Mrs. duPont also went to Europe that spring. In January she had the sudden inspiration that it would be delightful to take some of the family to England in May to attend the coronation of King George VI. Correspondence with the Countess of Kingston produced a few tickets for good seats at the ceremony, and Mrs. duPont embarked with her sister Elsie and General Bowley on the *Berengaria* on May 4.[15]

Before she left she had several long discussions with Denise, who was about to graduate from Bradford Junior College in Massachusetts. Unhappy at Sweet Briar College in Virginia, Denise had transferred to Bradford, where she had met Carl Zapffe, a robust, handsome young man who was completing his doctorate in metallurgy at Harvard. The two had fallen in love, and Denise was pestering Mrs. duPont to give her consent to their marriage. Always cautious about hasty marriages, Mrs. duPont asked Denise to wait at least until Carl had finished his dissertation and returned to his job at the DuPont Experimental Laboratory, a request that would have delayed their marriage until the spring of 1938. Denise was exasperated, not the least because her foster mother had another motive for wanting to delay the marriage: Wilmington was already agog over the coming wedding of Ethel duPont, daughter of Eugene duPont, Jr., to Franklin D. Roosevelt, Jr., that June. A second duPont wedding in the same Wilmington social season would hardly receive the attention of the first.[16]

While Mrs. duPont and the Bowleys were in England, Carl and Denise were married in a private service at historic Christ Church, just off the Harvard campus. Denise did not write to her mother about the event and now faced the trial of informing her face-to-face when Mrs. duPont, her two sisters, and General Bowley arrived in Boston for Denise's graduation. As often happens in such situations, Denise lost her nerve several times before finally blurting out the news to her mother at a most awkward moment. General Bowley was aghast at the announcement and rushed down to the courthouse to verify that the marriage had been legally recorded. Mrs. duPont took the news more calmly. She expressed her disappointment but never raised a single note of remonstrance or anger. She liked the young man, and he soon won her over completely with his intelligence, good humor, and engaging personality. Years later Carl Zapffe recalled Mrs. duPont's reaction to their marriage as a supreme example of her extraordinary bearing and strength of character.[17]

A few weeks later, when the Shandses were returning by ship from their tour of European hospitals, they received a radiogram from Mrs. duPont asking them to stop off in Wilmington on their way to Chapel Hill. Arriving in Wilmington on the day of the duPont-Roosevelt wedding, the Shandses could find no rooms at a suitable hotel, but Mrs. duPont insisted that they stay with her at Nemours. After weeks in Europe, Polly asked Mrs. duPont where she could have her hair done before they went out to the estate. Mrs. duPont shouted into the next office: "Miss Shaw, where can Mrs. Shands have her hair done in Wilmington?" Mrs. duPont always shampooed and set her own hair.[18]

After dinner that evening Mrs. duPont mentioned that the advisory board had recommended that a house for the Shandses be built on the grounds at Nemours so that the director could walk to the hospital. She was more than willing to build the house but wanted to know what sort of design the Shandses preferred. Mrs. Shands said she really did not care about the style, but she thought it would be convenient if the windows could be the same size as those in the house they had recently built in Durham. Mrs. duPont asked for the blueprints of their house and had the new home built with the same floor plans and dimensions, so when the Shandses moved into their new home at Nemours, the rugs, furniture, and even the pictures on the walls could go in the same relative positions.

Although creation of the institute claimed a large share of Mrs. duPont's time and attention in the late 1930s, she did not neglect the charities that she had supported in the years before her husband's death. The general pattern of giving remained much the same. In 1936 about 6 percent went to educational institutions, 21 percent to other charitable institutions, 66 percent in gifts to members of her family and Alfred's, 2 percent to individual college students, and 4 percent to needy individuals. Although Mrs. duPont's annual income increased more than ten-fold after her husband's death, from $250,000 after investment losses in 1934 to $2.9 million in 1936, the dollar amounts of her giving increased only gradually.[19]

A significant shift in the pattern of Mrs. duPont's giving was particularly evident in 1940, a trend away from individuals and toward institutions, or to put it another way, away from charity and toward philanthropy (see table 5-1).[20] Although more money went to educational institutions than to individual scholarships during all the years in the period, amounts for the former grew more rapidly, with a four-fold increase in 1940 alone. The trend in charities other than education was even more pronounced: gifts to charitable institutions more than doubled from 1936 to 1940 while gifts to individuals declined. The reasons for the shift were simple. First, some gifts to institutions were deductible for tax purposes; those to individuals were not. Second, the burden of administering gifts to individuals was stretching the capacities of Miss Shaw and

TABLE 5-1 Charitable Gifts, 1931–40 (in dollars)

Purpose	1931	1936	1937	1938	1939	1940
Educational institutions	15,860	18,211	17,972	16,052	19,328	76,306
Individual scholarships	7,251	6,091	13,921	14,972	12,569	14,137
Other institutions	3,620	61,093	113,673	43,035	142,494	146,267
Charity to individuals	7,966	12,964	12,648	9,828	7,601	6,088
Family gifts	119,044	192,591	315,359	389,776	346,177	450,622

the civic-minded individuals who were providing advice on who deserved support.

Wilmington, Delaware, enjoyed the largest number of gifts from Mrs. duPont during the late 1930s. Most of her contributions went to destitute families and those facing serious illness, channeled either through institutions like the People's Settlement or through Olive Byrne, a social worker who visited the families to verify their needs. Gifts to individuals were small, usually under $20, all under the watchful eye of Miss Shaw, who instructed Miss Byrne on one occasion: "Do not under any consideration let her know that you are investigating this case for Mrs. duPont. . . . Rather imagine that the fact her husband has left her, and that she was and is still a cripple, has become an hallucination with the woman, but if she can be helped, believe Mrs. duPont is more than willing to co-operate."[21]

In addition to her own Wilmington charities, Mrs. duPont inherited dozens of cases from her husband, who for years had met the needs of many of the city's destitute. Early in 1936 she was flooded with letters from former pensioners. She wrote to Laura Walls, who had managed the pensioner program in Delaware for Mr. duPont: "I am in hopes that the welfare bureaus in the various localities can render assistance to them, and especially through this severely cold weather. It is heart breaking to think of people not having the necessities of life, when they have fared so long on life's stormy seas and are close to the other Shore. You can readily realize that it is impossible for me to contribute to all the applicants."[22]

Before the end of the year Mrs. duPont decided to bring some system to the enterprise by establishing the Alfred I. duPont Foundation, to which she allocated $50,000. From this account the Jacksonville office drafted checks in accordance with Miss Shaw's instructions. In January 1938 the office dispatched thirty-three checks, mostly from $10 to $20 each.[23]

In Jacksonville the duPonts did not have the close ties to individuals at all social levels that Alfred had established in a lifetime in Wilmington. Accordingly, most of Mrs. duPont's Jacksonville contributions went to agencies rather than to individuals: $3,000 in 1937 to the American Red Cross relief fund; $5,000 to the Hope Haven Foundation; $3,000 in 1938 to Opportunity House, sponsored by the Jacksonville Federation of Christian Young People; $4,000 in 1940 to the Community Chest; and small annual donations to the Baptist Home for Children, the Episcopal Diocese of Florida, the Children's Home Society, and other institutions.[24] As she did in Virginia, Mrs. duPont relied in Jacksonville on people she knew for her larger gifts: on W. Hardin Goodman, trust officer at the Florida National Bank, for the Hope Haven Association; on George J. Avent, Jr., also at the bank, for Opportunity House; and on Bishop Juhan for the diocese of Florida.

Mrs. duPont did not forget Virginia in her charities in the 1930s. Ethel Tignor was still providing field evaluations for Miss Shaw, who forwarded funds for tax purposes through the county Red Cross chapter rather than to individuals. Dr. Thomas Wheeldon had incorporated his orthopedic clinic in Kilmarnock for the same reason and had arranged with Dr. Morgan E. Norris of Kilmarnock for treatment of black orthopedic patients at a hospital in Richmond.[25] Through her cousin Eoline Jesse, Mrs. duPont sent monthly checks to the White Chapel Ladies' Aid Society. "This is to be used," she directed, "for the poor people, as you deem wisest." But she could never completely escape the details. A few months later she wrote to Eoline: "It would seem wise to me to give Priscilla Campbell an allowance of $4.00 per month, as she has been bed-ridden for two years. Glad you notified the family that after June 26th the Society would discontinue the monthly allowance of $12.00 to Mrs. ———. There is no earthly excuse for these people living on the land not to be able to raise their food in the way of vegetables, meat, chickens, eggs, etc. There is too much shiftlessness, and I know on this you will agree with me."[26]

In Richmond Mrs. duPont's support went to institutions rather than individuals. She took a special interest in the Sheltering Arms Hospital, which treated indigent patients free of charge. She could not deny the elderly patients in the Home for Needy Confederate Women and regularly contributed to the Virginia Historical Society. Her greatest interest in Richmond was the new Virginia Museum of Fine Arts, which opened in January 1936. In addition to her large initial gift to the building fund, she agreed to serve as a vice-president and member of the executive committee. She usually attended board meetings and on occasion made up the balance of funds needed for special exhibits in the museum. Respected by the museum staff for her knowledge of art as well as of financial matters, Mrs. duPont was one of the museum's most valuable advisors.[27] Every year there were scores of small gifts to charities of all types, but Mrs. duPont had a consistent if modest interest in schools for underprivileged children. In Appalachia, she made small donations to the Mountain Mission School in Grundy and the Blue Ridge Industrial School. Since the early 1930s she had regularly sent checks to two industrial schools for black children in Mississippi: the Prentiss Normal and Industrial Institute and the Piney Woods Country Life School. These gifts reflected Mrs. duPont's conviction at that time that blacks as a race were incapable of higher education and that their education should be limited to the manual and domestic arts. She was not willing, however, during these years to go beyond token gifts for black institutions, as she made clear when she turned down requests from the Tuskegee and Hampton institutes on the grounds that they already had "heavy endowment[s]."[28]

By far the largest proportion of Mrs. duPont's gift dollars went to members of her family and Alfred's. Because none of these gifts were tax deductible, their motivation was simply the joy that came from making life a little easier and more pleasant for those she loved. As many as twenty persons on both sides of the family received regular monthly checks ranging from $250 to $500. For the most part these gifts were gratefully received, although Mrs. duPont's sisters, especially Belle Baker, thought at times that she could have been more generous. Under the circumstances that sort of tension was not surprising among three sisters who had been close in their youth. Mrs. duPont apparently understood the situation and tended to follow expressions of ingratitude with still more gifts, as if they might help to bridge the gap that her marriage and sudden wealth had opened between her and her sisters.

Soon after Alfred's death the harmonious relationships that Jessie had carefully nurtured with members of his family began to disintegrate. Her decision to have Alfred Victor and his partner design the hospital at Nemours had thrilled the young architects, but her insistence that another firm be retained to check the structural design placed Alfred

Victor in an almost impossible position. Although the final design was considered an outstanding success, this was the last assignment that duPont and Massena ever had at Nemours, and Alfred Victor soon drifted out of Jessie's life.

Even more disastrous was the open hostility that had arisen between Jessie and Alfred's sister Marguerite. Despite Jessie's best efforts to maintain a friendship with her sister-in-law, Marguerite had long since written off Jessie as a conniving, money-grubbing opportunist who preferred to spend vast sums on luxurious houses and gardens than on the poor and destitute. Marguerite was further alienated when she learned from Alfred's will that Reginald Huidekoper, and not her own son, Maurice duPont Lee, had been named as executor of the estate. She believed that Alfred had promised the appointment to Maurice and that Jessie was responsible for Alfred's change of heart. The final blow came in 1936, when Jessie and the executors refused her request for a copy of the trust agreement by which Alfred established annuities for members of his family. When Marguerite threatened to take the matter to court, the executors had finally relented. In a stinging letter to Henry Adair, Marguerite wrote: "Of course I know my rights in the matter (inasmuch as Mr. Goodman was dealing not with a stupid Ball, but with a smart duPont), and that you would get an opinion from the Court; and if you did not, I would. I knew the provisions of the Trust, and the names of the annuitants long before writing to the august Trustees; but Mrs. J. B. decreed that I should not have the information from the Trustees and I was bound I should. . . . Mrs. J. B. duPont cannot browbeat *me*."[29]

As Marguerite and other duPonts learned, Jessie had no intention of sharing her husband's wealth with members of his family who had had no part in creating it, but family members on both sides with real needs were another question. For years she supported one of Alfred's nieces who was confined to a sanatorium. She never gave up on trying to rehabilitate Elsie's son Tom, who was an alcoholic, or Belle's son John, who suffered from severe psychological problems. And then there was her extended family, people who were not blood relatives but really old friends like the Martins in California, to whom she felt a lifelong attachment. She broke her rule against granting people loans to help Billy Martin meet his financial crisis brought on by the depression and later paid college tuition for all his children.[30]

Deep in Mrs. duPont's personality was a keen empathy for the unfortunate, particularly for those who, despite their best efforts, had suffered adversity. She was particularly touched by a letter from an elderly friend in the Northern Neck who asked Mrs. duPont to accept her home as a gift in return for help in the past. Mrs. duPont wrote: "It is certainly dear and sweet of you to wish to give me the little home that has been so dear to you and your brother. Of course, I will be very glad to receive it, provided you will use it so long as you live, and provided you do not feel there is some near relative or relatives to whom you would [wish] to give it after your passing. What I did for your brother and for you gave me more pleasure than it did you to receive it."[31] Certainly the property was of no use to Mrs. duPont, but she could not think of refusing it.

Another letter to an old friend in Los Angeles:

> Just a word to tell you how terribly distressed I am to hear of the serious illness of your dear daughter. It does seem that you have had more than your share of illness these last few years, but let us hope that this is the last storm before the sun breaks forth in radiant splendor to envelope [sic] you and your loved ones in sunshine and happiness and health the rest of the journey. It is a joy to know that you had the happy day in your little home, and I am just in hopes that your daughter soon will be very well and able to supervise the children herself.
>
> I am herein enclosing a check for $200.00 to assist you with the extra expense that illness entails; only those who have had illness can in any way realize the expense incurred thereby, as well as the lowering of efficiency of loved ones. You keep your dear self well and don't work too hard or strain your eyes too much.[32]

Common in Mrs. duPont's gift correspondence is her desire for anonymity. When Belle's husband Addison Baker wrote to her for data on her giving to his family, she assured him that she did not appreciate the government's requiring this kind of information for tax returns. "I was trained," she replied, "in a school wherein if you did anything for anyone you never alluded to it, and it is decidedly distasteful and obnoxious to me to have every gift that I make to loved ones a matter of record." When the Virginia Academy of Sciences requested permission to use the letter accompanying her $1000 gift for campaign purposes, she responded: "I am not convinced that this is a wise thing to do. I have always, as far as it is humanly possible, refrained from publicity,—the press is more than willing to give me too much now,—but, if you think that by sending a copy of said letter it will be productive of good results . . . I will be willing to transgress my usual policy."[33]

One project that remained close to Mrs. duPont's heart was the restoration of the Lee mansion at Stratford. Through the late 1930s she remained one of the most active Stratties, along with May Field Lanier and Helen Knox, an officer in the Chase National Bank in New York. "Miss Jessie" not only attended the annual October board meetings at Stratford without fail, but she also, little by little, became the principal source of funds for the project. Her first endeavor was to restore the Stratford Landing, a boat dock on the Potomac below the mansion. In 1936 she began to receive requests for emergency funds to keep Stratford open during the lean winter months when there were meager revenues from tourists. She readily responded with a $1,200 loan in 1936, $2,000 in 1937, and $2,500 in 1939. There were also occasional gifts of $500 to $1,000 to support research by Ethel Armes or for emergency mainte-nance. She offered to purchase three hundred copies of Armes's book on Stratford Hall. Early in 1937 she recruited her brother Ed's wife to help organize a Stratford chapter in Jacksonville and offered to open Epping Forest that winter as a fund-raiser for Stratford.[34]

Mrs. duPont, however, did more than meet emergencies. She tried to stimulate interest in supporting restoration by offering gifts that would encourage others to give. In July 1936 she offered to restore the Southwest Dependency, one of the four outbuildings connected to the mansion by arcades, and funded research by Miss Armes to determine if the building indeed had been Thomas Lee's law office. In January 1937 she encouraged other directors to provide furnishings for the mansion as an added attraction for tourists and made an initial contribution of $2,500 for that purpose. In October she agreed to back a pledge of $20,000 by the Delaware committee for restoration of the interior of the mansion. Her contributions for the year totaled more than $17,000. During these years she supported much of the restoration work and met most of the shortfall in operating expenses.[35]

The frequent appeals from Helen Knox and Helen's nice touch in showing appreciation without being deferential were the beginning of a close friendship that blossomed in the late 1930s. Helen's background could hardly have been more different from Jessie's. The daughter of a

Texas banker, she had graduated from the University of Texas and spent the next ten years caring for her invalid mother. Many of her friends thought Helen was throwing her life away, but during those years she read widely and studied to be a writer. Coming to New York after her mother died, she found prospects for a literary career dim and took a job as a file clerk in the Chase National Bank in 1926. To learn more about modern banking methods Helen took night courses and soon moved up the corporate ladder to become manager of the women's department of the bank's Grand Central branch. Thus the two women, with very different origins, came to be part of the same business world and spoke the same language. Soon in their correspondence, Jessie became Big Owl and Helen, Little Owl. Their joint interest at Stratford became that of getting the project on a sound financial footing in order to avoid the continual flirtation with bankruptcy. In 1939 they began a campaign to raise an endowment of $1 million for Stratford. Jessie wrote letters to wealthy women all over the South and even purchased a racehorse, Time O' War, which she hoped would bring in some winnings for the fund.[36]

Ditchley claimed a significant amount of Mrs. duPont's attention, in terms not just of restoring the historic mansion but also of turning the property into a profitable farm. Mrs. duPont wrote scores of letters to Hugh Tait, the farm manager, with detailed instructions about which animals to purchase, what kinds of stalls to provide for the cows, what materials to use on the roads, how to design the new barn, and what crops to plant. "I am still of the opinion that we should plant a minimum amount of wheat or corn. The soya bean is a more salable crop. If we plant it in the Spring, we can harvest it in June or July and sell the beans for around seventy-five cents per bushel; then the second crop can be turned in and fertilize the land, thus saving the expense of fertilizer. Wheat and corn take everything from the soil and put nothing back."[37]

She wanted the Taits to raise enough chickens and vegetables to meet the needs of the mansion house when she and her guests were there, and she badgered Tait about obtaining proper discounts on the purchase of farm machinery. "We do not wish, in the future, to have to buy all of our food when there; what with our own oysters, chickens, eggs, milk, butter and vegetables, we need to purchase nothing." Quite clearly there was still in Mrs. duPont much of Miss Jessie Ball, who had learned the techniques of subsistence farming as a girl.

The natural beauty of the Northern Neck and the memories it held for this daughter of rural Virginia were still a strong pull on Mrs. duPont. In April 1939 she arranged to purchase the lands her father had sold in 1908, including the old homestead at Cressfield and the farm houses at Bay Plain and Hurstville. She placed title to the land in Ditchley Incorporated and asked her brother Tom to work out the details for family use of the properties after her death. Later she established a family burial ground at Cressfield and had the remains of their parents moved there from California.[38]

By 1938 Alfred duPont's executors had managed to sort through the vast holdings of his estate and were moving toward a plan for final settlement. Most of the assets, held by Almours Securities, were invested in scores of business enterprises in Florida, Delaware, and Virginia. Even at the highest level, the investment structure of Almours was complex. Almours directly held the stock in six real estate and building investment companies. All of the operations in Northwest Florida were held by two subsidiaries, Gulf Coast Properties, Incorporated, and the Panama Beach Development Company. Both subsidiaries shared in the stock ownership of the five companies that held the timber lands, railroad, telephone company, dock terminal, and other facilities in Port St. Joe. Gulf Coast Properties held Almours's 50-percent ownership in the St. Joe Paper Company and Apalachicola Properties, Incorporated. Stock in the thirteen Florida banks that Almours had acquired by the end of 1937 was held jointly by Almours and by the Florida National Bank Group, Incorporated. In addition to the properties in Florida, Delaware, and Virginia, Almours held a large portfolio of bonds and stocks, much of it in the DuPont Company.[39]

For Mrs. duPont, managing the estate was a new and fascinating experience. She wrote her sister Belle that she got more pleasure from her work on the estate "than do most women from their social life." The meetings were "intensely interesting," and she said she learned "a vast deal" from the skilled lawyers and accountants who took part. "It was because the business life appealed to me so strongly that made the tie between A. I. and me so much stronger than between most husbands and wives. That was why he left his business for me to direct, knowing that Eddie would always work in perfect harmony with me, and of course, he thought Colonel Huidekoper would, too."[40]

She found Huidekoper a skillful and seasoned advisor not only on legal matters but also on corporate management. He did not hesitate to express his own opinion on a variety of business issues, such as the bonus policy for Almours Securities, funding of real estate enterprises, or interpretation of tax law. Even with her brother Ed she had formed a new relationship after Alfred's death. Before 1935 Ed had worked for Mr. duPont and did not take orders directly from his sister on matters relating to Almours. Now she was president of Almours and had the final word on policy matters. Both Huidekoper and Ball could disagree with her, but they readily accepted her decision once she made it.

The harmony in their relationship was largely of her own making. On several occasions Huidekoper had been irascible in dealing with the Almours staff, and Ball already had a reputation for being obsessed with making money, despite his courtly Virginia manners. Mrs. duPont was candid and firm in her disagreements with Huidekoper, but she usually tempered her replies to his letters with statements of concern for his health or for the welfare of his family.[41] With both Huidekoper and her brother, her bearing was always correct, unperturbed, and considerate. She had a way of disarming them both in any dispute so that harmony reigned.

She also came to have great confidence in the trustees' legal and financial advisors. Her chief legal counsel was still Henry P. Adair, senior partner in the firm of Knight, Adair, Cooper, and Osborne in Jacksonville. Mrs. duPont considered Adair "one of the ablest lawyers in Florida, in fact his firm is said to be the ablest firm here."[42] To follow the Byzantine labyrinths of tax law, the trustees continued to use the services of Miller & Chevalier in Washington, D.C. Robert N. Miller took a personal interest in the estate's tax problems, not only in negotiating the final settlement of the estate but also in advising Adair on appealing decisions of the federal and state tax authorities in the intervening years.[43] On the financial side the trustees continued to have the expert advice of James G. Bright, who had served as comptroller of Almours since its establishment.

Mrs. duPont assumed many of the functions that the president of Almours might be expected to exercise. She presided at the annual meeting of stockholders and made quick trips to Florida to discuss investment decisions and tax matters with Ed, Huidekoper, and Adair. She received regular reports from the principal Almours subsidiaries. She also made inquiries at the Harvard Business School to find promising young men who could fill executive positions in Almours Securities.[44]

Mrs. duPont, however, made no attempt to take personal control of the Florida enterprises. That might have required her to spend most of the year in Florida and to devote most of her attention to business. Such a commitment was unthinkable now that the Nemours Foundation was being established and plans for the hospital were being drawn. The Nemours Foundation and her other charitable interests would keep her in Wilmington during much of the year. The result was that Ed continued to manage the day-to-day business of the estate.

Mrs. duPont's relationship with her brother was curious. On the one hand, she expressed complete confidence in his judgment and intentions and stood firmly with him on every important decision. Outwardly their views on any business matter were identical. On the other hand, no one knew whether they disagreed in reaching these opinions in their private discussions in her Jacksonville office or at Epping Forest. As the years passed, the intervals between their meetings lengthened. She seldom corresponded with her brother or talked with him on the telephone. During his infrequent trips north on business Ed might stop just overnight at Nemours if he stopped at all. In her letters to her sisters and her brother Tom, she occasionally remarked that she had not seen or heard from Ed in months, but her tone was always one of personal regret, not criticism.[45] So private was her relationship with her brother that one can only guess at her true feelings. One fact is certain: she almost always placed harmony above any other consideration in relations with her family, so she may well have decided to let Ed have his way in most business decisions unless they threatened her commitment to Alfred.

Peripheral as Mrs. duPont's role in the Florida enterprises appeared on the surface, her influence was probably greater in the four years after Mr. duPont's death than at any subsequent time in her life. It was true that Ed dominated the Florida organization. He held the title of president in fourteen of the twenty-four companies that made up the Florida empire in its mature form in early 1940. Jessie knew full well that without his extraordinary skill in financial management, his dedication to the task, and his complete loyalty to her, the vast structure that Alfred had erected with Ed's help might have collapsed. With this in mind, she gave her brother a comfortable rein, but never a full rein, in operating the companies. She concealed her influence by acting through her principal lieutenants, Will Edwards and Henry Dew, both her childhood friends, whom Alfred had hired to work in Florida. Within the twenty-four companies, Edwards held the office of vice-president in twelve (most of them in the Florida Panhandle), while Dew had the same title in four others.[46] They could warn her when Ed's thirst for profit seemed to be getting out of hand.

By the end of 1938, the executors had agreed on most of the tactics for settling the estate and were looking for cash to pay the federal and state inheritance taxes. For that purpose it seemed necessary to liquidate some of the assets held by Almours Securities. That requirement, however, did not explain the decision late in the year to liquidate Almours in its entirety.

One consideration, which was of great concern to Huidekoper, were the continual disputes with the Bureau of Internal Revenue and the difficulty of keeping up with the latest interpretations of the frequent changes in tax law. Earlier it had been possible to shelter some personal income from federal taxes by leaving earnings in Almours, but in search for more revenues during the depression, Congress had partly closed this loophole by lowering the limits on undistributed earnings. Late in 1936 the federal government filed claims against Almours for tax deficiencies of more than $1 million in 1931 and more than $750,000 in 1932. Adair at once filed an appeal and was prepared to take the matter through the courts on the grounds that the government, after challenging the company's returns for 1927–29, had accepted his defense of the income tax returns for those years. Huidekoper found Adair's appeals of tax determinations endless and on the whole fruitless. Was it worth all the trouble to keep Almours in business?[47]

Another factor, never even mentioned in correspondence, must have been of great weight in the decision to liquidate Almours. The problem went back to Mr. duPont's will, in which he left five thousand shares of Almours stock each to his children and Ed Ball and one thousand shares each to Mrs. duPont's two sisters and brother Tom. As stockholders these family members now had an interest in the Florida enterprise, and some of them were not reluctant to second-guess Ed's or even Jessie's management decisions, either at the annual stockholders' meeting or by letter at other times of the year.[48]

The problem became all too apparent in the stockholders' meeting in Jacksonville in February 1938. Elsie Bowley and her husband raised detailed questions about the status of the banks, Almours's investment in the paper mill, and construction of housing at Port St. Joe. Huidekoper questioned the cost overruns in constructing the Miami bank building, and Mrs. Bowley criticized the management for its liberal policy in paying a company officer's expenses during a prolonged illness. Huidekoper would not ratify the actions of the directors since the last stockholders' meeting because Ball had refused to send him copies of the minutes.[49] It was quite apparent that the stockholders' meeting was degenerating into a family squabble. Ed, no doubt with his sister's approval, saw to it that the Almours stockholders never met again.

At its next meeting the board of directors voted to liquidate the company, and James Bright set about the complicated task of determining how the company's assets would be distributed among the shareholders. He began by listing every asset on the balance sheet for June 30, 1938, and then determined their market value on September 22 for the purpose of liquidating all the preferred stock in full through cash payments. The remaining securities were to be distributed among the shareholders. Most of the assets were to go to the estate, Mrs. duPont, and Ed Ball. Bright estimated that Mrs. duPont would receive 61,751 shares of DuPont stock with a fair market value of $8,201,304.68. The total value of all assets she would receive he estimated at $10,352,990.56 (or more than 106 million in current dollars).[50]

With the Almours liquidation in December 1938, Mrs. duPont and the other executors could proceed with the final settlement of her husband's estate. They took the first step by paying the estate tax on April 1, 1939, when they gave the state of Florida a check for $2,927,338.62, the largest single tax payment ever made in Florida up to that time. The last step would be the actual transfer of the estate to the trustees in September.[51]

Whatever benefits Jessie and Ed saw in the liquidation of Almours, the action had some troublesome effects. The income from part of the Almours stock was dedicated to annuities that Alfred had established in a separate trust for members of his family. When, in accordance with the liquidation plan, the stock was redeemed with cash, the income for paying the annuities disappeared, at least until the estate could reinvest the cash in securities with an adequate yield. Fortunately for Jessie and Ed, Marguerite was no longer alive to rake them with her venomous pen, but her son, Maurice duPont Lee, took up his mother's battle. In January 1939 he warned Jessie that "the sudden and complete cessation of all monthly payments to the trust beneficiaries, without any warning whatsoever," had placed Alfred's brother Maurice and his family in such dire straits that Maurice Lee felt compelled to support them to the extent of $2,500 per month from "my meager resources." Maurice declared his determination to meet the needs of his uncle: "Should my resources fail in the doing, I am certain that a personal appeal to Pierre will not go unanswered."[52]

The tone of Maurice's letter was imprudent enough; but the threat to appeal to Alfred's estranged cousin Pierre was, as Jessie's friend Francis duPont pointed out to Maurice, a remark that surely would offend Jessie and damage his cause in the process. On Francis's advice, Maurice a month later wrote Jessie an abject letter of apology, which she quickly accepted. By late March she was writing him the sort of affectionate letters that she often sent to relatives. Maurice and his wife Gerry responded with equal warmth and frequently called on Jessie at Nemours. Beneath the outward show of affection, however, Maurice harbored a dislike for Jessie that he expressed from time to time for years afterward to third parties, but never directly to her. It was inevitable that some of these reports would filter through to her, but Jessie continued to ignore them. She was willing to play the game of social conviviality with Maurice, although she discounted his frequent complaints as irresponsible heckling.[53]

In the meantime, there were plenty of problems to be solved in setting up the Nemours Foundation and building the hospital. Because the estate had not yet been settled, the foundation had insufficient funds to finance construction of the hospital, and Mrs. duPont suggested that the foundation borrow $1 million for this purpose. When Colonel Huidekoper contended that a loan of this amount would be illegal under the foundation's charter, Adair had to go to court for a declaratory judgment on the matter. Huidekoper also objected to adopting the recommendation of the medical advisory board (a proposal probably initiated by Mrs. duPont) that the hospital be named the Alfred I. duPont Institute. The other executors finally approved both proposals, but resolution of the disagreement took time.[54]

Mrs. duPont and Alfred Shands were still struggling with details of the hospital design. She sent the architects back to the drawing boards once over the external design, which they had proposed to render in "modernistic" style. A second major revision in the plans came when she decided that the proposed building would be too costly. She spent hours poring over the fine points of the plans, from the functional assignments of space and the site elevations of the building to the theme of murals for the interior decoration.[55]

Impatient to begin the treatment of crippled children, Mrs. duPont made arrangements early in 1939 to set up Alfred's retreat at Cherry Island as a summer camp for handicapped children from Wilmington. She asked Frank Mathewson, Alfred's boyhood friend and hunting partner who now was caretaker at the island, to ready the smaller cottages for the children. The main cottage was to be reserved for her and the attending doctors. In May she visited the island with Shands and discussed arrangements with Marie L. Des Barres, who had already been selected as administratrix of the hospital. In July Miss Des Barres reported that the children were enjoying the swimming pool that Mathewson had just completed. They also appreciated the fresh vegetables that Mrs. duPont had sent down from the gardens at Nemours.[56]

As the hospital neared completion in 1940, Mrs. duPont's enthusiasm mounted. In January she wrote Dr. Tucker: "The hospital is progressing beautifully. It really is going to be lovely. The Medical Board is not going to be ashamed of it is my belief. The marble floors were being laid when I was there. Spent a couple of hours each morning with Mr. Watson in connection with the hospital, also went over some of the furnishings with Miss Des Barres."[57]

In May she wrote to Dr. Shands from Jacksonville: "It is quite a thrill to know that you and Miss Des Barres are moving your offices [to the

The Alfred I. duPont Institute, the hospital for crippled children, built by Mrs. duPont on grounds of Nemours and first opened in 1940.

hospital] not later than May fifteenth—to see the dream of Mr. duPont coming into fruition that the crippled child might benefit as a result of his life's labors,—gives me great satisfaction."[58] Her statement was hardly exuberant, but Shands must have known that the formality of her correspondence concealed a flood of emotion and pride in what had been accomplished at Nemours.

The year 1940 brought not only the completion of the hospital at Nemours but also a consolidation of the Florida companies. Without the organizational umbrella formerly provided by Almours Securities, Ed Ball and his associates had more than twenty companies and almost as many banks to manage. In May Ball completed negotiations with the Mead Corporation to purchase that company's interest in the St. Joe Paper Company. Edwards reported to Mrs. duPont that the mill was producing almost 10,000 tons of pulp per month and earning a net income after taxes and depreciation of more than $135,000, more than twice the income of a year earlier. In July Ball merged Gulf Coast Properties and the Panama Beach Development Company, which together held most of the duPont timber lands in Northwest Florida, into the St. Joe Paper Company. In November the three largest real estate companies in the old Almours empire were merged into the Florida National Building Corporation. By this time Ball had liquidated the Florida National Group, Incorporated, which, with Almours, had held the stock in all the Florida National Banks.[59]

Now the stock was no longer held by one large company but was distributed among the stockholders. With these moves Ball completed the process of excluding Alfred's and Jessie's families from a direct voice in the Florida enterprises and consolidating the Florida real estate and paper mill operations in two large companies, which he, Jessie, and the estate would control.

There is no evidence that Mrs. duPont ever questioned her brother's actions in any of these reorganizations. Presumably if they made good business sense, she was ready to approve them. After all, efficient operations with effective controls would help to assure good stewardship over the resources that Alfred had left them for the relief of human suffering. In this sense, she had reason to conclude that she was fulfilling Alfred's wishes. He had, perhaps quite deliberately, built an inescapable tension into the relationship between brother and sister. Ed would make the money that Jessie would spend on human welfare, and each of them would serve as a check on the enthusiasm of the other.

There was one more responsibility that Jessie wanted to discharge for Alfred's sake. In 1938 she began looking for a prominent author who could write Alfred's biography. Among those whom she consulted was Francis Pendleton Gaines, the president of Washington and Lee University. Gaines, eight years younger than Jessie, had graduated from Richmond College in 1912. For a decade he pursued graduate studies in the North while teaching in the South. Three years after receiving a doctorate in English at Columbia in 1924, Gaines was elected president of Wake Forest College and three years later took the same post at Washington and Lee. Although Jessie had known Gaines in her Virginia days, she had reestablished contact with him through his wife Sadie duVergne, who was on the Stratford board. Fluent in writing and public speaking, Gaines had quickly won Jessie's confidence and the couple soon joined Jessie's inner circle of friends. Gaines and Charles Hardwicke, both of whom Jessie had known before her marriage, were the only two men whom she ever addressed by their first names.

Frank Gaines was at once taken with the idea of the biography of Alfred and promptly suggested Marquis James, the popular biographer of Andrew Jackson and Sam Houston. James could be expected to write a solid and honest biography without being too scholarly. Gaines thought "the name of James on a life of Mr. A. I. would perhaps do more to guarantee a reception by the thinking public than the name of any other writer."[60]

James began research on the biography in the summer of 1939. Mrs. duPont wrote to many of her husband's old colleagues for reminiscences and opened the way for James to interview members of the family and close friends. She collected old letters and had dozens of files sent out to Nemours for James's review. Two long interviews with her gave James access to many stories that Alfred had told her about his early life. As the manuscript was completed in 1941, she read each chapter carefully and entered comments and corrections in the margin in red pencil. She directed most of her comments to factual details and only in two or three places differed with James on interpretation. James did not accept all of her suggestions by any means, and the book as published was almost exactly as he had written it.[61] In the end, Mrs. duPont was "deeply appreciative and delighted with the results of your work. It is a masterpiece."[62] By that time both James and his wife, Bessie, had become Mrs. duPont's close personal friends.

By the end of 1940 Mrs. duPont could take some satisfaction in her achievements in carrying out her husband's hopes for the future. His estate had been settled with no legal complications; she had provided for continuing his Wilmington charities through the foundation established in his name; she had realized his greatest dream in building the hospital for crippled children at Nemours; she had worked with Ed in consolidating Alfred's financial interests in their control; and she expected that Marquis James would at last bring to Alfred's name the public recognition that he had shunned in his lifetime. She had, in Alfred's words, proved "true to every trust."

6

Civilization on Trial

On a warm August morning in 1936 the *Queen Mary,* the magnificent new flagship of the Cunard Line, edged into her berth in the Hudson River. Among the first-class passengers were Jessie Ball duPont, the Bowleys, and Denise, who had just returned from six weeks in England, Switzerland, Germany, and France. Jessie's sister Isabel Baker and brother Ed were there to meet them. After clearing customs and stopping briefly at the duPont suite in the Ritz-Carlton Hotel, the party took the train to Wilmington, where they arrived in time for dinner at Nemours.[1]

It had been a marvelous trip, topped off by a week with Mr. duPont's daughter Madeleine and her family, who had a spacious home on the shores of Lake Amersee south of Munich. Madeleine had lived most of her life abroad, but while she was in Wilmington in 1907 she had eloped with John Bancroft, a Princeton undergraduate and the son of a prominent Wilmington family. On their honeymoon in Europe she had fallen in love with Max Hiebler, a dashing, debonair young German, who then fathered her three sons, the first of whom, Bayard, was born in Wilmington before her divorce from Bancroft. As her father had feared, Hiebler turned out to be a scoundrel interested only in getting his hands on the fortune he expected Madeleine to inherit. Madeleine finally rid herself of Hiebler by buying him off and then, in 1931, married Hermann Ruoff, the son of a fine old Munich couple whom she had known for years.[2] Madeleine's third marriage was as successful as the first two had been disastrous. Ruoff had all the qualities of a good husband and soon won Jessie's affection and Alfred's respect. Both were pleased to find the three boys intelligent and well behaved. Both Ruoff and Bayard, the oldest son, enjoyed visiting the duPonts twice during the early 1930s and

138

would have been happy to settle in America. However, neither Alfred nor Jessie nor Madeleine nor her sister, Victorine Dent, welcomed that idea—Madeleine, because she preferred to live in Germany; Jessie and Victorine, because they feared a revival of the scandal reported in the press during Bancroft's divorce proceedings.[3]

Jessie and Victorine were alarmed in 1934 when during a visit Bayard expressed a desire to move to the United States and claim his American citizenship. Under strong pressure from Jessie and Victorine, Madeleine prevailed on her son to remain in Germany.[4] The young man was not to be denied, however, and when Jessie returned from Europe in 1936, Bayard was back in the States looking for a job.

Madeleine and her family were certainly a topic of conversation around the dining table at Nemours that summer evening, but the more serious talk was probably directed to conditions in Europe. When she arrived in Wilmington that afternoon, Mrs. duPont had told reporters that the countries of Western Europe were building up armaments as quickly as possible as the fear of war mounted. "The [civil] war in Spain is a terrible thing," she said, "but I do not think there is any reason to fear it as a threat to the peace of Europe."[5] The next day, in a letter to Victorine, Jessie deplored the arms race. Apparently the European nations had learned nothing from World War I, "and this is evidently going to [be] a war of civilization versus Communism. If the latter wins, there is no place for our class. . . . Poverty would never awe me, but to live under distorted principles, with no ideals, disorder and dirt, would make life unbearable."[6]

As the years passed, however, Hitler and the Nazis became for Mrs. duPont a greater threat than communism. No doubt the long, serious discussions of politics and economics at her dinner parties at Nemours and Epping Forest led her to this conclusion, but her correspondence with the Hiebler brothers gave her a first-hand example of the danger. On the eve of the presidential election in 1936, Bayard, now working as a clerk in Los Angeles, wrote to her that if he could vote, he would cast his ballot for Alf Landon "because I hate to see this country run by a bunch of miserable foreign aliens and jews. Very many of them are nothing but international trouble-makers, wherever there is a chance to excite the masses they got [sic] their dirty fingers in it somehow."[7] For Mrs. duPont, Bayard's statement was not only a deplorable expression of anti–Semitism but also evidence of how the Nazis were distorting the minds of even educated people in Germany. In time Bayard, who soon became disillusioned with his failure to find a job equal to his social station, returned to Germany.

Mrs. duPont had no more success in making life in America amenable for Bayard's younger brother, Alfred, who came over in 1938 for his last two years of college at Washington and Lee University. Through her close friend Frank P. Gaines, the president of the university, Mrs. duPont arranged for Alfred's admission, and the Gaineses dutifully invited the young man to dine with them. Gaines found Alfred profoundly unhappy, not just because he was homesick and did not know English well enough to follow lectures, but because of the cultural shock he encountered in seeing his homeland through American eyes. The universal denunciation of Hitler after the annexation of Austria in the fall of 1938, in Gaines's words, "shocked Alfred into deep pain." Alfred was not belligerent or argumentative but had adopted "a sort of spiritual loneliness." "[H]e is almost tragically loyal with the assurance of his race that everything over there is perfect and that our failure to approve is the measure of our imperfection."[8] Bitterly disappointed and disillusioned with his grand-father's homeland, Alfred returned to Germany after spending the Christmas holidays at Nemours.

A few months later he wrote to his "Aunt Jessie" that he was thinking of coming back for a visit in the summer of 1939. Aunt Jessie responded in a letter that showed her sensitivity to the young man's frustrations, but she felt it necessary to remind him that he had been "so unhappy over your country, over our radio and the headlines in the daily papers, which gave to you information which you had never before had, then your days at Nemours, when you were so miserable because of the tense and bitter feeling." In recent months, she wrote, that feeling had "increased one hundred fold." She advised him to stay with his family in Germany.[9]

It was well that Alfred followed her advice, for before the end of the summer Germany was at war. Although the United States was still neutral, German and British censorship disrupted trans–Atlantic mail service. In the first eight weeks after war broke out, Jessie heard nothing from Madeleine. She was greatly relieved in October to receive a letter from a priest who had been rector of the American Church in Munich. He reported that all the family were well. Hermann was an interpreter on the general staff on the western front and the three boys were in the army. There was rationing of food and clothing but no real shortages. With few soldiers and automobiles on the streets, Munich had become a "quieter and pleasanter" city.[10]

Taking advantage of the priest's offer to provide more information, Mrs. duPont replied with four pages of questions: "Are the Jews still being herded into concentration camps? executed? and property confiscated?" Did the people really support Hitler? Could Madeleine operate her car? Were her letters getting through to Germany? Dare Germans listen to foreign radio stations? Was there any chance that the right wing might restore a constitutional monarchy in Germany? Did Madeleine have sufficient funds to operate her home?[11] Mrs. duPont's first concern was personal, for her husband's family, but she also revealed a broad interest in the international situation. Her questions about the fate of the Jews at this early point in the war now seem quite remarkable.

With the German blitzkrieg, the British evacuation at Dunkirk, and the fall of France in 1940, the outlook in Europe became desperate. Isolationism in the United States was paralyzing efforts to come to Britain's assistance. Jessie wrote to an old California friend now living in Toronto that she was supporting the Maple Leaf Society, which was raising money to supply aid to Britain. She was cancelling a $2,000 loan she had made to the society in 1938 and making the loan a gift. The saving of Britain was now imperative. "One needs," she wrote, "all one's strength and energy to do what one can do for the preservation of Christian civilization, which is certainly on trial."[12]

The threat to what Mrs. duPont called "civilization" came not only from the Nazis but from what she saw as profound ignorance among the "masses" in America. Political parties made no difference, she wrote to her brother Tom. The United States could not go against "the great tide of western civilization. People do not wish liberty, as they are all voting themselves on Government security." The loss of freedom, she averred, was the wish of the people. "While this momentous thing is being built up, the Nazis are diverting the attention of the American masses from the real issue by concentrating that attention on the jew as the menace of civilization. . . . [W]hoever is not an hundred percent Nazi and has power in the international world—are jews, and the colossal ignorance of the mass population—and that means your and my associates—accept this Nazi interpretation as one hundred percent correct—we being too lazy to look into an Encyclopedia."[13] Educated people, she thought, should have no trouble seeing through fascist propaganda.

As Britain stood alone against the Nazi onslaught in the West in 1941, Mrs. duPont gave her highest priority to helping those under attack. In turning down a request for funds for a questionable project in January, she wrote: "[A]ll available funds that are not absolutely allocated must go to Britain, to Greece and to China." She lectured her farm manager at Ditchley that "we should deny ourselves everything we can that we may give more to Britain."[14]

Aid to the Allies, however, was only a stopgap. Mrs. duPont was more willing than many Americans to admit that the direct involvement of the United States was inevitable in what she saw as the struggle for freedom. And she realized that involvement could imperil her foremost hopes for the hospital at Nemours. It seemed ironic that Alfred's dream was coming into reality just at the time that the international crisis was threatening to destroy it. The hospital was nearing completion in the spring of 1941. The administrative structure was in place. Under the trustees of Alfred's estate was to be the board of managers, with Henry Adair as chairman. The members in addition to Jessie were Francis I. duPont, her closest friend in Alfred's extended family; Charles M. Hanby, the Baltimore physician who had nursed her back to health in 1929; and Alfred Shands, medical director of the Alfred I. duPont Institute. Notably absent from the board was Ed Ball.[15]

The world crisis forced the board to cut back on plans even before the hospital was completed. The money was already in hand to construct convalescent cottages near the hospital, but defense priorities for materials and labor had caused indefinite postponement. The hospital, however, was dedicated as planned on June 14. Henry St. George Tucker, the presiding bishop of the Episcopal church, delivered the invocation, and Edmond J. FitzMaurice, the Roman Catholic bishop of Wilmington, gave the benediction. Alfred Shands described the origins of the institute and Frank Gaines delivered a tribute to Alfred duPont. It was, Jessie reported, "a most impressive occasion." Alfred's old friend Ellen LaMotte wrote Jessie that she "never saw such perfection of detail, such beautiful construction and wonderful equipment. You have indeed made it a fitting monument—and fulfillment of dear Alfred's wishes."[16]

As the clouds of war approached the United States in the summer of 1941, Mrs. duPont prepared for the changes that would inevitably touch her way of life. She had already heard rumors that the federal government was planning to requisition large yachts for the defense effort. Perhaps, she thought, this would be the last season for cruising on the "little boat" that had been so much a part of her life with Alfred.

In August she set off on an extended cruise on the *Nenemoosha* up the Atlantic coast from Wilmington. On the first leg of the trip to Long Island Sound, she enjoyed lazy days with the people closest to her at the time—Frank Gaines and brother Ed and their wives. The weather was perfect and the calm seas made the passage especially pleasant. Once in the sound they explored the Connecticut and Rhode Island shore, where she and Ed noted the rapid industrial development as the nation emerged from the depression and prepared for war. While the *Nenemoosha* was tied up in Manhattan, Mrs. duPont stayed at the Ritz-Carlton and enjoyed several Broadway shows, including *The Watch on the Rhine*. "It brings out quite forcibly not so much a fight against Communism, Nazism and Fascism as a fight for democracy that means the soul shall be free."[17]

New York friends and family joined the *Nenemoosha* the following week for a trip around Manhattan Island and two excursions up the Hudson to West Point. On the second run up the river with her sister Belle, the Edwardses, and Helen Knox, they stopped at West Point to call on the Bowleys and the commandant. In November Mrs. duPont invited several friends to join her on a cruise down the Inland Waterway from Norfolk to Charleston as the crew moved the yacht from the Chesapeake to Florida. Looking ahead, she arranged to have the extra china and glassware removed from the yacht and stored at Nemours. On December 18 she turned over the *Nenemoosha* to the government as an outright gift.[18]

By that time the Japanese had attacked Pearl Harbor, and the war Mrs. duPont had long feared became a reality. She wrote to her childhood friend Rebecca Harding Adams that the signs of war were already close to Epping Forest. The commandant of the Danish training ship that had taken refuge in the St. John's River had offered the ship and the services of the crew to the United States. Across the broad expanse of river opposite Epping Forest the navy was constructing an air base. Jessie

Mrs. duPont with her sister Elsie Bowley and Albert J. Bowley in Lakeland, Florida, in January 1941.

hoped the pilots would not mistake her home for the base. "If they did, it would be well for the base—better lose Epping Forest than an air base. All joking aside, it is quite serious."[19]

In March 1942 Jessie wrote Tom that eighteen men had been rescued from one of the tankers sunk by a German submarine off Jacksonville. Similar attacks were occurring up and down the Atlantic Coast. She thought the attacks "may do something to awaken the American people to their responsibility and what lay ahead, in fact eliminate that secure idea that the general public had, as it was told them by many of our leaders, that no power could ever touch the United States."[20]

The war was also having its impact on Nemours and the institute. All construction at the institute, including the convalescent cottages, had been set aside for the duration. Virtually all the equipment for the research department had been delivered, but use of the equipment was to be sharply limited. "There is no question but what we must curtail many expenses and concentrate [in] every possible way our efforts and our money upon the war."[21] Mrs. duPont did not attempt to open Nemours for the summer of 1942, but kept only a small staff and confined herself to the library on the first floor and her bedroom suite on the second. When weather permitted, she had her meals on a tray on the terrace. She was not concerned about gasoline rationing. "[It] is going to make people appreciate their homes more and find also that they have a pair of feet." She was planning to walk to Nemours from her office in downtown Wilmington; she had already walked from Nemours to the end of the streetcar line.[22]

At the age of fifty-eight, Mrs. duPont had boundless energy for work. That summer she wrote one of her cousins:

> You ask how I spend my day. This morning I had breakfast at eight fifteen. As I am absolutely alone in the house, I had it on a tray on the front terrace with my radio beside me, imbibing the war news, which is anything but cheerful these days. . . . I was through breakfast at nine o'clock, then I went into the kitchen to see the cook about the meals for the servants and my very light fare. Then I talked to the carpenter about work on the furniture. . . . Then I walked over the estate, or as much of it as I could, talking to the different men, who were pulling weeds, cutting hedges, trapping Japanese beetles, planting flowers, etc. . . . Next I went to town at ten thirty, where I selected some electrical fixtures for one of the employees' houses on the estate. Now at the office, where I arrived at eleven o'clock, and I shall be here in all probability until four o'clock. It takes me that much time to get through my work here, and then I am not through, even with the vast amount of work that Miss Shaw does. I shall go back to Nemours, then go to the Institute and sign the various checks, . . . and work up our plans for our meeting [of the board of managers], which will be held on the nineteenth. . . . This will put me at Nemours about six-thirty, when I shall reverse my cuffs, alias dress for dinner, which I shall have on the back terrace at seven o'clock, then take my two dogs for a walk. This is about a typical day, though sometimes I get to the office at ten o'clock, and stay until five. However, I enjoy every minute of it, Cousin Minnie, and I wouldn't change with one of the people who lead social lives, for anything in the world.[23]

Personal inconveniences were much easier to accept than were the reductions of staff and activities at the institute. The heaviest blow was the departure of Dr. Shands in September to join the Army Air Forces Medical Corps. Mrs. duPont wrote Shands that after seeing him off at the

New Castle airport, she "was just completely knocked out or sunk. . . . Somehow the darkness seemed so vast and heavy that I couldn't do anything." Shands had a major role in building the institute, but she had not anticipated his enormous help on financial matters. She missed him terribly. "Also, I didn't realize how much of my life and soul are in that Institute, until you moved on."[24] Within another month all of the medical staff had left for the armed services, and the research department was completely shut down. Dr. Bruce Gill, a retired orthopedist from the University of Pennsylvania, became interim medical director and with the help of one doctor and the nursing staff, he cared for the fifty children still hospitalized at the institute.[25]

One Sunday evening in October 1942, Mrs. duPont was alone at Nemours, "a right big house," she noted, "for one lone soul." The solitude gave her time to think about a letter she had received from her brother Tom, another of his bitter complaints about the social changes that had occurred in the United States under the New Deal. Tom was wrong, she thought, to see the upheaval solely in terms of the United States. "[T]he whole world," she wrote to him the next day, "is in a revolution—economic and social, and well might it be,—not because of the war. The revolution preceded the war. It has never been right—A.I. and I used often to discuss it—that one group should have so much and another group not even the bare necessities of life." She thought of India, where "because of religion—forty million untouchables are forever damned." Public education in America, however, had opened the eyes of the mass population to the inequities of the existing economic and social system, and American developments in transportation and communication were spreading revolutionary ideas abroad. The revolution, she predicted, might be "hard on a given class—you and I will be the recipients of some of those hardships," but the results would benefit "the vast majority of the peoples of the world, that is, if we believe in democracy."[26]

Democracy, she believed, was the answer to the world's problems if the masses could be educated to use it wisely. She had no patience with the House Un-American Activities Committee under Martin Dies, which was about to update its 1938 report on the communist threat to America. It was not the communists, she pointed out, but the Nazis who had enslaved Europe. "As bad as Communism is, if I had to live under one or the other systems [*sic*] of government, give me Communism. . . . Any land will work out of Communism, I believe if it is a land of literate people, which Russia is fast becoming."[27]

The Nazis, in contrast, had not only enslaved Europe, but she was convinced that they were behind the recent attacks on the Roman Catholic church and other groups in the United States. "Turning from the Catholics, they next went to the negro. . . . Next was the Jew, now it is the British." The last assault was the most unforgivable of all. "[W]e owe to that little group on those Islands an eternal debt, they held the fiends at bay with nothing to fight with except courage, faith, and a willingness to die to the last man rather than live in slavery, while we made our preparations."[28]

It was not surprising that Mrs. duPont was especially alarmed by anti-Catholic and anti-British propaganda. As early as 1932 she had expressed a fixed opinion that the church and the British government were the two strongest bastions of civilization as she understood it. At that time she had written: "In fact for many years [I] have felt that if a cultural civilization is to be saved, these two organizations . . . are the ones that will save it."[29] Over the ensuing decade she had expressed the same opinion in several letters, and the war had strengthened that conviction.

Mrs. duPont never revealed in her letters how she came to revere these two bastions of civilization. Her letters make it quite obvious that she had not developed these and other positions on social and economic issues in any systematic way. Rather they took the form of spontaneous expressions tossed off in the course of dictating chatty letters in private correspondence with Tom or other relatives. It is possible that the statement about the church and the British was a bit of hyperbole designed to catch the attention of the reader with an unexpected declaration. After all, she had been raised a Baptist and was proud of her lineage that included the mother of George Washington.

There must have been, however, some substance to her expressions of admiration for the Catholic church and the British. The church, after all, had kept civilization alive during the Dark Ages, and in her own day stood as a defender of traditional moral values, the sanctity of the family, and the importance of education based on Christian principles. Furthermore, admiration for the Catholic church had helped her as Jessie Ball and later as Mrs. duPont to maintain an independent stance as a Christian outside the confines of any denomination. In this stand for independence she had the support of her father, who considered all organized religion as a form of chicanery, and her husband, who, although a nominal Episcopalian, found more authentic religious belief among the Roman Catholic powdermen in the Hagley Yard than in the coldhearted duPonts who claimed membership in Christ Church, Christiana Hundred Parish.[30]

What the Catholic church offered Mrs. duPont in the moral and religious sphere, Britain provided her in the political and cultural world. American democracy had its roots in the individual rights the English had won in Magna Charta and in the parliamentary system of government for which Americans had fought during the Revolution. Even more important, however, was the cultural heritage that Jessie Ball received as a child of Virginia, the most British of all the American colonies. Her Florida home had been named not just for the family plantation in Lancaster County, Virginia, but also for the earlier Ball estate in England. Mrs. duPont's first trip abroad had been to England, she had sent Denise to school in England, she cultivated friendships with the Duchess of Northumberland and other British nobility, and she had organized a trip to England for the coronation in 1937. From her father she had learned to respect and love the English language. The correct use of English was the first rung on the ladder to success for her scholarship students.

In a world caught up in what Mrs. duPont believed was global revolution as well as global war, the Catholic church and Great Britain seemed to provide her with two solid footholds on the bedrock of "civilization." And because she was neither Roman Catholic nor English, she could extol the virtues of both the church and the government without risking a commitment to either.

However superficial and unsystematic Mrs. duPont's thinking may have been, it provided her with a clear-cut motivation for aiding the British during the war. After contributing generously to the Royal Air Force Visitors' Fund during the Battle of Britain, she turned her fund-raising energies to Bundles for Britain in 1941. A private corporation organized to provide food, clothing, and supplies for British families whose homes had been destroyed by bomb attacks, Bundles for Britain gave Mrs. duPont a direct outlet for her concern for the welfare of that country.

Although the sponsoring committee included many nationally known figures, the actual leadership was largely in the hands of Mrs. duPont and her friends. The president of Bundles for Britain was Aleen Bingham, the third wife of Robert Worth Bingham, the prominent Louisville publisher and U.S. ambassador in London when he died in 1937. Aleen, like Helen Knox, was also a Strattie, and the trio enjoyed many evenings at dinner and the theater in New York while attending to Bundles business. So close became their relationship that Aleen soon earned the title of Owlette in companionship with Big Owl and Little Owl. Also on the board of directors were Frank Gaines and Dr. Philip D. Wilson, who had been a member of the medical advisory board at the institute until he left for England early in 1940 to help establish hospitals for war casualties there.[31] Jessie must have been responsible for enlisting their services.

Mrs. duPont did more for Bundles than attend board meetings. She made substantial monetary contributions, solicited funds from others, and encouraged the formation of local chapters. Her personal project was to provide blankets for British families bombed out of their homes. She discovered that the felts used in processing kraft board at the St. Joe Paper Company could be cleaned, treated, dyed, and turned into blankets. As head of the board, she personally monitored the blanket project as a major contribution to the war effort by the company. By the spring of 1945 the company had shipped 1,500 blankets to England.[32]

The direct line from thought to action in Mrs. duPont's support of the British during the war did not extend to her admiration for the Roman Catholic church. She never considered becoming a Roman Catholic and continued during the war to preserve her stance as a nondenominational Christian. As she wrote to one of her goddaughters, who was planning in 1944 to marry a Roman Catholic: "To [me] Catholicism would never have stood in my way. It is the Christian religion and which church a man belongs to of the orthodox Christian religion would make absolutely no difference to me."[33]

Mrs. duPont's Christianity seemed at this time almost entirely a commitment to the moral principles to which the Christian church aspired rather than to the theology on which it was based. "Christianity," she wrote in 1945, "is the only religion that has recognized the dignity of man as an individual, therefore, it is to be hoped that the peoples of all parts of the world will in time recognize the teachings of Christ as a philosophy as well as a religion, by which man can live."[34] She seldom referred to Christ in her letters and then, as in this example, as a philosopher rather than as a personal saviour. In the 1930s she showed no reluctance in joining the Unitarian Church in Richmond, where Belle's husband Addison Baker was pastor. Her membership, however, was mostly an expression of personal support for Baker, and she promptly resigned when he left the church.[35]

It may be misleading, however, to accept these facts as evidence that Mrs. duPont was at best a nominal Christian. She, like her father, had never embraced the emotional expression of religious feeling that was common in the evangelical churches. It is even likely that the formalism of the Episcopal church, which screened one's personal religious commitments from public view, was one of the things that attracted her to this denomination. One as conservative and formal as Mrs. duPont did not wear her religious beliefs on her sleeve.

Despite her reluctance to accept formal affiliation with any Christian body, Mrs. duPont during the war was becoming involved in the work of the Episcopal church. She never explained the origins of this interest, but some of the roots seem obvious. Except for her immediate forebears, the Balls of Virginia had been Anglicans and Episcopalians, as the Ball family tombs at St. Mary's Church, White Chapel, in Lancaster County demonstrated. She had taken a personal interest in restoring St. Mary's and Christ Church, Irvington, both outstanding examples of colonial church architecture. Furthermore, her long relationship with Frederick D. Goodwin in her scholarship program had given her a favorable impression of a cleric who in 1944 became the diocesan bishop of Virginia, one of the most influential dioceses in the Episcopal church.[36]

In the church as at Stratford, it was the people as much as the cause that won her allegiance. Soon after the duPonts moved their residence to Jacksonville in 1927, they had met Frank A. Juhan, who had become bishop of Florida three years earlier. Just thirty-eight years old and three years younger than Mrs. duPont, Juhan was the youngest bishop in the church at the time of his consecration. Born in Georgia, he had grown up in San Antonio, Texas, and attended the West Texas Military Academy, where Douglas MacArthur was a fellow student. Juhan graduated from the University of the South at Sewanee, Tennessee, in 1910 and then from the Episcopal seminary that had been established there to train clergy to serve in the vast reaches of the American Southwest. In that tradition, Juhan had served as a missionary in Texas and then as rector of a parish in Greenville, South Carolina, before taking up his duties as bishop in Jacksonville. Florida at that time was divided into just two dioceses, Bishop Juhan's charge covering all of the state north of Palatka. Thus he was responsible for an enormous area stretching 350 miles west of Jacksonville all the way to Pensacola and, incidentally, including Port St. Joe and the surrounding Gulf Coast. There were fifty-seven parishes and missions in his diocese at the time, but they were widely scattered. Many were small with no regular clergy, and during the depression most of the rural parishes in the Panhandle struggled to survive.[37]

The duPonts entertained the Juhans at Epping Forest in the early 1930s and their daughter Frances attended parties there when Denise came down on her vacations. The bishop had presided at the funeral services for Alfred in Jacksonville in 1935, and within two years Mrs. duPont was making substantial contributions to the diocese of Florida. By 1941 the Juhans were becoming her close friends. "The Bishop and his wife are a charming couple and a very good-looking couple. He is a real Christian and a leader—something that is very much needed in all of the churches to-day."[38]

A significant event in Mrs. duPont's gravitation toward the Episcopal church was the meeting of the house of bishops in Jacksonville in February 1942. Intrigued with the idea that all the bishops of the church would be meeting in Jacksonville, she arranged with Bishop Juhan to have four of them stay at Epping Forest as her guests. Among them were Arthur R. McKinstry, who had recently been elected bishop of Delaware, and Bishop Goodwin of Virginia. McKinstry had called on Mrs. duPont at Nemours soon after taking up his new post in Wilmington. Almost as quickly he struck up an acquaintance with Henry duPont and other members of the family and later believed he had been instrumental in overcoming some of the social barriers that the family had erected against Alfred's third wife.[39]

McKinstry was no ordinary cleric. Although a Nebraskan by birth, he had spent most of his ministry in the Northeast and the South. While still in his twenties he was recognized as a rising star in the church and received successive calls to large parishes in Cleveland, Albany, San Antonio, and Nashville. In Albany Governor Franklin D. Roosevelt was a member of his parish, and in San Antonio he officiated at the wedding of a young congressional aide by the name of Lyndon B. Johnson. In 1933 Roosevelt tried to lure McKinstry to his parish in Washington, D.C., but McKinstry decided to stay in San Antonio. In 1938 he moved to a large parish in Nashville and just a year later was elected bishop of Delaware.

Endowed with a charming personality and plenty of self-confidence, McKinstry had a refreshingly direct approach that he tempered with just the right amount of flattery. He quickly won the confidence and then the friendship, not only of Jessie but also of the patriarchs of the other duPont families in Wilmington.

McKinstry's stay at Epping Forest in February 1942 gave him an opportunity to talk at length with Mrs. duPont and to instill in her some of his boundless enthusiasm for the mission of the church, not only in his own diocese, but also in the church at large. He spoke of the need for a chapel in the new diocesan house that R. Bland Mitchell, the bishop of Arkansas, was building in Little Rock. Mrs. duPont promptly gave McKinstry a check to cover some of the cost. Later that year she contributed to a fund to increase McKinstry's salary, which was too low at the time to support his family, and continued an annual $500 donation in 1943 and 1944. Through Bishop Mitchell, she helped to build a new church in Arkansas and supported an effort to provide a new residence for the bishop in Delaware. In Florida, she made regular contributions to Bishop Juhan's discretionary fund and often supplemented through the bishop the salaries of promising young clergy assigned to low-income parishes.[40]

Although Mrs. duPont began concentrating her giving to religious institutions in the Episcopal church in 1942, she continued to disperse a large number of small gifts to churches of all denominations, both Catholic and Protestant. Behind all these gifts was her conviction that the Christian church could build a new base for "civilization" at home while allied military forces defended it abroad. This conviction motivated her patriotic support of the war effort, and in turn the challenge posed by the war gave her a new appreciation of the vitality and practical value of Christian doctrine.

The war inevitably forced Mrs. duPont to assign new priorities to her civic and charitable interests. Although the Robert E. Lee Memorial Foundation continued to function during the war, the restoration work at Stratford came to a virtual standstill. Gasoline rationing made it all but impossible for the Stratties to assemble at the remote plantation for their semiannual meetings, and the same restriction reduced the tourist income to a trickle. Jessie wrote May Lanier early in 1942 that "[t]he Board must cut all expenses of every kind and dismiss some of the employees, which is hard to do—however, it is a time when they will be able to obtain work."[41] To avoid the monthly financial crises that plagued the operation, Jessie solicited prominent persons in all parts of the country for donations to the endowment fund. To one potential giver she wrote: "It [Stratford] is one of the best monuments in this country to democracy and holds a tremendous interest for everyone, but especially is it an ideal for young people."[42] By the spring of 1943 the fund had reached a total exceeding $137,000, of which Jessie had contributed more than $58,000. Later that year she joined Helen Knox and May Lanier in a trip to Richmond to appeal for state support for Stratford. By the end of 1945 the cumulative contributions to Stratford since the project was started in 1929 totaled more than $1,000,000. The contributions from individuals in Delaware were more than $187,000, surpassed only by Virginia, a fact reflecting Jessie's strong participation.[43]

Mrs. duPont's election as chairman of the board of the St. Joe Paper Company in April 1942 marked the beginning of a period of renewed interest in the business. She spent several days at Port St. Joe that month. In inspecting the paper mill she was impressed by the many improvements in equipment since her last visit. A new process developed by Will Edwards and an engineer from the Hercules Powder Company was extracting turpentine from the pulp and producing a net income of $100,000 per year. The mill was running at full capacity and the railroad was prospering since German submarine attacks along the East Coast had virtually eliminated shipments by sea. She expected that during the war the domestic market could absorb all the paper the mill could produce, and that after the war the British would once again become a major customer.[44]

Civic interests, however, commanded most of Mrs. duPont's attention in Port St. Joe during the war. Her influence sparked company support of the Bundles for Britain blanket project and participation in the American Red Cross War Relief Fund. J. L. Sharit, the mayor of Port St. Joe, soon found her to be the key to company support of local civic projects. In June 1943 Mrs. duPont wrote Sharit a long letter expressing her ideas for landscaping the boulevard coming into the town. "I would suggest the elimination of pittisporum and substitute mountain ash or pink mimosa, both small trees with beautiful color and foliage. . . . [A]ll of the shrubs and trees should clear the ground sufficiently to be able to mow the grass under them." Scarcely a single planting on the landscaping plot escaped her comment, but she was careful to commend the mayor and the community for "this artistic and practical plan."[45]

Mrs. duPont took a personal interest in completion of the new community hospital in 1943, and Sharit was careful to seek her opinion on the addition proposed a year later. She responded with a few comments on the nursery ward and praised the mayor for "having worked out such a perfect addition." She was at the time discussing with an architect the design of a new hotel to replace the one destroyed by fire. When Sharit had trouble getting a commitment from Ed Ball that the company would accept additional revenue debentures for the town water and sewer system, the mayor, at Edwards's suggestion, discreetly asked Mrs. duPont to intercede.[46]

She did not, however, allow her support of community projects to jeopardize the financial interests of the paper company. In 1945 she commended Edwards for enlisting the support of the mayor and company officials in defeating a three-mill tax levy for school buildings in the county. She was also pleased that Edwards had succeeded in electing "three good men" to the school board. Defeat of the tax levy had probably saved the company $25,000 per year, but she warned Edwards that the saving imposed an obligation. "[W]e must either as a company or I as an individual [must] assist just as soon as materials and labor can be procured in putting up a suitable school in Port St. Joe."[47]

The war quickly brought home to Mrs. duPont the need to modify the pàttern of her charitable gifts. During the late 1930s she had already begun to move from individual to institutional gifts, but when the war began, she was still giving more than $1 million per year to family and friends. The result was a virtual disaster when her federal income taxes for 1941 were calculated. As shown in table 6-1, her income that year was almost $2.2 million, two-thirds of which came from the residuary income from Alfred's estate after all other annuities had been paid. Her expenditures were close to $2.1 million, of which less than $500,000 was deductible. Under the new tax laws enacted to produce more revenue during the war, her income tax was more than $1.3 million, which left her a deficit for the year of $1.2 million.[48]

To bring her finances back on an even keel, Mrs. duPont cut back sharply on her operating costs. By keeping the mansion at Nemours

TABLE 6-1 Profit and Loss Statements, 1941, 1943 (in $ thousands)

	1941	1943
Income		
Trustee fee	5	5
Annuity	200	200
Residuary income	1,424	831
Salary St. Joe Paper	0	18
AIP Trust	6	10
Dividends	476	268
Interest	6	7
Other income	104	28
Losses	−49	−5
Total income	2,172	1,362
Expenditures		
Gifts	1,284	167
Charity to individuals	5	1
Education of individuals	12	7
Operating Epping Forest	25	23
Operating Nemours	45	11
Operating yacht	38	0
Personal	85	91
Biography	22	0
Ditchley expenses	18	0
Contrib. educ. inst.	45	9
Contrib. char. organ.	241	232
Contrib. yacht	140	0
Taxes	80	23
Interest paid	3	7
Other	18	8
Total expenditures	2,061	579
Income over expenditures	111	783
Federal income tax	−1,342	
Expenditure over income	1,231	

closed during most of the year, she cut operating expenses there from $45,000 in 1941 to $11,000 in 1943. Giving the *Nenemoosha* to the government eliminated an annual operating cost of $38,000 and provided a one-time tax deduction of $140,000. The big cut, however, came in the monthly checks to family and friends. These dropped from $1.3 million in 1941 to $167,000 in 1943. Under the new tax law all individual income over $200,000 was to be taxed at a rate of 94 percent. Furthermore, she wrote one of her cousins on her monthly check list, the limitation of personal gifts to $25,000 per year had raised her taxes above her estimated income and had forced her to borrow money. "You may not know it, but the gifts I make to relatives and friends on the $100.00 per month basis far exceed $25,000.00, therefore, it will be essential for me to eliminate many of these gifts."[49] The impact of federal tax laws on philanthropy could hardly have been more apparent.

The war had a similar effect on Mrs. duPont's charities. Contributions to needy individuals dropped below $2,000 in 1943 and all but disappeared before the end of the war. Unemployment had virtually evaporated as millions of men joined the armed forces, and war industries absorbed the rest of the labor pool. Mrs. duPont wrote to Ethel Tignor: "Where there are children in the Service, a dependent parent receives a contribution from the Federal Government; as you and I both know. Unless a person be ill, there is no occasion for anyone to be unemployed today."[50] She asked Mrs. Tignor to pare her list to the ill and elderly.

Many needy individuals, however, were still receiving aid from Mrs. duPont through her contributions to institutions. Closest to her heart was the Alfred I. duPont Foundation, which she saw as an instrument for continuing her husband's personal charities long after his death. In 1941 there were donations to ninety-nine organizations. Most of these were nominal gifts of twenty or fifty dollars. Those over $1,000 were as follows:

Nemours Foundation	$112,455
Hope Haven Association	70,625
Robert E. Lee Foundation	21,397
Alfred I. duPont Foundation	20,837
American Red Cross	5,155
Episcopal Diocese of Florida	4,500
British–Am Ambulance Corps	1,528
Christ Church Restoration	1,200

Included in the 1941 list were small gifts to sixteen churches of many denominations.[51]

Tax considerations also forced Mrs. duPont to cut her scholarship support to individual students, from $12,000 in 1941 to $7,000 in 1943. Because most of her contributions were now going to colleges rather than to individuals, the cut in institutional giving was more significant as it dropped from $45,000 in 1941 to $9,000 in 1943. Even these modest sums, however, could support a substantial number of students in the 1940s. In 1941, Mrs. duPont contributed to 30 colleges and universities: 19 in Virginia, 3 each in Maryland and North Carolina, and one each in the remaining 5 states. It is notable that only one Florida institution was on the list at this time: the Florida State College for Women in Tallahassee.[52] Her large contributions to Florida schools were to come after the war.

The reduction in scholarship funds was not entirely to be regretted. Bishop Goodwin was urging students in the Northern Neck to take practical courses that would prepare them for a trade in a year or so rather than attempting a four-year college program during the war. Mrs. duPont strongly approved. It was time "for the sixteen to twenty year old youngsters to take courses that will prepare them to be on their feet and independent within twelve to fifteen months—intensive mechanical, electrical or primary chemical courses." She had long since come to the conclusion "that too much stress was put on a college education, which very often unfitted the boy or the girl to fit into the work that he was qualified by nature and society to do."[53]

A new pattern in Mrs. duPont's college work emerged during the war—the granting of substantial funds to institutions for scholarship funds as opposed to gifts earmarked for specific students. These grants included three hundred shares of DuPont stock in 1941 to the College of William and Mary for the Thomas Ball Scholarship Fund; $10,000 to Hollins College in 1942; $10,000 to the Virginia Military Institute in 1944; $7,000 in 1945 to Mary Washington College for the Lalla Gresham Ball Scholarship; and $30,000, to be given over a period of three years to the University of the South in memory of Charles Juhan, Bishop Juhan's son, who was killed in military service. That many of these gifts were made at the end of the calendar year suggested that they were motivated in part by a desire to keep Mrs. duPont's net income close to the ceiling established in the federal income tax law, but they also represented a sincere personal commitment to the work of these institutions. These scholarship funds augmented the provisions of a 1942 codicil to Mrs. duPont's will, in which she designated one thousand shares of DuPont stock each to these institutions and to a number of others.[54]

The scholarship program did bring Mrs. duPont moments of great satisfaction, especially when she received letters from former students whom she had helped. A young woman whom Mrs. duPont had sent to college from the Northern Neck wrote to her in 1942 to relate how she had gone on from college to business school in Baltimore and eventually became the private secretary to a prominent attorney in Washington, D.C. "You can never really know how delighted I was when I received word that your generosity would make it possible for me to attend school, and little did I know that it was to be the turning point in my life." Mrs. duPont replied that the young woman's letter had thrilled her with pride. "There are spirits, you know, who are going to win in life's battle—they cannot be held down. . . . You know the person who succeeds in life is not necessarily the most brilliant one, but given a normal degree of intelligence, background, etc., it is the person who has a sense of responsibility, a willingness to work and a determination to win. These characteristics you unquestionably have."[55]

The shift in Mrs. duPont's emphasis from individual scholarships to general scholarship funds suggested that she was beginning to look at education more and more in terms of institutional support rather than individual needs. Historians today would say that she was moving from charitable activities to philanthropy, although she never used the term *philanthropy* during these years.[56] There were indications during the war, however, that she was moving toward a broader institutional perspective in her other civic activities.

Early in 1943 she established the Alfred I. duPont Radio Awards, to be granted each year "for outstanding performance of public service, by aggressive, consistent and accurate gathering and reporting of news by radio" and for "outstanding meritorious public service of [a] radio station to its community."[57] The awards thus were motivated by an institutional rather than an individual perspective.

Initially the awards of $1000 each were funded by banks in the Florida National Group, under the direction of W. Hardin Goodman, trust officer of the Jacksonville bank. Goodman assisted Mrs. duPont in choosing members of the selection committee, screening the large number of entries for the committee, and, most important of all, assuring that leaders of the major radio networks and wire services attended the first presentation. The first selection committee included Frank Gaines, Bishop Henry St. George Tucker, Mrs. duPont, and representatives of the radio industry and of a national women's organization.[58]

Mrs. duPont was more than pleased with the results of Goodman's efforts in staging the first presentation. The presidents of two of the radio networks, heads of the Associated Press and United Press, and Madame Chiang Kai-shek's press officer for her American tour were in the audience. Mrs. duPont thought Frank Gaines made an excellent presentation address and was disappointed only that Fulton Lewis, Jr., recipient of the commentator award, could not be there in person. Mrs. Lewis, however, was there to receive the award for her husband, who made "as gracious and as appreciative an acceptance speech as I have ever heard" from a radio station in San Antonio.[59]

So successful was the first presentation that Mrs. duPont took steps that summer to establish the Alfred I. duPont Radio Awards Foundation with a trust fund that she set up in the Florida National Bank of Jacksonville. The same judges continued to select the winners and Goodman performed the administrative functions during the war years. Mrs. duPont considered the annual award ceremonies in New York one of the highlights of her year. She wrote Gaines after the 1945 ceremony that she thought it the best yet "except for one thing. I did not like the absence of some of the radio chiefs. This, I believe, can be and should be corrected another year." She and Goodman were also concerned that other groups were following their lead in setting up radio awards, a trend that would dilute the prestige of the duPont awards.[60] These, however, were problems to be resolved after the war ended.

The new will that Mrs. duPont signed in May 1943 also gave evidence of the shift of her interest toward an institutional perspective. Like the 1927 instrument, it did provide individual bequests to scores of individuals,[61] but the 1943 will also included endowments for scholarships at seven colleges and universities and for memorials at the Home for Needy Confederate Women, the Robert E. Lee Memorial Foundation, the Virginia Museum of Fine Arts, and the Alfred I. duPont Foundation. Her motivation was essentially philanthropic: "It has ever been my belief that monies invested in the youth of our country pays [sic] the greatest dividends that it is possible to obtain on an investment; as it equips boys and girls with tools to take their place in life's great battle."[62]

The will also provided that the principal of the bequests to both the educational and charitable institutions be held intact and that only the income from the securities be disbursed. Her intent was to address what she saw as fundamental social and economic problems rather than the immediate needs of individuals.

The relentless pace of Mrs. duPont's activities during the war did not mean that there were no moments of relaxation or personal enrichment. In the summer of 1943 she visited Denise and her family in Columbus, Ohio, and then went on to the West Coast to see Tom for a week and then to San Diego to visit old haunts. She found that the city had changed since the last war, and the Coronado Hotel, the scene of many happy events of her youth, was now an old "fire-trap . . . filled with service men and their families."[63] In September she went to Lake George in the Adirondacks with the Gaineses and the Juhans for three weeks of fishing and conversation. She later wrote to Bishop Juhan to thank him for a glorious vacation: "Groups who have ideas and exchange them, who have a spirit of mirth and are not afraid to laugh, have a spirit of solemnity and are not afraid to express their spiritual views[,] to be with such a group has ever been to me life's greatest joy, and just such a group I considered the one on Lake George. We did veer to the gay side rather than the serious one, but the gay side was much more needed at that time for that group of hardworking people."[64]

In September Mrs. duPont took her nephew John Baker to Ditchley in hopes that some quiet time in the country would help to bring him out of the deep mental depression from which he seemed unable to escape. Unfortunately her therapy had little effect on John, but it did give her some time alone to think. When she returned to Nemours, her thoughts on many subjects poured forth in a long letter to Billy Martin's brother Charles, who was now an army officer stationed in Washington. "Would that we could sit down and argue a while, exchanging ideas, because I have very definite ones and so have you on the psychology of the race and the opportunities afforded all. It was never God's intent," she wrote, "that all [persons] should be alike." No matter what advantages were made available to all, some would be successful, others would not. "Out of it will come some leaders in one line or another, some great musicians, some derelicts, some misfits and some cripples. One cannot go against natural law. I believe in equal opportunity, I believe in it for black and white alike, but equal opportunity isn't going to eliminate the derelicts. . . . Where I believe the weak link in all our troubles is that the baby is not trained to a sense of responsibility, and as little as the child was given responsibility in my day, it is given none to-day."[65]

She pursued the same theme two days later in a letter to Tom. She was shocked by the reports on juvenile delinquency at all levels of society. "There was a day when such was not countenanced by a Christian society." When such behavior was applauded by the upper classes, there was no hope for the lower classes, and the fault lay in parents who would not accept responsibility for their children. "Perchance, when this war is over and we are trying to recover from the fearful tragedy that lack of responsibility has precipitated on the world, we may again take a firm hand under Christian guidance and try to teach something of life's values."[66]

In another letter Mrs. duPont wrote that after the Civil War the people of the South were poor in terms of money, "but Oh! they were rich in a heritage and love, and that has been what has brought them back." They thought nothing of having a meal for ten or twenty in a family including not only their own children but distant relatives who had lost their parents. "I do not believe that a civilization can hold together that is not built on just such a foundation."[67]

World War II, however, was long from being over. Mrs. duPont hoped and prayed that the Russians would sweep westward and defeat the Germans before the Japanese became entrenched in Southeast Asia, but in 1943 the Germans were so deep in Soviet territory that an early end to the war seemed unlikely. In the meantime she made the best of living with the shortages and restrictions imposed on domestic life. At Epping Forest the military presence was inescapable. In May 1943 a Catalina flying boat from the naval air station crashed into the breakwater in front of the estate. She and the servants rushed out to help and pulled the injured pilots from the wreckage. Mrs. duPont maintained close ties with the officers at the base and regularly invited them to come across the river for evening dancing parties with young women from Jacksonville.[68]

Rationing of food and fuel also posed problems. Mrs. duPont found that "these fashionable cooks" tended to expect the best cuts of beef and the best fish for their menus, an expectation that was unrealistic during the war. As a result, she had to do much of the marketing herself. "[O]perating with three gallons of gasoline [per week] and the number of servants that must go in to the movies occasionally and the number of guests we have, and to get the marketing done is kind of like a jig-saw puzzle."[69] To save gasoline she usually took the bus home in the evening, a hot stuffy ride because the bus was always crowded. In the mornings the bus went to town too early for her, so she had Dolan, her chauffeur, take her part of the way, and she walked the rest.

Life was even more spartan at Nemours. By the summer of 1943 all of the able-bodied men in the grounds crew had entered military service, and the few old-timers left could not keep up with the work. "You know we haven't a single plant in any of those flower beds or vases, not a bloom. Our grass is not properly mowed and our hedges look as though they had never seen a barber. That is quite as it should be, though, as we are so short of men. All are doing the best that they can and the place will not suffer only its looks. . . . I have no servants except Jorgine and Olga, the laundress, who have been with me since 1922."[70] Vegetables, not flowers, were the order of the day at Nemours. Mrs. duPont urged Miss Des Barres, the executrix at the institute, to grow as many vegetables as possible for the children.

During the winter of 1944 Mrs. duPont continued her wartime regimen at Epping Forest. There were dinner dances for the naval officers every two weeks and the usual string of visitors, both friends and relatives, who came by train from the North. That winter she saw less of her brother Ed. Now that his wife, Ruth, was seeking a divorce, Ed had sold his home and moved into a hotel in downtown Jacksonville across the street from the bank. If possible, his life was more consumed with business affairs than ever before. When he did take some time away from the office, he was often in Edgewater Park, Mississippi, where he owned the fashionable Edgewater Gulf Hotel.[71]

Mrs. duPont was back at Nemours on June 6, 1944, the day of the Normandy invasion. She wrote to Tom: "I know you like the rest of us to-day are praying as we have never prayed before and God knows we should,—The safety of the civilized men of the world, who are yielding their lives second by second that civilization and freedom may survive. I am going to stay at the office only a short time, as I want to be close to the radio. I listened for two hours this morning. I am rather glad I didn't know of the invasion last night, as it would have meant being awake all night."[72]

That same day she expressed similar thoughts in a letter to Ed, but she went on to reiterate her prediction that "a great revolution over the entire world" would change the way of life everywhere after the war. Some nations of the world were living with a technology thousands of years old while some people in those nations were employed in plants using the most modern technology, and were earning wages that to them seemed incredible. Such people would never return to their primitive way of life. "We are responsible for the great industrial age—we must be the ones to help these vast countries in their development, but at the same time make our own lives and people as near to self-sufficiency as is possible." Europe, she thought, could not continue as a group of small nations. She expected them to "ask for some kind of federation in the British Commonwealth."[73]

One of the monumental changes in American society during World War II was the entry of women into the work force. As the military services depleted the nation's manpower, women took over jobs in war plants, shipyards, and offices. The popular tune "Rosie, the Riveter" reflected the sense of novelty and pride that Americans attached to the new role of women. Jobs for women resulted in more income, which in turn sparked the entry of women into the banking industry as tellers and cashiers. Some financially independent women entered banking as officers.[74] Mrs. duPont, who had led the way in her own career, encouraged this trend.

Mrs. duPont's close friend, Helen Knox, was one of the women in the banking business who moved into the upper ranks in the industry. During the war she became head of the women's department of the Grand Central branch of the Chase National Bank in Manhattan. Mrs. duPont herself may have reached the highest position attained by a woman in the banking business up to that time when she became a director of the Florida National Bank in Jacksonville in 1935. Three years later she attended her first national convention of the Association of Bank Women. By the end of the war banks employed more than 140,000 women, a fact that Helen Knox attributed as much to Mrs. duPont's influence as to economic opportunities opened to women during the war. Mrs. duPont's interest in the association peaked in 1944, when Helen Knox served as national president. In 1946 Mrs. duPont attended the national convention in New Orleans and probably had some role in electing Willa A. Riley of the Florida National Bank as president. In urging women to join the association, Mrs. duPont wrote: "Women in business are and must be a constructive factor; as the combined force of all able men and women is needed if our civilization is to survive. . . . [W]omen are in the banking world to stay, whether a few men like it or not is beside the issue,—many women might prefer to return to the home of the 90s and the peace that went with it,—such cannot be."[75]

The end of the war was still more than a year away, but Mrs. duPont was already looking to the future. She knew that the United States and the world would never return to the way of life that had existed before the war. Still vigorous and healthy at sixty, she looked forward to the future not as a golden age but as one of challenge and opportunity. On the day the war ended she launched her first postwar plans in a letter to Ed: "While the hurrahing and the shouting are going on, as it should over the surrender of Japan and the word has just flashed over the wires that gasoline and fuel oil coupons and blue points have all been eliminated, . . . I suppose some of the other restrictions will go very shortly. This bring[s] to mind that I do want to get the plans in some kind of shape for the hotel at Port St. Joe."[76]

Three days before Christmas in 1945 Mrs. duPont walked through the snow from Nemours over to the institute for the annual Christmas party. She had arranged for a local department store to send out a Santa Claus to distribute the gifts she had purchased. The children "were all in the auditorium in their cots or wheel chairs, etc.—they were the sweetest little things one could wish to see. . . . It was really an inspiring sight. . . . I believe A. I. from afar knew it."[77]

How Firm a Foundation

*O*ctober 12, 1951, was an auspicious day at Stratford, the now restored ancestral home of the Lees in Virginia's Northern Neck. Stratties from many states gathered to dedicate the new Council House, which would provide a meeting place for the directors on the plantation grounds. Not only was Douglas Southall Freeman, the distinguished biographer of Robert E. Lee and George Washington, present to extol the character of the Lees, but the directors of the Robert E. Lee Memorial Foundation also had successfully prevailed on Mrs. duPont to say a few words in public. Dismayed at the thought of addressing a large audience, she had agreed only because she would be honoring May Field Lanier, an old friend and founder of the Stratford restoration project. If anyone had proposed to announce that she had provided the funds for the new building, she certainly would have refused to speak.[1]

At the close of the dedication exercises, the audience stood and sang General Lee's favorite hymn, "How Firm a Foundation." The choice of hymn was significant, not just because it was closely associated with the sainted leader of the lost cause, but also because the words must have touched the hearts of many of those present:

> How firm a foundation, ye saints of the Lord,
> Is laid for your faith in his excellent word!
> What more can he say than to you he hath said
> To you that for refuge to Jesus have fled?
>
> Fear not, I am with thee; O be not dismayed!
> For I am thy God, and will still give thee aid;
> I'll strengthen thee, help thee, and cause thee to stand,
> Upheld by thy righteous, omnipotent hand.[2]

For an aging generation of Virginians born in the closing decades of the nineteenth century, the revered virtues of honor, of loyalty to one's family, of dedication and self-sacrifice—all epitomized in the Lee legend—seemed to be slipping away in the maelstrom of social, political, and economic change that was sweeping across the Old South.[3] The hymn called upon those who raised their voices that October afternoon to persevere. With the Lord's help, the words suggested, it was still possible to save the best of the old for the benefit of the future.

For Jessie Ball duPont the words spoken and sung that day must have had a special meaning. She had seen the agrarian world of her youth ravaged by the Great Depression in the 1930s, and she had used her own resources to keep family, old friends, and institutions alive in the Northern Neck. With the outbreak of World War II she had expanded her horizons to come to the defense of "Christian civilization" and the traditions of the Old South. Once the global battle had been won, she had returned to the task of fulfilling Alfred's dream and finding new ways to shore up the old foundations on which her life had been built. Looking back on the hectic years following the war, she may have noticed how well the words of the old hymn expressed the convictions that governed her life.

Even before the Japanese surrendered, Mrs. duPont was impatient to resume activities that she had been forced to set aside during the war. She badgered Ed now to make a decision about the plans for the hotel at Port St. Joe, and she looked forward to the fall meeting of the Owls at Stratford. Early in 1946 she wrote a prominent Strattie in Dover: "Now that the war is over, don't you think our Delaware Committee of the Robert E. Lee Memorial Foundation, Inc., might do some active work [?]" She suggested that her friend might be able to "organize some entertainment in Dover" that would help to raise money for Stratford. Perhaps the local chapter of the Daughters of the Confederacy might be willing to help.[4]

The Alfred I. duPont Radio Awards had survived during the conflict, but now that the war was over, Mrs. duPont was anxious to establish the awards on a solid footing. She was especially pleased that the heads of the national press services and radio networks were present at the annual award dinner in March 1946. She thought that "they thoroughly understand what we are aiming to do, which supports what they realize is the power of radio, to guide and educate the public." All to the better,

Mrs. duPont with six representatives of the major radio and television networks at a meeting at Washington and Lee University in November 1951. At the far left is O. W. Riegel, newly appointed curator of the radio awards foundation. On Mrs. duPont's left is Francis P. Gaines, president of Washington and Lee.

two of the three network presidents were southerners and in Mrs. duPont's opinion "very high type men."[5]

There was, however, a need to plan for the future. The novelty of the annual award broadcasts was wearing off, and some of the radio people thought other forms of publicity might be more effective. Mrs. duPont was still concerned that other organizations might establish competing awards in the postwar years, and she gave some thought to the suggestion that the duPont awards carry the official recognition of the National Association of Broadcasters. In June 1946 she sent Hardin Goodman to New York to sound out leaders in the radio industry. After meeting with a dozen or more radio executives, Goodman wrote a long report of his findings. With New York opinions divided on what changes might be made, Mrs. duPont decided to continue the existing format for the awards, at least through 1946.[6]

Postwar conversion was also starting in the Alfred I. duPont Institute at Nemours. By the spring of 1946 Alfred Shands and most of the medical staff had returned to the institute, but the war years had brought some inevitable changes. Dr. Osgood resigned in the fall of 1945 as head of the medical advisory board, and Dr. Farr found it necessary to cut back on his commitments. To replace him, Shands recruited Donald D. Van Slyke of the Rockefeller Institute to serve on the medical advisory committee and to assume the new post of chairman of the research advisory committee. The first order of business in the spring of 1946 was to open the research department, which was still in the construction stage when the war began. With Van Slyke's help and with the assistance of two other doctors who were joining the institute staff during the summer, Shands hoped to have research activities in full swing by fall. Mrs. duPont concurred in these plans although she continued to warn Dr. Shands that "the already crippled child comes before the research."[7] She believed that research projects should start small and should never exceed 25 percent of the total budget.

Chairing the board of the St. Joe Paper Company, Mrs. duPont was not involved in daily operations, but she did keep a close eye on the business. Will Edwards continued to scout new business opportunities and to keep her informed of events in Port St. Joe. In June 1946 he reported on a recent trip to Houston, which he found a vibrant and fast-growing industrial area with an obvious need for a container manufacturing plant. Edwards hoped the St. Joe company would build it. Mrs. duPont received monthly operations reports from the company and kept abreast of current production figures. In December she offered several suggestions for modifying the design of the proposed hotel in Port St. Joe. J. L. Sharit, the former mayor who also worked for the company railroad, encouraged Mrs. duPont to pursue the hotel project in the face of Ed Ball's foot-dragging. Ed was not about to oppose openly a project in which Jessie had a longstanding interest, but he could still kill it by offering deferential objections and by failing to act on her recommendations. When Ed refused to commit company funds for a water treatment plant at Port St. Joe, Jessie prodded Sharit and Edwards to obtain equipment from closed military bases and eventually made a personal gift of $15,750 to the project.[8]

Despite her efforts to follow business affairs in Florida, Jessie found it difficult to keep tabs on Ed. In June 1947 she wrote: "We might as well be on separate continents for the amount of time we spend together." In the same letter she reiterated an earlier request that the offices in Jacksonville be closed on Saturdays during the summer. The staff worked hard, and she thought "we should show that much consideration and appreciation for them." Will Edwards, she wrote, supported the idea, and a "great majority of the successful and large companies are closing on Saturdays."[9]

Jessie had no more success in changing Ed's mind on other operational matters. She urged him to buy new office furniture, hire more secretaries, and bring in younger men to help him and Will Edwards. "I think we ought to try to get the office on a very efficient basis." Then, recognizing the implications of her statement, she added: "[D]on't mean by this that it hasn't been on an efficient one. I realize it has been very, very efficient always."[10]

One of Jessie's protégés was Seabury Stoneburner, a distant cousin on her mother's side, whom Ed had hired at the end of World War II at her prodding. Stoneburner was a graduate of the Harvard Business School and a young man of considerable promise. He had known Ed Ball before the war and had some reservations about taking the job, but Jessie made it almost impossible for him to refuse. When she learned that he did not earn enough money to purchase a house that she would consider suitable for an executive of the paper company, she gave him $21,000, which, with a loan from Elsie Bowley, enabled Stoneburner to buy a house for his growing family. Although salaries at the paper company were low, Stoneburner found the work challenging and in a few years became treasurer of the company.[11]

On major issues, Jessie stood as one with her brother, particularly in Ed's seemingly endless battle to gain control of the Florida East Coast Railway. The railroad was a consolidation of smaller lines rebuilt by Henry M. Flagler to bring northerners to the new communities he was developing along the coast from Jacksonville to Key West. Hard hit by the depression, the Florida East Coast had gone into receivership in 1931. A decade later as the nation headed toward war, Ed noticed that the road's mortgage bonds were selling for six cents on the dollar, but under the receivership the road was keeping up interest payments on its mortgage bonds and accumulating a surplus. Employing the technique he had used in acquiring the original duPont holdings in Florida, Ball quietly began buying up the mortgage bonds for the St. Joe Paper Company. By the end of the war the paper company held 51 percent of the bonds.[12]

Ed Ball had two reasons for buying up the Florida East Coast bonds, and the first was surely profit. The road's $20 million surplus at the end of the war was a plum too tantalizing to pass up. In addition to the right-of-way and equipment, the railway owned large blocks of land that he thought would increase in value as the East Coast developed. Also he was outraged by arguments voiced by liberal politicians in both national parties that takeover by the federal government was the only way to salvage the nation's financially strapped railroads. To Ed Ball, this was the kind of left-wing New Dealism that was destroying free enterprise in America. Acquiring and rebuilding the Florida East Coast Railway would demonstrate that it was possible to operate an independent railroad under the free enterprise system.

When the railroad went from receivership to outright bankruptcy in 1940, Ed, on behalf of the St. Joe Paper Company, presented the Interstate Commerce Commission with a reorganization plan that, he argued, would protect the company's financial interests and give it control of the railway. The commission rejected Ed's plan and two others; but in the ensuing struggle for control, Ed kept buying up bonds in the name of the St. Joe Paper Company from creditors who had tired of the years of court battles. By 1944 the paper company had 53.5 percent of all the outstanding bonds, holdings worth more than $23 million.[13]

It now seemed that Ed Ball had control of the railway and could go about rebuilding it. His hopes were thwarted, however, in 1944, when the small remaining group of bondholders petitioned the Interstate Commerce Commission to give operational control of the road to the Atlantic Coast Line. ACL officials argued that the proposal would best serve the public interest by making the FEC "part of an existing major railroad system."[14]

At this point the fight for control of the Florida East Coast became a public issue when Claude Pepper, who had been championing the cause of organized labor in the U.S. Senate since 1936, joined the debate. Pepper personalized the issue by charging that control of the road by the duPont estate would not be in the public interest "when it is public knowledge that the estate is operated principally BY ONE MAN, Mr. Edward Ball."[15]

Both men had come from poor rural Baptist families in the South, but there the similarity ended. Ball had left elementary school to begin his insatiable quest for money; Pepper had struggled to get an education and succeeded in graduating from the University of Alabama and then from Harvard Law School. Ball was a hard-hearted realist with his eye on the main chance; Pepper was a kindhearted idealist with a penchant for taking what he considered the correct position on unpopular issues. In the U.S. Senate, this meant pushing New Deal programs and the cause of organized labor in the Deep South.[16]

Ball had tried to woo Pepper away from his New Deal persuasions during his first years in the Senate, but Pepper was not about to be bought off. The final break between the two came in February 1944, when Pepper had been the only member of the Senate to speak in support of Roosevelt's veto of a revenue bill that had been loaded with tax loopholes for the wealthy, including exemptions for the holders of bonds bought at bargain rates for speculative purposes.

The impatient Senate brushed aside Pepper's oratory and quickly overrode the veto, but for Ed Ball and other conservative business interests in the Deep South, Pepper's speech was beyond the pale. Within a few days Ball and a few others had raised $62,000 to oppose Pepper in the 1944 senatorial primary. It was too late in the year to mount an effective campaign, but Ball and his associates succeeded in nominating Ball's old friend J. Ollie Edmunds to run against Pepper. Edmunds had been a Jacksonville attorney who as a state judge had probated Alfred duPont's will in 1935; he was now president of Stetson University. Pepper won the nomination but only by a very small majority, and the Ball group set out at once to build a war chest for the 1950 election.[17]

There is no reason to believe that Mrs. duPont took any direct part in her brother's political attack on Pepper; nor is it likely that Ed would have bothered his sister with the details of his vendetta. In fact the only reference to the 1944 election in Jessie's correspondence suggests that she did not grasp the central motivation in Ed's endeavors. She wrote nothing about Pepper's politics but concluded that he had been "unfair to Ed." Her chief complaint was the senator's implication that she was not pulling her weight in company affairs. She wrote Frank Gaines: "I am a little tired of one Senator stating and re-iterating and re-iterating that Ed is the only one who takes an active interest or is the controlling factor. I assure you such is not true."[18]

Just as she was moving her household north to Nemours in the spring of 1947, the Interstate Commerce Commission accepted the Atlantic Coast Line's proposal. Ed was more than ready to continue the fight in the courts, and she was quick to echo the ideological argument of conservative business interests. "If the Court upholds that decision," she wrote Tom, "then we might as well say good-bye to private property." She observed that according to the press, 80 percent of the Florida East Coast stockholders favored control by the duPont estate, but Pepper, she wrote, was demanding that "the most valuable property of Florida be transferred to an alien corporation."[19]

What Mrs. duPont considered the growing intrusion of the federal government in private enterprise was a frequent theme in her letters in the postwar years. In March 1947 she commiserated with an English friend as Britain faced nationalization of public service industries by the Labour government. "The world has progressed rather far under a democratic form of government," but communism, socialism, and nationalization threatened to undo all the advances of the past. She took heart in a recent decision of the U.S. Supreme Court that upheld an injunction against John L. Lewis, president of the United Mine Workers. "Many have felt that our Supreme Court was too communistic to do this. It is the first real blow that we have had at labor dictatorship." She hoped the Supreme Court's decision would encourage Congress to amend destructive laws such as the Wagner Act. The great hope for democracy lay with the middle class, "which, of course, is the backbone of every country."[20]

The problem with U.S. society, she wrote an old San Diego friend, was that children were not brought up to accept responsibility; young people expected the government to provide them with a living. The government, she asserted, was "not an earner," but simply took from those who had a sense of responsibility and gave to those who did not. She hoped that the states would adopt a constitutional amendment that would tax estates at the same rate as ordinary income. "Do you realize that the death taxes in the high brackets is 77% of what a man has accumulated, worked and slaved for. If he gives anything away, he soon goes into the 57–¾% gift tax. All of this amounts to so little in operating the Federal Government, that it is hardly worth mentioning, but these same fortunes are the ones that create new industries, as the people who have accumulated these fortunes are the ones with creative minds."[21]

She never for a moment doubted that Alfred's financial success had been the result of his creative ability, which in turn was the source of his dream for the institute at Nemours. Now she was trying in her own way to augment her financial resources and to put them to good use in charitable activities.

Federal tax laws continued to influence the patterns of Mrs. duPont's giving in the postwar years. In both 1946 and 1947 she followed her wartime strategy of making carefully measured gifts at the end of the year to a few favored institutions so that her federal income and gift taxes would be held to a minimum. In 1946 her major year-end gifts, ranging from $35,000 to $60,000, went to four educational institutions: Hollins College, Washington and Lee University, the University of the South,

Mrs. duPont received an honorary doctorate at the University of the South in June 1945. Other honorees (*left to right*): Angus Dun, Episcopal bishop of Washington; Henry I. Loutitt, bishop of South Florida; Captain Anthony S. Adams, Navy chaplain; and the Reverend Holly W. Wells.

and Mary Washington College of the University of Virginia. Other large gifts went to the Alfred I. duPont Institute and the foundation, Stratford, the Young Women's Christian Association of Jacksonville, and the Virginia museum.[22]

The large gifts to the universities were in the form of corporate stocks, most often shares in the DuPont Company, and were to be used to provide scholarships or increase faculty salaries. The same institutions also received small gifts, either in cash or stocks, at other times of the year. Individual scholarships were still going each year to students in some twenty colleges and universities, mostly in the South, but for tax reasons very few of these gifts went directly to students.[23]

Avoidance of taxes surely motivated Mrs. duPont's increasing use of endowments during the 1940s, but the endowment form had other important implications. It removed Mrs. duPont and Miss Shaw from the direct administration of giving, and that change in turn inevitably modified the rationale for giving. Direct gifts to individuals required an evaluation of individual need; the criterion for endowments had to be an assessment of the institution's ability to foster the social and cultural values to which Mrs. duPont was committed.

The war years and the sweeping changes that they brought to American life raised in Mrs. duPont new concerns and even anxieties, but they did not upset her fundamental values. The mass movement of blacks into urban areas outside the South, particularly in Southern California, where her brother Tom was present to sound the alarm, was a problem explored at length in many of her letters. In October 1946 she wrote to Tom of "the darkie problem in California." "You and I know it is a problem, more difficult for the west and far northwest than for those of us who have been accustomed to dealing with the negro, knowing what allowances, etc. to make."[24]

The danger was that northern whites, with no appreciation of the carefully crafted structure of racial segregation that underlay southern society, would accept blacks as equals. "It does look," she wrote to Tom, "as though the white man has gone crazy putting the negro on the faculties of some of our foremost colleges. Vassar has a negro man as the professor of Sociology, Wellesley has a negro woman as a teacher, and also Smith College, and I assume most of the other colleges."[25]

She elaborated her fears in a letter to her California teaching companion, Winifred Stephenson. "Why should we the white race be forced to have negro children in the schools with our children[?] They should have schools just as good as ours and let them have them. I don't wish a negro professor on the staff of a white school, nor would I send a child to a school where there is a negro on the staff. . . . There are not a sufficient number of educated negroes to staff the negro schools, . . . then why should we have negroes on the staff of Vassar. . . . It just isn't logical."[26]

Her many acts of charity supported her protestation that she had a certain affection for blacks, but like a true Southern conservative, she insisted that blacks had their place. As she put it, "I do not wish them sitting in the drawing room with me."[27]

The ultimate danger, however, was not the collapse of social distinctions but the threat to civilization and the white race. In her letter to Winifred, Jessie stated the conviction that she had expressed scores of times in writing and probably in conversations: "What is more history shows that no race has ever been strong enough to raise the negro race up that [sic] race has carried every race down that has ever mingled with it. Why do we feel that we would be the exception?"[28]

Given this conviction, Mrs. duPont could rationalize a policy of refusing to contribute to colleges that hired black teachers. She announced in March 1947 to a friend who was an Episcopal priest that "I will give no scholarship to a boy or girl entering a white college where there are negro instructors, if I know it." She would, however, continue to give scholarships to black students attending black colleges.[29]

That same month she complimented one of her scholarship students who had sent her a newspaper account of a black history exhibit. "You, as a well trained, high-class young negro woman, have great opportunities to help your people." But Mrs. duPont went on to quote what she called Booker T. Washington's "admonition to his people, viz., 'to develop your racial traits, be proud of your race and encourage your race to associate with each other and not to attempt to associate or mix socially with the white race.' "[30]

Obviously Mrs. duPont still carried the social convictions of the young Jessie Ball, who had grown up in the segregated world of the Northern Neck. For Jessie, the war had not dimmed that tradition but in a way reinforced it. The loss of the *Nenemoosha* and travel restrictions during the war had made visits to the Northern Neck infrequent. As if to make up for lost opportunities, she took a new interest in the world of her childhood after the war. She made short trips to Ditchley with members of her family, scolded her younger cousins for not maintaining the Ball graveyard at Cressfield, took time to visit the colonial church at White Chapel, and gave detailed suggestions for the design of the new parish house. She consulted architects about restoring Woodlawn, the home of her Gresham grandparents in King and Queen County. Later she visited the Morattico Baptist Church, where she had gone to Sunday school as a girl, and with modest gifts encouraged the local clergy to provide regular Sunday services for the congregation.[31]

She was not immune, however, to the flood of new ideas that were threatening her way of life from the outside. During a whirl of social events in Washington in January 1948, she met the justices of the Supreme Court and their wives at a party given by her sister Elsie Bowley. The next morning, at the invitation of Justice Harold Burton, she sat in the courtroom as Thurgood Marshall and other attorneys argued the landmark segregation case of *Sipuel* v. *Oklahoma,* which involved the rights of a black woman to attend law school at the state university.[32]

Perhaps it was the Washington experience that stimulated Mrs. duPont to read Gunnar Myrdal's *An American Dilemma,* which had stirred dismay and controversy in the South since its publication in 1944. "As a plain theoretical book written by a man from a theoretical standpoint it is excellent—from an appraiser of the negro it is extremely poor." Most southerners, she noted, who had lived with blacks all their lives would not have felt competent to write a book on such a complicated subject. "The Swede has had no experience with the negroes. . . . Yet he could come to America, stay two years or a little less and write an authoritative treatise."[33] She had no more respect for Americans who went to China for a short time and came home with an authoritative book on that subject. Mrs. duPont's reaction was typical of most southerners of that time, both liberal and conservative.

The postwar years were a time for a renaissance of social life after four years of stringent living. Mrs. duPont could once again staff the mansion house at Nemours and her winter home at Epping Forest as she tried to reestablish the familiar routines of the prewar period. Of course, things would never be quite the same again. Domestic servants were hard to find, and those who were available lacked the training and standards of those who had served her in the 1920s and 1930s. Perhaps the major change in her life was the loss of the *Nenemoosha,* which the federal government had offered to return in its existing condition. To reclaim the yacht, Mrs. duPont would have had to pay federal tax on the $140,000 that she had taken as a deduction when she gave the vessel to the government in 1941. To restore the yacht to anything like its prewar condition probably would have required that much or more.[34] So it was that the pleasant cruises on the St. Johns, the Chesapeake, and Long Island Sound were for Mrs. duPont a thing of the past.

Even a year after the war ended, vacation travel was still difficult in America and impossible in Europe. Trains were crowded, and many of the resort hotels taken over by the government during the war had not been reconditioned for commercial use. Under the circumstances, Mrs. duPont entertained at home in Delaware or in Florida, where in May 1946 she had sixty-five guests seated at a wedding breakfast for a naval officer and his bride. In August she took the Juhans, the Gaineses, Will Edwards, and her two sisters and their families to the Homestead at Hot Springs, Virginia, for ten days, and then spent two weeks in New England.[35]

The following summer she took an extended trip to California, where, with her brother Tom, she visited old haunts in San Diego and Los Angeles. On the way home by train she stopped to see the Hurleys in Santa Fe and then visited the Juhans in their summer home at Sewanee, Tennessee. She reported to Tom that the parties at Sewanee began at ten-thirty in the morning and lasted until midnight. Within a few days after her return to Nemours she began a round of house parties. During the hot summer evenings the pool at Nemours was popular. To Denise she wrote: "Don't laugh—I went swimming last evening at ten o'clock, Miss Knox, Mrs. Juhan, Mrs. Gaines and 'yours truly.' The men went to bed. Then after swimming we bowled a while and had a glass of beer. I took tomato juice and sauerkraut juice. Then we went to bed. Am going swimming again this afternoon as we missed our swimming period yesterday afternoon due to going to a party."[36]

She was now almost sixty-four years old, and she admitted to an old California friend that she was beginning to look her age. But she did not think that age had yet slowed her down.

> For instance, I left here Saturday, went to Florida, attended all the meetings there it was essential to attend, took the night train Tuesday evening to Richmond. Got off in Richmond and attended

the meeting of the Executive Committee of the Virginia Museum of Fine Arts, of which I am Vice-President. Then we entertained the Governor and the Budget Commission for luncheon, hoping to get the State to appropriate enough money to build a new wing on the Museum. Visited my great nephew, newly arrived, Jessie Gresham Baker's baby, took the five o'clock train to Wilmington, got here at ten o'clock. I have been trying to get caught up with the work ever since. I have guests arriving to-morrow and Sunday. I am off to New York on Tuesday, then to a house party down in the Valley of Virginia on the fourteenth. This is about my average speed.[37]

By the spring of 1948 conditions in Europe had improved enough for Mrs. duPont to plan her first trip abroad since 1939. She was anxious to see old friends in England and particularly Elizabeth Chamberlain, the daughter of Placidia and Will Edwards, who had stayed with her husband through the Battle of Britain and the hard times of the war. All during the war Mrs. duPont had sent food packages to Elizabeth and other friends in England, and with severe food rationing still in effect in 1948, the food packages from America were arriving regularly.[38]

When Mrs. duPont learned that the bishops of the Anglican Communion would be meeting in London and Canterbury during July, she asked Bishops Juhan and McKinstry if she could "tag along." They were happy to have her company, not suspecting that she intended to cover all their expenses. Mrs. duPont embarked with the Juhans on the *Queen Mary* on June 24 and met the McKinstrys at Claridge's in London, where she had reserved an elegant suite for her companions. Bishop McKinstry and his wife had never before visited London and were dismayed at the prospect of having to pay for such opulent accommodations until it became apparent that they were guests of Mrs. duPont. It was an experience they would never forget—elegant dinners at Claridge's with distinguished members of British society, tea at the queen's garden party with the royal family, and transportation about London in limousines with liveried chauffeurs. When the Lambeth Conference neared its end, Mrs. duPont invited her guests to join her on a tour of Europe. Completely unprepared for this development, the two couples at first demurred but then hastily revised their travel plans. For six weeks they toured Switzerland and Italy before returning to Paris early in September. For her guests, the trip was beyond anything they could have imagined. For Mrs. duPont it was a joyous summer with good company. As she wrote to Arthur B. Kinsolving, the distinguished rector of St. Paul's Church in Baltimore: "Traveling with Bishops and their ladies is a rare privilege."[39]

The European trip drew Mrs. duPont closer to the Episcopal church than she had ever been before. Her growing friendship with the Juhans had been moving her in that direction since the early 1940s, and through that relationship she had come to know many of the prominent clergy in the church. In January 1947 she had traveled to Washington with Henry Adair to attend the installation of Henry Knox Sherrill as presiding bishop in Washington Cathedral. Those weeks in London, however, at the Lambeth Conference gave her new contacts and a new vision of the Anglican Communion that reached far beyond the American church. To guide her on that pilgrimage she could have selected no one better than Bishop McKinstry, that congenial but circumspect extrovert who seemed to know everyone who mattered and who had a knack for keeping himself at the center of events. In London Mrs. duPont had struck an immediate friendship with Geoffrey F. Fisher, the archbishop of Canterbury, and his wife, and she and Mrs. Fisher corresponded regularly for years thereafter.[40] Then those six weeks on the continent with the Juhans and McKinstrys cemented a relationship that would not fade with the passing years.

Mrs. duPont's formal mode of address belied the warmth and affection of these friendships. She had never addressed males in her own social cohort by their first names, the only exceptions being Frank Gaines and Charles Hardwicke. So McKinstry and Juhan were always addressed as "Bishop." In fact friends said that Juhan's first name was really Bishop because everyone, including Mrs. duPont, always called him that. Her informal letters to the Juhans always began: "Dear Bishop and Vera." In reply, they (and this included Frank Gaines) never thought of using a form of address more familiar than "Miss Jessie," a term that implied the intimacy of southern kinship but still carried a note of respect. To everyone else, including her closest associates, she was always "Mrs. duPont."[41]

The months abroad in the summer of 1948 gave Mrs. duPont a healthy respite from the fast pace of her normal routine, but as usually happened she was soon enmeshed once again in her hectic schedule. During the winter of 1949 she concentrated her attention on the Florida enterprises.

The legal battle with the Atlantic Coast Line over the Florida East Coast Railroad was still making its tortuous way through the courts. In February there was an encouraging note when a federal judge remanded the earlier decision of the Interstate Commerce Commission favoring the merger back to the commission for new hearings. Whether the commission could be induced, however, to change its earlier decision was uncertain, and it seemed likely that the case would ultimately go to the Supreme Court. Jessie, and certainly her brother Ed, were not about to abandon the cause.[42] A hard fight for what one believed to be right might be good for the soul, but it did not make life easier. Ed's pugnacious manner, his stubborn refusal to court any compromise, and his open disdain for his opponents fed the fires of hostility.

A new sign of trouble appeared in February 1949, when the antitrust division of the Department of Justice informed Ed that it was investigating complaints that the St. Joe Paper Company and other duPont interests in Florida were violating the antitrust laws. Ed suspected this was another form of harassment by his old adversary, Senator Pepper, and Senator Pat McCarran, who had conducted a Senate investigation of the St. Joe Paper Company in 1945. To respond to the government complaints Ed retained James F. Byrnes, the former Supreme Court justice, with whom Jessie had established a personal relationship. He also enlisted Ollie Edmunds, who had run unsuccessfully for Pepper's Senate seat in 1944, to take the case directly to Attorney General Tom Clark. When Edmunds reported that Clark seemed determined to pursue the case, Ed took another approach. It happened that Jessie had strengthened her acquaintance with Attorney General Clark when he and Mrs. Clark spent a weekend with Jessie at Nemours in November 1948 and visited the Alfred I. duPont Institute. In May Ed had his staff in Jacksonville prepare a briefing paper that Jessie could use in approaching the attorney general informally to explain the company's position on the case. Whether Jessie ever actually saw Clark or whether he intervened, the antitrust division apparently never pursued the investigation.[43]

The antitrust charges against Ed, however, did not end with the Department of Justice investigation. In December 1949 Roy E. Crummer, one of Ed's oldest enemies, filed a $30-million antitrust suit against Ed, Jessie, and the St. Joe Paper Company. Crummer had been a prominent municipal bond salesman back in the 1930s when Ed and Will Edwards were encouraging small towns in the Florida Panhandle to sell bonds for the Gulf Coast Highway. By bidding up the price of bonds to give the towns a fair sale, they incurred Crummer's displeasure. Ed also used his influence in the state legislature to gut several bills that Crummer had introduced, calling the bills "a swindle on the taxpayers of Florida."[44]

Crummer's suit charged that Ball and his associates had ruined his reputation and were instrumental in bringing mail fraud and other criminal charges against Crummer's company, all for the purpose of converting "the state of Florida into a duPont-Ball dominated and controlled proprietary domain." When the Department of Justice dismissed the antitrust charges against Ball, Crummer sued the duPont group for slander and libel.[45]

Although the Crummer suit and Ed's struggle to gain control of the Florida East Coast Railway were to drag on for years, they ceased to be a matter of primary concern to Mrs. duPont after 1949. Ed's attorneys were confident of their defense in the Crummer suit, and things seemed to be going Ed's way in the Florida East Coast struggle. He probably enjoyed the irony in the attacks by some of the railway unions on Senator Pepper, who for years had championed the cause of organized labor. Pepper had been warning labor leaders that control of the railroad by Ball would strike a severe blow at the unions. The Florida Brotherhood of Railway Clerks, however, saw Pepper's support of the Atlantic Coast Line merger as a scheme to turn over a Florida enterprise to "outsiders." Then in January 1950 the Fifth Circuit Court of Appeals affirmed the district court's opinion that found the proposed merger with the Atlantic Coast Line "contrary to law."[46]

Senator Pepper's support of the merger played directly into the hands of Ed Ball and his coalition of reactionary business interests, which had been mounting a campaign since 1944 to defeat Pepper in his bid for reelection in 1950. For six years Ball had worked behind the scenes to build a war chest of large contributions collected from wealthy individuals like H. L. Hunt and conservative organizations like the U.S. Chamber of Commerce, the National Association of Manufacturers, and Sears Roebuck. Even the American Medical Association contributed from the conviction that Pepper's support of medical benefits under Social Security would open the door to "socialized medicine." Most of the money went to a Jacksonville public relations firm that planted anti-Pepper articles and editorials in newspapers and other publications all over Florida.[47]

Until early 1950 the coalition was merely anti-Pepper. No viable opposition candidate appeared until the choice finally settled on George A. Smathers, a handsome, ambitious war veteran whom Pepper had befriended and introduced to the ways of Washington when the young man was elected to Congress in 1946. Smathers promptly turned on his old friend and, as one journalist put it, "fell into Ball's pot of senatorial campaign money and refused to struggle."[48] In a vicious campaign built on the crudest forms of super-patriotism, anticommunism, antiunionism, and racism, Smathers anticipated by several years the worst tactics of McCarthyism.[49] Outdistanced ten to one in campaign funds and caught on the defensive, Pepper never had a chance.

There was general rejoicing in the paper company's Jacksonville office in May 1950 with the news of Smather's victory. Jessie wrote a friend: "I believe Mr. Claude Pepper is through with Florida politics. . . . He made the duPont estate, Ed Ball and me one of the platforms of his campaign. He was just going to remove us entirely from the State,—stop us from doing any work in the State. Really, his activity with the Atlantic Coast Line versus the Florida East Coast was one of the main causes of his defeat."[50]

Except for comments such as these on the outcome of the election, Mrs. duPont never mentioned the campaign in her correspondence. There is no evidence that she knew Smathers personally, took any part in the campaign, or contributed any money to it. The comprehensive list of donors to Smathers's campaign from Duval County includes neither Ed Ball nor his sister. Whatever money she may have given probably went by way of her brother, who would have made certain that his contribution and his sister's were well concealed.[51]

Business interests and politics were not Mrs. duPont's only concern in Florida during the postwar years. As news of the accomplishments of the Alfred I. duPont Institute spread across the nation, crippled children's associations and physicians began calling Wilmington for assistance. Mrs. duPont had little patience with many of the requests, which she recognized simply as attempts to extract funds for salaries and high-overhead operations. "It is strange," she wrote Shands, "they all want office work and field work, therefore, no money is left for the crippled child,—all is spent on literature and salaries."[52] But she could not resist pleas for direct aid to individual children. As the number of cases in Florida began to pile up, she consulted with Shands about bringing the children to Nemours for treatment, but they concluded that would not be economical.

Shands, however, soon found a better approach to the problem. He had learned that health care programs for crippled children in Florida were "almost at a standstill principally because of the lack of proper organization and strong leadership."[53] Furthermore, the state's society for crippled children was seeking a new executive director, and Shands saw this as an excellent opportunity to organize the disparate efforts of the state society and the many local groups.

Within the duPont organization itself Shands had access to persons who were deeply involved in health care projects in Florida. Hardin Goodman was the spark plug of the Hope Haven Hospital in Jacksonville, and Will Edwards had been working for years to obtain state funds for tuberculosis hospitals. After visiting hospitals across the state in the spring of 1948, Shands concluded that there were reasonably adequate facilities for the care of crippled children but insufficient funds to operate them. Although there were empty beds in the institute at Wilmington, Shands concluded that it would be less expensive to treat Florida children in local hospitals than to bring them to Nemours. On this premise Shands proposed that the board of managers allocate $35,000 for treating children in Florida. After Shands worked out a plan for the Florida Children's Commission to administer the funds, the board approved the proposal, with direct financial aid to begin in October 1949.[54]

To gain local support, Shands arranged with the Florida Children's Commission to hold a conference on the care of crippled children in Tallahassee early in 1949. Mrs. duPont attended the conference, provided a buffet supper for all the participants, and agreed to meet with a reporter who wrote an excellent story on the conference for Jacksonville's *Florida Times-Union*. People from all parts of the state found that they had common interests that could best be met by joint action.[55]

The Tallahassee conference marked the beginning of a coordinated effort to aid crippled children in Florida, but it remained for the Nemours Foundation to move, as Mrs. duPont put it, "from talk to action." In April 1949 she called a joint meeting of the trustees of the estate and the directors and board of managers of the foundation to consider a new proposal that she and Shands had drafted. Shands had found that in April 1949 there were more than four hundred children in Florida who needed immediate hospital care and who fell within the category of "curable," as specified in Mr. duPont's will. At an estimated cost of $300 per child, it would take more than $100,000 to treat all the children on the waiting list. That is precisely what Mrs. duPont and Dr. Shands proposed to do.[56]

The plan was not only bold, it was also practical. Under the watchful eyes of Mrs. duPont and her brother, Dr. Shands and Miss Des Barres had exercised strict control over expenditures at the institute, with the result that they had accumulated a surplus of $300,000, "in excess of all requirements and reservations contemplated" in Mr. duPont's will. From that surplus, Mrs. duPont proposed to allocate $150,000 to treat all the children in the backlog. The proposal received unanimous approval.

The treatment of children began within a few weeks, and Shands reported early in June that the Nemours Foundation was paying for an average of sixty-three patients a day in Florida hospitals at the very low daily cost of $5.28. He was confident that the program was giving the maximum benefit for the money available. There was also good news that month from the Florida legislature, which increased the appropriation for the Children's Commission by $150,000. By the end of the year, the foundation had paid for the hospitalization of more than five hundred children.[57]

Before Mrs. duPont left for Europe with Helen Knox and Aleen Bingham in the spring of 1949, she consulted with Henry P. Adair and William B. Mills about the specifics of an endowment fund that they had drafted. Adair, a trusted and skillful legal advisor for more than twenty years, never shunned an opportunity to be of service to Mrs. duPont, despite his advancing years and fragile health. On this particular assignment he had the assistance of Mills, a much younger lawyer whom Ed Ball had hired away from the Bureau of Internal Revenue in Washington to handle the complex tax problems faced by the St. Joe Paper Company and the duPont estate. Mills, a native of Maine and a graduate of Bowdoin College, had never lived in the South, but his competence and knowledge of tax law made him a valuable addition to the Jacksonville staff. Mrs. duPont found Mills and his wife, Helen, personally charming, and she greatly enjoyed the informative, slightly humorous, but always cordial letters that Bill Mills wrote. She must have appreciated the opening paragraph of a letter he wrote to her later that summer:

> A letter greeting your return home should be one, I think, devoted to that pleasant event and should not properly concern itself

at all with the "dismal science" of economics. It is also an invigorating thing for one who customarily writes letters eternally about carry-overs and carry-backs, drawbacks, regulations here and regulations there, the wherefore of this decision, or the remotely implied insinuations of that decision, and the other thousand and one pains associated with taxation, to take time out and write only about such a good event.[58]

The proposed endowment fund had two aims. The first was to relieve Miss Shaw of the onerous task of sending out monthly checks to more than thirty of Mrs. duPont's relatives and friends and incidentally to insulate her from occasional but troublesome appeals for additional funds from those already on the list. The second aim was to avoid the federal tax that Mrs. duPont had been paying on income that she used for these gifts. In 1948 she had given more than $175,000 in nondeductible gifts to individuals. Furthermore, her deductible gifts to charitable and educational institutions fell far short of 15 percent of her adjusted gross income, the upper limit on gifts then permitted by the tax laws. Mills estimated that in 1948 Mrs. duPont could have increased her charitable contributions by $155,000 before reaching the 15 percent limit and thereby could have realized a tax saving of $119,000.[59]

The attorneys' proposal was that Mrs. duPont should set up a trust funded with enough DuPont Company stock to yield the $175,000 then required annually for nondeductible gifts to relatives and friends. The thirty-two named individuals would continue to receive approximately the same amounts for the rest of their lives. As each of them died, that portion of the interest income would revert to the trust. Mrs. duPont at any time, or her estate after her death, could give portions of the residual income and principal to charitable and educational institutions. The trust would terminate upon the death of the last surviving beneficiary. Because the institutions would eventually own all the stock in trust, Mrs. duPont would not be taxed for the income.

Drawing on his government experience, Mills thought it would be wise to spell out the details of the proposed trust and present it to the Bureau of Internal Revenue in Washington for formal approval before Mrs. duPont signed the document. While she was in Europe that summer, Mills and Adair made several trips to Washington, where they discussed the details of the proposal with Robert Miller of the tax firm of Miller & Chevalier and with officials at the bureau. By the time Mrs.

duPont returned from Europe in August, Mills was confident that the bureau eventually would give its approval.

In the meantime, Adair and Mills reached agreement with Mrs. duPont on the details. She would place in the trust 22,000 shares of DuPont stock worth something more than $1,300,000. To avoid any problems with the bureau, the Barnett National Bank of Jacksonville and the Florida National Bank would be parties of the trust agreement. At the outset, Mrs. duPont provided in deeds of gift that the residual income from the trust would be divided among three educational institutions. The University of the South at Sewanee would receive 15.75 percent, and Hollins College and Washington and Lee would each receive 13.5 percent. In letters to the institutions she indicated that she intended during the next four years to increase these percentages so that the three educational beneficiaries would eventually share the entire corpus of the trust.[60]

The magnitude of the gifts overwhelmed the recipients. Frank Gaines felt speechless when he tried to compose a letter of thanks to his old friend. "If I am not getting ludicrous in trying to find an outlet from these compulsive emotions that stir within my spirit, I should say that I feel much like a man who has been given, from dearest and trusting hands, a Holy Grail to keep."[61] Not only were the gifts unusually large, but they came with no restrictions. Mrs. duPont requested that, when the institutions received their share of the principal, they would put these gifts in their permanent endowment funds "and that the income from this addition be used to augment the salaries of the teaching staff."[62] The residual income received in the meantime could be used for any purpose, but she hoped some of it would go for faculty salaries.

The trust agreement, which became effective just before the end of 1949, proved in the following year to be satisfactory to all concerned. The individual beneficiaries continued to receive their monthly checks from the banks, and the Bureau of Internal Revenue accepted the arrangement. Convinced that the plan was working, Mrs. duPont sent the institutions a second deed of gift in December 1950, increasing the shares to Sewanee and Washington and Lee to 35 percent each and to Hollins, 30 percent. Thus she had allocated the entire corpus of the trust to the three institutions. During the year the value of the stock had appreciated considerably, so that the principal in the trust now exceeded $1,850,000. Bishop Juhan, chairman of the capital campaign at Sewanee, joyfully announced that the ultimate gift of $650,000 would be the largest ever received by the University of the South and would be in addition to the $566,000 that Mrs. duPont had already given.[63]

The general trust proved such a convenient charitable device that Mrs. duPont asked Mills to set up a second trust of the same nature late in 1950. The new trust provided a way to establish tax-free lifetime annuities for twenty more friends and members of her family. Like the first general trust, the second named Washington and Lee, Hollins, and the University of the South as the residual beneficiaries, each to receive eventually 12 percent of the principal of the trust, which was created with shares of DuPont stock. A year later Mrs. duPont increased the share of each institution to 24.1 percent.[64]

In addition to the two general trusts, Mrs. duPont also sharply increased her annual gifts to her favored institutions. Whereas the average annual gift in the first postwar years was around $50,000, the amount was close to five times as large by 1950 (table 7-1).[65]

Mrs. duPont's motivation for these large gifts stemmed in part from her conviction that the small independent college was an essential cultural resource. "It is my earnest belief," she wrote in 1946, "that if leaders and statesmen are to be developed in our country, it is going to be through the small colleges, where there is a hand-picked faculty, so to speak, who come in daily communication with the students."[66] She was most concerned about the small southern colleges, whose best faculty might be lost to wealthier northern institutions. This conclusion explained her special interest in increasing salaries in colleges below the Mason and Dixon Line, especially in Virginia, and prompted a $1,000 gift to Sweet Briar College in 1948. The following year, when she was setting up her general trust to avoid taxes, she found a new reason for support. To her friend L. Valentine Lee, rector of the largest Episcopal parish in Jacksonville, she explained that independent colleges "must secure their

TABLE 7-1 Major Gifts in Securities, 1946–50 (in dollars)

Institution	1946	1947	1948	1950
Hollins College	36,750	54,675	36,700	220,143
Washington and Lee	62,450	47,868	44,500	256,834
University of the South	54,450	51,587	36,350	256,834

endowment within the next few years, as under the present form of government, fortunes are not going to be accumulated in the future."[67] With inheritance taxes at 77 percent, there would not be much to pass on to future generations.

Two years later a new threat to the independent colleges appeared on the horizon. The United States' entry into the Korean War had revived the military draft, with the danger that the men's colleges might once again suffer a severe loss in enrollment and tuition income. When both Frank Gaines and J. Ollie Edmunds, president of John B. Stetson University in Deland, Florida, raised this specter, Mrs. duPont responded by sending each of their institutions shares of corporate stocks with a market value of close to $50,000. "These colleges," she declared, "are fortresses on the last defense line of freedom and our Christian commitments; they are fountains for the free flowing of forces that will keep vigorous our heritage and our hope; they are seed-beds of true leadership for the generations yet to come."[68] She had already written to Niles Trammel, chairman of the board of the National Broadcasting System, who had supported her interests in the radio awards, to suggest that "a number of wealthy men and women in each State be interviewed to see if they won't underwrite the loss of tuition that the reduced enrollment is obliged to cause."[69]

As Mrs. duPont focused her interest on the independent colleges, new patterns appeared in her scholarship program. In January 1951 she decided to give no more scholarships to students attending colleges outside Virginia, Delaware, and Florida. Even in those states there were some changes. She was still receiving detailed reports from Bishop Goodwin on scholarship applicants from the Northern Neck, but she noted that none of those recommended intended to study at William and Mary. Perhaps this fact and the change in the college administration after the death of President Julian Chandler explained the college's failure to be included in Mrs. duPont's general endowment trusts.[70]

A less explicit, but certainly potent source of Mrs. duPont's interest in the independent colleges was her hope that they would prove a last refuge against racial integration in educational institutions. In June 1950, the University of Virginia announced that it intended to accept black students. For Mrs. duPont, the decision portended "a revolution" that, she was happy to say, she would not live to see completed. She took some comfort in the election of her friend, F. Bland Mitchell, the Episcopal bishop of Arkansas, as the new chancellor of the University of the South. Both Bishops Juhan and McKinstry could assure her that Mitchell would stand firm against any "radical" attempts to integrate the faculty or student body of the university.[71]

By the end of 1951 black students were attending the Medical College of Virginia and the Richmond Polytechnic Institute as well as the University of Virginia. She wrote to Bishop Juhan:

> For Virginia to have admitted negroes is betraying the trust that was left to us by those splendid ones who gave all in the Sixties that principle and spiritual values should survive. . . . Had they have [*sic*] accepted the negroes and the carpet baggers, much poverty would have been averted, but no standards would have been maintained, no spiritual values carried on. They could have furled their banner of truth and culture and gone in with the mob to degradation, but they chose the reverse and with smiling lips they carried their banner, maintaining a code of morals and culture. Little did they dream that we to-day would be a party to destruction and surrender of what heart and life holds dearest.[72]

The world she had known and loved as a girl seemed to be fading into the past on all fronts, and it was doubly distressing to see the vortex of the whirlwind in Virginia. She was dismayed to learn that the Virginia Theological Seminary in Alexandria had that fall admitted a black student from Detroit. Had she known this at the beginning of the term, she would have withdrawn her scholarship for the one student she was supporting there. She dashed off a letter to the seminary dean "to know the status of conditions."[73]

In his prompt reply, the dean defended the student as "exceedingly able and most satisfactory . . . whose presence among us seems to have created no problem whatever." The dean was not convinced himself that "the attempt to merge the two races in this way was advisable," but he reminded Mrs. duPont that the seminary was a postgraduate institution where "men are more mature." He also pointed out that there was no Episcopal seminary that was exclusively training blacks for the ministry. "Somehow we must provide clergy for our negro congregations unless we are to abandon them entirely."[74]

Mrs. duPont's response was bitter and emotional. She saw the admission of the black student as a plot by the same persons who had closed down the Bishop Payne Divinity School, the only one that had trained blacks in the South. The church would do well to reopen that school, whatever the cost, or to start a new school, as several bishops advocated, at an accredited black college in North Carolina. She listed seven other Episcopal seminaries outside the South that admitted blacks. Why did this student not choose to enter one of those schools where "he does not present the problem that he does in the South"? So long as the Virginia seminary was open to blacks, she declared, "I have made my last contribution to it and many more will have made theirs. . . . Never has my reason and sense of fairness been so disturbed as by this insult to Virginia and to every Virginian—I am a Virginian!"[75]

Virginia was still very much a part of Mrs. duPont's life although she spent little time in the state during the course of a year. Few projects generated more correspondence for Mrs. duPont than did the Robert E. Lee Memorial Foundation at Stratford. She continued to be the largest annual contributor and wrote dozens of letters soliciting contributions to the endowment fund. When the directors decided in 1949 to build the Council House as a permanent meeting place on the grounds, Mrs. duPont funded the project, took a personal interest in the design of the building, and sent detailed comments on the plans to the architect. At her suggestion in 1950, the foundation sent six thousand booklets describing the Stratford project to trust officers and lawyers who were known to write wills for affluent clients.[76]

In Mrs. duPont's mind, the arts stood beside tradition and education as part of the cultural heritage she was trying to preserve. That conviction explained her faithful support of the Virginia museum. She provided funds to augment staff salaries, helped raise funds for the new wing, scouted works of art to be purchased for the museum, served on the executive committee, and helped to recruit Leslie Cheek as the new director.[77] During the same years she supported the Barter Theater, which staged dramatic presentations in Abingdon, in the remote reaches of southwestern Virginia. She considered the theater unique in both Britain and the United States in "carrying drama to the hinterlands."[78] She served on the board of directors for many years and provided annual gifts and several loans. The museum and the theater were cultural resources that she hoped to preserve for all the people of Virginia.

Mrs. duPont attends the Scandinavian exhibit at the Virginia Museum of Fine Arts in Richmond, January 1954. She was a founding member of the museum board.

The leaves of the dogwood were already a deep red and the tulip poplars a bright yellow when the Stratford directors convened at the Council House in October 1951. The dedication exercises ended, the words of General Lee's hymn wafted through the autumn air. "How firm a foundation, ye saints of the Lord." How apt these words must have seemed to Jessie Ball duPont as she stood straight and tall on the steps of the Council House. The battle was far from won, but the foundations of her life were still intact. The singing audience now reached the fourth verse:

> When through fiery trials thy pathway shall lie,
> My grace, all-sufficient, shall be thy supply;

The flame shall not hurt thee: I only design
Thy dross to consume, and thy gold to refine.

Even at the age of sixty-seven, Mrs. duPont felt her life was far from over. Perhaps all the years that had gone before—her teaching career in California, her golden years with Alfred, the hard times of the depression, the tragedy of war, and the frustrations and disappointments of the postwar era were merely a preparation for new tasks ahead. In any case, she was in full command of her resources and had no qualms about the principles that would guide her in the future. On the firm foundation of her heritage she was attempting to support a structure of moral principles and social philosophy that represented her deepest convictions. The question was whether she could reinforce this structure, and, even if she could, whether it would prove functional in the New South that was coming into existence.

Giving with a Purpose

By the 1950s it was clear that Mrs. duPont was no longer engaged simply in charitable acts for the needy but also in a determined effort to apply her financial resources in ways that would support the moral precepts and social principles that she espoused. It was probably presumptuous on her part to believe that she alone could have a significant impact on society. But if she was naive, she was also supremely confident in her ability to manage her resources and in the validity of her analysis of the evils that she saw threatening American life. In establishing an endowment fund in 1954, she declared: "This fund is to assist the University of the South in its continuing effort to draw to its faculty men with mental, moral and spiritual endowments, who are capable of training youth to be intellectual, Christian, moral and Godly leaders. A few LEADERS and THINKERS can change the minds and hearts of men,—in these terrible times when Satanic forces have been released, attempting the destruction of Christian civilization, men's hearts and minds must be changed. Such a change is our only hope for the future."[1]

The statement revealed a deliberate plan to concentrate her resources on educating individuals who would be most likely to carry her message through the schools to society at large.

In one respect Mrs. duPont's strategy was similar to that which the Carnegie and Rockefeller foundations had employed for years: to use educational institutions as instruments for effecting social change.[2] In other respects, however, her intent could hardly have been more different. The established practice of the foundations was to fund selected fields of research, usually in the social sciences, that would investigate critical social problems and propose solutions. In contrast, Mrs. duPont's gifts went primarily to scholarships and faculty salaries and thus carried with them no imprint of social policy, even though she clearly had a social agenda.

There is no evidence that the thought of sponsoring social science research ever occurred to her, but it is quite likely that she would have found the idea abhorrent. The concept of research suggested to her that the answers to critical social problems were not apparent but could be discerned only by study and analysis. For Mrs. duPont the answers were already clear from her own observations of society: the world's social and economic problems would be solved only when the populace adopted the moral and ethical principles that she saw as the foundations of Western civilization. She thought the paramount function of educational institutions was to teach these values, not to engage in research that might well produce solutions unrelated to them.

In recent years, since the archives of the great foundations have been opened for research, historians and social scientists have turned their attention to the motivation of philanthropists. This research has in turn stimulated a debate over whether the managers of foundations have supported university research in an effort to build an intellectual hegemony that would dominate public policy.[3] At first glance, Mrs. duPont's philanthropic activities seem to lie completely outside that debate. She did not fund research and did not identify her gifts with a social agenda. Yet it is clear that she intended her benefactions to have a social impact. She might well have admitted, at least to her intimate friends, that she was trying to establish a hegemony with the faculty and students of the institutions she was supporting. She exerted this influence, however, not by sponsoring research, but rather by supporting the institutions that were most likely to advance her views of society.

Mrs. duPont's goal was ambitious and could hardly have been contemplated by a person lacking the wealth at her disposal. She was fully aware, however, that even her substantial resources were limited in terms of the task she hoped to accomplish. To achieve maximum effect, she adopted two courses of action. The first, already described, was to exercise great care in distributing her money. The second, equally important, was continually to replenish her assets and to avoid unnecessary taxation. These two strategies governed her actions in the 1950s.

Mrs. duPont's financial position at the beginning of the decade explained the importance of increasing assets. At first glance, she was an extraordinarily wealthy woman. In January 1950, her assets were about $10 million (or $55 million in current dollars). Her income for the first eight months of 1949 was $1.1 million, of which about 80 percent came from Alfred's estate and 20 percent from her own investments. Her deductions, including about $85,000 in educational and charitable contributions, brought her net income for the eight months to about $1 million. Her nondeductible expenditures included: $91,000 in gifts, about $63,000 for operating Epping Forest and Nemours, about the same amount for personal expenses, and $690,000 in taxes. This left a profit for the first eight months of $151,000, which, if all went well, could be added to principal.[4]

True, the figures show that she was not rapidly gaining assets, but why was this important in light of the large income she was receiving? Would it not have been sufficient, as William B. Mills advised, to increase contributions to the legal limit and thus maximize tax avoidance? There is no evidence that Mrs. duPont ever specifically confronted that question, but the answer certainly was no, and the reason lay in the terms of Alfred's will.

The probated will, unlike the conditional instrument that never took effect, placed a heavy obligation on Mrs. duPont because it left the disposition of the income from the estate almost entirely in her discretion. She had a moral obligation to preserve the corpus of the estate and to use at least part of the income, as she saw fit, to create and maintain the Nemours Foundation. The discretion allowed by the will posed a dilemma for Mrs. duPont. Having decided to create the foundation in her lifetime (and she was not required to do so), she had to determine how much of the income she would divert to it. In 1950 she was giving 12 percent. She never hesitated to give enough money to the foundation to assure its efficient operation, but there were good reasons for not moving most of the income from the estate into the hospital. Neither she nor Alfred Shands was convinced that the hospital could responsibly use that much money. It was also likely that such a decision might create an institution far different from any Alfred had ever contemplated. For example, the institute might become more a research center than a clinic. Even more important, such a move would have poured all the available resources into a project conceived more than a decade earlier. Times were changing, as Mrs. duPont knew only too well, and the needs and agenda of the foundation were changing too.

Another factor to be considered was that the income from Alfred's estate would be available for her own projects only during her lifetime. Under the provisions of Alfred's will, all the income from the estate would go to the Nemours Foundation at the time of her death. It was therefore essential to augment her own estate if she expected her influence to outlive her.

It made sense to withhold some of the estate income to produce more principal in her own portfolio and to provide immediate funds for the projects to which she was committed. Contrary to what some critics later claimed, she was not withholding funds from the foundation to squander them in outrageous luxury but rather to husband resources for her own philanthropic purposes.[5] She would never have put it this way, but she intended to apply her own income to causes that seemed pressing in her lifetime rather than to commit her resources to the dead hand of the past.

It was essential to Mrs. duPont's interests that she maintain and even augment the income from Alfred's estate. Because the estate owned most of the stock in the Florida National Banks, the St. Joe Paper Company, and its subsidiaries, the financial condition of the estate depended to a large extent on the profitability of those companies. In one respect, Mrs. duPont was fortunate in having her brother Ed as overseer of the Florida enterprises. No one else could possibly have taken on the task of augmenting the estate with more zeal and even relish. In the sixteen years since Alfred duPont's death, Ed had more than fulfilled his boss's dreams and built a financial empire so large and powerful that, in the minds of some at least, it threatened to dominate the economy of the entire state. Not only did Jessie have unwavering confidence in Ed's ability and integrity, she was also inextricably linked to him as the little brother whom she had brought to a position of power and who had fully justified her faith in him.

With Ed Ball's remarkable talents, however, also came decided disadvantages, a combination that became more apparent in the 1950s. Jessie admired Ed's stubborn determination in fighting the Florida East Coast Railway and Crummer cases, but that same quality thwarted her attempts to bring new people and new ideas into the Florida companies. She believed that Ed's harsh treatment of company personnel was responsible for the frequent resignations by valued employees, among them the head of the bank in Miami Shores in 1950. She was particularly distressed by what she saw as her brother's efforts to drive from the paper company and banks the last of Alfred's associates and those closest to her. In April 1951 Ed had threatened to fire Will Edwards for questioning an order that he remain in Washington to follow the course of legislation critical to the company. Taking Edwards's side in the dispute, Jessie quickly intervened and worked out a compromise. Ed, moreover, had never been comfortable with Jessie's old friend Henry Dew, who, as vice-president for sales, had insisted upon retaining a degree of independence, which Alfred duPont had allowed. Jessie felt a special obligation to Edwards and Dew because they had been hired by Alfred and had served his interests long and faithfully. Although Jessie never accepted her sister Elsie's accusation that Ed was disregarding Alfred's wishes in order to promote his own interests, she was not about to permit Ed to drive these loyal subordinates from the company.[6]

In addition to Edwards and Dew, Mrs. duPont could rely on other officials in the company to provide her with information and support her views. Elbert Dent, the husband of Alfred's daughter Victorine, had replaced Reginald Huidekoper as a trustee of the estate after Huidekoper's death in 1943. Jessie did not always agree with Elbert's opinions, but she enjoyed the company of the Dents, and they were often dinner guests at Nemours. She also had a friend in Seabury Stoneburner, whom she had brought into the paper company in 1945. As a distant relative, Stoneburner had an access to Jessie that other employees with similar status would not have enjoyed, and he often proved a valuable source of information. Edwards, Dew, and Dent all served on the board of directors along with Frank Gaines and W. Hardin Goodman, who were both close to Mrs. duPont. William B. Mills, a trusted assistant to Ed Ball and vice-president of the company, had established close ties with Mrs. duPont and gradually came to serve as a liaison between sister and brother.

Of lesser rank in the company hierarchy but essential to maintaining Mrs. duPont's interests was Hazel O. Williams, her Florida secretary. Miss Williams had responded to a newspaper want ad in 1947 and had been Mrs. duPont's eyes and ears in Jacksonville ever since.[7] Raised and educated in Florida, Miss Williams was bright, personable, and an excellent legal secretary. Her soft southern accent, her nice sense of language, and her genteel manner made her instantly acceptable to Mrs. duPont. Even more important to her success were her quiet manner, patience, and discretion in working with such strong personalities as Mr. Ball, Mr. Dew, and Irene Walsh, Ball's longtime executive secretary.

This same gift for quiet diplomacy was especially valuable in dealing with Miss Shaw. With the passing years, Mary Shaw had become ever more possessive in her role as Mrs. duPont's agent in Wilmington. Although technically an employee of the paper company, Miss Shaw had gone to Jacksonville only once, in 1938, to work with Mrs. duPont. But Miss Shaw's inflexible and officious manner had raised havoc with the staff, and Ed had told Jessie never again to bring her to Jacksonville. That situation left Miss Williams in sole control of Mrs. duPont's affairs in Florida, but she never enjoyed Miss Shaw's full confidence. Miss Shaw jealously guarded all of Mrs. duPont's correspondence files and financial records in Wilmington and never passed on to the Jacksonville staff any more information than was absolutely required. In time, Miss Williams began building her own set of duplicate files.[8]

Ed took special pains to mollify his sister after the Edwards incident. "It is my opinion," he wrote, "that there are few brothers and sisters who, over such a long period of years, have been as close to each other as have you and I, and I do hope that . . . we can again put in lots more time together." He wanted to get back "on the same old basis, which, I have to admit, we should never have gotten off; and, if we have gotten off it, I believe it was my fault."[9] He probably thought it would comfort Jessie when he reported that the excellent earnings of the paper company would have justified a higher dividend than was being paid. It is just possible that Jessie would have preferred a higher dividend to increase her own income.

Ed's words may have reassured Jessie for the moment, but his actions spoke louder. A few weeks later, after Jessie had sailed for Europe, Ed asked the St. Joe board to approve a proposal to grant pensions to company officials and salaried employees. Jessie did not oppose the idea; in fact she had long urged Ed to increase salaries and pensions as a means of retaining good employees. It is also likely that she had in mind the interests of the old faithful, like Edwards and Dew, who were nearing retirement. At the May 1951 meeting, while Jessie was traveling in Europe, the board of directors finally approved the provisions of a plan that had been under study for more than a year.[10]

When Jessie read the final version after her return, she found the plan too restrictive and stingy and demanded that it be reconsidered. By that time Mills and others had already begun discussing the plan with company officials and were about to send it to the federal government for approval. To calm the troubled waters, Ed sent Elbert Dent and a pension plan consultant to Wilmington to discuss the details with her. Ed followed this action with a long letter to his sister in which he rehearsed the need for orderly procedures in making corporate decisions and even saw fit to invoke their responsibilities as trustees to carry out the provisions of Alfred's will. Still not satisfied, Jessie pursued her inquiry for several more weeks before the St. Joe board, this time in her presence, gave its final approval.[11]

Much of the misunderstanding between Jessie and Ed resulted from their increasingly infrequent meetings. Ed almost never came to Nemours and seldom to Epping Forest. While in Jacksonville, he stayed at his modest hotel rooms across the street from the bank, but in the 1950s he was spending more and more time at his farm, Southwood, southeast of Tallahassee. In July 1951 he embarked on a five-month trip with Elbert Dent to the South Pacific and Australia. From all he had read about the big country down under, he was convinced that Australia offered rare opportunities for investment. Somehow he also had the idea that the relatively young economy blossoming there would not be so encumbered with government regulations and restrictions as that in the United States, which, to Ed's way of thinking, had lost its vitality under the "socialistic" programs of the New Deal.[12]

A few weeks later Jessie was faced with new responsibilities that would leave her less time for company affairs and contacts with Ed. In September 1951 Governor Fuller Warren asked her to serve on the Florida Board of Control, which reported to the governor through the state board of education. The board of control had oversight of the three state-supported universities, the Florida School for the Deaf and Blind, and the Ringling Museum of Art in Sarasota. At first Mrs. duPont declined. She already had more than she could do, and she could not imagine how she could fit monthly board meetings in Florida into her schedule. Although the board's responsibilities for higher education attracted her interest, she was wary of the inevitable involvement in state politics. However, a call from Judge B. K. Roberts, who was representing the paper company in the Crummer suit, and conversations with Mills and Adair soon made it clear that Mrs. duPont's acceptance of the position would help to dispel the charges that the duPont companies were an alien interest attempting to dominate the economy of the state. As she wrote to Tom: "[O]ur own officers wanted me to take it, and perchance,

Mrs. duPont served as a member of the Florida Board of Control from 1951 until 1955.

at this particular time, in the midst of the Florida East Coast Railway litigation and the Crummer blackmail suit, it may be best. I can resign later, I suppose."[13]

The appointment fulfilled a promise Warren had made during his 1948 gubernatorial campaign to appoint a woman to the board of control. Although he had named thirty-three women to minor state offices during the first two and a half years of his term, his first three appointments to the board had been men. With only fifteen months of his term left, he could not delay much longer. In announcing the appointment, Warren made much of the fact that Mrs. duPont would be the first woman to serve on the board. He spoke of her as "perhaps the state's top taxpayer, [who] heads Florida's biggest business-banking empire." Although she had "attained her highest fame in the field of finance and business, . . . her acknowledged business acumen" would be of great value in the board's work.[14]

Judge Roberts, with his close ties to Ed Ball and the St. Joe Paper Company, obviously had a hand in the appointment, but it is most likely that the idea of selecting Mrs. duPont came from J. Hillis Miller, president of the University of Florida since 1947. As Mrs. duPont had turned her attention from Virginia to Florida charities in the late forties, she had come to know Miller well, and her increasing contributions to the university reflected her growing confidence in him.[15] Miller, like the presidents of the other two state universities, appeared monthly before the board of control to defend budget requests and equipment purchases. The board had great respect for Miller's opinions, and it is reasonable to speculate that his recommendation of Mrs. duPont would have had great weight with the board. Miller himself surely must have seen personal advantages in the appointment. Mrs. duPont's presence would give him a sympathetic voice on the board and help to assure that his university would remain near the top of her list of scholarship grants.

Ed's long absence gave Jessie a rare opportunity to turn the tables on her brother and effect some of her own ideas in the St. Joe Paper Company. Ed's obsession with profit and acquisition of capital had made him notoriously stingy in corporate charities. On one occasion, when Boy Scout leaders appealed to him for a contribution, he offered them half his salary as an officer of the railroad on the condition that they would not come back for additional funds. When they later received a check from Mrs. Walsh for five dollars, Ed held them to the bargain.

While Ed was in Australia, Jessie presented the executive committee of the paper company a proposal to contribute $20,000 to the Baptist Memorial Hospital in Jacksonville. In Ed's absence and with Edwards and Henry Dew on the committee, the proposal was approved unanimously. She probably did not reveal that she had matched the company gift with her personal contribution in the same amount.[16]

She then proposed that the company grant college scholarships to the children of employees. The company would follow the procedures that she and Miss Shaw had established for her own scholarships: applications would be carefully reviewed to determine eligibility and the funds would go directly to the institutions. From Sydney, Australia, Ed pleaded with Jessie to delay the proposal until the next board meeting, presumably when he would be present. He thought the scholarship program would put too much strain on his sister and was "in actual conflict with Mr. duPont's will. I do hope that you will wait until we can all sit down and discuss this . . . as neither the Directors nor the Officers have the right to give away the stockholders' money."[17]

By the time Ed Ball returned to Jacksonville, the issue was all but settled, and the company announced the scholarship program in December 1951. The contribution was to be $20,000, to be administered by the City of Port St. Joe, presumably to take the administrative burden off the company. The contribution was "to be used to provide scholarship awards to boys and girls of employees of the St. Joe Paper Company or its subsidiaries, who graduate from high school and are eager to further their educational training."[18] One can imagine that Mrs. duPont dictated those words—the stipulation on high-school graduation and the emphasis on "training."

Despite her heavy commitments, Mrs. duPont was determined to carry out her plans for a Mediterranean cruise during the winter of 1952 with the Juhans and the Gaineses. A few days before the ship was to sail from New York, she learned that the Florida East Coast Railway case would come up for a hearing in the district court in Jacksonville during the first week in February. In order not to disappoint her traveling companions, she did not inform them that she would be staying in Jacksonville for the hearing. Every day that week Mrs. duPont sat in the courtroom from ten in the morning until four-thirty in the afternoon as the Atlantic Coast Line attorneys "droned on," as she put it, in presenting their case. Even Mrs. duPont, who often found legal proceedings interesting, was bored as the old arguments were rehearsed, but she was glad she attended. She wrote to Tom that Henry Adair had asked her to appear with Ed and Henry Dew, the other two trustees, to thwart the opposition's charge that "there is just one person—Ed Ball. I'll tell you they didn't emphasize that this time before Judge Strum when we three sat there each day."[19] Once the outcome appeared favorable, she made her first and only transoceanic airplane flight to join the cruise ship in Casablanca.[20]

When Mrs. duPont and her party returned from Europe late in March 1952, they found the racial segregation issue boiling up again in the Episcopal church. Late in 1951 the synod of the fourth province, representing twenty-two dioceses in nine southern states, adopted a resolution noting the shortage of black clergy in the province and the absence of any theological seminary for training black candidates for the ministry. The synod also concluded that "it would not be desirable or advisable to establish a segregated seminary" in the province.[21] Most of the dioceses in the province had had a part in establishing the University of the South at Sewanee, and most of the clergy in the province had been trained at the seminary that was part of the university. In referring the report to the university, the synod was placing the issue squarely before the university trustees.

Several southern bishops, including Juhan and McKinstry, had attempted to defuse the issue by urging the province to reconsider a segregated seminary to replace the Bishop Payne Divinity School. McKinstry, obviously reflecting the views of Mrs. duPont and Bishop Juhan, thought that the Virginia seminary could not admit "any considerable number of Negro students" without losing a substantial amount of financial support. The best solution, in McKinstry's opinion, was to set up a theological school in St. Augustine's College in Raleigh, North Carolina.[22] When that idea failed to attract support, the trustees at Sewanee had to face up to responding to the synod's report at their annual meeting in June 1952.

With her friend F. Bland Mitchell, the bishop of Arkansas, as chancellor of the university and Bishop Juhan on the board, Mrs. duPont had no fear that Sewanee would now desert the cause of segregation, and she was right. The board in its response admitted that there was nothing in the ordinances of the university to prevent the admission of blacks but concluded that to encourage the enrollment of blacks at that time was "inadvisable." The admission of blacks, the board contended, would be a violation of Tennessee law. Furthermore, the school of theology at Sewanee was an integral part of the university, which was located on a remote mountain top, which the board considered "an isolated domain." The board concluded that "furtherance of the Church's work and the happiness and mutual good will of both races will not now be served by the action requested by the Synod."[23]

It was not surprising that Mrs. duPont asserted the same arguments in defense of segregation in her strongly worded letters to Frederick Goodwin, who as bishop of Virginia was president of the board of trustees of the Virginia seminary, and to Ben R. Lacey, Jr., president of the Presbyterian seminary in Richmond. Three days after the Sewanee board's decision, she wrote Lacey that she could not understand how the two southern seminaries, "which are totally independent private schools," could do what Virginia law forbade. She was much more direct than the Sewanee board in making the second point: the Supreme Court had opened the graduate school at the University of Virginia to blacks, but to admit them as undergraduates in private institutions would soon mean that blacks would be going to school with white children "from kindergarten up. . . . We, as leaders, know what the results are compelled to be when we mix adolescent blacks and whites and indoctrinate them with the equality of the two races, which is far removed from fact. 'Being equal' has been misinterpreted by those seeking to destroy our Government, our independence and our freedom."[24]

A few days earlier Mrs. duPont had expressed the same sentiments in a letter to Bishop Goodwin. The letter was pointed enough: she wanted to know whether the seminary would admit blacks in the coming academic year. "As you know, it is nearing the time when I make up my educational budget. It is my considered belief that such action will utterly ruin the Seminary."[25] Bishop Goodwin knew Mrs. duPont too well to give her a perfunctory reply. In a five-page, typewritten letter, he tried to put the issue in its national and historical context. The fact was, the bishop wrote, that blacks would no longer attend the segregated Bishop Payne Divinity School, and with no students the school had no choice but to close. He did not think that the admission of blacks to Virginia seminary was "the final [or] the effective answer to the problem of educating Negro clergymen," but it was essential to train blacks in the

South because "Negroes trained in the northern seminaries do not fit into the needs of our southern parishes." The bishop was still hoping that arrangements could be made to transfer the assets of Bishop Payne to the school of religion at Howard University in Washington, D.C.[26]

Before Mrs. duPont could reply to the bishop's letter, the Sewanee issue hit the public press. On June 11 the *New York Times* reported that eight professors at Sewanee had announced that they would resign their academic positions unless blacks were permitted to enter the university's school of theology. The group included the dean of the theological school and five of the professors, the university chaplain, and the head of the university department of religion. Deploring the trustees' "failure to state any Christian principle involved," the professors found the trustees' position "untenable in the light of Christian ethics and of the teaching of the Anglican Communion." The trustees' decision would do "irreparable harm to the reputation of Sewanee as a center of Christian education" and would compromise the protesters as priests and teachers in a university supported by the Episcopal church. Unless the board reversed its position at its next meeting in June 1953, all eight would resign.[27]

The dissidents' action stunned Mrs. duPont and her clergy friends. It seemed incredible that southern Christians could take such a position, but to throw the dispute into the public arena seemed beyond the pale. Bishop Mitchell tried gamely to explain the board's position but found little support in the church press, even in the *Episcopal Churchnews,* the most widely read Episcopal periodical in Virginia. Bishop Juhan seemed utterly crushed by the incident, and Bishop McKinstry told Mrs. duPont that if he were in command, he would accept the resignations of the eight men immediately.[28]

Mrs. duPont railed against the dissidents in her private letters: "It is a trifle difficult to understand how American citizens, much less clergymen, could condemn Communists, when their act is an absolutely communistic act, namely, giving ultimatums and threats to the Board that with an overwhelming majority of votes had taken action, not as dictators but as those in whom power was entrusted. For eight professors to set themselves up as a Stalin in an American college is I believe without parallel."[29]

However reprehensible the action of the Sewanee professors seemed to Mrs. duPont and her friends, it was clear that the protest had posed a challenge that could not be ignored. Realizing that the university could not let the challenge go unanswered until the following spring, Bishop Mitchell arranged a two-day meeting of the board of regents with the professors. Several of the professors privately apologized for taking their protest to the press rather than to the board, and after the meeting they issued a statement maintaining that they had not intended their protest to be "an ultimatum of eight people acting as a corporate pressure group, threatening the University, but as an expression of the deepest personal convictions of eight individuals." For its part, the regents noted that the board of trustees had "erected no permanent bar to the admission of qualified Negro students," and Bishop Mitchell announced that he was appointing a special committee of the trustees to study the problem and to make recommendations to the board.[30]

Mrs. duPont was far from satisfied with the outcome of the meeting. Noting that the professors had used the pronoun *we* throughout their protest, she thought their "clarification" either was less than forthright or reflected their inability to understand the English language.[31] She was probably relieved when the eight faculty members, citing the administration's refusal to raise the Christian principles involved, submitted their resignations in November 1952. In August she had written to Bishop Mitchell: "The elimination process one by one sounds very wise. I trust it has already begun."[32]

The Sewanee dispute soon took on national dimensions. The deans of the other Episcopal seminaries questioned the action of the Sewanee board, and the faculty of the General Theological Seminary in New York supported the statement by the deans. In February 1953, James A. Pike, dean of the Cathedral of St. John the Divine in New York and outspoken liberal theologian, announced that he would not deliver the baccalaureate sermon at Sewanee in June or accept an honorary degree because of the university's refusal to admit blacks. The graduating class at Sewanee applauded Pike's decision.[33]

By the time the Sewanee trustees assembled for their annual meeting in June 1953, it must have been clear to all but a few people like Mrs. duPont that the university would have to reverse its stand of the previous year. The week following the board's overwhelming vote to end discrimination in the theological school, Mrs. duPont wrote to a friend at Sewanee who had sent her an article entitled "Sewanee's Capitulation to Communism." "It is amazing that the Board bowed to the orders of the Saboteurs and Pike, the latter advocated breaking the law of a sovereign state."[34]

By this time Mrs. duPont was incensed over an exchange of letters with Peter Day, editor of *The Living Church,* the national weekly of the Episcopal church. Day had written to her about "a persistent rumor" that her gifts to Sewanee were conditioned on the continuation of the discrimination policy and that she had terminated her gifts to the Virginia seminary because it had changed its policy. In her reply she denied that it had ever been her intent to dictate how her contributions should be used, and she assured Day that her contributions to Sewanee "have never been, nor will they be, conditioned or restricted."[35]

In a strict sense Mrs. duPont's response was accurate, but obviously it was not the whole truth. Although she had given moral support to Juhan and Mitchell at Sewanee, she had never suggested that she might terminate her gifts to the university. And, although she avoided Day's question altogether in her reply, she had not made an iron-clad decision about the Virginia seminary. When Day promptly printed her reply in *The Living Church* under the heading "Unrestricted Gifts," she accused him of a gross breach of ethics and law in neglecting to obtain her permission to publish the letter.[36] It was one more bit of evidence that outside forces were trying to destroy the foundations of southern life. As she wrote to the vice-chancellor at Sewanee: "I haven't much hope that the persecution from outside will cease. They have but one objective, which is the destruction of a culture—the easy way to implant Communism, forcing the highest to the lowest level of Society. From there it is easy for dictators to take over."[37]

In the introduction to his classic study, Gunnar Myrdal defined the American dilemma as "the ever-raging conflict between, on the one hand, the valuations preserved on the general plane which we shall call the 'American Creed', where the American thinks, talks, and acts under the influence of high national and Christian precepts, and, on the other hand the valuations of specific planes of individual living."[38] From his study Myrdal concluded that Americans were particularly troubled by the contradiction between their democratic ideals and their racial practices. Deep in the American psyche he found a powerful if irrational belief in racial purity. A southern historian summarized Myrdal's findings in terms that seemed to fit Mrs. duPont perfectly: "Even the most liberal whites frowned on race mixing. He reported that the sexual aspect of the race problem lay deep in the subconsciousness of whites, filling them with personal insecurities about blacks. Fear of interracial sex explained why whites condemned social equality and why they extended segregation to education, religion, recreation, and housing."[39]

Mrs. duPont may have been a typical southerner by Myrdal's definition, but she did not experience the moral dilemma in the way he suggested. She saw no contradiction between her convictions on segregation and the ideals of a democratic society. Quite the contrary, for her the attack on segregation was a threat to democracy. "At one time we were governed by the will of the majority—their wishes prevailed—not so today! The minority group (negroes) must be given all the power and they must dictate the policies and way of life to, as well as initiate the laws for the majority group (white). We no longer in our business can employ whom we wish. We no longer must be permitted to give our child, as we were given, the privilege of an education in an all white school. . . . It is all right to teach Communism and break down of all our culture."[40]

That same summer of 1953 she thanked her friend James F. Byrnes, governor of South Carolina and former Supreme Court justice, for standing firmly for "American principles" at the Democratic National Convention. Whichever candidate was elected president in November, she hoped that freedom would be returned to the individual citizen. Byrnes, Governor John S. Battle of Virginia, and Senator Harry F. Byrd "were the three fearless fighters at the Convention for white supremacy and the preservation of state's [sic] rights."[41] With Judge Byrnes she dreaded the coming decision of the Supreme Court in Brown v. Board of Education, which would strike down the doctrine of separate but equal in elementary schools. When the court announced its decision in May 1954, Mrs. duPont termed it "the most disastrous decision that the Supreme Court has made in over a hundred years or since the Dred Scott decision."[42]

When it came to morals and religion, however, Mrs. duPont did feel the pangs of conscience that Myrdal described in his book. Her feelings were best expressed in a letter she wrote to Presiding Bishop Henry Knox Sherrill in sending him a check for $5,000 for the Episcopal Church Foundation. She noted his concern about crime and delinquency in U.S. cities. This problem she attributed to church leaders and the judiciary. The clergy preached to parents that "unless they have always associated with negroes on an equality basis and will from here forward continue to do so, they are not following the teachings of Jesus." The judiciary accused the same parents of failing to live by the Constitution. Children interpreted these charges, she wrote, as meaning that their parents did not live by the moral and religious principles they expected their children to follow. "[T]herefore, why should not the youth, if they wish to steal automobiles or commit crimes do so[?]"[43] Sherrill and many of his fellow bishops probably did not accept so simple an explanation of cause and effect, but the gulf between racial practices in the United States and Christian doctrine as expressed in the fourth chapter of Galatians continued to trouble Episcopalians, both northern and southern.

Perhaps no issue dogged Mrs. duPont's thoughts more in 1953 than did the race question, but it far from immobilized her. In fact, the new year brought twelve months of constant activity—board meetings, business conferences, conventions, and a steady stream of house guests, all interspersed with dozens of train trips. After moving the household to Epping Forest early in January, she returned north for the inauguration of President Eisenhower and a meeting of the judges for the annual radio awards. On her way south again, she stopped in Richmond for a board

Alfred R. Shands, Jr., director of the Alfred I. duPont Institute, and Mrs. duPont visiting crippled children at a hospital in Coral Gables, Florida, in April 1950.

meeting of the Virginia Museum of Fine Arts. February and most of March she devoted to business affairs in her Jacksonville office. After another trip to Washington in March for the radio awards dinner at the Mayflower Hotel, she returned to Florida for visits to crippled children's clinics in Miami and Coral Gables with Dr. Shands.

Her almost constant travels during the winter of 1953 made it impossible to attend two meetings of the board of control during that period. Although she felt an obligation to attend, she must have realized by this time that her contributions to the work of the board were marginal at best. She had missed half the meetings during her first year on the board, and when she was present she apparently limited her comments to issues on which she had some experience. No doubt her attendance at board meetings of the Virginia museum explained her interest in matters affecting the Ringling museum in Sarasota. Likewise her experience with Alfred's deafness sparked her interest in the affairs of the Florida School for the Deaf and Blind. Occasionally she took part in the discussion of salary increases, land purchases, contracts, and personnel matters. At no time, however, did she seem to take any leadership or initiative in the work of the board.[44]

After a vacation trip in the Deep South in April 1953 she stopped in Tallahassee for a board of control meeting, then in Jacksonville for a meeting of the English Speaking Union with the Juhans, and then in Miami for a hospital visit and five hours of lectures on orthopedics. After a banquet that evening with the doctors, she set off for Key West to see the new wing of the company bank. "[H]ad a nice visit with the President; went around and talked to each of the employees."[45] She was back in Miami the next day for the banquet of the Florida Medical Association. On her way up the east coast of Florida she visited a handicapped clinic in Palm Beach and the company banks in West Palm Beach and Fort Pierce, arriving at Epping Forest in time for dinner with eight guests. The next evening she invited ten friends for dinner and then attended the Rotary dance for the benefit of retarded children.

No sooner had Mrs. duPont moved her ménage north to Nemours in June than she was off to New York to replenish her wardrobe and to bid the Shandses farewell as they sailed for Europe. To make the June meeting of the board of control in Gainesville she took the train direct from New York and on her way back stopped in Virginia for a board meeting at Hollins College. John R. Everett, president of the college, had become a close

Jessie Ball duPont with her close friends Polly and Alfred Shands and Vera and Frank Juhan on a cruise to Alaska in July 1953. At the time Shands was director of the Alfred I. duPont Institute and Juhan was the Episcopal bishop of Florida.

friend of Mrs. duPont and one of her allies in supporting racial segregation in the schools. Born in Oregon, Everett graduated from Union Theological Seminary in New York before earning a doctorate in philosophy at Columbia University. He taught philosophy at Columbia and at Wesleyan University in Connecticut before his election at Hollins in 1950. Both Everett and his wife, Elizabeth, were charming hosts and always invited Mrs. duPont to stay at the president's house during her visits to Hollins.[46]

Before she left in July for a long vacation in the Canadian Rockies and Alaska, she wrote to her brother Ed to give him her itinerary and to chide him for not writing to her. "I do not like not hearing from you, not knowing how you are and not knowing what is going on."[47] She also took the occasion to prod him on company scholarships by sending him an article from the *Kiplinger Letter* on gifts from large U.S. companies. The import was that, if the DuPont Company could give $600,000 in scholarships, the St. Joe Paper Company could offer more than $20,000.

When Ed did write to Jessie in Vancouver, he wrote a business letter and not a pleasant one. He complained that Hardin Goodman, who served as trust officer in the bank, had been so hard on employees that several had left the trust department to work for competitors. In a sharp reply, Jessie took issue with the allegations Ed reported from the company "grapevine." She noted that some years earlier the grapevine in the Jacksonville office had criticized Miss Shaw and made it impossible to bring her to Florida again. "She realizes that if anything were to happen to me, she would not be with the Company but for a brief time."[48] Jessie suggested that the loss of good employees extended far beyond the trust department.

> I do not think we are working on the right angle to build permanent structures. It has been evidenced in the main office by elimination, as far as possible, of the last old friends that Mr. duPont had there, and so it goes. I am deeply concerned over this procedure. Yes, via the grapevine, the present president, who, in my opinion, would wreck any organization, was elected lest I promote the one that now is marked for elimination. Such a thought never dawned on me. . . . There has been no one for me to talk to, of course, as I seldom see you and then only with groups, whether it be at the farm or in the office.[49]

Jessie also sensed that she was drifting away from her sisters. When Belle complained that they never had time for more than a "church speaking acquaintance," Jessie responded with a long conciliatory letter in which she attempted to explain the difficulty. They no longer had the same friends or similar interests, and there was always "the trust that Mr. duPont left me to carry on."[50] Of all the family, she still felt closest to Tom, whose good nature and easy manner suggested that he had more time for friendly chatter and camaraderie than did his sisters or brother. Whenever she went west she always stopped to spend a week with Tom

Mrs. duPont's sister Isabel Baker with her husband, Addison Baker, her daughter Jessie Gresham Baker Thompson, and her three grandchildren, Addison B. Thompson, Jessie Ball Thompson, and William T. Thompson III, at Tuckahoe, their home near Richmond, about 1954. Private collection.

in Los Angeles, and she continued to prod him to come east for Christmas and other occasions.

Such an occasion occurred in October 1953 when Tom came east for the celebration of the three-hundredth anniversary of Westmoreland County at the Stratford plantation. Jessie was once again caught up in a frenzy of travel as she hurried back from a board of control meeting in late September. On the way she stopped for two days with the Gaineses at Washington and Lee and a board meeting at Hollins. Belle's daughter, Jessie Baker Thompson, and her husband, Dr. William T. Thompson, who was now a member of the medical advisory board at Nemours, had invited the board to a cocktail party at their home in Richmond preceding a dinner that Belle and Addison Baker hosted at the Commonwealth Club. After a day of meetings with the board, Jessie left with Tom for the anniversary celebration at Stratford. She did manage to squeeze into her schedule two pleasant days at Ditchley with Tom, but much of her time there went into decisions about maintaining the house and farm.[51]

While in the Northern Neck, Mrs. duPont took part in three celebrations that her gifts had made possible. For several years she had been corresponding with John Dos Passos, the author, who lived in Westmoreland, Virginia, and was spearheading a drive to build a gymnasium in Cople. In the end she had provided most of the funds for the building, which was named in her honor. On Sunday she attended services at the Morattico Baptist Church and turned the first shovelful of earth for the new education building, which could not have been built without her support. After attending the annual meeting at Stratford on Monday, she went to Fredericksburg, where the governor of Virginia received the Artmobile, a traveling art exhibit organized by the Virginia Museum of Fine Arts. Mrs. duPont not only provided much of the funding for the project but also helped Leslie Cheek, the museum director, to convince the board to approve the project.[52]

In the midst of all her travels and committee work, Mrs. duPont never completely abandoned the personal charities that she had supported since her marriage. Miss Shaw, who knew Mrs. duPont's mind in most of these cases, could handle the dozens of routine appeals that arrived each month. Eoline Jesse and Ethel Tignor continued to receive requests from needy families in the tidewater counties, but few of the appeals seemed as desperate as those during the Great Depression, when survival in some

Mrs. duPont breaks ground for the addition to the Morattico Baptist Church, which she attended as a child, near Kilmarnock, Virginia, October 1953.

cases literally depended on gifts from Mrs. duPont. "As you say," she wrote to her Cousin Eoline in Nuttsville, "you are swamped with requests, and the more you give, the more request[s] you will have." Tax-supported social welfare programs were now available, and the needy, she thought, should turn to them. "I hope you do not think I am unjustly harsh, but since the Government and the State have taken over charities and welfare, the individuals are not going to be able to handle it as was originally done, and as I think it should be done."[53]

Mrs. duPont's declaration to Eoline was of course more of a political statement than one of serious intention. She could never ignore appeals from the truly destitute, particularly from families she had known personally as a young woman. To an elderly black woman who had been on the charity list for decades, Miss Shaw sent two of the St. Joe blankets with a note in her formal but sympathetic style: "It is to be hoped that these blankets will be of service to you through this cold weather, and serve to keep you warm on your new bed throughout the winter."[54]

A few weeks later Mrs. duPont wrote directly to a widow in Byrdton, Virginia, who had appealed for help: "[W]ith the vast amount of sickness that has befallen your family over these last years, it is amazing that you have been able to keep on, and it was the training, I am sure, in your youth, that your Mother and Father gave you around their knee,—to bear one another's burdens and share one another's blessings. It is from this that one derives the greatest pleasure and it is what has made for strong family units, which . . . form the foundation of our civilization."[55]

With the letter Mrs. duPont sent a check for $400. "Divide it equitably, or pay off the accumulated bills. It goes with full appreciation of what you have been up against and hoping it will alleviate some of the pressure."

For tax reasons, most of Mrs. duPont's charitable contributions continued to go, not to individuals, but to institutions. Money for Mrs. Tignor's list went to the Wicomico Church fund and that for Eoline Jesse to the ladies' aid society at White Chapel Church. Most of the contributions outside the Northern Neck were funneled through the Alfred I. duPont Foundation, which Mrs. duPont had established in Jacksonville expressly for that purpose. Although the need to protect the status of the foundation as a charitable institution precluded her from taking a direct role in its administration, she still considered it her primary charity.

Not all of Mrs. duPont's charities were in response to appeals. At

Christmas and Easter she still sent small gifts to shut-ins and the elderly. To the Home of Merciful Rest in Wilmington Miss Shaw sent the usual check for $450 at Easter 1955. "Will you be good enough to have this check cashed, and with the proceeds, please place a crisp $10.00 bill in each of the addressed envelopes enclosed with this letter for each guest in your Home, and at the same time on Easter morning please extend to each one Mrs. duPont's best wishes for a very Happy Easter Day."[56]

The plight of suffering children never failed to arouse Mrs. duPont's sympathy. When polio struck the young son of a worker at Port St. Joe, Mrs. duPont arranged to have the child moved to the institute in Wilmington for treatment. Six months later, she wrote to his parents:

> This note is prompted to you and your dear wife, realizing that you would like to have some outside direct news of your precious little boy, Neal. I was over at the . . . Institute last evening for their Hallowe'en Party. . . . All the children were in costume and masked, and so were we. Your little son had the cutest rabbit outfit and mask that I have ever seen. He was all animation. . . . His cheeks were as pink as if he had been the healthiest child in the world. Dr. Shands said outside of his crippling condition, he is a very healthy youngster, . . . and feels the most of that condition he would outgrow.[57]

With Miss Shaw's help, Mrs. duPont had devised routines that made it possible to acknowledge personally scores of events, such as births, graduations, marriages, and deaths, among her friends and even among her business associates. To newborns she sent a savings bond and a letter addressed to the child, noting "your safe arrival on this mundane sphere." It was a small but thoughtful gesture, one that Eli Fink, who served with her on the board of control, remembered three decades later as something that touched him personally.[58]

The birthday letters were just one example of Mrs. duPont's sensitivity to the joys and sorrows that her friends and relatives met in the course of daily living. She wanted to share those moments with her "loved ones," as she put it. A short note with a small check could mean much more than its monetary value indicated; to the recipient the important thing was that "Cousin Jessie" was thinking of them that day. Ever since the 1930s she had been sending food packages to the Chamberlains and other friends in Britain. The packages continued to arrive, not only during the war, but for years thereafter, until food rationing in Britain finally ended in 1953.[59]

Another wartime project still operating in the 1950s was the St. Joe blanket distribution. The appeals for blankets did not end with the war, and Mrs. duPont continued to send hundreds of blankets to England and the continent for homeless families. There was also a pressing need at home. In January 1953 the Children's Service Bureau in Miami reported that the ten single blankets and eight crib blankets sent by Mrs. duPont "were beautiful in varied colors as well as warm and practical for daily use. My foster mothers here said they are too pretty to be hidden from view and are folding them across the foot of the beds."[60] A year later Mrs. duPont requested the paper company to send two hundred blankets to Wilmington for needy families. She was prepared to provide blankets as long as they were needed.

Since the 1930s Mrs. duPont had contributed generously each year to Jacksonville charities, with the largest gifts going to the Community Chest, the Red Cross, and the Salvation Army. These were essentially perfunctory gifts that reflected a sense of civic obligation as much as her personal interest. World War II, however, brought her somewhat closer to the community. Like many Americans, she had been caught up in local efforts to support the war effort. Gasoline rationing had even led her to use public transportation between Epping Forest and her office in downtown Jacksonville. The dances and parties she gave for officers from the naval air station brought her personal contacts with the families of some of the young women who came to Epping Forest on these occasions. These new relationships with the Jacksonville community sparked a greater personal interest in the welfare and cultural development of the city.

Even before the war Mrs. duPont had tried to promote interest in the fine arts and music in Jacksonville, as evidenced by her contributions to the Civic Art Institute and the Civic Music Association. In the 1950s she welcomed even the modest accomplishments of the Jacksonville Art Museum. She wrote to a friend: "To me it is a disgrace that Jacksonville hasn't done more in regard to the Arts. There is plenty of money in Jacksonville and plenty of talent. I talked to Mr. Ed Lane, deceased, on this subject many years ago; so maybe in time we will have a museum worthy of the name. First, we must use the one we have to the greatest advantage."[61]

When the DeEtte Holden Cummer Museum Foundation was established in 1959, Mrs. duPont agreed to serve on the board of trustees and drew on her experience on the board of the Virginia Museum of Fine Arts to help in initial planning for the new museum. The opening of the Cummer Museum in 1961 not only stimulated interest in the arts in the city but also prodded the Jacksonville Art Museum in 1963 to embark on its own building fund, to which Mrs. duPont contributed $10,000.[62]

In support of music in the city, Mrs. duPont each year bought blocks of tickets for concerts by the Jacksonville Choral Society and the Jacksonville Symphony. In 1955 she helped finance the choral society's trip to New York, and her year-end gifts in 1957 and 1958 included substantial amounts to the symphony, totaling more than $71,000 in the years after 1957. In gratitude for her gifts the symphony board elected her a life member in 1963.[63]

Plans to broaden the base for college education always attracted Mrs. duPont's interest. She applauded the efforts of the fledgling Jacksonville Junior College, which gave local high-school graduates from low-income families an opportunity for at least two years of college. When the board decided in 1944 to buy a residence on Riverside Avenue for classrooms and to increase enrollment by offering daytime as well as evening classes, she questioned the move on practical grounds, but still encouraged the board with a donation of $5,000. Larger contributions followed after the war as the daytime program expanded. She was "delighted" when the first building on the new campus on University Boulevard was erected in 1950. The educational mission of the college fitted her philosophy perfectly. "The college has done splendid work here. . . . I do hope it will continue its night school, as so often from the night school come our great leaders, as they are the boys and girls eager for an education and have a willingness to work for it."[64] When the college became a four-year university in 1956, she turned down an offer to serve on the college council that was planning the transition, but she continued to make regular contributions, totaling more than $220,000 for scholarships and faculty salaries.[65]

Of all Jacksonville institutions, hospitals received some of the largest gifts from Mrs. duPont during the 1950s and 1960s. Through her friend

W. Hardin Goodman, Hope Haven Hospital continued to receive steady support. When St. Luke's and the Baptist Hospital launched building funds in the midfifties, she responded generously. In the years after 1957 these two hospitals together received more than $450,000. Smaller amounts during these same years went to St. Vincent's and to Brewster Hospital (now Methodist Hospital).[66]

Scores of charitable institutions in Jacksonville came to rely on regular support from Mrs. duPont. The biggest gifts continued to go to the United Fund, the Salvation Army, and the Young Women's Christian Association, but those caring for children, such as Opportunity House, the Boys' Service Council, the Daniel Memorial Home, and the Florida Children's Home Society, were always on the list. Churches of all denominations counted on regular gifts as well as extra amounts for fund drives, the largest gifts going to Episcopal churches. The Clara White Mission and many black congregations received small gifts. With funds provided by Mrs. duPont, the Alfred I. duPont Foundation continued to respond to the needs of individuals in the Jacksonville area.[67]

Virginia and especially the Northern Neck would always have a place in Mrs. duPont's heart, but as the 1950s wore on, the concerns that had challenged her in earlier years seemed to fade in importance. Stratford was in good hands as a new generation was taking over the responsibilities of the "Owls." With Mrs. duPont's help, the Virginia museum in Richmond had succeeded in raising the funds needed for its new wing. The education building at Morattico church was under construction, and the historic colonial structures at Christ Church, Irvington, and St. Mary's White Chapel had been restored. Now that Mrs. duPont seldom visited Ditchley, the problems of maintaining the house and farm seemed less important. And by 1956 the number of appeals from the needy in the Northern Neck had declined to the point that Mrs. duPont closed out her account at Wicomico Church on Ethel Tignor's recommendation.[68] It had been twenty-eight years since Mrs. Tignor wrote her first evaluation.

Amid the changes engulfing America in the 1950s Mrs. duPont, as a southern conservative, held fast to the moral values and social principles on which she had fixed her course in her adolescence. When social and moral issues arose, she did not hesitate to exert the influence she had gained through her large gifts to southern universities and the Episcopal church. There was no question that she recognized the power that her generosity accorded her.

Although Mrs. duPont was channeling larger portions of her giving into what could be called philanthropy in the 1950s, she would never cease to respond to appeals from the disabled and destitute. Philanthropy was something to be planned, with a long-term goal in mind, and was therefore somewhat impersonal. Charity, in contrast, was personal and almost spontaneous. The impulse toward charity was deeply imbedded in her character; philanthropy was something she learned.

The balance between philanthropy and charity, however, was always fluid. Intent and motivation were not the only factors involved. Age and declining vitality made it increasingly difficult for Mrs. duPont to maintain the pace of earlier years. Growing resources and new opportunities would demand the kind of rational management that philanthropy entailed. In the years ahead the balance would inevitably shift in that direction.

The Practice of Philanthropy

*T*here is no record that Mrs. duPont ever in her life used the word *philanthropy*. Perhaps in her mind it was too elegant, too high-flown a term to apply to an activity that was personal and private. She may also have thought it a needless abstraction invented by social scientists and others who seemed intent on dissecting and analyzing what was to her a perfectly natural impulse toward charity. The course of events in the late 1950s, however, pushed her into a mode of operation that clearly fit the modern definition of philanthropy in at least two respects: it was directed toward the long-term solution of fundamental problems rather than toward the immediate alleviation of human suffering; and it was deliberate, rational, and controlled rather than impulsive and intuitive.

The first signs of philanthropy appeared in Mrs. duPont's contributions to educational institutions. Over the three decades since she began to award college scholarships to individual students, Mrs. duPont and Miss Shaw had built an elaborate structure of giving that involved both charity and philanthropy. In the early days her scholarships represented charitable acts designed to provide worthy individuals with an education they could not otherwise attain. From the beginning, however, a hint of philanthropy was evident. A college education could lead to economic security and a better life for the indigent student, and that was a matter of charity. But education could also produce leaders who could be relied on to make wise decisions in the public interest, and that idea suggested a philanthropic motive.

Practical considerations and the growing importance of tax avoidance accelerated the transition of the scholarship program from charity toward philanthropy. The more scholarships Mrs. duPont awarded, the more difficult it was to keep track of individual students, and the need to move more of her giving into the tax-deductible category did force her to deposit scholarship money with the colleges rather than to send it directly to individuals. Mrs. duPont, however, never entertained any thought of relinquishing control. The application form, revised and printed in 1951, posed more questions about family background and income than about the applicant's high school record, the main purpose being to ascertain that the parents did not have adequate means to send the student to college.[1] High grades in school were important too, as well as the proposed course of study and estimated annual cost. Miss Shaw reviewed all the applications and referred the borderline cases to Mrs. duPont, who sometimes rejected students recommended by others. There was no uniform rate for scholarships, each one being based on a close estimate of actual need. When a student was accepted, Miss Shaw sent a check for the proper amount to the college. The transfer of funds to the college rather than to the student was, therefore, little more than a bookkeeping detail. Mrs. duPont selected the students and determined the amount of the scholarship.

Mrs. duPont's oversight did not end with the initial award of the scholarship. At the close of every semester she and Miss Shaw faced the onerous task of reviewing the grades of each student and determining which ones should be dropped.[2] In 1953, after consulting with several college presidents and deans, she asked Miss Shaw to prepare a form letter stating that no student would continue to receive a scholarship who did not attain a "C" average by the end of the first year and stay "above average" thereafter. Students were invited to submit a report on their college activities at the end of each academic year. "When they have an earning capacity, scholarship students are requested to assist some struggling student in the same amount that they have received." No more than one student in a family was to receive a scholarship.[3]

The students, by their choice of colleges, determined which institutions were on the scholarship list in any one year. Information on the number of students and institutions receiving scholarships from 1951 to 1956 (table 9-1), incomplete though it is, suggests that the number of institutions gradually declined and the number of students increased during the period. This trend reflects in part Mrs. duPont's decision to restrict her scholarships to students attending colleges in Virginia, Delaware, and Florida. The majority of institutions on the scholarship list had only one of Mrs. duPont's students in any one year (see table 9-2).

TABLE 9-1 Scholarships Awarded, 1951–56

Year	No. of Institutions	No. of Students
1951	41	110
1952[a]	30	100
1954	42	137
1956	35	142

a. Figures for 1953 and 1955 were not available.

TABLE 9-2 Distribution of Scholarships by Institution, 1951–56

Institution	Number of Scholarships Awarded			
	1951[a]	1952[b]	1954	1956
Armstrong College	0	0	1	0
Bennett College	1	1	0	0
Berea College	1	0	0	0
Bluefield College	1	0	0	0
Blue Ridge School	0	0	1	0
Carson Newman College	1	1	0	0
Centre College of Kentucky	0	0	1	0
Chipola Jr. College	1	0	0	0
Columbia Theological Sem.	0	0	0	1
Columbian School	0	0	1	0
Cornell University	0	0	1	0
Episcopal High School	0	0	1	1
Erskine College	1	1	0	1
Ferrum Jr. College	1	0	0	0
Flora MacDonald College	0	0	1	2
Florida Normal College	0	0	0	1
Florida State University	8	3	8	9
Fork Union Military Acad.	0	0	1	0
Greensboro College	0	0	1	1
Hampden-Sydney College	4	3	2	3
Hollins College	0	0	2	5
Hood College	0	0	1	1
Jacksonville Jr. College	0	0	0	1
Johns Hopkins Medical Sch.	0	0	1	0
Johnston-Willis Hospital	0	2	0	0
King College	7	3	2	1
Longwood College	18	16	26	31
Lynchburg College	1	3	2	0
Madison College	1	8	5	4
Mary Washington College	1	3	7	5

a. For the academic year ending as indicated.
b. Figures for 1953 and 1955 were not available.

(continued)

TABLE 9-2 *Continued*

Institution	Number of Scholarships Awarded			
	1951[a]	1952[b]	1954	1956
Maryland Institute	0	0	0	1
Maryville College	1	0	0	0
Medical College of Va.	1	0	0	0
Meredith College	0	0	0	1
Middlebury College	0	0	1	0
Montreat College	1	1	0	0
Nazareth College	1	0	0	0
Neighborhood Playhouse	1	0	0	0
North Carolina State Col.	1	0	0	0
Oberlin College	0	0	1	0
Pembroke College	0	0	1	0
Radford College	1	1	0	0
Randolph–Macon College	1	2	1	2
Randolph–Macon for Men	5	4	6	0
Richmond Prof. Institute	7	5	12	14
Roanoke College	0	1	0	0
Sewanee Military Acad.	0	0	1	1
Stetson University	0	0	1	1
Shorter College	2	1	0	0
Sweet Briar College	0	0	0	1
University of Alabama	4	0	0	0
University of Delaware	0	0	8	9
University of Florida[c]	3	4	6	5
University of Georgia	1	0	0	0
University of Maryland	1	0	1	0
Univ. of North Carolina	1	0	0	0
University of Oklahoma	1	0	1	0
University of Richmond	1	2	3	3
University of the South	0	0	0	1
University of Virginia	1	1	3	4
U. of Va. Sch. of Nursing	0	1	0	0
Virginia Military Inst.	3	4	2	1
Va. Polytechnic Inst.	5	6	5	9
Va. Theological Seminary	0	1	0	0
Wake Forest College	0	0	1	0
Washington & Lee Univ.	2	3	4	2
Wellesley College	1	1	1	0
Westhampton College	3	2	1	3
William & Mary College	3	1	1	2
Wingate Junior College	10	11	10	10
Winthrop College	1	0	0	0
Wofford College	0	0	2	2
Yale Divinity School	0	0	0	1

c. Does not include more than 40 Alfred I. duPont scholarships provided under an endowment fund.

Longwood College, which had been the state normal school when Jessie Ball was a student there in 1900, received by far the largest number of scholarships, presumably for young women from the Northern Neck who were training to be teachers. The figures also reflect Mrs. duPont's preference for small independent colleges, trade schools, and junior colleges, where students could be expected to acquire a "practical" education that would prepare them to make a living. The number of scholarships in institutions outside Mrs. duPont's three-state preference declined after 1951, but the data show that for exceptional cases she was willing to support a worthy student at almost any institution.

This scholarship program was only one of several that Mrs. duPont supported. In addition to these direct scholarships, she had as early as 1940 established endowed scholarships at several institutions. These included scholarships in Alfred's name at Washington and Lee and at the University of Florida; in her father's name at William and Mary; in her mother's name at Mary Washington College; and in memory of Bishop Juhan's son at Sewanee.[4] Because the funds for these scholarships came from endowments, Miss Shaw did not include them in the budget for the direct program, but she used the same method of selecting and monitoring students in both programs. These procedures did not apply to the scholarships set up in 1951 for children of St. Joe Paper Company employees.[5]

In a final category were those scholarships awarded annually by the Alfred I. duPont Awards Foundation, which had evolved from the radio awards first granted in 1943. Mrs. duPont expanded the radio awards in 1950 to include television and the allied sciences of communication. She rewarded the tireless efforts of Hardin Goodman in setting up and maintaining the program's administrative machinery by making him executive secretary of the awards foundation, a position he filled in the postwar years with a mixture of enthusiasm and anxiety. By 1951 Goodman's responsibilities as trust officer of the Florida National Bank in Jacksonville and as executive secretary of the foundation, among other assignments, were proving too heavy for him to bear indefinitely. So, with Mrs. duPont's approval, he arranged through Frank Gaines to have the award process administered by the school of journalism at Washington and Lee University. Along with the reorganization, Mrs. duPont decided after months of correspondence with Gaines, Goodman, and network officials in New York to invite winners to convert their cash

Francis P. Gaines, president of Washington and Lee University and chair of the Alfred I. duPont Awards Foundation, with Mrs. duPont presenting the 1950 station award to Walter Annenberg for station WFIL in Philadelphia.

awards into scholarships for students who intended to enter the field of communications. The winners were to be free to do whatever they wished with the cash awards, including the creation of scholarships, but the scholarships would not bear the name of the foundation unless they complied with the foundation's criteria.[6]

Exactly how much Mrs. duPont was contributing to scholarships during these years is almost impossible to determine. Her federal tax returns for 1953 suggest that she gave almost $75,000 for direct scholarships that year and more than $38,000 in 1955.[7] These figures, however, could not have included the endowed scholarships or those established by radio and television award winners.

Running the scholarship programs was a burden in terms of time, but in terms of dollars they were a small part of Mrs. duPont's contributions to education, and even to the institutions on her scholarship lists. By 1953

Hollins, Sewanee, and Washington and Lee were already receiving more than $20,000 each year as residuary income from the general trust which she had set up in 1949. In addition, Mrs. duPont made frequent gifts of securities, not just to these three institutions, but also to Stetson, Rollins, Mary Washington College, and William and Mary, with a total market value of about $410,000 in 1953. This figure, added to the $75,000 in direct scholarships that year gave a total contribution to education of $485,000 (or $2.5 million in current dollars).

The very large gifts to educational institutions that began in 1954 resulted from a concerted effort by George B. Webster, Mrs. duPont's accountant, to minimize federal income taxes (see table 9-3). Mrs. duPont's tax situation at the end of 1955 illustrates the problem. In October Webster estimated Mrs. duPont's adjusted gross income for the year to be $4,716,000. Under the existing tax law, she would be entitled to deduct contributions up to 30 percent of adjusted gross income, or $1,415,000. Through October 13, she had made contributions of $530,000, leaving $885,000 still to be given in order to achieve maximum benefit of the deduction for contributions. Webster estimated that if Mrs. duPont's contributions came up to the 30 percent limit, her income tax would still be $2,715,000.[8]

For a person with Mrs duPont's deep sense of responsibility for her gifts, determining how best to give away $885,000 in less than three months was no small matter. To make the situation worse, Webster

TABLE 9-3 Major Grants to Educational Institutions, 1953–56 (in dollars)

Institution	1953	1954	1955	1956
Univ. of the South	144,863[a]	284,112	227,419	241,505
Washington & Lee	9,703	254,112	209,231	205,868
Hollins College	69,936	254,112	237,426	210,624
Stetson University	55,105		22,881	28,067
William & Mary	32,878		33,000	
Rollins College	20,950	9,320		26,432
Mary Washington		26,843		
Centre College, Ky			17,900	20,125
Sweet Briar College			10,775	20,150
Woodberry Forest School			36,159	
All Saints Jr. College			21,937	
Davidson College				31,031

a. Figures do not include direct scholarships.

learned on November 22 that the DuPont Company would pay a year-end dividend of three dollars per share, which would raise his estimate of Mrs. duPont's total allowable contributions to $1,698,000 and further increase the amount she should give away before the end of the year. It was not surprising that she spent hours on the telephone during the last two weeks in December seeking suggestions for large gifts to her favorite institutions.[9]

The three universities that were the beneficiaries of the first and second general trusts received the largest amounts in these year-end disbursements, but Bishop Juhan and the Episcopal church were not far behind. In response to her 1955 appeal, the bishop had compiled a list of projects totaling almost $180,000. By juggling the list of securities she intended to give, Mrs. duPont came up with a total of $173,000 and promised to make up the difference in 1956.[10]

By the end of 1955 Mrs. duPont was almost seventy-two years old. In the two decades since Alfred's death she had not only realized many of his hopes but had also built a career of her own. She was only too aware that advancing age would bring changes in the years ahead. On the way to the West Coast in August she had sprained her left foot and had to go aboard the ship for Honolulu on crutches. In Honolulu she had inexplicably sprained her thumb, and after returning she had sprained both feet. She wrote Addison Baker, "I must take it easy. I have stayed in bed the last two days and am doing the same thing to-day."[11]

The series of disabling accidents in 1955 prodded Mrs. duPont to give serious attention to revising her will. The legal instrument in effect at the time had been written at Nemours during the spring of 1943. A codicil added in 1948 made a few minor adjustments.[12] Now, in the closing weeks of 1955, the situation was quite different from those she had faced in earlier decades. Even the generous bequests and annuities that she intended for individuals would claim only a small portion of her estate.

As the first and second general trusts and her large year-end gifts indicated, she wanted most of her assets to go to educational institutions that appeared to espouse her social and moral values. To achieve that purpose, a completely new approach would be necessary. She had tried her hand at a draft, which would have made large bequests to the University of the South, Hollins, Stetson, Rollins, and Washington and Lee for scholarships for students "of the white race," but the document contained little more than scattered thoughts on paper.[13] Obviously she would need legal assistance to draft a document that would pass muster with the Internal Revenue Service.

Mrs. duPont had always been careful to exclude members of her family and the inner circle of her friends and business associates from any matters relating to her estate. She kept all such documents separate from her business files in Wilmington and Jacksonville, and it is possible that no one (probably not even her brother Ed) knew what her old wills contained or what her intentions were. Likewise, in planning a new will she did not rely on William Mills, Hardin Goodman, or any of the other lawyers who usually handled her business affairs. Instead she called upon Robert N. Miller of the Washington law firm of Miller & Chevalier, which had been advising her, Ed Ball, and the St. Joe Paper Company for many years on tax matters. To assist him in the task, Miller selected Charles T. Akre, who had been involved in the paper company's tax problems. Neither Miller nor Akre ever discussed Mrs. duPont's affairs with Ed Ball or with anyone in Jacksonville. Mrs. duPont went to Washington several times to discuss her thoughts on the will; when drafts of various sections were complete, Miller and Akre would go to Wilmington upon Mrs. duPont's invitation to work out the details. Mrs. duPont found the two men knowledgeable, pleasant to work with, and discreet.[14]

The document that emerged from Mrs. duPont's discussions with Miller and Akre in the autumn of 1955 was long and complex. Consisting of forty-two typewritten pages in its final form, the new will, like the earlier ones, provided bequests and annuities for scores of relatives, friends, and business associates. A completely new feature, however, was the creation of a perpetual trust that was to receive her entire estate, except for bequests otherwise stated in her will. The trustees were requested, but not directed, to include thirteen specified institutions among the beneficiaries in distributing the income from the trust. Relative weights were assigned to each of the designated institutions to indicate her feelings about how she would have apportioned the income at the time she signed the will. The University of the South received the heaviest weighting, 12; Hollins and Washington and Lee, the next heaviest, 10; the Alfred I. duPont Foundation next, 8; and the remaining nine, a weighting of 1 or 2. The nine were: Sweet Briar, Rollins, Stetson, Randolph-Macon, Randolph-Macon Woman's College, the Robert E. Lee Memorial Foundation, Sheltering Arms Hospital, Home for Needy

Mrs. duPont at her desk in Jacksonville, June 1955. By permission of the *Tampa Tribune*.

Confederate Women, and the Jessie Ball duPont Home, yet to be established.[15]

The lawyers' skillful drafting would give the trustees sufficient flexibility to meet unforeseen developments in the future while at the same time imposing a strong moral commitment to use the trust for the purposes Mrs. duPont intended. They convinced Mrs. duPont to delete the racial exclusions that she had written into her own drafts on the grounds that such provisions were likely to be challenged in the future. They wanted to leave nothing in the will that the government or disgruntled individuals could challenge.

Miller and Akre also took great pains to build an impregnable wall around the estate to protect it from tax claims by the Internal Revenue

Service. The most important precaution was to make absolutely clear the charitable nature of the trust. For this purpose, the two attorneys decided to adopt the precise wording of Section 501(c)(3) of the Internal Revenue Code, which defined an eligible institution as "any . . . foundation organized and operated exclusively for religious, charitable, scientific, testing for public safety, literary or educational purposes." The new trust was to be called the "Jessie Ball duPont Religious, Charitable, and Educational Fund," and the income from the fund was to be "devoted exclusively to general religious, charitable, scientific, literary, or educational purposes and . . . no deviation from these purposes shall be made."[16]

Other institutions were to receive fixed amounts: Grace Chapel, near her Epping Forest home, $250,000 for a new church, and $20,000 each for: the Virginia Museum of Fine Arts; St. Margaret's School in Tappahannock, Virginia; Stuart Hall, which her mother had attended in Staunton, Virginia; and the Piney Woods Country Life School and the Prentiss Normal and Industrial Institute, two schools for black students in Mississippi. Through the Alfred I. duPont Foundation she would also provide $200,000 for three Northern Neck institutions: Morattico Baptist Church, St. Francis Roman Catholic Chapel in Kilmarnock, and White Chapel Church in Monaskon. The gifts for Morattico and St. Francis were intended "to assist those churches in securing ministers of talent and ability." The fund would provide for maintenance of the Ball burying ground that she had established at Cressfield and old Ball tombs at White Chapel.[17]

Because the Nemours Foundation and the Alfred I. duPont Institute would receive all of the income from Alfred's estate after her death, Mrs. duPont's bequest to the foundation included nothing more than the tangible property (except her personal effects) in the mansion house at Nemours. Epping Forest and its contents were to go to Denise, and the tidewater farm at Ditchley was to be maintained for use by her brothers, sisters, their children, and their grandchildren during their lives. Eventually the property was to go to the Alfred I. duPont Foundation.[18]

In designating trustees for her estate, Mrs. duPont followed the pattern Alfred had established in his will. The trustees were to be Ed Ball, her distant cousin Seabury Stoneburner, Bishop Juhan, and the Florida National Bank of Jacksonville. William Mills was designated as alternate trustee. The will was in final form for Mrs. duPont's review at Nemours

just before Christmas in 1955. On December 27 she went to the
Washington offices of Miller & Chevalier to sign the completed document.

On her seventy-second birthday on January 20, 1956, Mrs. duPont spent a
quiet day at Epping Forest. She was determined in the new year to avoid
the hectic schedule that she had pursued in 1955, and she accepted the
incapacitating injuries suffered during that year as a sign of advancing age.
Even more to the point, she was just plain tired, and the thought of a full
calendar of travel and meetings had somehow lost its appeal. In a letter to
Miss Shaw she announced her resolution to clean house and free herself of
the piles of mail that continually inundated her. She listed a dozen
magazines that were no longer to be sent to Florida. Miss Shaw was to hold
applications for scholarships in Wilmington and not send them on
piecemeal to Jacksonville as she had in the past. Annual reports to
stockholders were to be discarded except those from the DuPont
Company, General Motors, and Radio Corporation of America.[19]

In February she enjoyed a week of complete rest and relaxation at the
Riomar Club in Vero Beach with the Everetts, the Gaineses, and
probably the Juhans. "We were in bed every night, except one, by 10:30;
didn't see each other until noon the next day, breakfast being served to
each in his own apartment. We had luncheon together daily, then took a
siesta immediately thereafter, until the 'sun crossed the yardarm' at five;
then reversal of our cuffs, dinner, back to our apartments, as we were not
there for social promotion. Thus you see, we had in the neighborhood of
eighteen hours sleep out of twenty-four."[20]

Denise and her seven children invaded Epping Forest in March. It was
a joy having them and the house seemed strangely quiet and deserted after
they left. But Mrs. duPont confessed to her old friend Rebecca Harding
Adams that she could not take many weeks of having the children
underfoot. Early in April she was off to Port St. Joe with Bishop Juhan
for four days. She inspected the paper mill while the bishop visited one of
his parishes. This was to be the last such trip because Juhan had officially
retired in February to become director of development at the University
of the South.[21]

Perhaps in anticipation of that event, Mrs. duPont had at long last
agreed to accept formal membership in the Episcopal church. In most
instances, and especially for a person as close to the Episcopal church as

was Mrs. duPont, the formality would take the form of confirmation by the bishop. The surprising fact was, however, that she had never been baptized. As a child she had attended the Baptist church, which did not practice infant baptism. After she moved to California, she made no positive commitment to any denomination and had never bothered to be baptized. Thus Bishop Juhan both baptized and confirmed her in a private service at St. John's Cathedral in Jacksonville on her birthday. The following week she gave the bishop a check for $225,000 for his discretionary fund, to be used either in the diocese or at Sewanee.[22]

No sooner had she returned to Jacksonville than she was off once again to Miami to visit a friend and drop in on the Florida National Banks in the area. Five days later she was off on a quick trip to Wilmington. The trip was tiring but she did not let that bother her. "I think the one thing that gives me strength and courage to do it all, is [that] I look at those who don't; who are considerably younger than I am, and they are always talking about being tired."[23]

The truth was, however, that the spirit was willing but the flesh was weak. Mrs. duPont spent the rest of the spring in Jacksonville quietly attending to her correspondence. She took the time to rewrite a letter that Miss Shaw had drafted to the widow of one of her oldest employees at Epping Forest. She started by changing the salutation from "Dear Madam" to "Dear Gladys," and then transformed Miss Shaw's cold formality into a warm and sympathetic response. She sent off $15,000 to Helen Knox for the new administration building at Stratford, but regretted that she could not be with her in the Owls Roost for the spring meeting. As much as she loved Stratford, the memories now meant more to her than the realities.[24]

It seemed more work than ever, she confessed to her sister Elsie, to close Epping Forest that spring and move north. The physical effort somehow seemed overwhelming, and the difficulty of obtaining servants to staff the mansion house at Nemours was becoming every year more and more a headache. Despite her best intentions, she admitted that she indulged in more social life than her energy would allow her. She was looking forward to a quiet summer at Nemours, where she could concentrate on refurbishing the main rooms on the first floor and cataloging the works of art in the mansion. Now that she had committed herself in her will to leave the furnishings with the mansion, she felt a responsibility to keep the house in good order. Many of the paintings needed restoration, some of the antique furniture needed repair, and all the draperies on the first floor were overdue for replacement. Unwilling to trust unknown artisans with such delicate work, she sought the advice of David E. Finley, director of the National Gallery of Art and chairman of the National Trust for Historic Preservation in Washington.[25]

Mrs. duPont was of two minds about houseguests that summer. On the one hand, she wanted to avoid the continuous run of house parties and dinners that had filled earlier summers at Nemours; on the other hand, she found being alone in the mansion depressing and too full of memories. Having one guest was no solution either because "no one wants to come and spend several days alone." She urged Rebecca Adams, her brother Ed, her sisters, and her nephew Thomas Ball Wright to come whenever they could.[26]

Old habits, however, were hard to break. In July she was off to California to visit Tom, now seventy-seven years old and in poor health. Nothing ever lifted her spirits more than being with Tom, the one member of her family to whom she could speak her mind without fear of misunderstanding. The long train ride across the continent, however, was exhausting. Upon her return Miss Shaw reported to Will Edwards that "she is still as nervous as ever, though she admits staying in bed for a whole day every now and then. All she talks about is resting."[27]

A long-planned trip to Nova Scotia with the Juhans and Shandses in August proved refreshing, and Mrs. duPont even found the energy to take a few golf lessons in addition to the usual fishing. During her brief stays at Nemours she filled her weekends with house parties. The autumn brought more refurbishing at Nemours and a round of parties in Washington and at Nemours in connection with the dedication of the Woodrow Wilson bay in the Washington Cathedral and the visit of her old friend, the dowager Duchess of Northumberland.[28] The parties filled her life and her home with treasured hours of warm friendship and refreshing conversation about art, literature, politics, and religion. She genuinely enjoyed the role of a generous hostess who could delight her guests by entertaining them in a style that few others could afford or emulate. But all too often the glow faded with the departing guests, and she realized how much the pleasant occasion had sapped her strength.

In her business activities as well as in her social life, Mrs. duPont often found herself overextended, and she adjusted only slowly to a more modest regimen. She looked forward to June 1955, when her term on the Florida

Board of Control would end. The commitment to attend the monthly meetings of the board in various Florida cities had become onerous, especially when she was not in residence at Epping Forest. She found the board members congenial and conscientious, and she was pleased that she could make some contribution to the board's deliberations.

It so happened, however, that the last eighteen months of her term turned out to be the most demanding. The board faced a daunting crisis in November 1953, with the sudden death of J. Hillis Miller, the president of the University of Florida. Of all the heads of the institutions under the board's purview, Miller had been by far the most capable and influential. Mrs. duPont had always been partial to Miller because he was a native Virginian, but she also appreciated the broad experience he had gained in the field of education before coming to Florida in 1947. During his six years as university president, Miller had earned a national and international reputation as an educator. It was a man of this stature that Mrs. duPont and some other members of the board wanted in the next president. She was determined to find a respected leader, a man of integrity, an experienced administrator, and, off-the-record, one who was "sound" on the question of racial segregation.

In the search for the new president, Mrs. duPont took a much more active role in the work of the board than she had in earlier years. She attended most of the board's meetings in the spring of 1954 and hosted a luncheon and daylong meeting at Epping Forest on April 28. Through her scholarship program, she had many contacts in the field of education, and she used these to find likely candidates, several of whom she proposed to the board. Some members of the board were enthusiastic about Milton S. Eisenhower, the brother of the president and head of Pennsylvania State College, but Mrs. duPont considered him far too liberal. Finally, on June 17 the board agreed to recommend Philip Grant Davidson, president of the University of Louisville.[29]

Because the board had taken pains to consult an advisory committee representing the university faculties and several state organizations, there was some reason to believe that approval of Davidson's appointment by the state board of education and the governor would be only a formality, but this was not to be. Three months before Miller's death Governor Dan McCarty himself had died, leaving Charley E. Johns, president of the state senate, as acting governor. Johns had represented Starke, a rural town in North Florida, in the senate for eighteen years and was known as a "porkchopper," an unsophisticated conservative who cast a jaundiced eye on educated liberals with their fancy ideas. Johns was especially suspicious of left-wing New Dealers who seemed to have an affinity for blacks and communists. Vague reports that Davidson had such leanings led the acting governor to reject the board's nomination. As it turned out, this was just the beginning of Johns's notorious career as a red-baiter that earned him the epithet "the Joe McCarthy of Florida."[30]

Johns's action threw the board of control into turmoil; there was nothing left to do but start the search process from the beginning. Determined to select the best man available in a nationwide search, Mrs. duPont began to collect the names of prominent educators. By December 1954 the board had a total of thirty-two names, which it soon reduced to twelve. The final choice, however, proved more difficult. Mrs. duPont joined other members of the board in supporting Richard A. Harvill, president of the University of Arizona, who met her requirement for a man with a national reputation, but when the board could not meet Harvill's salary request, consensus within the board collapsed. Forgetting the lofty criteria agreed upon at the beginning of the search process a year earlier, the board broke into three factions, each supporting a different member of the University of Florida faculty. Mrs. duPont joined two other members of the board in insisting on a man who seemed to the majority clearly unsuited for the position. Only the intervention of LeRoy Collins, the new governor, broke the deadlock, and the board on March 17 voted unanimously to nominate J. Wayne Reitz, a professor of agricultural economics and provost for agriculture at the university.[31]

When Governor Collins called Mrs. duPont in July 1955 to inquire about her interest in a second term, she mentioned her disappointment that politics had been allowed to interfere with the work of the board, notably in the Charley Johns affair. The governor was careful to offer her a second term without urging her to accept, and he was no doubt relieved when she confirmed his assumption that she would not accept.[32] She had been in part responsible for the dissension within the board that had nearly resulted in a disastrous appointment. Collins may also have thought it wise to distance himself from Ed Ball and his nasty machinations.

During the late 1950s Mrs. duPont's gifts to educational institutions followed the pattern established in earlier years. Hollins, Washington and

Lee, and the University of the South continued to receive large year-end gifts in the form of securities. In 1959 each institution accepted more than $150,000 in this form. Three others, Stetson, Rollins, and Sweet Briar, were recipients of securities in lesser amounts.

Cash contributions to educational institutions usually fell into one of two categories: scholarships and special fund drives. Cash gifts to a college varied from year to year as the number of scholarship students changed. More than thirty institutions received cash gifts of $1,000 or more from 1957 through 1960, but the number declined sharply thereafter. The total annual amount of cash gifts likewise declined from $379,000 in 1958 to $53,000 in 1961.[33]

Whatever type of contribution Mrs. duPont made to educational institutions, she usually requested that the funds be used for scholarships or faculty salaries. She was reluctant to support building funds because she believed it was relatively easy to raise money for that purpose. In her later years, however, she relented in a few special cases and allowed her gifts to be used for buildings. One of her first exceptions was the new gymnasium at Sewanee, to be dedicated to Bishop Juhan, who in his college days had been an all-American in football. In 1955 Mrs. duPont promised the board of trustees that she would contribute, if necessary, as much as $400,000 of the $500,000 needed to complete the building. "[N]or is it my wish that there should be any impediment to hinder the completion of the gymnasium by the opening of the University in September, 1956."[34] The building was not completed until the spring of 1957, but Mrs. duPont made a special trip to Sewanee to attend the dedication ceremonies.

For quite a different reason she decided to provide funds for the new chapel at Hollins College. She had made a small contribution toward that purpose in 1952, but when her friend John Everett failed to find a major donor, he came back to Mrs. duPont. She was not averse to giving two or three hundred thousand dollars to supplement the funds already raised, but first she warned Everett "that the Chapel will have to look like a church building." She wanted none of "these modernistic monstrosities" that she found so offensive "that they might be productive of criminal ideas to ones who are criminally inclined." Everett was quick to reassure her that Hollins wanted a traditional design, and on this condition Mrs. duPont agreed to fund the chapel. The Jessie Ball duPont Chapel was dedicated on February 22, 1959.[35]

Of all the buildings a college might wish to construct, a library was closest to Mrs. duPont's heart. Libraries were for scholarship and learning, and she considered them the center of intellectual life in a college or university. In 1959 she made a commitment to President Ollie Edmunds at Stetson University to give $100,000 for a new library, and even took the risk of making a similar pledge for her brother. Ed was hardly enthusiastic about the idea, but he agreed to honor her commitment only because of her interest. "Personally," he wrote his sister, "I think we have passed the stage where independent universities or anybody else can save us. I think we are going to have to go on this present socialistic spending spree until the Government collapses and we start back around the cycle of change."[36] Jessie did not share her brother's view and honored her commitment to Stetson. The new libraries at Stetson and the University of the South were among the very few exceptions to her insistence that buildings not be named for her.[37]

Mrs. duPont's monetary gifts and her personal interest in education gave her considerable influence at critical times in the three institutions that received her largest contributions. When Frank Gaines decided in November 1958 to retire as president of Washington and Lee, she readily agreed to serve on the search committee for Gaines's replacement and promptly recommended three men for the position. Before the search was completed, she had agreed to serve as the first woman on the university's board of trustees. In May 1960 she was in Lexington for the inauguration of Fred C. Cole as the new president.[38]

Earlier that year Mrs. duPont was disappointed to learn that John Everett had resigned as president of Hollins to become chancellor of the City University of New York. In February she had discussed the situation at a meeting of the board of trustees without suggesting any candidates. Recurring trouble with a twisted knee prevented her from attending board meetings during much of the year, but by correspondence she took an active role in selecting John A. Logan, a young history professor from Yale, as the new president. A resumé prepared for the board noted that Logan "is the type of person Mrs. duPont would approve of. About integration he recognized the problems in Virginia, and the integration of schools is entirely foreign to his way of thinking. . . . Dr. Logan is a cultured gentleman and is fine looking."[39] Mrs. duPont could hardly expect a finer recommendation.

Almost as burdensome as the educational program for Mrs. duPont and Miss Shaw was the management of charitable giving. In reviewing the hundreds of requests received each year from charitable institutions, Miss Shaw could respond to letters from those already on the gift list; new and unusual appeals she referred to Mrs. duPont. During the late 1950s changes in the list of charitable institutions from year to year suggest that Mrs. duPont and Miss Shaw were still scrutinizing the applicants to see that the gifts continued to reflect current needs. In 1958 and 1959, for example, the total number of tax-deductible gifts of one thousand dollars or more to charitable institutions was about eighty in each year. Of these, the number of new gifts was close to thirty and the number of institutions dropped from the previous year was almost the same. Of the twenty-six gifts in 1958 that were dropped in 1959, twenty were one-time special contributions. Thirty-nine of the seventy institutions on the 1957 list were still receiving annual support in 1966.

The dollar amounts suggest that any donation under one thousand dollars was for Mrs. duPont a token gift representing the fulfillment of an obligation rather than an attempt to make a significant impact on the institution. The number of small and large gifts was about the same, but the dollar total of the large gifts far exceeded that of the small contributions. About twenty of the large gifts each year were one-time donations for special fund drives.

The names of many of the individuals and institutions receiving relatively small gifts appeared on Mrs. duPont's lists year after year. The Ladies' Aid Society of White Chapel Church received at least five thousand dollars every year to provide the funds that Eoline Jesse distributed to the needy in the Northern Neck. The two technical schools for black students in Mississippi had not been overlooked since the 1920s and were now receiving five hundred dollars a year. Children's hospitals, homes for the aged, and church charities in Wilmington, Jacksonville, and Richmond could count on annual gifts of several thousand dollars. Also on the annual lists were local churches of several denominations, mostly in the same three cities. Dozens of routine charities received fifty or one hundred dollars. Several Episcopal bishops and Maurice Sheehy, a Roman Catholic priest and old friend, received generous contributions for their discretionary funds.[40]

Over a period of nine years beginning in 1957, the following institutions received the largest totals in tax-deductible cash gifts:

Institution	*Total*
A. I. duPont Foundation	$343,375
A. I. duPont Institute	289,875
A. I. duPont Awards Foundation	242,375
Bishop Juhan, discretionary fund	231,000
R. E. Lee Memorial Foundation	227,380
Salvation Army	160,000
Christ Church, Greenville, Del.	146,000
YMCA, Jacksonville	141,000
W. C. Munds, discretionary fund	131,000
City of St. Augustine restoration	115,000
Home for Needy Confederate Women	113,000
Catholic Charities, Jacksonville	102,000

That the largest contributions went to the two foundations and the institute named for Mrs. duPont's husband demonstrated her continuing dedication to these charities even when her personal participation in their operation was declining (see table 9–4 for major cash gifts in 1957 and 1958).

All these charitable donations, however, covered only tax–deductible contributions in cash. In addition to the $625,000 in cash gifts in 1957, Mrs. duPont gave almost $200,000 in corporate securities to the Alfred I.

TABLE 9–4 Charitable Cash Contributions over $20,000, 1957–58 (in dollars)

Institution	1957	1958
Alfred I. duPont Foundation	54,500	50,000
Delaware Academy of Medicine	100,000	
William C. Munds, discretionary fund	15,000	48,000
St. Luke's Church, Smithfield, Va.	50,000	
United Fund, Jacksonville	22,000	26,000
Frank A. Juhan, discretionary fund		41,200
Christ Church, Greenville	27,000	7,000
Alfred I. duPont Institute		31,500
Opportunity Center, Inc.	6,000	25,000
Christian Herald Association		29,000
Virginia 350th anniversary	22,010	
All gifts over $1,000	537,984	551,840
All gifts under $1,000	87,746	37,953
Total charitable cash gifts	625,730	589,793

duPont Foundation. As in the past, the foundation dispensed small monthly checks and emergency funds to scores of needy individuals, mostly in Florida but some in Delaware. Thus Mrs. duPont's deductible contributions for charity in 1957 totaled more than $823,000. There were also more than $320,000 in nondeductible gifts, most of which probably went to members of the family and others who may already have been receiving monthly checks from the first and second general trusts. Included in this category were a hundred Christmas gifts ranging from $50 to $2,000.[41]

Although Mrs. duPont accepted the fact that advancing age would force her to reduce her involvement in many of her projects, she knew it was important to maintain her official connection with them. Her formal presence alone was important to the organizations, and her continuing affiliation made it possible for her to intervene if necessary. Now that management of the Alfred I. duPont Awards Foundation had been turned over to Washington and Lee University, she restricted her role to endorsing the annual selections and making the trip north each winter to attend the award ceremony. She continued to serve as an officer and member of several committees in both the Association of Bank Women and the Robert E. Lee Memorial Foundation, but she gave them little of her personal attention. After a terminal illness struck her dear friend Helen Knox in May 1957, Mrs. duPont's involvement in both organizations soon began to wane. She resigned as assistant treasurer of the Lee foundation in September 1958 and limited her participation to brief visits to Stratford during the annual October meetings.[42]

So many of her responsibilities were tied so closely to personal friends and congenial social occasions that Mrs. duPont found it no insuperable burden to continue them. The spring and fall meetings of the boards of trustees at Hollins and Washington and Lee gave her an opportunity to spend a few days with the Gaineses and Everetts. Apparently the two presidents arranged their schedules so that Mrs. duPont could attend both meetings on a single trip. From Lexington she often went to Richmond for the board meeting at the Virginia Museum of Fine Arts. Her interest in art had grown steadily since her trips to Europe with Alfred early in their marriage to purchase paintings and sculpture for Nemours, and her considerable knowledge of the art world gave her membership on the board something more than financial importance. An added attraction at the museum was her admiration for Leslie Cheek, the director, and her affection for his wife, Mary Tyler Cheek, the daughter of historian Douglas Southall Freeman and one of the new generation of Stratties. In 1957 Mrs. duPont began extending her spring round of meetings by going to the Homestead at Hot Springs, Virginia, for the annual meeting of the Virginia Foundation for Independent Colleges. In later years, she invited the Gaineses, Juhans, Everetts, and members of her family to be her guests at the Homestead for a week.[43]

After 1955 Mrs. duPont gave less attention to the routine business affairs of the St. Joe Paper Company and the Florida National Banks, but she was always ready to make her presence felt at critical moments. After Henry Adair died in the spring of 1956, she had come to rely on Frederick H. Kent and other attorneys retained to protect the company's interests in Florida. She spent several days in June 1956 attending the Interstate Commerce Commission hearings on the Florida East Coast Railway case. She found the all-day hearings "tiresome" but very interesting.[44] The case was to drag on for two more years, until the spring of 1958, when the commission's examiner rejected the petition of the Atlantic Coast Line Railroad to take over the Florida East Coast line. Mrs. duPont was pleased when W. Thomas Rice, the new president of the Atlantic Coast Line, decided not to file exceptions to the examiner's report. Rice, who had been one of Mrs. duPont's first scholarship students, wrote his benefactor that "continued litigation . . . was certainly not in the interests of either the people living on the east coast of Florida or the railroads involved."[45] Ed Ball had won his thirteen-year battle for the railroad.

Mrs. duPont was also pleased that Rice had agreed to serve on the board of directors of the Florida National Bank. She thought his business experience and ability would be a great asset and, incidentally, might be a moderating influence on her pugnacious brother, who was still waging his thirty-year legal battle against his old adversary, Roy E. Crummer.[46]

Now that Mrs. duPont was cutting back on her office work and personal participation in charitable organizations, she had less opportunity to perceive new needs and to discover additional institutions worthy of support. For new ideas she came to rely more and more on her associates. In December 1957 William Mills submitted a list of Jacksonville organizations deserving support. The list included four Jacksonville hospitals, the Visiting Nurses Association, the Society of Former Special

Agents of the F.B.I., the Jacksonville Symphony Association, and the Boys Service Council. All of these appeared on the charitable list for at least the next five years. Alfred Shands frequently recommended children's hospitals and other charities for Mrs. duPont's support. In November 1958 on Shands's advice she gave $25,000 to the building fund of Opportunity Center, Incorporated, a workshop for handicapped persons in Wilmington. This was a one-time donation, but in 1964 the center began receiving an annual gift of $10,000, probably on Shands's recommendation.[47]

In providing funds for the Alfred I. duPont Foundation, Mrs. duPont had gradually learned to follow William Mills's advice to leave day-to-day decisions to the foundation staff in Jacksonville in order to steer clear of problems with the Internal Revenue Service. As president of the foundation, Henry Dew took charge of investigating appeals for help in Jacksonville, and Mary Shaw, as treasurer, kept close tabs on finances. Miss Shaw, in her usual officious manner, did not hesitate to question Dew's recommendations or to prod him to invest some of the foundation's funds when disbursements fell behind receipts from Mrs. duPont's accounts.[48]

Most of Mrs. duPont's contributions to educational and charitable institutions could be considered simple charity or altruistic philanthropy. That is, they were designed to alleviate human need or were part of a systematic plan that would bring benefits to society in general. Gifts to hospitals and churches could be seen as improving the quality of life, but they did not support specific social or economic policies. Scholarships likewise could be expected to produce good citizens who would be an economic asset to the community, but these gifts carried no social agenda.

As we have seen, however, in earlier chapters, Mrs. duPont did deploy her philanthropic resources to support institutions that she believed espoused her moral and social values. In the 1950s there were new examples of such tactics, and, as in earlier years, they were often attempts to prevent racial integration in the schools. A case in point was All Saints' Junior College in Vicksburg, Mississippi. Bishop Juhan had urged support of the junior college as a model of an independent institution providing a Christian education with a firm policy of racial segregation. Mrs. duPont had been giving the school modest support for some years but, on the bishop's recommendation, had increased her gift in 1956 when the Reverend John M. Allin, whom the bishop considered an able administrator, took over the college.[49]

Mrs. duPont's generosity toward institutions of the Episcopal church stemmed in large part from her confidence in Bishop Juhan and her personal affection for the bishop and his wife. After attending the general convention of the church in Boston in 1952 as a guest of the Juhans, Jessie wrote to Tom that they were "one of the world's loveliest couples and it is always a joy to be with them. The Bishop and I have much in common and many traits that are very much alike."[50]

After Bishop McKinstry retired in January 1955, Mrs. duPont's view of the church was almost entirely through Bishop Juhan's eyes. He not only helped her in working out stock portfolios for gifts to Episcopal institutions but also drafted letters on national church affairs for her signature. In July 1954 he had drafted a letter to the presiding bishop protesting the decision to move the general convention that year to Honolulu because blacks were not admitted to hotels in New Orleans, which had been selected earlier.[51]

The protest, however, did not prevent the three friends from attending the convention in Honolulu that summer. Mrs. duPont enjoyed the convention, but she did not appreciate the decision to hold the next convention in Miami Beach. How could the church, she wondered, seek funds when it held consecutive conventions in two of the most expensive resort cities in the nation? The selection of Miami Beach was, she thought, a gesture to the South after the "insult" at New Orleans, but she did not accept the decision as such. In a letter to Francis B. Sayre, Jr., dean of Washington Cathedral, she noted that not only blacks but also Jews were excluded from many hotels in Miami Beach. "No Southerner," she wrote, "would take Miami Beach as a Southern city."[52] Having expressed herself on the race question in the church, she went on to inform the dean that she was contributing $10,000 for completion of the Woodrow Wilson memorial in the cathedral. For Mrs. duPont, Dean Sayre was hardly an ordinary clergyman. As the grandson of Woodrow Wilson, the last "genuine" Democrat to occupy the White House (and a southerner), the dean and Wilson's widow were favored friends of Mrs. duPont.

Mrs. duPont had long held the conviction that gifts to tax-supported institutions would simply encourage state and local governments to divert school funds to other purposes. She also believed that independent colleges were more likely to meet the personal needs of students and to foster the ethical and religious values essential in a Christian society. Most important of all, however, was the freedom of the independent college from federal control, specifically from racial integration decreed by federal courts. As she wrote to the president of Davidson College: "Our private individual colleges for the white race must be supported; if we are going to have leaders and maintain a cultural, Christian society. I have endeavored to use my funds for this purpose. . . . I make no contribution to a white school in the South that accepts negroes. As yet the private school is out of the jurisdiction of the Supreme Court Order. By this statement I do not wish you to think that I make no contributions to negro schools, as I give to many of them."[53]

Mrs. duPont did not hesitate to ask college presidents to state their policy on integration and to inform her if the student body was multiracial. Unfavorable replies usually meant termination of scholarship funds. Mrs. duPont never revealed the reason for her action but simply informed the college that all her scholarship funds had been allocated.[54]

The racial implications of the U.S. Supreme Court's decision in the Girard case were not lost on Mrs. duPont. Stephen Girard, a Philadelphia financier and philanthropist, had several times used his personal fortune in the early days of the Republic to rescue the federal government from financial disaster. When he died in 1831, he left his estate to the city of Philadelphia to be used in founding a "college" for "poor white male orphans between the ages of six and ten years." Under state law the board of city trusts in Philadelphia operated the college. In 1954 the board refused to admit two applicants solely on the grounds that they were black. The Pennsylvania Supreme Court upheld the board's decision, but in May 1957 the U.S. Supreme Court found that the college, as an agency of the State of Pennsylvania, was subject to the court's decision in *Brown* v. *Board of Education* and could not deny admission of the students on the basis of race.[55]

The decision aggravated Mrs. duPont for several reasons. Most obvious, it would force integration of the school; but even worse, it enabled the federal courts to dictate the admission policy of what she considered essentially a private institution. She had staked her support of independent colleges on her hopes that they would prove a safe refuge from federal control. Now it seemed that this last refuge had been denied.

The Girard case was also troubling because it showed that the state could ride roughshod over the intent of an individual making a bequest for philanthropic purposes. Did the Girard decision portend a day when the courts could set aside the provisions of her husband's will or, closer to home, thwart the carefully laid plans set forth in her own? To her way of thinking, the decision was a blatant assault on private property, another step in the direction of what she called "communism." She was somewhat relieved when the city transferred control of the college to private trustees to escape the court's ruling. On a second appeal the Supreme Court dismissed the case, thus preventing the admission of black students, at least temporarily. For Mrs. duPont, however, the decision was an uncertain victory. Her experience in the Florida East Coast Railway and Crummer cases had taught her how transitory a court decision could be. She never quite recovered from the shock of the Supreme Court's initial decision in the Girard case.[56]

In the 1950s the varied patterns in Mrs. duPont's giving coalesced in a course of philanthropy. The sheer weight of the scholarship program forced her to adopt systematic procedures for handling applications. The need to reduce net income in order to avoid excessive federal taxes encouraged large annual cash gifts to favored colleges and universities rather than many small donations for individual students or specific projects. A similar trend was evident in charitable giving: larger grants to a smaller number of institutions and a sharp decline in the amounts given to family and friends.

Advancing age was also a factor in the shift toward philanthropy. Now in her seventies, Mrs. duPont was no longer able to give personal attention to the hundreds of appeals that came to her office each year. More and more she left these decisions to Miss Shaw or passed them on in the form of large gifts to institutions. The general trusts and the new will that she signed in December 1955 were logical extensions of the new reliance on philanthropy. These instruments established the ground rules for continuing Mrs. duPont's philanthropies after her death.

Philanthropy, however, was more a matter of last resort than a positive choice for Mrs. duPont. She never lost the deep sense of compassion that she had for individuals in need and she preferred to see her gifts bring about practical, visible results rather than disappear in an amorphous sea of institutional funding. For a woman brought up in the traditions of the Old South, people and her relationships with them were more important than abstract policies.

Only on the issues of racial integration and the role of the federal government in educational policy did Mrs. duPont attempt to exercise any hegemony through her philanthropy. She was for a time able to exclude colleges and universities with multiracial student bodies or faculties from her scholarships, but legal considerations prevented her from including such provisions in the general trusts or in her will. Her outrage over the Girard case reflected the frustration that she felt as she saw federal law and the decisions of federal courts threaten the traditional exclusionary policies of private institutions. Neither her strong will nor the millions of dollars at her disposal could stem, or even temporarily divert, the tide of change that would sweep over the South in the 1960s. In her declining years her world would shrink to the grounds of Nemours, delimited by Alfred's great walls. There she would devote the last full measure of her energy to maintaining the practice of philanthropy that had become her reason for being.

10

The Last Full Measure

*T*he passing years inevitably brought changes not only in Mrs. duPont's life but also in the lives of those closest to her. When her brother Ed suffered a severe heart attack in July 1957, she rushed to his side in Jacksonville and never left the hospital until he was out of danger. She wrote Tom: "I have been staying at the hospital at nights [*sic*]. . . . This has made it less strenuous for me, realizing I was right in reach, on a moment's notice, just across the hall from Ed. We try to keep all business from him. He is perfectly good natured and happy. The Doctor lets him have three ounces of bourbon a day."[1]

No sooner had she returned to Wilmington than she began sending Ed flowers and followed with a nostalgic letter designed to cement old relationships:

> Never in my life have I hated to say good-bye to anyone as I did to you. It is hard to part with a pal,—the best pal in the world. You know we were pals from very young children. I remember the last fight we had with Tom,—the day that Mr. Sam Luttrell was buried. It was over the croquet when Tom wanted to croquet a ball for Belle and I objected. As the croquet set was mine, I pulled up the wickets quickly and you sat on the box while I did something to the mallets. We were little tykers [*sic*] then and have been good friends and pals since, therefore, I cannot afford for anything to happen to you being the only pal I have left.[2]

Probably both Jessie and Ed knew in their hearts that the sentiments expressed in the letter were strained. If they had been "pals" before the turn of the century, their relationship had hardly been that close for at least two decades. This sort of hyperbole, however, was characteristic of Jessie's letters when she wanted to express sympathy, and probably few of the recipients, including Ed, saw anything disingenuous in the sentiment behind the exaggeration.

Ed recovered more rapidly than anyone expected, and Jessie was off to Europe in late August with the Shandses for eight weeks of leisurely touring and an orthopedic conference in Spain. The two siblings drifted apart once again as Jessie immersed herself in her philanthropies and Ed, now half-retired, spent more of his time at his Southwood estate or at the baronial castle he had purchased with some of his friends in Ballynahinch, Ireland. Although Jessie found traveling ever more taxing, it did have the advantage of removing her from the responsibilities and loneliness she faced at home. The permanent move of the Juhans to Sewanee left a void in her life at Epping Forest, and the growing burden of keeping up Nemours seemed to overshadow what little pleasure she derived from living there.[3]

As her family and friends aged, the occasions for parties and weekend guests became less frequent. For Jessie's sisters Nemours aroused a sense of resentment more than pleasure. Jessie, out of her devotion to Alfred, had maintained the house almost exactly as he had left it in 1935. Thus for Elsie and Belle, Nemours was still very much Alfred's home, and thoughts of him took them back to their girlhood on the Northern Neck, where Alfred had treated all of them with avuncular impartiality. Although Jessie had been thoughtful as well as generous with an endless flow of gifts to her sisters, she would never have considered lavishing a third of her fortune on each of them. Both Jessie and Ed would have considered that a violation of Alfred's trust in them, but Elsie and, especially, Belle considered that protestation a transparent excuse devised by Ed and Jessie for amassing a fortune for themselves.[4]

The Christmas holidays were especially lonely for Jessie, now that Denise's family and others in that generation had busy lives of their own. For the second generation it must have been increasingly difficult to identify with the imposing mansion that seemed more like a museum than a home. Had Jessie not been able to persuade Tom to come for Christmas in 1958, she would have been alone at Nemours, and even then he left in a few days so that she had no guests in the house on New Year's Eve. She tried to call Ed on the phone, but could not get through. "No word has come from you this Christmas," she wrote, "and no word has gone to you either."[5]

Jessie was relieved to see that Tom had lost weight and seemed in good health for his age, but she still worried about him. She feared that both she and her older brother drove themselves too hard, and she worried that Tom did not take care of himself. Fortunately she could rely on Tom's longtime personal secretary to keep her informed on his condition. When Tom suffered a heart attack in August 1959, she asked Shands to have two specialists review the medical report, and they confirmed that the attack, while not immediately threatening, had caused severe damage. Despite these warnings, Tom insisted on coming east that fall, and was stricken again in Kansas City. Jessie arranged for specialists to attend her brother in Kansas City and eventually had him transferred to a Wilmington hospital and then to Nemours for a month's convalescence. Jessie doted over him and reluctantly let him return to Los Angeles, where he died in May 1960.[6]

A month later Jessie went to Ditchley for the first time in years for the interment in the family plot on the bay just east of the site of Cressfield, the old family home. Tom's death was the greatest personal blow she had suffered since Alfred's death twenty-five years earlier. She was also deeply distressed that Ed had refused to come home from his vacation in Ireland to attend the funeral. Those who were close to her thought some bit of sparkle went out of her with Tom's death.[7]

The loss, however, did seem eventually to bring her closer to Ed, who in the years ahead became more solicitous and even comforting. In July he wrote his sister an unusually long letter in which he congratulated her on catching a "big striper" on a fishing trip with the Juhans and Shandses in Maine. He also urged her to consider giving up the ever heavier burden of maintaining Nemours as a home. "[I]t would be a grand idea," he suggested, "for you to turn it over to the Foundation at this time so that in the next few years you can get it organized as a museum, just the way you want it." It was probably sound advice, but nothing Jessie was prepared to take seriously.[8]

No doubt, like many older people, Jessie would have found it difficult to give up a way of life and the familiar surroundings that she had enjoyed for almost four decades, but she was also concerned that the mansion house would not be adequately maintained in her absence. She had done

her best to refurbish the interior, but she could not cope with repairs on
the outside or in the gardens. A year earlier, in July 1959, she had written
Ed an unusually strong letter in which she complained that the trustees of
Alfred's estate were not keeping up with necessary repairs. The tiles
needed to be replaced on the third-floor terrace, there were several
cracked and loose stones in the carillon tower, and the ceiling in the
Temple of Love at the end of the garden needed repair. She reminded her
brother: "As you know, that Estate was what Mr. duPont dwelt upon
especially. He built it as a memorial to his parents and to Pierre Samuel
duPont,—I don't talk [about] this very much, as there is no use.
However, we must keep the place up. That is a charge made upon the
Trustees in his Will."9

As the horizons of her interests gradually shrank, Mrs. duPont concentrated much of her remaining energies on the children's hospital just a few
hundred yards from the mansion house. She supported Shands's proposal
to enlarge the institute building to provide more classrooms so that the
research department could expand on the second floor. As she had on
other construction projects, she personally consulted with the architects
and engineers on design details and recommended changes to provide
adequate facilities at reasonable cost.10

Now that Hardin Goodman had retired as vice-president of the bank,
she retained him to help her on legal matters at the institute. Goodman
may well have had a hand in drafting what were to become almost annual
memorandums from Mrs. duPont setting forth her expectations for the
future program of the institute. In the 1959 memorandum she endorsed
the relationship between child care and research that the institute had
followed since 1946. "It is my hope that the Institute should always be
known primarily for its work with the child. I am, and have always been,
interested in research, but do not desire the Institute to ever become what
some might call a 'research institution'."11

This longstanding preference may have been the source of her decision
the following year to add a codicil to her will eliminating the word
scientific from the description of eligible institutions.12

In the 1959 planning document Mrs. duPont advocated continued
support of the state conferences that made possible cooperation between
state and private agencies in providing medical care for children. As more
funds became available, she hoped they would be used in those states where

the need was greatest, with the highest priorities going to Delaware, Florida, and Virginia in that order. Funds were not to be used in competition with other institutions and only for direct care of specific children.

With the help of Goodman and Shands, Mrs. duPont could feel that she was keeping abreast of affairs at the institute, but by late 1960 she worried that she had lost touch with Ed, Alfred's estate, and Jacksonville activities in general. She had hoped that her brother might come to Nemours for Christmas so that they could have a relaxed conversation, but once again he had disappointed her. She reminded Ed that she found it difficult to discuss serious matters on the telephone. "I think that you, Elbert [Dent] and I should sit down calmly together and talk things over and make some decisions."[13]

Some of the anxiety in this letter must have stemmed from her realization that she was slowly losing her grip on events. She seemed extremely tense and tired that winter. Before she embarked on a Caribbean cruise with her sisters, she told Dr. Shands that she thought they were taking her to a sanitarium. Shands was concerned about her lapses in memory and occasional confusion. Early in February 1961 she complained for the first time of a heart condition. Shands wrote to Mrs. duPont's physician in Jacksonville that her physical condition on the whole was quite good, but he urged the Florida doctor to see her as soon as she arrived at Epping Forest.[14]

When Ed failed to take any action on her request for regular meetings, Jessie finally lost her patience and fired off a letter in March 1961: "As I have told you recently, I am gravely worried about the situation of our organization. The matter is one of increasing concern, and I sometimes feel I cannot longer put up with the strain of it. I need your understanding and help."[15]

Perhaps reflecting her recent trouble with memory lapses, she complained that she found it difficult to discuss matters "across the table"; rather she preferred to have issues in writing so that she could reflect upon them. She then proceeded to set forth her views on several issues. She had found a younger man to take charge of the St. Joe Paper Company, and she wanted the board of directors to give him enough authority to make the position attractive. She wanted the board to revoke the decision made at a recent meeting at Nemours requiring senior officers to leave the board of directors when they reached retirement age.

She had not had time at that meeting to think through the issue, and she asked Ed to submit his views on these matters in writing so that she could study them.

Fully aware that her own physical and mental stamina was waning, she also realized that Miss Shaw was no longer able to maintain the pace of earlier years. On several occasions she had deftly suggested the need for adding a younger person to the Wilmington staff to relieve Miss Shaw of the heavy burdens she was carrying. She could have guessed, however, that the proud and devoted woman, who felt it necessary to apologize even for a single day of illness, would never consent to having an assistant.[16]

In March Mrs. duPont informed Miss Shaw that she would have to revise the scholarship program before another year passed. No doubt the memory lapses that Shands detected that summer made it difficult for Mrs. duPont to face the issue, but early in 1961 she asked Miss Shaw to draft a letter informing the colleges and universities that she would no longer designate scholarships for individuals but would instead let the institution decide how her contributions were to be used for this purpose. "I find that it is impossible for my office and me to do all of the detail work and write all of the letters that must be written to ascertain whether students are really worthy or not."[17]

In the future she intended to concentrate scholarship funds on institutions in Virginia, Florida, and Delaware, as well as the University of the South. Each college would receive "a stipulated amount with a request that the colleges disburse these funds to worthy students, who are of college material." The academic standards she had already established were still to hold. In the first year, the student was "to put forth his best effort." In the second year students were to have no grades below "C" and none below "B" thereafter. Any student who married would lose the scholarship, and all scholarships were to be limited to "students of the white race." She hoped that former students would repay their scholarships by helping other needy students to attend college.[18]

The response of the colleges and universities to the new plan was favorable, but under the strained circumstances of that summer, it was impossible for the two women to put the new system into effect before the end of the year. As a result, the total of cash contributions of one thousand dollars or more fell from $327,000 in 1960 to $53,000 in 1961, while the number of institutions receiving large sums dropped from thirty-eight to nine. Gifts of securities in 1961 were limited to the handful of favored institutions and the total sum dropped by more than a third.[19]

The decline in philanthropic activities in the early 1960s affected charitable as well as educational institutions. The number of large donations fell gradually between 1958 and 1962 while the number of new institutions added to the list dropped even more sharply during each of the same years (table 10-1). Most of the drop in the dollar total could be attributed to a sharp reduction in the number of small gifts, presumably because it was almost impossible to process the volume of correspondence that the work generated.

The pattern of giving for large donations supports the impression gained from Mrs. duPont's correspondence that, except for a few special gifts, she and Miss Shaw were no longer monitoring charitable contributions closely but rather tended to carry over the same list from year to year. December cash reports and other documents show that most of the contributions were made with checks written during the last few days of the year. Obviously in this situation there was little time to consider the merits of each recipient.[20]

When Mrs. duPont came north in the spring of 1961, it must have been apparent to Miss Shaw and Kennard Adams that she had slowed down considerably. She did her best to disguise the change by coming up with excuses for declining invitations. She explained her decision not to attend her granddaughter Denise's wedding by saying that she could not hope to make the usual round of trustees' meetings and graduation exercises at the Virginia colleges and so had declined them all. Her sister Elsie had asked her to consider a trip to Europe, but Jessie confided to Belle that she did not have the strength even to make preparations. "What is more I have no

TABLE 10-1 Summary of Tax-Deductible Cash Gifts, 1958–61 ($1,000 or more)

Year	Total amount ($)	Total number	New	Dropped	Resumed[a]
1958	556,840	81	37	26	0
1959	497,445	79	21	26	3
1960	285,300	67	13	30	5
1961	253,800	63	4	12	4

a. Denotes number of institutions dropped in earlier years but returning to the list this year.

clothes. I haven't bought anything for a couple of years, and I haven't the energy to do it. That is not my style, generally speaking. I am not sick,—I haven't a pain or an ache but I reckon the engine just needs priming."[21]

It was also evident that Mrs. duPont would no longer be able to make quick business trips to Jacksonville. To honor her March request, Ed arranged to hold business meetings in the mansion house at Nemours. The procedure was to have a one-day session that would include formal meetings of the trustees of the Alfred I. duPont estate and the executive committee of the paper company. According to Miss Shaw's formal minutes, Mrs. duPont presided at the meetings held in July and October.[22]

Mrs. duPont, however, was far from being in good health. "[A] slight but painful back injury" had prevented her from attending a meeting of the Hollins board early in October. By December she was feeling better and, despite Miss Shaw's misgivings, took the train to Jacksonville on December 13, 1961, for a trustees' meeting just before Christmas. Old-time employees at the bank noted how slowly she walked from her limousine to the elevator, but she found the meeting stimulating and admired the offices on the eighth floor of the new Florida National Bank building, which bore unmistakable signs of her brother's simple, if not parsimonious, tastes in architecture.[23]

Within weeks she was scolding Ed again for making decisions without taking them to the trustees.

> There is no reason why you, Elbert, and I can't meet once in six weeks or two months, if we are in the western hemisphere, and talk some of these things over. . . . Please don't think that I am being pig-headed about all of this or trying to dictate to anyone. I want to see you sometime is one of the main things. It used to be, and we had right much business in those days, that you, A. I. and I would sit down and talk for an hour or two hours, not all the time on business, sometimes there were some good jokes. I haven't heard a good joke for a century.[24]

Ed responded by calling a meeting of the trustees of the estate and the executive committee of the paper company at Nemours on February 3, 1962. Jessie welcomed the opportunity to discuss business matters, but she was even more pleased to have Ed visit with her for a few days. She was planning a trip to New York the following week to begin a Caribbean cruise with her sister Elsie and Miss Shaw. A relaxing cruise in a warm climate might relieve some of the tension and fatigue that were plaguing her. After her return, she expected to spend most of her time at Epping Forest.[25]

In fact, Mrs. duPont never went to Florida again. On February 10 she fell in her room at Nemours and fractured the femur in her right leg. After two weeks in the hospital, she returned to Nemours, where she spent the rest of the winter in her suite on the second floor with three nurses around the clock. During these weeks her sisters took turns staying with her, but Mrs. duPont asked them and Miss Shaw not to tell others about her accident. In fact, she never mentioned the fracture at all in her conversations. Miss Shaw honored this wish by turning aside inquiries and explaining Mrs. duPont's true condition only when necessary.[26]

By April 1962 Mrs. duPont was well enough to inspect the gardens at Nemours from a wheelchair and by July she was able to walk without crutches. The long convalescence seemed over as she made plans to spend several weeks at the Greenbrier with the Bakers, the Shandses, and Miss Shaw. The weather at White Sulphur Springs was delightful, and she seemed to regain some of her old spirit and energy. In September she chaired a trustees' meeting at Nemours, but Miss Shaw was concerned that her "patient" no longer walked more than a few steps and seldom went for a ride in the car.[27]

Despite her lack of mobility, Mrs. duPont had never given up the idea of returning to Epping Forest, at least for the winter season if not year around. When she found in January 1963 that she would not be able to move her household south that winter, she asked her physician in Jacksonville to investigate the possibility of installing an elevator in the house at Epping Forest so that she could have access to her bedroom suite at the south end of the second floor. The idea proved feasible, but by the time her brother had blueprints, another year had passed. Ed Ball probably thought the elevator was a silly waste of money, but he used his old strategy of simply delaying the project rather than openly opposing it. The elevator was in fact installed in 1964, but Mrs. duPont never had an opportunity to use it.[28]

Some of the Jacksonville staff agreed privately among themselves that Mr. Ball had effectively banished Mrs. duPont from Jacksonville so that he would have free rein in running the Florida businesses. There was no question that Mrs. duPont's absence had that effect, but Ed Ball had other reasons for wanting his sister to remain in Wilmington. For one thing, Mrs. duPont no longer had the mental and physical stamina to deal with substantive issues, so having her in Jacksonville would simply be more frustrating for her. The second reason was even more important: Ed agreed with Dr. Shands that it made sense to keep her at Nemours, where she would be close to the best doctors and health facilities. She often talked bravely of returning to Epping Forest "next year," but at the same time she admitted that her doctors opposed the idea.[29]

The wisdom of this opinion was evident as Mrs. duPont's physical condition worsened rapidly in 1963. She suffered a heart attack in February and in May had a fall that resulted in multiple fractures of the pelvis. In August she was seriously ill with a kidney infection. In the face of these troubles she made every effort to give others the impression that she was only temporarily incapacitated. Miss Shaw came out to Nemours every weekday from Wilmington with the mail, and when Mrs. duPont was up to it, she dictated letters to members of her family and friends. At other times Miss Shaw answered correspondence, often shielding Mrs. duPont from information or requests that might upset her.[30]

Miss Shaw's intentions were admirable. Mrs. duPont was finding it increasingly difficult to discuss issues, particularly if they presented unpleasant alternatives. On such occasions she refused to participate or simply changed the subject.

In protecting Mrs. duPont, however, Miss Shaw was depriving her of any voice in matters close to her heart. In the spring of 1963, a group of protestors picketed the annual Alfred I. duPont Radio Awards ceremony in Washington. This incident brought to a head a smoldering controversy between Washington and Lee University, which administered the awards, and the Florida National Bank, which was the trustee of the fund supporting the award program. The bank asked Hardin Goodman to investigate the growing reservations within the bank about the university's performance.

Goodman was a natural choice for this assignment because during his years as trust officer of the bank, he had been close to Mrs. duPont and had conducted many negotiations with the university. Goodman had never liked the arrangement with Washington and Lee, and he relished this opportunity to compile a critical report. In conducting his investigation, however, Goodman stirred up a hornet's nest within the university and the broadcast industry in New York. Alarmed by the furor, William

Mills decided that the bank should take no action on Goodman's report. When rebuffed in the past, Goodman had always taken his criticisms directly to Mrs. duPont; now that was impossible. Instead, Goodman appealed to Mrs. duPont through Miss Shaw, who, after some thought, concluded that "presenting such a lengthy report to her might tend to upset her. . . . I am afraid she is entirely too weak to cope with these matters."[31]

Thus the issue lay unresolved for several years until Mills, now president of the bank, concluded in 1966 that a new arrangement was necessary. After a series of negotiations, the bank concluded a contract with Columbia University to administer the awards foundation, and by that time there was no possibility of explaining the situation to Mrs. duPont.[32]

Other issues might have been settled quite differently in 1963 if Mrs. duPont had been able to address them. As Alfred Shands approached retirement age, he became increasingly concerned about providing for his successor as director of the Alfred I. duPont Institute. His hope was that G. Dean McEwen, chief surgeon at the institute, would succeed him, but Ed Ball, now free to impose economies without his sister's moderating influence, had refused to give McEwen a salary increase. Afraid that McEwen would leave the institute for a higher paying position, Shands was ultimately forced to strike a demeaning deal with Ball: he offered to take a five-thousand-dollar salary cut so that McEwen's income could be increased by the same amount. He also offered to vacate the residence that Mrs. duPont had built for the Shands family on the grounds at Nemours so that McEwen could have acceptable living quarters. Ed Ball promptly accepted the offer.[33] It is hard to believe that Mrs. duPont would have tolerated such an arrangement. Apparently neither Ball nor Shands ever troubled her with the true story.

Shands was also hoping to realize Mrs. duPont's dream of establishing a home for the aged on fifteen acres adjacent to her estate at Epping Forest. Caring for the elderly had been one of Alfred's interests, and she had for decades provided regular support to institutions in Richmond, Wilmington, and Jacksonville. In 1955 she had declared in her will her intention to establish a home for retired clergy and schoolteachers and provided $750,000 as well as the land to support the project. The will made clear that she hoped to start the project before her death, and in the first codicil to her will in October 1960 she expressed a similar intent. In the press of business, however, Mrs. duPont had never found time to launch the project, although she must have discussed her interest in the idea with Shands. Because he may not have been aware of the provision for the home in the will, he probably saw little chance that Ed Ball would release funds to build the home after Mrs. duPont's death. When Shands approached Ball in November 1963 for permission to begin some planning for the home, Ball put him off by saying it was "too soon" to consider the project.[34] It was apparent that Shands was already too late. Without Mrs. duPont's direct intervention, the home for the aged would never be built.

As Miss Shaw became more protective and more suspicious of the motives of others, Mrs. duPont's contacts with the outside world gradually decreased. Soon her ties to Jacksonville were limited to occasional weekend visits by her brother, periodic short business sessions with William Mills, and correspondence with Hardin Goodman and Charles Akre. Her old friend Will Edwards had long since left the paper company and died late in 1962. Frank Gaines died after a long illness early in 1964.[35]

Over the years Mills had cultivated a cordial relationship with Mrs. duPont, and he was usually able to clear legal and financial matters with her in a few minutes of friendly conversation. It was not so easy, however, for Mills to expedite the processing of charitable contributions and scholarship funds. Miss Shaw had always maintained those files in the Wilmington office, and she was not prepared to turn them over to anyone else, even Mills. Probably for that reason contributions rose only slowly in the first two years after the breakdown of the system in 1961.

From bank and tax records, however, Mills and the Jacksonville staff knew something of Mrs. duPont's interests in the past. If it was not always possible to get her views on individual cases, a judicious use of the records assured that institutions that had received contributions for many years were not overlooked. In some cases Mills restored to the list institutions that presumably had been dropped unintentionally during the early 1960s. Contributions to charitable institutions in 1964 almost tripled over 1963 while those to educational institutions rose almost four times. It was also significant on the charitable side that twenty-eight new institutions and thirty-seven that had been on the list in earlier years received donations in 1964, while only sixteen were dropped.[36]

The desire to minimize federal income taxes explained much of Mills's interest in overhauling the system for processing gifts, but not all of it.

Mills accepted Mrs. duPont's premise that her money should be used for the maximum benefit of those in need. It was ironic that, at the very moment he was putting the gift machinery back in order, the federal government raised new questions about the status of the Alfred I. duPont estate as a charitable enterprise.

As in the past, the problem arose not from Mrs. duPont's philanthropic activities but rather from her brother's heavy-handed business practices. When Ed Ball had finally won control of the Florida East Coast Railway in 1959, the local unions were elated that the road would be retained by Florida interests. But, as Claude Pepper had predicted in the 1950 senatorial campaign, the unions would rue the day that Ball seized control. Once he was in the driver's seat he set about making the road a profitable operation. This meant cutting costs and refusing to include feather-bedding provisions in union contracts. When the nonoperating unions called a strike in 1961, proposing a 25-cents-per-hour wage increase and some rule changes, Ball refused to negotiate and ran the railroad with nonunion workers. When a special mediation board appointed by President Kennedy recommended in 1963 a 10.28 cents per hour wage hike, the national unions and 192 railroads accepted, but Ball would not.[37] He was determined to wage a one-man war to keep the unions and the federal government from telling him how to run his railroad.

As frustrations grew, strikers and others began derailing trains, blowing up bridges, and vandalizing equipment. Ball later reported 270 acts of vandalism or sabotage against the railroad. On the other side of the dispute, only a few of the union members charged with sabotage and vandalism were ever convicted. It also became painfully apparent that Ball's stubborn defiance was wreaking a devastating hardship on the railway workers and on the whole economy of the Florida's east coast.[38]

When the strike entered its second year in 1964, the unions took their cause to liberal Democrats in Washington, and a group of legislators, led by Representative Wright Patman of Texas and Senator Wayne Morse of Oregon, launched an attack on Ball and the duPont empire. Patman, an old-time southern populist, for years had been fighting a one-man battle against big business, the banking industry, and private trusts set up by the wealthy to avoid income taxes. Unable to win the support of the House Ways and Means Committee, Patman conducted his lonely campaign as chairman of the Select Subcommittee on Small Business. Beginning in 1962 he had published a series of annual reports designed to "[lay] bare for the first time . . . the detailed anatomy of . . . America's great fortunes."[39] The Alfred I. duPont estate was the subject of his third installment, published in March 1964. Tax evasion was the main target of Patman's report. He warned that the duPont "fortune will one day slip away forever from the payment of any income taxes." The "cream" of America's income was escaping taxation while the "skim-milk" income of "average hard-working families must then shoulder an increasing part of the tax burden. . . . Our earlier findings, now supplemented by the study of the DuPont Estate and The Nemours Foundation, show clearly the ever-increasing drift of wealth into tax-exempt foundations and the serious problems this creates for tax policy."[40]

Patman's report, containing more than three hundred pages of income and tax tables on the duPont estate, provided all the ammunition that he and Morse needed for an attack on Ed Ball. The charge was that the duPont estate was not really a charitable enterprise and therefore should not have been exempt from the provisions of the Bank Holding Company Act of 1956. Patman introduced a bill in the House that would effectively revoke the duPont exemption from provisions of the 1956 act; in April 1964 he opened a series of hearings on the amendment.[41]

Ball's opponents made no attempt to disguise his refusal to settle the strike as the real motivation for the bill. The first witness was the mayor of Miami, who declared that Ball's stubborn opposition to negotiation was damaging the economy of the city. Leon Keyserling, a lobbyist for the unions, and George Meany, president of the AFL-CIO, both argued that Ed Ball's power base in Florida made it possible for him to defy the American labor movement.[42]

Ed Ball relished the opportunity to match wits with Patman when he testified before the committee on June 24, 1964. He noted that no one from the duPont estate had testified in support of the exemption granted in the 1956 act, and, if the exemption was such a mistake, he wondered why the Congress had waited until 1964 to remove it. Reading into the record pages of financial data, he tried to show that the companies controlled by the estate did benefit the economy and did pay substantial taxes. He could not, however, counter Patman's insistent observation that the estate itself paid no federal income taxes.[43]

In taking up Patman's attack on the Senate floor, Morse turned his attention to Mrs. duPont. He pointed out that she had received more than $8.5 million from her husband's estate in 1963. He admitted that Mrs.

duPont had assigned 12 percent of the income from the estate to the Nemours Foundation, but that left her more than $7.5 million for her own use. By not mentioning any of Mrs. duPont's own philanthropic activities, Morse left the impression, at least in the minds of her friends, that he was accusing her of squandering these enormous sums on herself.[44]

Associates and old friends were quick to come to Mrs. duPont's defense. Mills in a public statement noted her extraordinary gifts "in the range of $40 to $50 million" and the "many thousands of worthy students" who had benefited from her scholarships. Because Mrs. duPont was "a person of very real humility" and seldom permitted institutions to identify her with her gifts, Mills claimed that neither he nor anyone else knew the full extent of her generosity.[45]

Bishop McKinstry, who was in Florida at the time, wrote a strong but tactful letter to Lady Bird Johnson, at whose wedding he had officiated many years earlier in Texas. Mrs. duPont, the bishop wrote, was being "ruthlessly attacked by Senator Morse," but she was "loved by a fierce loyalty by many thousands of alumni and alumnae of numerous colleges and universities in the South" for her generous scholarships. These former students would never forget the senator's misrepresentations about her "alleged lack of generosity." The real target of the attack, McKinstry wrote, was the railroad, which had become the "whipping boy" of the unions. He hoped that the president would "in no way give support to all this, or even the insinuation of support."[46]

It was understandable that those who loved and admired Mrs. duPont should see Morse's statement as a personal attack on her, but as the senator pointed out, what Mrs. duPont did with her money was beside the point. The large sums she was receiving from the estate did suggest that it was not merely a charitable enterprise. Furthermore, her insistence that most of her gifts receive no publicity made it difficult to describe the extent of her philanthropy. Even when an individual recipient knew that the gift had come from Mrs. duPont, there was no way of knowing how many similar gifts or scholarship grants she had made. Few third parties, not even her daughter Denise, ever knew what she gave to others.[47]

It was noteworthy in the Morse affair that Mrs. duPont never thanked her friends for defending her record of generosity, only for their personal concern and support. The one thing that did make her bristle was a statement in an Associated Press article that "the principal mission" of the

Nemours Foundation was "to maintain a family mansion . . . and its grounds and gardens, including a 'classic temple of love,' for the pleasure and benefit of the public."[48] That the article overlooked the hospital for crippled children was to her unpardonable.

Ed Ball would fight to retain the estate's exemption from the Bank Holding Company Act for two more years, but Mrs. duPont soon forgot the Morse affair. She no longer had the strength to follow her brother in his seemingly endless battles or to keep track of the skirmishes from one month to the next. Ed had no wish to trouble her with details, and even Miss Shaw complained that she knew very little about activities in the Jacksonville office after Will Edwards died. So the summer of 1964 was a quiet one at Nemours. Mrs. duPont spent most of her life on the second floor with her three nurses. Occasionally she came downstairs for dinner with the Dents or the Shandses or enjoyed having the Juhans or the Dews as houseguests for a few days.[49]

Mrs. duPont felt well enough to drop in on the annual Halloween party for the children at the institute that fall, but as the dark days of winter set in, she retreated more and more into a private world from which Miss Shaw found it increasingly difficult to recall her. Christmas, once a joyous occasion for family reunions at Nemours, now meant only a quiet visit with Belle and her husband, Addison Baker, who came to Nemours for a few days. The uneventful routine dragged on through the winter of 1965 until March 4, when the way of life Mrs. duPont had followed for almost forty years suddenly came to an end. Early that morning, Mary Shaw suffered a heart attack and died later that day.[50]

It seemed that no one could ever replace Miss Shaw. She had known Mrs. duPont's heart and mind so well that letters written by the two women could hardly be distinguished one from the other. By insisting that every piece of correspondence for Mrs. duPont pass through her, Miss Shaw had achieved a degree of authority that no one but Ed Ball could challenge. Furthermore, she had wrapped the Wilmington office in such a cloak of secrecy that it was impossible for anyone in Jacksonville to catch more than an occasional glimpse of what Miss Shaw did.

It was fully apparent to Ed Ball that, despite these difficulties, a replacement was needed in Wilmington immediately, and there was only one logical candidate. Hazel Williams had served as Mrs. duPont's secretary in Jacksonville since 1947. She was devoted to Mrs. duPont and enjoyed her complete confidence. Although she had never been to Wilmington and had never seen Miss Shaw's files, she knew how Mrs. duPont worked and she had set up her own filing system for Mrs. duPont's correspondence in Jacksonville. Since Mrs. duPont's last full winter in Jacksonville in 1960, Miss Williams had had little contact with Mrs. duPont except for an occasional friendly letter, but during those years she had become an ever more trusted member of the Jacksonville staff. Ed Ball had no hesitation in offering her the position as Miss Shaw's successor.[51]

For Miss Williams, the decision was difficult. She enjoyed her associates in the Jacksonville office and had purchased a home in Jacksonville Beach. She was not willing to move to Wilmington permanently but agreed to take the position if she could return to Jacksonville every few weeks. While in Wilmington, she would live at the DuPont Hotel.

When she arrived in Wilmington a few days after Miss Shaw's death, Miss Williams found the office in the Delaware Trust Building in disarray. It was obvious that Miss Shaw had been struggling to maintain the office during the months since Mrs. duPont had last come into the city from Nemours. Years of correspondence were unfiled and dozens of signed checks had not been dispatched. The disorganization made the situation especially difficult for one who knew almost nothing about her predecessor's method of operation. Fortunately Miss Williams understood some of the grant procedures from working with George Webster, the Jacksonville accountant who prepared Mrs. duPont's income tax returns.[52]

The most rewarding part of Miss Williams' assignment was her weekday visits to Nemours. She continued Miss Shaw's practice of taking some of the correspondence to the mansion in hopes that Mrs. duPont would consent to discussing it or even on occasion to dictating a reply. The task was the same, but Miss Williams added to it a warmth and empathy for Mrs. duPont that was sometimes lacking in Miss Shaw's all-business approach. With her cheerful personality Miss Williams tried to brighten Mrs. duPont's days and to restore her interest in life. In reporting to others Miss Williams stressed Mrs. duPont's good days and overlooked the bad. She was a breath of fresh air in a quiet and sometimes lonely household.

Miss Shaw's death was not the last shock to hit Nemours in 1965. Elbert Dent, who had succeeded Reginald Huidekoper as trustee of Alfred's estate in 1943, died in May. At the time of his death Dent was also on the board of managers of the Alfred I. duPont Institute and a director of the Nemours Foundation, the Florida National Bank, the Florida East Coast Railway, and the St. Joe Paper Company. His role in these organizations had been significant, not only because he was a good businessman, but also because he succeeded in maintaining a close personal relationship with both Ed and Jessie. Elbert could hold his own in business meetings with Ed and proved himself a good traveling companion and hunting partner. He no doubt helped to build Jessie's relationship with his wife, Victorine, the only one of Alfred's children who was still a close friend.

Thus Elbert Dent's death was more than the loss of a personal friend. Among the four trustees, the bank representative was at least neutral and more often a safe vote in Ed's pocket. Elbert usually voted with Ed, but his assurances came often enough to convince Jessie that her fears about the issue at hand were unfounded. It was probably a foregone conclusion that Elbert's replacement would be someone from Alfred's family, but none of the aspirants had Elbert's business ability or his close ties to Ed Ball. Maurice duPont Lee, who had inherited much of his mother, Marguerite's, suspicious nature, had been nipping at Jessie's heels ever since 1936, when Ed had delayed payment of the annuities established in Alfred's will for members of his family. Although Maurice and his wife maintained a sort of friendship with Jessie in face-to-face relationships and even came to see her from time to time at Nemours, Miss Shaw had reported Maurice's less than charitable comments in the office about Mrs. duPont's generosity. Under the circumstances Maurice's hopes that his son would succeed Elbert as trustee were unrealistic.

The choice seemed to fall naturally to Victorine's son Alfred duPont Dent, who as his grandfather's namesake had always held a warm spot in Jessie's heart. She must have welcomed the idea, but Ed Ball obviously had second thoughts about it. If young Alfred should decide to champion the claims of the duPont family, he could upset the delicate balance of power among the trustees and perhaps threaten Ed Ball's hold on the estate. Two days after Elbert's death the minutes of a trustees' meeting showed that Mills, and not young Alfred, had been selected as Dent's replacement. Then, on Ed's motion, the number of trustees was increased from three to six, and Alfred duPont Dent and two officials of the St. Joe Paper Company were elected to fill the new positions.[53]

The spring of 1965 also brought significant changes in Mrs. duPont's provisions for her own estate. For some time Robert Miller and Charles Akre, the Washington attorneys who drafted Mrs. duPont's will a decade earlier, had been concerned about the small number of institutions singled out to receive income from her large estate. Item 2 of her will requested but did not direct her trustees to include thirteen institutions among the beneficiaries of the income from the trust. Most but not all of the institutions specified in the will were the favored independent colleges that had received large grants for many years. The thirteen recipients named, however, could not begin to represent a cross section of the hundreds of institutions that had enjoyed her benefactions. Did not such a small number reflect an unnecessarily arbitrary distinction or perhaps the influence of a few close friends?

Because the thirteen designated institutions seemed to enjoy a preferential but not exclusive position, the two attorneys asked themselves how the trustees in the future would apportion income beyond those named and on what basis they would decide which applicants would receive funds and which would not. And would the thirteen always be worthy of receiving grants in the future? Mrs. duPont had offered no guidelines or standards that the trustees could apply. Under the circumstances, Miller and Akre thought it would be desirable to enlarge the number of institutions that the trustees might consider as possible recipients. To help Mrs. duPont feel more secure, they came up with a plan that would do what they thought she wanted. After several conferences with them, she agreed to define eligible institutions as those to which she had made contributions in the five years ending December 31, 1964.[54]

The five-year term was completely arbitrary but seemed logical as the most recent history of her philanthropies. Some argument might have been made for including some earlier years, when Mrs. duPont was more directly involved in the annual selection of recipients, but this alternative had the danger of including some institutions that had been dropped in later years. In order to comply with the incorporation-by-reference rule of law, it seemed wise to include the most recent past years. The change might also have included all institutions receiving gifts up to the time of Mrs. duPont's death. If she should live for several more years, however, that provision might well have included recipients known only to her advisers. All in all, the five-year period, spanning the years 1960 through 1964, seemed a reasonable compromise.

The codicil also deleted the weights that Mrs. duPont had assigned to each of the thirteen designated institutions in her 1955 will, since they no longer represented her thinking. Also dropped was the thirteenth recipient on the original list—the home for retired schoolteachers and clergy. The draft explained that since 1960 Mrs. duPont had transferred Epping Forest, including the land to be used for the home, to the Alfred I. duPont Foundation. Thus "a substantial reason for establishing the home . . . [was] now gone."[55] The fact was Ed Ball had fended off the project for so many years that it had lost much of its initial impetus. Social Security benefits had reduced the immediate need for the home, and Mrs. duPont could no longer expect to see the project started. When Miller and Akre were convinced after several visits that Mrs. duPont was fully satisfied with the content and import of the codicil, they took it to Wilmington for signature. In a faltering but clearly legible hand, Mrs. duPont signed the codicil on June 23, 1965.[56]

Hazel Williams reveled in her new job. She understood Mrs. duPont's personality and interpreted her sometimes crisp commands as a spark of returning vigor rather than as a note of disapproval. In July 1965 she was delighted to arrange with William Mills's wife, Helen, to purchase some new dresses for Mrs. duPont. She reported to Helen: "I took them out yesterday and you never saw such a reception. Mrs. duPont loved every one of the dresses and wanted to keep all of them."[57]

Handling correspondence took much of Miss Williams' time. Routine matters addressed to Mrs. duPont she answered in her own name. Personal letters she read to Mrs. duPont, who would occasionally dictate a reply to old friends like Rebecca Harding Adams or Elizabeth Chamberlain. From business correspondence Miss Williams selected only a few items to have on hand if Mrs. duPont felt disposed to discuss them. Sometimes these business sessions during the afternoon at Nemours would continue for an hour, sometimes for only a few minutes. The purpose was not just to determine Mrs. duPont's wishes but also to attract her attention and stimulate her interest. It was, as Miss Williams sometimes wrote, "heartbreaking" to see a once vigorous and talented woman struggling to hold on to a life that was fast disappearing. There were, however, compensations. She wrote to Bishop Juhan in August,

"You realize, I am sure, Bishop, what a real privilege it is and how very proud and happy I am to have had those years with Mrs. duPont, which gave me the opportunity to come up here and be with her at this time."[58]

For Miss Williams, life was a series of ups and downs as Mrs. duPont's condition shifted from day to day, and sometimes from hour to hour, from animated participation in conversation to complete withdrawal. She often perked up when her sister Elsie came for a few days or when Denise brought several of her children to Nemours for the day. Ed Ball now came to Wilmington every few weeks, sometimes only for an overnight visit, but even the anticipation of his arrival could lift her spirits. Elsie was often trying because she talked too much, stayed too long, and persisted in silly squabbles with her sister. As Miss Williams once observed, "I must say one thing for her. She may tire Mrs. duPont, but she does seem to stimulate her."[59]

Interspersed in the ups and downs were incidents that were potentially life threatening for Mrs. duPont—a slight stroke in December 1965 and a fall in her bedroom in July 1966 that broke the femur in her left leg. It would be six months before she took another step, but she always seemed to recover from these setbacks just as Miss Williams and her three nurses were fearing the worst.[60]

As the months passed, the periods of inactivity grew longer, but there were days, even a few intervals of a week or more, when Mrs. duPont was surprisingly alert and active. For all her ailments, she had retained the fair complexion that she had enjoyed throughout her life. Lovingly tended by her nurses and dressed in one of the pretty frocks selected by Miss Williams, she still had the appearance of a much younger woman.

During his visits to Nemours Ed sometimes reported favorable developments in the Florida business enterprises. Jessie enjoyed his descriptions of how he was outmaneuvering both the unions and the federal government in the Florida East Coast Railway strike.[61] Ed, however, did not trouble her with business details that might upset her. Because she could not follow events from one week to the next, he considered that such news would be merely frustrating. For that reason he told Miss Williams that she should not say anything to his sister about Jacksonville or the Florida businesses. Miss Williams knew enough not to argue with "Mr. Ball"; she simply disregarded his instructions. She was convinced that boredom and the enforced isolation of Mrs. duPont from her life and friends in Jacksonville were the cause of much of her depression.[62]

On occasion Mrs. duPont could assert herself in ways that mattered. In 1966, when a Senate subcommittee in Washington chaired by Willis Robertson of Virginia reported out a bill that would remove the duPont estate's exemption from the bank holding company act, she took part in drafting a letter marshaling opposition to the bill. She was "shocked and grieved over the discriminatory [b]ill" that would force the estate to divest its holdings, either in the Florida banks or in the other business enterprises within five years, while labor unions continued to be exempt from the act and other family-held corporations were given as long as fourteen years to divest. "The action is particularly heart-breaking to me, being so aware of the many tedious months Mr. duPont spent drawing up what he hoped to be an iron-clad Will, trying to benefit the little crippled child and old people, his appointed Trustees working untiringly in an effort to carry out his wishes."[63]

The invocation of Alfred duPont was a stock formula that Ed Ball used in his fight against the bill, and he probably instigated his sister's letter. It is significant, however, that he felt it necessary to draft the letter in this form in order to gain her approval. Miss Williams would have made certain that Mrs. duPont understood the letter before it was sent, and it is quite likely that Mrs. duPont would never have approved the letter without making some editorial changes of her own. In the end neither this letter, nor Bishop McKinstry's appeal to Lady Bird Johnson, nor any other tactic by Ed Ball succeeded in diverting congressional action on the bill, which became law later in 1966.[64] Now the indomitable Mr. Ball began a new campaign that would continue long after his sister's death to thwart the application of the law.

At least through 1966 Mrs. duPont continued to have some voice in her philanthropic work. When Miss Williams went out to Nemours, she usually had with her a list of institutions to which Mrs. duPont had contributed in earlier years, and occasionally Mrs. duPont would consent to consider them. Ed Ball, Mills, and to a lesser extent Dr. Shands took the initiative in suggesting new institutions that they believed deserved support. As Mills read the list with suggested dollar amounts, Mrs. duPont would nod her assent or in a few words suggest a change. Because it was impossible to check each of the large number of small donations with Mrs. duPont, the total amounts for donations under one thousand dollars declined sharply after 1963. Mills and Ed Ball compensated for this by adding each year a dozen or so new institutions, each receiving a substantial gift (table 10-2). In this way they were able to keep the total amounts of tax-deductible giving high enough to approach the 30-percent limit on deductions for contributions under the federal tax laws.[65]

Now that Mrs. duPont had terminated the awarding of individual scholarships, it was possible to give lump-sum amounts to a larger number of institutions. Thus the number of institutions receiving cash gifts increased from six in 1963 to forty-five in 1967, and the totals increased from $60,500 to $826,000 in the same period. Likewise, gifts of securities increased from $428,506 in 1963 to $1,847,433 in 1966. The list of twenty-five or so institutions receiving securities did not change appreciably.[66]

Except for occasional brief discussions of her contributions with Hazel Williams, Kennard Adams, George Webster, or William Mills, Mrs. duPont took no active part in her affairs after 1966. The last letter that she actually dictated herself was probably one to Elizabeth Chamberlain in May 1968.[67] Thereafter Miss Williams took drafts to Mrs. duPont and signed them herself if Mrs. duPont approved. In December Miss Williams informed one applicant for a grant that Mrs. duPont had more or less limited her contributions to those organizations to which she had contributed over the years, and that before adding new ones to the list, she must depend and rely on the advice of her attorneys and other confidential advisers.[68]

After 1967 the pattern of contributions established by Ball and Mills showed few variations and consisted exclusively of gifts in round numbers. They added thirty-five new charitable institutions to the 1967 list, which reflected a broad spectrum of churches, hospitals, and civic organizations of the type Mrs. duPont had supported in the past. Substantial

TABLE 10-2 Cash Contributions to Charitable Institutions, 1964–67

Year	Number[a]	Total amount ($)
1964	109	1,804,925
1965	140	1,361,824
1966	153	1,416,237
1967	164	3,666,826

a. Denotes the number of gifts over $1,000. The total dollars are for all gifts.

gifts to the new recipients and larger amounts to the regulars helped to achieve a sharp increase in cash gifts to charitable institutions. Because large gifts of securities to educational institutions were curtailed in 1967 and all but eliminated thereafter, the larger cash contributions helped to keep tax-deductible gifts close to the 30-percent limit (table 10-3).[69]

As the months slowly took their toll in the late 1960s, Miss Williams did her best to be optimistic. Mrs. duPont still had her good days, but she took little interest in anything beyond family visits. Dr. William T. Thompson, the husband of Mrs. duPont's niece, Jessie Gresham Baker Thompson, now chaired the board of managers of the institute and came to Nemours with his wife for the periodic meetings. Ed continued to come regularly to see his sister and to attend trustees' meetings, which were now often held at Nemours even though Mrs. duPont no longer attended. The Shandses frequently came to dinner, and Elsie was never far away.[70] In July 1970 Miss Williams reported: "I find very little change from day to day, other than Mrs. duPont's interest and energies are not as sustained as formerly. She looks wonderful and as lovely as ever. The greatest change I have noted in the past several months is that more and more she is leaving it up to me to keep up with her correspondence, which I try to do as promptly as possible."[71]

A month later when Elsie Bowley came to Nemours, she was pleased that her sister had enough spark to smile at some of her humorous stories. Miss Williams reported the incident to Denise and Carl Zapffe, but she added: "This isn't to build up your hopes or paint a false picture, as Mrs. duPont is still very frail and is only up once in the morning and once in the evenings—mealtimes—and, of course, isn't permitted downstairs yet."[72]

Miss Williams actually knew the end was near. During the late summer she tried to keep Mrs. duPont's correspondence and accounts up

TABLE 10-3 Income and Tax-Deductible Contributions, 1963–70 (in dollars)

Year	Total income	Federal tax	Contributions
1963	8,440,757	4,832,664	2,574,508
1967	12,458,766	6,042,027	3,745,874
1968	9,315,590	4,832,009	2,946,198
1969	8,847,861	4,698,234	2,523,895
1970	6,062,563	3,210,613	1,517,754

to date in painful anticipation of the moratorium on business activities that would begin on the day of her death. In September Mrs. duPont grew steadily weaker. There was no longer any possibility of real communication. Early on Saturday morning, September 26, 1970, Mrs. duPont died quietly in her sleep.

Later that morning Alfred Shands called members of Mrs. duPont's family and Bishop McKinstry to tell them of her death. Mills was in Scotland and Akre in Bermuda on vacation, but Shands managed to reach them in time for them to fly home for the funeral. Ed Ball, in Washington on business, was able to reach Nemours that evening as did Elsie Bowley and the Zapffes. When the family assembled with the bishop on Sunday morning, Ed, never comfortable with ceremonial occasions, especially funerals, proposed that services for Jessie be held the following afternoon at Nemours. Elsie was outraged at the unseemly haste, but Ed offered the excuse that business commitments left him no choice. Despite the short notice, the drawing room was packed with family and friends when Bishop McKinstry conducted the Episcopal burial service on Monday afternoon.[73] From the mansion it was scarcely a thousand yards to the carillon tower, where Jessie's body was interred beside that of her beloved Alfred.

Events moved so swiftly that September weekend that there was little time for those present at Nemours to contemplate what Mrs. duPont had meant to each of them and to the times in which she lived. Alfred Shands perhaps put it best on a happier occasion five years earlier, when he spoke of her at the dedication of the Jessie Ball duPont Library at the University of the South: "[S]he is truly one who has had a full, rich, productive, and meaningful life; one who is a devout Christian, a great humanitarian, and a wise philanthropist; and certainly one of the greatest ladies ever claimed by the South. So great has been the impact she has made on the South during the last four decades, I am sure that her name will live on for long years to come."[74]

It was perhaps predictable that Shands, himself a southerner, should see fit in his eulogy to stress Mrs. duPont's ties to the South. She was indeed a daughter of the Old South and her loyalty to that region colored everything that she thought and did. Shands, however, could just as well have pointed out the ways in which she did not fit the stereotype of the southern lady. Her great wealth, her professional career, her independent life-style, her abilities in business and finance, all suggested that culture and gender did not always confine southern women to conventional roles. It was also clear that the kind of exceptional woman whom historians have usually identified with the North did exist in the South. In fact, her life foreshadowed the emergence of the woman professional who would transform American society in the closing decades of the century.

Under the circumstances, Shands could not have been expected to dwell on what Mrs. duPont must have seen as the failure of her professional career, but that failure was nonetheless significant. She had staked much of her philanthropy, and especially her large gifts, on the idea that she could somehow influence the direction in which her own culture was developing. All her appeals, all her letters, all her gifts could not stem the tide of social change accelerated by the intervention of the federal government in striking down the barriers against racial discrimination in the United States.

If she failed to achieve this larger goal, however, Mrs. duPont could be confident that the philanthropic activities she had pursued during her life would continue after her death. The fund she established by her will would assure that future generations would benefit from her generosity. That in itself was no small achievement.

11

Giving for the Future

The day after Mrs. duPont's funeral Hazel Williams returned to her office in the Delaware Trust Building to begin acknowledging letters of condolence and formal resolutions of appreciation from charitable and educational institutions. For the moment that was the most pressing concern. In anticipation of Mrs. duPont's death, Miss Williams had kept all accounts and correspondence as current as possible, so few creditors were affected when access to Mrs. duPont's bank accounts was temporarily suspended. Before he left Wilmington, Ed Ball had authorized Miss Williams to charge travel and hotel expenses for those invited to the funeral to the St. Joe Paper Company until new accounts could be opened. The long-established domestic routines in the mansion house ended abruptly with the funeral, but the household staff of ten, including the butler, cook, kitchen help, chambermaids, and chauffeur were to be retained indefinitely. In the weeks ahead Ball, Mills, and others would come frequently to Nemours on a host of matters, and it made sense to keep the mansion in operating condition.[1]

Later that week Hazel Williams and Kennard Adams opened Mrs. duPont's personal safe in the mansion house and removed the original copy of the will, carefully embossed with red sealing wax. Charles Akre in Washington had a copy, but the original would have to be filed with the county judge in Jacksonville to begin the long process of settling the estate.

The first order of business was formally to identify the persons named in the will to serve as executors of the estate and trustees of the Jessie Ball duPont Religious, Charitable, and Educational Fund when it was established. In addition to the Florida National Bank of Jacksonville as corporate executor, the will named three individuals. Of the three men designated in the 1955 will, only Ed Ball had not been superseded by later codicils. In 1963 Mrs. duPont had replaced Seabury Stoneburner, who had left the paper company in 1961, with William Mills. The following year she named the Reverend Alexander duBose Juhan as successor trustee to his father.[2] Since Bishop Juhan had died in 1968, his son would now serve in his place.

Sandy Juhan seemed at the time a logical replacement. Born at Sewanee in 1916 while his father was chaplain of the military academy there, Sandy had attended the academy himself and graduated from the University of the South in 1940. He decided to follow his father into the ministry and after graduating from the Virginia Theological Seminary served in several parishes before becoming dean of the Episcopal cathedral in Havana. Sandy had known Mrs. duPont since college days and with his sister, Frances, and his parents had often been a guest at Epping Forest and Nemours. Now fifty-four years old, Juhan was rector of a fast-growing suburban parish in the Jacksonville area and thus had good working knowledge of the diocese of Florida and the church institutions that Mrs. duPont had supported there. There is little doubt that Mrs. duPont expected Juhan to stand with Mills in representing her philanthropic interests and thus provide a balance for the more conservative tendencies of her brother and the corporate executor.

Ball and Mills had no hesitation in selecting Irvin P. Golden as the representative of the corporate executor. Golden had joined the trust department of the Florida National Bank in Jacksonville soon after his graduation from law school at the University of Florida. Working first under Hardin Goodman and later under Kenneth E. Haefele, Golden had become the bank's expert in managing personal trusts and estates. At the time of Mrs. duPont's death he was managing as many as a hundred trusts for the bank. Except for the size of her estate, Golden foresaw no unusual problems in carrying out the provisions of the will.[3] Quiet, unassuming, and efficient, he was ideally suited to mediating disputes that were likely to arise among the executors.

Because no one in the Jacksonville office had seen the will, it took some time for Mills and others to digest its contents and begin to formulate plans for the years of legal procedures that would be required to close the estate and establish the fund. As an executor of the estate, Mills could hardly serve as attorney, and it was quite natural that Ed Ball should appoint his personal lawyer, Frederick H. Kent, to serve with Charles Akre as cocounsels for the estate. Kent was one of the most prominent members of the Jacksonville bar and had worked closely with Ed Ball for many years.

When the will was entered into probate and became public record on October 16, 1970, it must have been clear to anyone who read it that the fulfillment of Mrs. duPont's wishes would pose legal and tax questions of some complexity and import. The size of the estate alone made the case unusual. As a Jacksonville newspaper reported, the estate was "expected to be one of the largest ever filed in Florida. . . . There has been no official accounting of the estate, but unofficial estimates indicate the total value may be between \$50-\$100 million."[4] Actually, George Webster in the Jacksonville office computed the total assets on the date of Mrs. duPont's death to be something more than \$42 million.[5]

One of Hazel Williams's first tasks was to identify the scores of beneficiaries named in the will and codicils. The 1955 will included legacies of \$20,000 to each of five educational and religious institutions; a trust of \$200,000 to supplement the salaries of clergy in the Northern Neck; scores of cash gifts ranging from \$1,500 to \$50,000 for close relatives and friends; \$10,000 each to nineteen godchildren; \$6,000 each to fifteen distant cousins; and lifetime annuities to more than eighty individuals, many of whom were already included in the legacies. In addition the will provided for gifts based on years of service for employees at Nemours, Epping Forest, Ditchley, and the offices in Wilmington and Jacksonville.[6]

Further complicating matters, the first codicil to the will replaced many of the legacies with annuities, increased the dollar amounts of many legacies, and completely eliminated others. In some bequests there were rights of survivorship; in most of them, not. Just to draw up a list of eligible recipients and to find their current addresses was a monumental task, especially since Florida law required prompt notification of legatees once the will had been probated.[7]

In addition to this administrative burden, the executors faced a host of state and federal laws and regulations relating to estate taxes, income taxes, and the untested provisions of the recent federal tax reform act. After studying the situation for several weeks, Charles Akre went to Jacksonville in late October 1970 to discuss a plan of action with Fred

Kent. The two attorneys compiled a checklist of legal steps that the executors would need to take in the next few weeks and a brief summary of the strategies that might be followed in settling the estate.[8]

Interpreting relevant law would be especially difficult on the heels of the Tax Reform Act of 1969, which was just then coming into effect. The new law was yet further evidence of Congressman Wright Patman's persistent efforts to regulate the affairs of private foundations. In opening hearings before the House Committee on Ways and Means in February 1969, Patman declared that his bill would "end a gross inequity which the country and its citizens can no longer afford: The tax-exempt status of the so-called privately controlled charitable foundations, and their propensity for domination of business and accumulation of wealth. Put most bluntly, philanthropy—one of mankind's more noble instincts—has been perverted into a vehicle for institutionalized deliberate evasion of fiscal and moral responsibility of the Nation."[9]

By the time the executors held their first formal meeting on November 3, 1970, Hazel Williams had moved back to Jacksonville to take over the administrative work in settling the estate. As Kent and Akre presented their recommendations, the full magnitude of the task ahead became evident for the first time. The resolution of legal and tax questions would involve months of study by the attorneys and voluminous correspondence with the executors. There were still bank accounts to be closed, safe deposit boxes to be opened, inventories to be completed, employees to be terminated or reassigned, dividends to be recorded, and accounts to be maintained.[10] Miss Williams was able to get some temporary help on financial matters from paper company personnel in Jacksonville, but Ed Ball saw no need of going to the expense of adding more staff.

In February 1971 Charles Akre undertook to explain to the executors the complexities and ambiguities presented by the tax reform act. Because the law was just coming into effect and had not been tested in the courts, his interpretation of the statute was based largely on his own reading of its provisions.[11]

Akre's greatest concern was the requirement that the "governing instrument" of a private foundation contain certain provisions that would assure its performance as a charitable institution. In the case of the duPont fund, the governing instrument would be Mrs. duPont's will, which clearly did not include the specific provisions required by the law, and the will could not be changed without a lengthy court procedure. Akre wanted to avoid reforming the will, but he could not be certain whether interpretation of the new law would make that necessary. The new law did contain some grandfather clauses, but unfortunately there was no possibility that the fund could be set up in time to take advantage of them. Akre thought the best course was to ask the Treasury Department for an interpretation that would make reforming of the will unnecessary as long as the fund complied with the restrictions that the new section imposed.[12]

The central provisions of the new law had several implications for both the estate and the new fund. There was no certainty that, without reforming the will, the estate could obtain a charitable deduction for a bequest to the fund. An unfavorable ruling on this point would greatly reduce the potential resources from the estate. Nor was it certain that the fund, once established, would be exempt from federal income taxes unless the will was reformed.

Even with a revised will, the new law and regulations posed other difficulties. The first was the requirement that the foundation distribute for charitable purposes an amount equal to its entire adjusted net income or 6 percent of its total assets, whichever was greater.[13] This provision was obviously intended to prevent foundations from sitting on low-income investments and using very little for philanthropic purposes, but the requirement raised severe problems for the executors. Akre estimated that stock in the St. Joe Paper Company comprised about half of the assets of the estate, and that the stock was paying far less than 1 percent in dividends. The Florida National Bank stock was not doing much better. Unless these stocks were exchanged for better paying securities, the fund might have to dip into principal in order to meet the minimum distribution requirement in the tax reform act. Such a penalty would not only deplete the resources of the fund but also violate the provisions of the will, which prohibited expenditure of the principal of the estate. It seemed clear that the estate would have to sell the stock.

Selling the paper company stock, however, involved its own difficulties. Because the stock was closely held and not traded publicly, it would be difficult to sell on the open market. An obvious recourse might have been to sell the stock back to the paper company, but Akre suggested that such a transaction might violate the "self-dealing" provisions of the act, which prohibited a private foundation from selling its property to a "disqualified person," either directly or indirectly. As a trustee of the fund and a substantial shareholder in the paper company, Ed Ball seemed to fit the definition of a "disqualified person."[14]

Akre warned the trustees that the restriction on disqualified persons also seemed to apply to gifts of fund income to the Alfred I. duPont Foundation and the awards foundation. Under the new tax code, a distribution to either of these foundations would be a taxable expenditure if either foundation was controlled by a disqualified person. Whether Ed Ball or the bank fit that category was uncertain. Even if they did, the tax could still be avoided if the foundations made qualifying distributions in the same amounts they received. In this case, however, the fund would be required to obtain records or other evidence that the gift had been so used. This requirement threatened to impose an additional administrative burden on the fund and create a potential liability over which the fund would have no direct control.[15]

Obviously the executors could not address all of these complex questions at the same time. Only opinions from the federal government and the courts could resolve some of them, and a well planned course of action seemed advisable to avoid unnecessary legal tangles. On the advice of Akre and Kent, the executors first sought a ruling from the Treasury Department that the fund would qualify for a federal estate tax deduction. They also asked their attorneys to request that the executors be authorized as trustees of the fund so that they could petition the court to reform the will. Favorable rulings on both requests were in hand before the end of the summer.[16]

Another provision of the will called for immediate attention. Because the Alfred I. duPont Foundation was a private foundation under the tax reform act, any bequest it received from the estate would have to be used for charitable purposes. Mrs. duPont, however, had left the foundation her tangible property at Epping Forest, and it seemed unlikely that a charitable use could be found for these items. Thus the property would probably have to be sold and the proceeds given to the foundation for charitable use if a substantial tax penalty was to be avoided.

Akre and Kent also urged that title to the mansion house at Nemours be transferred from the Alfred I. duPont Estate to the Nemours Foundation in order to assure that it would not be declared a private foundation under the new tax law. If this should happen, the foundation could be subject to all of the restrictions imposed by the Tax Reform Act of 1969, and Mrs. duPont's bequest of her tangible property in and about the mansion house would not qualify for a charitable deduction in the estate tax. In addition to the transfer of title, the attorneys also recommended that the institute make use of the mansion house in a way that would make clear that it was an integral part of the hospital.[17]

Timing emerged as a cardinal strategy in settling the estate and establishing the fund. A careful reading of the amended tax code revealed that the restrictions imposed on private foundations would not come to bear until assets were actually transferred to the fund. Thus it made sense for the executors to sell the stock in the St. Joe Paper Company and to purchase securities with a higher yield before the fund began operation.

Nor was there any hurry about closing the estate. The executors had obtained permission from the court to borrow money from an outside party to pay the estate tax, which would be more than $2 million. Because the estate and not the fund was paying off the loan, the expenditure was not taxable under the amended tax code, and Akre estimated that the loan could be paid off from annual income by February 1974. The amended tax code did provide that if the settlement of an estate was "unduly prolonged," the restrictions on a private foundation would be applied, but Akre and Kent were confident that this would not happen as long as the executors were still paying off the loan.[18]

The big question facing the executors early in 1971 was whether the will would have to be reformed. Fortunately some answers to that question began to appear before the end of summer. In July the Internal Revenue Service ruled that the bequest to the fund would qualify for a charitable deduction in the estate tax even if the will were not reformed. The ruling, however, also covered a point on which the executors had not asked an opinion. The government ruled that a charitable deduction on income tax would also be available if the executors reformed the will within two years of Mrs. duPont's death. Even more promising was an act by the Florida Legislature providing that all trusts established in Florida before November 1, 1971, would be deemed to have the provisions required by the tax reform act incorporated in their governing instruments. If the legislation was upheld in the courts, it would mean that the fund would qualify as a private foundation under the 1969 act. The Florida law would also have the effect of revoking the stipulation in Mrs. duPont's will that prohibited distributions to charities from the trust's principal. Thus it would be possible for the fund to make distributions out of principal if grants from annual income fell below 6 percent of assets.[19]

Now under no pressure to settle the estate precipitously and confident that the legal obstacles imposed by the new tax law would be overcome, the executors and the lawyers moved ahead with great deliberation. The cautious inquiries directed to the Internal Revenue Service, the repeated analysis and dissection of statutory and regulatory language, and correspondence with the court were not unique to Mrs. duPont's estate. Tax experts who studied the impact of the new legislation during the first few years after its enactment found that it had caused widespread confusion and uncertainty, not only among foundation managers, but also among government officials. One commentator remarked that the statute could properly be called the "Lawyers' and Accountants' Relief Act."[20]

The analysts also noted, however, that there had been enormous and perhaps unprecedented cooperation and correspondence between the foundations, the Internal Revenue Service, and the Treasury Department in developing regulations to interpret the new law. The focus of several books and many journal articles on the law and its implications in the early 1970s supported this view.[21]

While the lawyers and accountants were groping for answers, it seemed likely that some foundation managers were overreacting to the legislation or were reacting with "excessive caution." If Mrs. duPont's executors did not overreact, they certainly fit the pattern of not moving precipitously. Some experts on tax law feared that in exercising caution, foundations might neglect innovative or controversial projects that otherwise would have received support.[22] This was certainly not a concern of the duPont executors in 1971.

The legal questions that Akre and Kent raised early in 1971 had been resolved by the end of 1973, and Mills and Juhan were ready to settle the estate. Two obstacles, however, remained. First, the estate could not be settled until the low-yielding stocks in the St. Joe Paper Company and the Florida National Bank had been sold. The paper company stock had not been sold because Ed Ball had as yet found no way to determine its market value without filing a report with the Securities and Exchange Commission and offering the stock for public sale. Until the summer of 1971 he had been struggling to escape the 1966 law that required the

Alfred I. duPont Estate to divest its holdings in the bank, and he did not want to release financial information about the companies. He was also convinced that the bank stock was greatly undervalued, and he wanted to delay the sale until the market improved.[23]

The second obstacle was a prolonged debate among the executors over the size of the fee to be paid out of the estate to the executors and how it would be distributed among them. Ed Ball, in his characteristic approach, complained that the statutory fee was entirely too large for the amount of work the executors had done, and he particularly objected to the portion that the bank was claiming. Mills and Juhan wanted to accept the statutory fee and close the estate promptly. Faced with an impasse on these matters, the executors had no choice but to take their differences to McKenney J. Davis, the county judge who was ruling on the settlement of the estate. Davis held that the executors had no choice under the law but to pay the statutory fee, which would amount to $1.7 million, and he threatened to replace the executors if they did not agree among themselves how the fee was to be divided. Under this threat, Ed Ball reluctantly agreed that the bank would receive 40 percent; he and Mills, 22.5 percent each; and Juhan, 15 percent.[24]

By the summer of 1976 these differences between the executors had been resolved, and the attorneys took steps to close the estate. On August 10 Fred Kent informed the executors that the final report to the court was nearing completion. He had prepared a plan for disbursement of the funds in the estate. The Jacksonville properties held by the estate and the stock in the Florida East Coast Railway had been sold to the St. Joe Paper Company. The last of the estate's stock in the paper company was to be sold in a few days. The settlement of the income tax on the estate would be completed with receipt of the refund agreed upon with the Internal Revenue Service. The last items to be settled were the final fees for the executors and the attorneys.[25]

When Judge Davis accepted the executors' final report and fee proposal, Mrs. duPont's estate could be closed and the estate's assets transferred to the fund. Golden made the paper transfer at the bank in November, and the Jessie Ball duPont Fund was in operation.

When the trustees of the Jessie Ball duPont Fund met for the first time in January 1977, their titles were new but the faces the same. The three individual executors—Ed Ball, Bill Mills, and Sandy Juhan—were now trustees. Golden was still serving as representative of the Florida National Bank, now the corporate trustee. Without breaking stride, Hazel Williams moved into her duties as executive director of the fund, and Fred Kent continued to serve as the fund's attorney.[26]

Now that the fund was in active operation, the trustees were subject to all the restrictions imposed by federal and state tax law on private foundations. The meetings of the executors had always been businesslike, but the trustees now followed more formal procedures to assure full compliance with the law. They decided to meet regularly to consider investment recommendations that Golden would bring to them from the bank as well as proposals for grants to institutions based on data that Hazel Williams had assembled from Mrs. duPont's files in Wilmington. Miss Williams had already compiled a preliminary list of institutions eligible to receive grants under the will, and Fred Kent with all the precautions exercised by a veteran attorney drafted a letter informing the institutions of their eligibility.

The notification letter made clear that Mrs. duPont had attached no dollar amount to the bequest to any institution named in the will, nor did she make a grant to any of them mandatory. Any of the recipients of the notification letter were welcome to submit applications for grants, which the trustees would judge on their merits. Early in May Miss Williams reported that 176 replies had been received to the 318 letters sent out. She now sent each of the respondents a copy of the instructions for preparing a grant application. She still had on hand the names of a substantial number of individuals and institutions that had received donations from Mrs. duPont during the specified years. Many of these had received small, one-time gifts, and it would take the trustees some time to determine their eligibility.[27]

The biggest challenge facing the trustees was how to disburse responsibly the income that was rapidly accumulating from securities held by the fund. Under the new tax law, the fund was required to disburse all of its income by the end of the fiscal year following the year of its receipt; and if, under the latest regulations, the amount disbursed did not equal 5 percent of the fund's assets, the difference would have to be taken from principal. One approach was to make substantial donations to the twelve institutions listed in the will. By this method the trustees could have quickly moved large sums of money out of the estate, but they would not have complied with the spirit of the will. Instead they adopted a formula for making grants during the first fiscal year only. Under this proposal, the fund would pay out its first grants based on the actual contributions Mrs. duPont had made during the specified five-year period from 1960 through 1964. On October 13, 1977, the trustees approved the first list of grants totalling $1,174,223 to ninety-eight institutions.[28]

The 1977 formula did enable the trustees to make substantial grants to the eligible institutions, but they did not begin to meet the federal requirement for disbursement of at least 5 percent of the fund's total assets. With assets of more than $76 million, the 5-percent rule brought the minimum required payout to more than $3.7 million; the initial grants were less than half that amount.[29]

The trustees had hoped to make all future awards strictly on the merits of grant proposals for specific projects, but the sheer magnitude of the remainder to be disbursed in 1978 made that procedure impossible. As an alternative the trustees asked Miss Williams, using her intimate knowledge of the eligible institutions, to draw up a list of proposed grants totaling $4 million. In reevaluating proposals and reviewing new ones, Miss Williams considered each in the context of Mrs. duPont's philosophy and interests. By the autumn of 1978 Miss Williams had recommended grants totaling more than $4.2 million for 113 organizations.[30]

Both settling the estate and establishing the fund demonstrated the profound effect that federal tax and estate laws had on American philanthropy. Designed to prevent foundations from becoming tax shelters for private fortunes, the laws not only imposed restrictions on philanthropic activities but also defined the areas in which foundations could operate. Federal law still encouraged private philanthropy, but the government had assumed a major role in its administration.

In his recent analysis of the thirty-six largest foundations in the United States, Waldemar Nielsen has found a pattern of evolution. When the donor dies, the fortune established in a trust passes into the hands of family members or old business associates. Over a period of years the influence of family and associates declines and "the institution comes under the control of a self-selected board of trustees, with no personal links to the donor and, to some degree, of the professional staff. It has then achieved its 'mature' character, adhering to some extent to the traditions and patterns it has acquired but also reshaped by the changing social and political context within which it operates."[31]

During its first decade of operation the Jessie Ball duPont Fund followed the Nielsen pattern of evolution. For the first five years, all of the original trustees and staff were still active, and the spirit of Mrs. duPont's will governed their actions. Grants were strictly limited to institutions eligible under the terms of the will, and the size of the grants for the first year was similar to the amounts awarded by Mrs. duPont. Unlike many of the foundations in Nielsen's sample, the duPont Fund operated under specific instructions from the donor, a circumstance that introduced a degree of stability in grant profiles. As Nielsen pointed out in his study, however, exact adherence to the records of the past was neither possible nor desirable, and the grant profile underwent significant changes even during the first five years (table 11-1).[32] The percentages for 1977 closely approximated the pattern of Mrs. duPont's giving because the trustees determined them with a formula based on her gifts during the five-year period stipulated in the will. The pattern, however, began to change even in 1978 with a significant shift from educational to health institutions, a change caused mostly by a few large grants. During the next three years the percentages for health institutions gradually declined while those to religious institutions increased, mostly for grants to the Episcopal church in Florida.

The grant-making procedure established by the trustees made such changes inevitable. Eligible institutions could not expect automatic grants but each year had to submit proposals, which the trustees evaluated on their relative merits. In this respect the trustees were more closely following Mrs. duPont's approach than had they slavishly accepted her own pattern of giving. Her first principle in giving had

TABLE 11-1 Distribution of Grants by Type, 1977–81 (percentage of annual total dollars, for fiscal years ending October 31)

Type	1977	1978	1979	1980	1981
Religious	3.4	3.7	3.7	21.1	24.6
Charitable					
Health	5.6	24.7	14.5	13.8	11.3
Historical and cultural	9.0	8.2	17.6	5.8	7.0
Other	8.9	6.7	24.6	11.8	13.6
Educational	73.1	56.7	39.6	47.5	43.5
Total	100.0	100.0	100.0	100.0	100.0

always been to determine actual need or merit and then to distribute her gifts accordingly.

The duPont fund reached the next step in Nielsen's pattern of evolution early in the 1980s when the original trustees began to leave the scene. When Ed Ball died in the spring of 1981, Hazel Williams replaced him under the terms of the will, but a new generation of trustees began to appear in 1985, when Mills and Juhan resigned. By 1986, when Hazel Williams retired, the transition was complete. The new trustees and the executive director would come from a generation younger than those they replaced; none of them had known Mrs. duPont personally. For them, Jessie Ball duPont would be a remote figure, whose personality, motivation, and private world were buried in the thousands of pages of letters, bank statements, photographs, and mementos that she had left in her voluminous office files. One of the purposes of this book has been to retrieve from that mass of paper the essence of her life and career.

The highly technical and rapidly changing world of the 1990s bears little resemblance to the times in which Jessie Ball duPont lived. The way of life she experienced as a child in the Northern Neck of Virginia and even as a dowager presiding over her estates at Nemours and Epping Forest now seem as remote as the setting of a nineteenth-century novel. Many of her convictions about the shape and nature of American society are already outdated and will become little more than curiosities in the new century. But through the fund that she made possible her compassion for the less fortunate and her commitment to the value of education, religion, and the arts will continue to enrich the lives of Americans for generations to come.

The duPont and Ball Family Trees

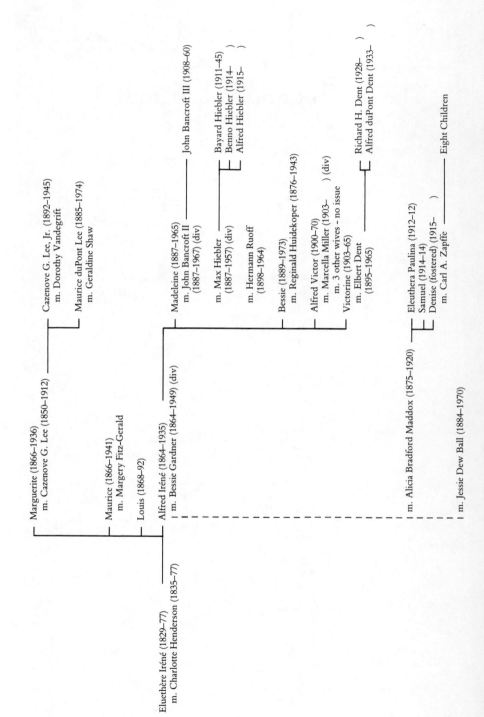

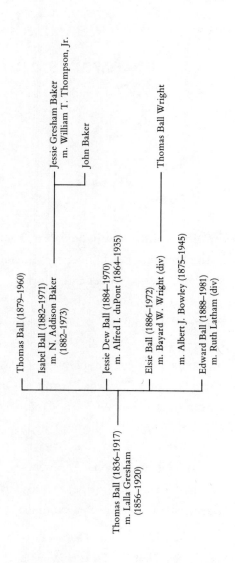

Thomas Ball (1879–1960)

Isabel Ball (1882–1971)
m. N. Addison Baker
(1882–1973)

Jessie Gresham Baker
m. William T. Thompson, Jr.

John Baker

Jessie Dew Ball (1884–1970)
m. Alfred I. duPont (1864–1935)

Elsie Ball (1886–1972)
m. Bayard W. Wright (div)

Thomas Ball Wright

m. Albert J. Bowley (1875–1945)

Edward Ball (1888–1981)
m. Ruth Latham (div)

Thomas Ball (1836–1917)
m. Lalla Gresham
(1856–1920)

Jessie Ball duPont,
Awards and Honors

Honorary Degrees

1945   D.C.L., University of the South, Sewanee, Tennessee

1947   D.H.L., Washington and Lee University, Lexington, Virginia

1952   H.H.D., Stetson University, DeLand, Florida

1953   L.L.D., Rollins College, Winter Park, Florida

1954   L.L.D., College of William and Mary, Williamsburg, Virginia

1954   H.H.D., Centre College, Danville, Kentucky

1954   L.L.D., University of Delaware, Newark, Delaware

1958   Honorary Fellow, Trinity College, Toronto, Ontario

1959   D.H.L., Western College for Women, Oxford, Ohio

1959   D.H.L., Women's Medical College of Pennsylvania, Philadelphia, Pennsylvania

1959   D.H.L., Hollins College, Hollins, Virginia

1970   L.L.D., Bethune-Cookman College, Daytona Beach, Florida

1970   D.H.L., Jacksonville University, Jacksonville, Florida

Citations and Awards

1943   Meritorious Service Citation, Florida War Fund

1943   Meritorious Service Citation, Community War Chest, Jacksonville

1946   Ribbon of the King's Medal for Service in the Cause of Freedom, United Kingdom

1954   Lafayette Citation, Newburgh Chapter of the Empire State Society, Sons of the American Revolution

1956   Distinguished Service Citation, Virginia State Chamber of Commerce

1957   Distinguished Service Citation, Military Chaplains of U.S.A.

1957   Tennessee Colonel Citation

1957   Godmother's Certificate, Florida Crippled Children's Association

1963   Associate Commander (Sister), Venerable Order of the Hospital of St. John of Jerusalem

1964   Certificate, National Trust for Historic Preservation of the U.S.

1967   Hollins Medal, Hollins College

Appendix 3

Jessie Ball duPont, Positions Held

Vice-president and member, board of directors, Almours Securities, 1926–35; president, 1935–38

Member, board of trustees, Hollins College, 1944–70

Member, board of directors, Florida National Banks, 1934–64

Chairperson, board of directors, St. Joe Paper Company, 1942–70

Trustee, the Estate of Alfred I. duPont, 1935–70

Founder, Alfred I. duPont Foundation, 1936

President, board of directors, The Nemours Foundation, 1936–70

Member, board of managers, Alfred I. duPont Institute, 1936–70

Founder and Member, awards committee, Alfred I. duPont Awards Foundation, 1943–62

State director, Robert E. Lee Memorial Foundation, Inc., 1930–67; assistant treasurer, 1933–58

Founder member and vice-president, board of directors, Virginia Museum of Fine Arts, 1934–66

Member, board of trustees, Stetson University, 1942–45

Member, Florida State Board of Control, 1951–55

Member, board of trustees, Washington and Lee University, 1959–70

Founder and trustee, Virginia Foundation of Independent Colleges, 1952–70

Notes

AIP Papers of Alfred I. duPont, Washington and Lee University, Lexington, Virginia

EB-STJ Edward Ball Files, St. Joe Paper Company, Jacksonville, Florida

FSA Florida State Archives, Tallahassee

JBP Papers of Jessie Ball duPont, Washington and Lee University, Lexington, Virginia. The two numbers following the symbol are box and folder numbers respectively.

JBP Fund Files of the Jessie Ball duPont Religious, Charitable, and Educational Fund, Jacksonville, Florida

WBM Papers of William B. Mills, private collection held by Mrs. Mills, Jacksonville, Florida

CHAPTER ONE

1. Los Angeles *Examiner,* Jan. 23, 1921, p. 3. The headline and first quotation were in an unidentified paper, a clipping of which is in *JBP 254-1.*

2. San Diego *Union,* Jan. 25, 1921, p. 8.

3. Los Angeles *Express,* Jan. 27, 1921, p. 3.

4. JBP recalled the Pauline Frederick story in a letter to Marquis James, Dec. 19, 1940, *JBP 58-4.*

5. "Genealogy—Ball Family," and "Relation to Mary Ball Washington," *JBP 188-12;* Robert O. Norris, "Mary Ball Washington and Her Family," *Northern Neck of Virginia Historical Society* 3 (1953):190–97.

6. "Information for the National Cyclopedia of American Biography, re: Honorable Thomas Ball," *JBP Fund.*

7. Dallas *Weekly Herald,* June 22, 1871, p. 2.

8. C. C. Rister, "The Significance of the Jacksboro Indian Affair of 1871," *Southwestern Historical Quarterly* 29 (Jan. 1926):181–200.

9. Tax Rolls, Jacks County, Texas, 1872–78, Texas State Library, Archives Division, Austin, Texas.

10. Dallas *Weekly Herald,* Mar. 4, 1876, p. 1, Apr. 29, 1876, p. 1; a copy of the marriage license, dated Feb. 26, 1878, from Marriage License Book F, p. 257, Galveston County Texas, is in *JBP 187-4.*

11. "Colonial Families of Virginia—Gresham," Mar. 1, 1935, copy in *JBP 188-12;* Lalla Gresham Ball, "Reminiscences of Plantation Life in Virginia," *Northern Neck Historical Quarterly* 12 (1962):1060–67 (copy in *JBP 254-1*).

12. To Mrs. Henry Stoeckle, Nov. 18, 1954, *JBP 132-43.*

13. Rupert Norval Richardson, *Texas: The Lone Star State* (Englewood Cliffs, N.J.: Prentice Hall, 1970), pp. 232–37; Thomas to Lalla Ball, Sept. 29, 1880, *JBP 254-1.*

14. Northumberland County, Va., Deed Book G, p. 284, copy in *JBP 188-12;* from Jennie Harding Cornelius, undated, *JBP 188-12;* Clement Eaton, *The Waning of the Old South Civilization, 1860–1880s* (Athens: University of Georgia Press, 1968), pp. 150–60.

15. William H. Pease, "The Saints and Sinners of Bertram Wyatt-Brown," *Reviews in American History* 15 (June 1987):179–80; Bertram Wyatt-Brown, *Southern Honor: Ethics and Behavior in the Old South* (New York: Oxford University Press, 1982), p. xv.

16. Virginia Dept. of Health, Delayed Certificate of Birth, Jessie Ball, Jan. 20, 1884, certificate issued Apr. 22, 1947, copy in *JBP 189-15;* to Arthur McKinstry, Apr. 17, 1954, *JBP 132-3;* to Robert Carter Ball, July 13, 1954, *JBP 129-25.*

17. To James Finnie, Mar. 12, 1958, *JBP 151-12.*

18. On Ditchley, see JBP to O. W. Riegel, May 13, 1954, *JBP 132-23;* "Ditchley," undated, *JBP 188-12;* from Cazenove G. Lee, Jr., Feb. 5, 1938, *JBP 47-26.* I am indebted to Robert Carter Ball for pointing out these landmarks for me on a cold, blustery March day.

19. C. Van Woodward, *Origins of the New South, 1877–1913* (Baton Rouge: Louisiana State University Press, 1971), p. 448; Kenneth K. Baily, "Southern White Protestantism at the Turn of the Century," *American Historical Review* 68 (April 1963): 619–20; Robert C. McMath, Jr., "Community, Religion, and Hegemony in the Nineteenth Century South," in *Towards a New South? Studies in Post Civil-War Southern Communities,* ed. Orville V. Burton and Robert C. McMath (Westport, Conn.: Greenwood Press, 1982), p. 288; Wyatt-Brown, *Southern Honor,* pp. xviii, 34; to Helen Knox, May 16, 1955, *JBP 191-24;* Thomas Ball to Ella Haile, Aug. 3, 1896, *JBP 254-1;* Thomas Ball to Mollie Pinckard, Sept. 15, 1909, *JBP 254-1;* to the

Rev. Wilbur Sims, Mar. 4, 1954, *JBP 129-22;* to Father McDonald, Mar. 25, 1954, *JBP 132-36.*

20. Woodward, *Origins,* pp. 264–65.

21. Thomas Ball to W. L. Colby, Asst. Attorney General, May 4, 1892, Court of Claims, Indian Depredations, R.G. 205, National Archives.

22. To Mr. and Mrs. Taliaferro Thompson, Jr., July 3, 1956, *JBP 142-5;* to Thomas Ball Wright, Jan. 11, 1956, *JBP 142-21.*

23. Indian Depredations Letter Book, 1892–93, R.G. 205, National Archives; to Mrs. Robert Ball, Aug. 11, 1942, *JBP 68-84.*

24. Charles D. Howry, Asst. Attorney General, to Thomas Ball, Jan. 19, 1894, Indian Depredations Letter Book no. 4; Ball to Howry, Jan. 24, 1894, Court of Claims, Indian Depredations, Box 4; Ball to Richard Olney, Attorney General, Mar. 19, 1895, Court of Claims, DOJ Section, Letters Received, "B," Box 1–5; Howry to Ball, Mar. 20, 1895, Letters Sent, books 2–16; all in National Archives.

25. To Tom Ball, Apr. 28, 1941, *JBP 63-12;* to Mary Peck, Jan. 14, 1959, *JBP 157-44;* Richard Wilson, "Personality Profile," Richmond *Times-Dispatch,* Apr. 8, 1958, copy in *JBP 191-83.*

26. Thomas Ball to Ella Haile, Jan. 10, 1899, *JBP 254-1;* Lalla Ball to her daughters, Dec. 15, 1901, *JBP 254-1;* Lalla Ball to Isabel Ball, Jan. 11, 1902, *JBP 254-1.*

27. To Denise duPont Zapffee, May 27, 1958, *JBP 154-6;* to Beverley Broun, Feb. 5, 1959, *JBP 195-45;* to Rebecca Harding Adams, Jan. 4, 1941, *JBP 63-6;* to Mrs. Robert Ball, Aug. 11, 1942, *JBP 68-84.*

28. To Beverley Broun, Feb. 5, 1959, *JBP 195-45;* Carroll Smith-Rosenberg, "The Female World of Love and Ritual: Relations between Women in Nineteenth Century America," *Signs* 1 (Autumn 1975):27.

29. Marquis James, *Alfred I. duPont: The Family Rebel* (Indianapolis: Bobbs-Merrill, 1941), pp. 135-36. This paragraph is based on James's account, which in turn came from an unrecorded oral interview with Rebecca Harding Adams.

30. To Rebecca Harding Adams, July 29, 1939, *JBP 50-4;* from Adams, Aug. 22, 1939, *JBP 243-1;* Maria Ball to AIP, Apr. 1, Oct. 12, 1920, both in Folder 121, *AIP.*

31. J. L. Blair Buck, *The Development of Public Schools in Virginia, 1607–1952* (Richmond: Virginia State Board of Education, 1952), 35:81–83; Circular of the State Female Normal School at Farmville, Va., Aug. 1, 1887, pp. 6–7, in the Virginia State Library, Richmond; Charles A. Harper, *A Century of Public Teacher Education* (Westport, Conn.: Greenwood Press, 1970), p. 106; Jessie M. Pangburn, *The Evolution of the American Teachers*

College (New York: Teachers College, Columbia University, 1932), pp. 14–18.

32. Copies of Jessie's and Isabel's original grade sheets were obtained from Longwood College, Farmville, and are now on file in the Jessie Ball duPont Fund's file on Mrs. duPont.

33. To Rebecca Harding Adams, Mar. 22, 1955, *JBP 190-55;* to Mary Peck, Jan. 14, 1959, *JBP 157-44.*

34. Wytheville (Va.) *Dispatch,* Aug. 20, 1897, p. 2, Sept. 1, 1898, p. 3; to Devall L. Gwathmey, Nov. 10, 1954, *JBP 131-16;* to Knox Chandler, Feb. 15, 1955, *JBP 191-24;* Buck, *Public Schools,* p. 98.

35. Thomas Ball to his daughters, Dec. 17, 1901, *JBP 254-1.*

36. Thomas Ball to his daughters, Jan. 1, 1902, *JBP 254-1.*

37. To Mrs. Robert Ball, Aug 11, 1942, *JBP 68-84;* Wyatt-Brown, *Southern Honor,* p. 131.

38. Virginia State Board of Education, *Bulletin,* vol. 3, Jan. 1921, no. 3, supplement 2, *Certification of Teachers* (Richmond, 1921), p. 6; ibid., Apr. 1926, no. 4, *Annual Report of the Superintendent of Public Instruction,* school years 1918–19 and 1919–20, pp. 74–78.

39. Anne Firor Scott, *The Southern Lady from Pedestal to Politics, 1830–1930* (Chicago: University of Chicago Press, 1970), pp. iii, 5–7; Sally Schwager, "Educating Women in America," *Signs* 12 (Winter 1987):333–72; Sophonisba P. Breckinridge, *Women in the Twentieth Century: A Study of Their Political, Social and Economic Activities* (New York: McGraw-Hill, 1933), pp. 188–89; Thomas Woody, *A History of Women's Education in the United States* (New York: Octagon Books, 1966), pp. 516–18.

40. Anne Firor Scott, "The Ever Widening Circle: The Diffusion of Feminist Values from the Troy Female Seminary, 1822–72," *History of Education Quarterly* 10 (Spring 1970):3–25.

41. Sondra R. Herman, "Loving Courtship or the Marriage Market? The Ideal and Its Critics, 1871–1911," *American Quarterly* 25 (May 1973): 360; James R. McGovern, "The American Woman's Pre–World War I Freedom in Manners and Morals," *Journal of American History* 55 (Sept. 1968): 320; Scott, *The Southern Lady,* p. 225; Sheila M. Rothman, *Women's Proper Place: A History of Changing Ideals and Practices, 1870 to the Present* (New York: Basic Books, 1978), pp. 56–60; Scott, "The Ever Widening Circle," pp. 3–25.

42. To Rebecca Adams, July 29, 1939, *JBP 50-4.*

43. The quotation is from James, *The Family Rebel,* p. 187 (I did not find the letter cited in Mrs. duPont's files); Joseph Frazier Wall, *Alfred I. duPont: The Man and His Family* (New York: Oxford University Press, 1990), pp. 240–41. Leonard Mosley (*Blood Relations: The Rise & Fall of the duPonts of Delaware* [New York: Atheneum, 1980], pp. 186–87), describes in graphic

detail a budding romance between Jessie and Alfred. I have found no evidence to substantiate Mosley's account.

44. James, *The Family Rebel,* pp. 142–60; Wall, *duPont,* pp. 180–96; to Mrs. Arthur Chamberlain, Jr., Feb. 8, 1957, *JBP 193-10;* Alfred D. Chandler and Stephen Salsbury, *Pierre S. DuPont and the Making of the Modern Corporation* (New York: Harper and Row, 1971), pp. 47–54.

45. To Mamie T. Edwards, Aug. 19, 1944, *JBP 78-40.*

46. James, *The Family Rebel,* p. 328; Wall, *duPont,* p. 471; Captain Ball to his daughters, Dec. 17, 1901, *JBP 254-1.*

47. To Tom Ball, March 31, 1944, *JBP 78-3;* from Tom Ball, Oct. 14, 1906, *JBP 254-1.*

48. From Tom Ball, Oct. 14, Dec. 30, 1906, *JBP 254-1;* to Charles Hardwicke, Nov. 6, 1929, *JBP 6-2.*

49. James, *The Family Rebel,* p. 188; Wall, *duPont,* pp. 241–42.

50. Wall, *duPont,* p. 217.

51. James, *The Family Rebel,* p. 187.

52. Wall, *duPont,* pp. 224–32.

53. Wall, *duPont,* pp. 253–55.

54. The verse, in JBP's handwriting, appears undated on stationery of "W. C. Dickinson, Wheatland, Loretto, Virginia, 190_," *JBP 254-1.* There is no contemporary evidence of JBP's feelings for AIP in 1907, but evidence in later documents cited below convinced me that my interpretation is close to the mark.

55. Commonwealth of Virginia, Professional Certificate for Jessie D. Ball, Sept. 1, 1907; from Thomas Ball, June 4, 1908, both in *JBP 254-1.*

56. JBP Diary, 1908, *JBP 241-1;* San Diego City Directories, 1908–15; to Arthur Gould, Sept. 18, 1942, *JBP 70-40;* County of San Diego, Grammar School Certificate, Jessie Ball, Oct. 24, 1914, *JBP 254-1.*

57. Three letters to Winifred Eldred Stephenson: Dec. 29, 1952, *JBP 122-11;* Feb. 20, 1956, *JBP 192-43;* Aug. 2, 1956, *JBP 141-37.*

58. Dance programs, Christmas 1908, *JBP 248-1;* San Diego *Union,* Dec. 3, 1910, p. 6, July 6, 1911, p. 10, July 7, 1911, p. 10.

59. J. Stanley Lemons, *The Woman Citizen: Social Feminism in the 1920s* (Urbana: University of Illinois Press, 1973), pp. 41–43; to Isabel Ball Baker, Dec. 16, 1948, *JBP 97-5;* to Isabel Baker, Dec. 1, 1937, *JBP 37-43.*

60. From Rebecca Harding Adams, May 15, 1967, *JBP 180-14;* to Jessie Baker Thompson, June 8, 1956, *JBP 142-5;* to Winifred Stephenson, March 1, 1934, *JBP 23-45;* to Henry H. Bawden, May 3, 1944, *JBP 77-80;* to Winifred Stephenson, July 13, 1944, *JBP 81-12.*

61. Margaret Snydelaar to the author, June 3, 1987.

62. To AIP, Apr. 19, 1920, *JBP 254-2;* Duncan A. MacKinnon, super-

intendent of schools, letter of recommendation, July 1, 1916, *JBP 248-1;* JBP carried on a lifelong correspondence with the Rosses, e.g., from Pete Ross, Jan. 31, 1921, *JBP 248-1;* Woody, *A History of Women's Education,* pp. 516–18.

63. As the text states, JBP must have destroyed almost all of the secret letters to Alfred, if indeed she actually wrote them. She revealed the existence of the fantasy letters in one more that she wrote to Alfred, Apr. 19, 1920, *JBP 254-2;* to Charles Hardwicke, Aug. 13, 1943, *JBP 75-36.*

64. From Lalla Ball, May 19, 1917, *JBP 254-1;* to Mrs. Charles C. Sanford, Nov. 21, 1957, *JBP 193-60;* to A. J. Bowley, June 6, 1938, *JBP 44-22;* to Isabel Ball Baker, June 8, 1942, *JBP 68-85.*

65. San Diego City Directories, 1909, 1918, 1919. On Edward Ball, see James, *The Family Rebel,* pp. 358–59.

66. AIP to Rebecca Harding, Jan. 28, 1918, *AIP.*

67. From AIP, Dec. 8, 1918, *JBP 254-2.*

68. From AIP, May 6, 1919, *JBP 254-2.* Mosley states that Alfred met Jessie and Ed Ball at Ball's Neck in January 1911 (*Blood Relations,* pp. 218–19). Such a meeting was highly unlikely because both Jessie and Ed were much involved in their own careers in California at that time.

69. To AIP, Oct. 8, no year, but almost conclusively 1919, *JBP 254-2.* Mosley claims that Jessie wrote to Alfred "regularly" and that Alicia found Jessie's letters in Alfred's desk (*Blood Relations,* pp. 229–30).

70. Wall, *duPont,* pp. 322–53; James, *The Family Rebel,* pp. 254–81, 286–92, 302–8, 321–25.

71. To AIP, Oct. 8, [1919], *JBP 254-2.*

72. To AIP, Oct. 10, 1919, *JBP 254-2.*

73. Draft transcript of Mrs. duPont's interview with Marquis James, undated, *JBP 52-4;* James, *The Family Rebel,* p. 329; Wall, *duPont,* pp. 417–18. Mosley gives a garbled account of the meeting (*Blood Relations,* pp. 279–80).

74. From AIP, Jan. 17, 1920, *JBP 254-2.*

75. AIP to Madeleine Hiebler, Feb. 2, 1920, *AIP.*

76. Hotel bills, March 30–April 3, 1920, *JBP 248-1.* Wall, *duPont,* pp. 270–72; James, *The Family Rebel,* p. 337.

77. JBP, handwritten on Cherry Island stationery, undated, *JBP 254-2;* to AIP, May 16, 1920, *JBP 254-2.*

78. To AIP, June 20, 1920, *JBP 254-2.* Five other letters written to Alfred during that week are in the same file. Mosley, *Blood Relations,* p. 285.

79. From AIP, June 15, 1920, *JBP 254-2.*

80. To AIP, undated but probably June 13, 1920; to AIP, June 28, 1920, both in *JBP 254-2.*

CHAPTER TWO

1. From Miller M. Montgomery, Jan. 31, 1921, *JBP 248-1*.
2. From Pete Ross, Jan. 31, Mar. 13, 1921, *JBP 248-1*.
3. Nemours House Servants, Feb. 1921, *JBP 248-1*; to Wm. Taliaferro Thompson III, Oct. 19, 1964, *JBP 176-28*. Mrs. duPont's roadster is preserved in the garage at Nemours.
4. Joseph Frazier Wall, *Alfred I. duPont: The Man and His Family* (New York: Oxford University Press, 1990), pp. 402–4.
5. Marquis James, *Alfred I. duPont: The Family Rebel* (Indianapolis: Bobbs-Merrill, 1941), pp. 253, 313; Wall, *duPont*, pp. 405–6.
6. AIP to Mrs. John Sebree, Mar. 16, 1921, Folder 1586, *AIP*.
7. James, *The Family Rebel*, pp. 326–28, 331–34; Wall, *duPont*, pp. 426–32.
8. James, *The Family Rebel*, pp. 340–42, 345–50; Wall, *duPont*, pp. 434–40.
9. James, *The Family Rebel*, pp. 22–24, 93–95; Wall, *duPont*, pp. 150–51; from Margery duPont, Feb. 2, 1921, *JBP 248-1*.
10. To Ella G. Haile, Dec. 28, 1923, as quoted in James, *The Family Rebel*, p. 367.
11. Wall, *duPont*, pp. 445–46.
12. James, *The Family Rebel*, pp. 370–71; Wall, *duPont*, pp. 460–62.
13. James, *The Family Rebel*, pp. 370–74.
14. Ibid., pp. 375–80; Wall, *duPont*, pp. 463–64; Leonard Mosley, *Blood Relations: The Rise and Fall of the duPonts of Delaware* (New York: Atheneum, 1980), pp. 320–25.
15. To Madeleine duPont Hiebler, Dec. 30, 1927, *JBP 3-12*.
16. To Mrs. Alex B. Francis, July 16, 1925, *JBP 1-18*; to Mrs. S. C. Kendall, June 28, 1926, *JBP 2-5*.
17. Interview with Denise duPont Zapffe, June 12, 1987; James, *The Family Rebel*, pp. 371–72.
18. To Tom Ball, June 29, 1925, *JBP 1-7*; AIP to Tom Ball, June 17, 1925, Folder 1924 A-Z, *AIP*.
19. To Mrs. Thomas Ball, Nov. 13, 1925, *JBP 1-7*.
20. To AIP, June 21, 1927, *JBP 254-2*.
21. "Checks Drawn by Marion Gillespie, April 30, 1926," *JBP 2-21*; Monthly Gifts, 1927, *JBP 3-40*; List of Registered Mail Sent Out, Dec. 1927, *JBP 3-32*.
22. List of beneficiaries, undated but in 1927 files, *JBP 2-29*. This list was probably incorporated in the 1927 will. Codicil, Apr. 21, 1927, to Last Will and Testament of Jessie Ball duPont, Mar. 2, 1927, *JBP 251-2*; Codicil, Dec. 18, 1935, *JBP 241-11*; Codicil, June 11, 1948, to Last Will and Testament, May 17, 1943, *JBP 251-4*.

23. Warren Weaver, "Pre-Christian Philanthropy," in *America's Voluntary Spirit,* ed. Brian O'Connell (New York; The Foundation Center, 1983), p. 8; Daniel J. Boorstin, "From Charity to Philanthropy," ibid., p. 135.

24. Edward Grubb, "Philanthropy," in *Encyclopedia of Religion and Ethics* (1917), 9:837.

25. Kathleen D. McCarthy, *Noblesse Oblige: Charity and Cultural Philanthropy in Chicago, 1849–1929* (Chicago: University of Chicago Press, 1982), p. 151; Robert H. Bremmer, *American Philanthropy* (Chicago: University of Chicago Press, 1960), p. 90. The Rockefeller foundations are a striking 1920s example of the application of philanthropy to the study of contemporary society. See Warren Weaver, *U.S. Philanthropic Foundations: Their History, Structure, Management, and Record* (New York: Harper & Row, 1967), pp. 27–80; Donald Fisher, "The Role of Philanthropic Foundations in the Reproduction and Production of Hegemony: Rockefeller Foundations and the Social Sciences," *Sociology* 17 (May 1983):206–33.

26. Mary G. Shaw obituary, Wilmington *Evening Journal,* Mar. 6, 1965, p. 5.

27. To H. J. Edmonds, Apr. 30, 1928, *JBP 4-21.*

28. M. G. Shaw to Edmonds, June 16, 1927; Edmonds to Shaw, undated; Shaw to Edmonds, July 18, 1927, all in *JBP 2-65;* to Mrs. James D. Jesse, Sept. 29, 1927, *JBP 3-15;* from Powhatan Stone, Oct. 21, 1927; to Powhatan Stone, Oct. 28, 1927; from Powhatan Stone, Nov. 2, 1927; to Powhatan Stone, Nov. 8, 1927, all in *JBP 3-40;* from Sallie H. Taylor, Jan. 9, 1928, *JBP 5-15;* Shaw to Mary Haile, Jan. 19, 1928, *JBP 4-28;* from Morgan E. Norris, June 8, 1928, *JBP 4-47;* from Stella Brubaken, Oct. 30, 1929 and Shaw to Brubaken, Nov. 5, 1929, *JBP 5-53.*

29. To J. A. C. Chandler, Aug. 31, 1926, *JBP 1-69;* Chandler to Mary G. Shaw, Aug. 9, 1929, *JBP 6-64.*

30. To W. T. Rice, Jan. 25, 1961, *JBP 162-14;* to F. D. Goodwin, Aug. 22, 1923, Folder 589, *AIP;* from Goodwin, Aug. 15, 1927, *JBP 2-70.* Many of Goodwin's reports are in *JBP 4-18* and *JBP 6-60.*

31. To Mrs. E. P. Tignor, June 26, 1928, *JBP 4-16.*

32. To Mrs. E. P. Tignor, May 11, 1928, *JBP 4-16.* Many reports from Mrs. Tignor in 1928 and 1929 are in *JBP 6-57.*

33. To Thomas Ball Wright, Jan. 28, 1927, *JBP 3-49.*

34. To William Wellons, June 18, 1928, *JBP 4-17.*

35. From J. A. C. Chandler, Feb. 9, 1928; to Chandler, June 28, 1928, both in *JBP 4-17.*

36. To Virginia Lee Cox, May 10, 1927, *JBP 2-63;* from J. A. Turner, Aug. 13, 1928, *JBP 4-31.* Hollins had not raised the matching funds by 1939,

and Mrs. duPont was unwilling to honor the pledge at that time. See JBP to Bessie C. Randolph, Apr. 11, 1939, *JBP 53-20*.

37. Total Amounts Appropriated by Mrs. duPont for Education, 1928–29, *JBP 6-44*.

38. To John R. Saunders, Sept. 24, 1927, *JBP 3-36*.

39. To J. Franklyn Dew, Sept. 22, 1925, *JBP 1-12;* to James L. Howe, Aug. 18, 1930, *JBP 7-8*.

40. Daniel A. Wren, "American Business Philanthropy and Higher Education in the Nineteenth Century," *Business History Review* 57 (Autumn 1983):321–34; Rosemary Higgins Cass and Gordon Manser, "Roots of Voluntarism," in O'Connell, *America's Voluntary Spirit,* p. 14.

41. To Virginia Church, Oct. 20, 1926, *JBP 1-63*.

42. To Lee G. Crutchfield, Jr., Sept. 16, 1930, *JBP 7-12*.

43. To Denise duPont, Nov. 30, 1928, *JBP 4-2*.

44. To L. R. Combs, Jan. 19, 1928, *JBP 199-7*.

CHAPTER THREE

1. Marquis James, *Alfred I. duPont: The Family Rebel* (Indianapolis: Bobbs-Merrill, 1941), pp. 354–56; Joseph Frazier Wall, *Alfred I. duPont: The Man and His Family* (New York: Oxford University Press, 1990), pp. 469–71; AIP to Tom Ball, Dec. 27, Folder 117, *AIP*.

2. AIP to Ed Ball, Mar. 26, 1923, and Ed Ball to AIP, Apr. 2, 1923, both in Folder 1130, *AIP;* Raymond K. Mason and Virginia Harrison, *Confusion to the Enemy: A Biography of Edward Ball* (New York: Dodd, Mead, 1976), pp. 11–20, 30–31.

3. Wall, *duPont,* p. 472; Leonard Mosley, *Blood Relations: The Rise and Fall of the duPonts of Delaware* (New York: Atheneum, 1980), pp. 317–20; AIP to Maurice duPont Lee, Dec. 31, 1923, Folder 695, *AIP*.

4. AIP to Tom Ball, Apr. 22, 1924, Folder 606, *AIP;* James, *The Family Rebel,* pp. 356–58; Wall, *duPont,* pp. 473–75.

5. AIP to Tom Ball, Oct. 15, 1924, as quoted in James, *The Family Rebel,* p. 360.

6. To William A. Martin, May 2, 1937, *JBP 41-10*.

7. James, *The Family Rebel,* pp. 392–96; AIP to Tom Ball, Jan. 7, 1924, Folder 606, *AIP;* Wall, *duPont,* pp. 480–85.

8. James, *The Family Rebel,* pp. 396–97; William J. Oven to Ed Ball, Oct. 22, 1924, Folder 1924–26, EB-*STJ;* AIP Memorandum, Dec. 15, 1924, Folder 1130, *AIP;* interview with Frederick H. Kent, Jr., Mar. 17, 1987.

9. "No Income or Inheritance Taxes for Florida," *Suniland: The Magazine of Florida* (Dec. 1924), pp. 15–16, 92.

10. James B. Crooks, "Changing Face of Jacksonville, Florida, 1900–1910," *Florida Historical Quarterly* 62 (Apr. 1984):439–40; Herbert J. Doherty, Jr., "Jacksonville as a Nineteenth-Century Railroad Center," *Florida Historical Quarterly* 58 (Oct. 1977):373–86.

11. Ibid., pp. 442–43.

12. Ibid., pp. 444–45.

13. Ibid., pp. 454–58; James B. Crooks, "Jacksonville in the Progressive Era: Responses to Urban Growth," *Florida Historical Quarterly* 65 (July 1986):58–59; Wallace M. Nelson, "The Economic Development of Florida, 1870–1930" (Ph. D. diss., University of Florida, 1962), University Microfilm 62–6541.

14. T. Frederick Davis, *History of Jacksonville, Florida* (St. Augustine: Florida Historical Society, 1925), pp. 279–85; Jacksonville *Florida Times-Union,* Dec. 3, 1924, p. 1; Jacksonville *Journal,* Nov. 6, 1925, p. 1.

15. As quoted in Mason and Harrison, *Confusion,* p. 41.

16. Clifton Paisley, *From Cotton to Quail: An Agricultural Chronicle of Leon County, Florida* (Gainesville: University of Florida Press, 1968), pp. 40–71.

17. Ed Ball to AIP, Apr. 2, 1925; telegrams, Ed Ball to AIP, Apr. 30, 1925 and May 1, 1925; telegram, AIP to Ed Ball, May 2, 1925, all in Folder 1924 A-Z, Edward Ball 1925, *AIP.*

18. Ed Ball to AIP, July 3, 1925, Folder AIP/1924–26, EB-*STJ.*

19. Telegram, Ed Ball to AIP and JBP, Sept. 3, 1925; AIP to Ed Ball, Sept. 15, 1925; telegram, AIP to Ed Ball, Sept. 13, 1925, all in Folder 1924 A-Z, Edward Ball, 1925, *AIP;* AIP to Ed Ball, Oct. 11, 1925; Ed Ball to AIP, Oct. 14, 1925, in Folder AIP/1924–26, EB-*STJ.*

20. James, *The Family Rebel,* pp. 398–401; Ed Ball to AIP, Dec. 4, 1926, in Folder AIP/1926, EB-*STJ.*

21. To Tom Ball, Apr. 20, 1926, *JBP 1-62;* Susan Caven, "Epping Forest," in *Show House XI, Epping Forest* (Jacksonville, 1984), p. 31.

22. James, *The Family Rebel,* pp. 402, 405.

23. American National Red Cross, *The Florida Hurricane, September 18, 1926: Official Report of the Relief Activities* (Washington, D.C., 1926); Charlton W. Tebeau, *A History of Florida* (Coral Gables: University of Miami Press, 1971), pp. 377–88; W. H. Harper, *A Pictorial History of the Florida Hurricane, September 18, 1926* (Miami: L. L. Tyler, 1926).

24. William T. Edwards, "Recollection of Alfred I. duPont's Early Interests in Florida" (undated manuscript), *AIP.*

25. Ibid.

26. J. G. Bright to Marquis James, Feb. 15, 1941, *JBP 243-1.*

27. Edwards, "Florida Recollections"; and Ed Ball to AIP, Apr. 30, 1927, both in Folder 1927, Edward Ball, *AIP;* James, *The Family Rebel,* pp. 451–52.

28. Ed Ball to AIP, May 14, 1927, Folder 1927, Edward Ball, *AIP*.

29. James, *The Family Rebel,* pp. 403–6, 429–33; Wall, *duPont,* pp. 485–88.

30. To Inga Orner, April 25, 1925, *JBP 1-34.*

31. To Tom Ball, Feb. 28, 1927, *JBP 199-34;* to Mrs. John F. Sebree, May 9, 1927, *JBP 3-37;* Christmas gift list, 1928, *JBP 4-6.*

32. From Mary G. Shaw, Mar. 21, Apr. 18, 1928; to Shaw, Apr. 13, 1928, all in *JBP 4-3.*

33. Wall, *duPont,* pp. 457–58.

34. To Tom Ball, Mar. 17, 1926, *JBP 1-62;* to Ed Ball, July 9, 1928, Folder 1928, EB-*STJ;* to Isadore Muller, Nov. 30, 1928, *JBP 4-47;* to F. C. Bowen, undated, but probably Mar. 1929, *JBP 199-69;* to Mrs. Fennimore Cooper, Oct. 31, 1929, *JBP 5-56;* James, *The Family Rebel,* p. 433.

35. James, *The Family Rebel,* pp. 429–36.

36. To Dr. Dewitt B. Casler, Jan. 6, 1930, *JBP 189-15;* AIP to Tom Ball, Feb. 11, 1930, Folder Thomas Ball, 1930, *AIP;* to Mr. and Mrs. William A. Martin, Mar. 4, 1930, *JBP 8-16.*

37. To Mamie T. Edwards, Mar. 20, 1930, *JBP 8-46.*

38. As quoted in James, *The Family Rebel,* p. 443.

39. To William Martin, May 2, 1930, *JBP 8-16.*

40. To Mrs. Arthur Chamberlain, Jr., Nov. 15, 1944, *JBP 78-21.*

CHAPTER FOUR

1. JBP Financial Report for the Year Ended Dec. 31, 1927, *JBP 3-3.*

2. "Women in Business: III," *Fortune* 12 (Sept. 1935):81; JBP Report for Period Ended Sept. 30, 1929, *JBP 5-69.*

3. JBP Annual Report for the Year Ended Dec. 30, 1930, *JBP 8-38;* to Almours Securities, Nov. 21, 1930, *JBP 9-10.*

4. To Charles F. Ball, Nov. 10, 1930, *JBP 9-16.*

5. From Ethel Luttrell, Oct. 24, 1930; to Luttrell, Nov. 5, 1930, both in *JBP 8-20.*

6. From T. F. Wheeldon, Nov. 21, 1930, and to H. J. Edmonds, Nov. 24, 1930, both in *JBP 8-45;* from Wheeldon, Nov. 25, 1930, and M. G. Shaw to Wheeldon, Dec. 2, 1930, both in *JBP 7-20;* to Edmonds, Dec. 8, 1930, *JBP 8-45.*

7. Robert H. Bremmer, *American Philanthropy* (Chicago: University of Chicago Press, 1960), pp. 143–44.

8. From F. D. Goodwin, July 28, Aug. 15, 1931, and to F. D. Goodwin, Aug. 21, 1931, all in *JBP 11-8;* to F. D. Goodwin, June 24, 1932, *JBP 12-37;* to W. A. R. Goodwin, June 13, 21, 1932, and from W. A. R. Goodwin, June 15, 1932, all in *JBP 13-7.*

9. List of Money Appropriated to Assist Students Attending College During School Year 1932–33, undated, *JBP 24-23;* List of Questions to be Answered by Applicants, 1933–34, *JBP 16-67.*

10. From W. T. Rice, Apr. 8, 1934, and to Rice, Apr. 13, 1934, both in *JBP 24-41;* to Lucille Hurst, May 7, 1934, *JBP 24-32;* from Ada Kelley, May 13, 1934, and to Kelley, May 18, 1934, both in *JBP 22-38.*

11. To Madeleine Ruoff, June 22, 1931, *JBP 10-13.*

12. To Margery duPont, May 4, 1932, *JBP 14-26.*

13. Ibid.; to Olga Anderson, Apr. 30, 1932, *JBP 200-39;* Marquis James, *Alfred I. duPont: The Family Rebel* (Indianapolis: Bobbs–Merrill, 1941), pp. 511–12; to W. A. Martin, Apr. 14, 1932, *JBP 200-55.*

14. To Denise duPont, Apr. 12, 1932, *JBP 200-44;* to Mrs. Alec B. Francis, Apr. 12, 1932, *JBP 14-43.*

15. To Joseph W. Chinn, Sept. 22, Oct. 9, 1930, *JBP 9-13;* to Chinn, Nov. 8, 1931, *JBP 12-1.*

16. From Ed Ball, July 19, 1932, *JBP 14-27;* to Wilmot Ball, Nov. 11, 1933, *JBP 16-74;* to Wilmot Ball, Feb. 14, 1934, *JBP 20-70;* to Carter Keane, Aug. 1, 1934, *JBP 21-32.*

17. The text of Sidney Lanier's address was printed in Ethel Armes, *Stratford on the Potomac* (Greenwich, Conn.: United Daughters of the Confederacy, 1928), pp. 5–8 (copy in *JBP 8-17*).

18. Barbara J. Howe ("Women in Historic Preservation: The Legacy of Ann Pamela Cunningham," *The Public Historian* 12 [Winter 1990]:31–39) describes how women's interest in site preservation stemmed from the project at Mount Vernon.

19. To Mrs. Charles D. Lanier, Dec. 21, 1929, *JBP 6-12.*

20. From Mrs. Lanier, Apr. 16, 1930, and Roster, Robert E. Lee Memorial Foundation, 1930, both in *JBP 8-17.*

21. From Mrs. Lanier, Oct. 1, 1930, *JBP 8-17;* from Mrs. Lanier, Nov. 13, 1931, *JBP 10-37;* to Helen Knox, Oct. 26, 1934, *JBP 23-2.*

22. James, *The Family Rebel,* pp. 464–69; from Mrs. Lanier, Sept. 12, 1932, and reply, Sept. 13, 1932, both in *JBP 13-21;* to Thomas Wright, Sept. 21, 1932, *JBP 13-42.*

23. To Tom Ball, Oct. 24, 1932, *JBP 200-40.*

24. To Mrs. Lanier, Jan. 4, 1933, *JBP 18-45;* to Elsie Bowley, Mar. 24, 1933, *JBP 17-14;* to Tom Ball, Oct. 23, 1933, *JBP 17-8.*

25. Reminiscence by Mrs. Pratt Thomas, director for Mississippi, in *Jessie Ball duPont, 1884–1970* (Stratford, Va.: Robert E. Lee Memorial Foundation, 1985), p. 33.

26. Leila J. Rupp, "Reflections on Twentieth-Century American Women's History," *Reviews in American History* 9 (June 1981):279–81.

27. From Mary G. Fendall, National Woman's Party, Sept. 15, 1927, *JBP 3-27;* M. G. Shaw to Mrs. William S. Hilles, Jan. 28, 1929, *JBP 6-4;* to Representative Louis Ludlow, Mar. 15, 1933, *JBP 187-3;* to Richard A. R. Marische, July 10, 1934, *JBP 23-10.*

28. To Winifred Stephenson, Mar. 12, 1929, *JBP 199-95.*

29. To H. Thompson Holladay, July 17, 1931, *JBP 10-48.*

30. To T. B. Wright, June 30, 1931, *JBP 9-54;* to T. B. Wright, Mar. 24, 1932, *JBP 13-42.*

31. Wilbur J. Cash, *The Mind of the South* (New York: Alfred A. Knopf, 1941), pp. 38–39, 83–85, 108–10.

32. Ibid., p. 116.

33. Joel Williamson, *The Crucible of Race: Black-White Relations in the American South Since Emancipation* (New York: Oxford University Press, 1984), pp. 1–3.

34. Ibid., p. 6.

35. To J. Bland Dew, Feb. 23, 1926, *JBP 1-64.*

36. To Tom Ball, Apr. 25, 1927, *JBP 2-54.*

37. To Minnie J. Edwards, Dec. 1, 1930, *JBP 8-45.*

38. To T. B. Wright, Nov. 11, 1932, *JBP 13-42.*

39. To Tom Ball, June 25, 1931, *JBP 11-49.*

40. To J. G. Pollard, July 20, 1931, *JBP 10-20;* from Pollard, Feb. 9, Apr. 26, 1934, both in *JBP 23-34;* to Mrs. W. F. Rhea, May 5, 1934, *JBP 23-35;* from Genie P. Lapsley, Feb. 10, 1934, *JBP 24-13.*

41. Ed Ball to AIP, May 20, June 3, 1930, both in Folder 1930, Edward Ball, *AIP;* Ed Ball to AIP, June 1, 1931, Folder Edward Ball, 1931, *AIP;* James, *The Family Rebel,* pp. 445–48, 457–60.

42. W. T. Edwards, Memo on Paper Mill Project, undated but probably 1936, *JBP 35-34;* James, *The Family Rebel,* pp. 495–98.

43. To Mrs. Maurice duPont, Apr. 12, 1932, *JBP 14-26;* to Dr. Arnold Lorand, Apr. 7, 1930, *JBP 8-20;* to Richard A. R. Marische, Feb. 23, 1934, *JBP 23-10.*

44. James, *The Family Rebel,* pp. 482–87.

45. To Tom Ball, Feb. 20, 1933, *JBP 17-8.*

46. To Elsie Bowley, May 11, 1933, *JBP 17-14;* to George H. Dern, Apr. 26, 1934, *JBP 21-26;* from J. G. Pollard, May 4, 1934, and to Pollard, May 11, 1934, both in *JBP 23-34;* to Tom Ball, Apr. 9, 1935, *JBP 25-36;* to Elsie Bowley, Apr. 14, 1935, *JBP 25-44.*

47. To N. Addison Baker, June 19, 1933, *JBP 17-2;* to Tom Ball, June 26, 1933, *JBP 17-8;* Raymond K. Mason and Virginia Harrison, *Confusion to the Enemy: A Biography of Edward Ball* (New York: Dodd, Mead, 1976), pp. 150–51, 189–95.

48. Leonard Mosley, *Blood Relations: The Rise and Fall of the duPonts of Delaware* (New York: Atheneum, 1980), pp. 345–46; James, *The Family Rebel,* pp. 511–14.

49. James, *The Family Rebel,* pp. 525–29. Joseph Wall has achieved a major reinterpretation of the roles of Alfred duPont, Ball, and Edwards in the decision to build the mill for kraft paper production. See Joseph Frazier Wall, *Alfred I. duPont: The Man and His Family* (New York: Oxford University Press, 1990), pp. 497–506.

50. To Tom Ball, Feb. 15, 28, 1934, both in *JBP 21-4.*

51. To General and Mrs. A. J. Bowley, Mar. 27, 1934; to Elsie Bowley, Apr. 23, 1934, and to A. J. Bowley, May 14, 1934; all in *JBP 21-12;* James, *The Family Rebel,* pp. 530–31.

52. Jacksonville *Florida Times-Union,* May 3, 1934, copy in *JBP 187-3;* from N. Addison Baker, June 9, 1934, *JBP 21-1;* Memorandum to AIP, Sept. 14, 1934, *JBP 21-28.*

53. To Warner and Helen Ball, Jan. 11, 1935, *JBP 25-29.*

54. *The Blue Book: A Social Register of Jacksonville, Florida, 1935* listed the duPonts, Balls, Adairs, Dews, and Edwardses. Only the duPonts made the 1929 register, and only Ed Ball was added in 1929.

55. To Elsie Bowley, Jan. 11, 1935, *JBP 25-44.*

56. To W. T. Edwards, Apr. 24, 1937, *JBP 41-10.*

57. James, *The Family Rebel,* pp. 422–25, 463–64; to Julia Harding, Jan. 7, 1931, *JBP 12-24.*

58. Will and Testament, Nov. 19, 1932, *In Re the Estate of Alfred I duPont, Deceased: True and Correct Copy and Literal Transcript,* pp. 2–3. The original of the will is filed in the Duval County Courthouse, *Last Wills and Testaments,* Book 5, pp. 42–63.

59. 1932 will, pp. 4–5, 13–15.

60. Ibid., pp. 16–18.

61. Codicil to the Last Will and Testament of Alfred I. duPont, Mar. 4, 1933, *Last Wills and Testaments,* Book 5, pp. 64–66.

62. James, *The Family Rebel,* pp. 532–33.

63. Second Codicil to Last Will and Testament of Alfred I. duPont, Jan. 15, 1935, in *Last Wills and Testaments,* Book 5, pp. 68–81.

64. Conditional Instrument of Alfred I. duPont, Jan. 15, 1935, filed in the Court of the County Judge, Duval County, Florida (copy in *JBP 241-11*). Also in this file is a draft memorandum to the other trustees, undated but written in 1956, in which Mrs. duPont explains the differences between the 1932 will and the conditional instrument and her understanding of the reasons for the changes.

65. The conditional will is on file with the original will in the Duval County Courthouse, Jacksonville.

66. To Tom Ball, Feb. 20, Mar. 6, 1935, both in *JBP 25-36.*

67. James, *The Family Rebel,* p. 537.

68. To Elsie Bowley, Apr. 27, 1935.

69. James, *The Family Rebel,* pp. 540–42.

70. Christine Donahue, "The death of Alfred I. duPont—a postmortem," *Forbes 400* (Oct. 28, 1985):62–68; Hazel Williams, Notes on Conversation with Joseph Wall, Nov. 8, 1982, *JBP 241-11.*

71. Mason and Harrison, *Confusion to the Enemy,* pp. 149–55.

72. To Tom Ball, May 7, 1935, *JBP 37-45.*

CHAPTER FIVE

1. To Tom Ball, May 11, 1935, *JBP 25-36.*

2. To Tom Ball, May 15, 28, 1935, *JBP 25-36.*

3. To Tom Ball, May 11, 1935, *JBP 25-36;* to Tom Ball, Sept. 4, 1935, *JBP 213-25.*

4. To William duPont, Sept. 12, 1935, *JBP 25-26.*

5. To Tom Ball, Sept. 4, 1935, *JBP 213-25.*

6. To W. T. Edwards, Sept. 5, 1935, *JBP 213-31;* Balance Sheet, Almours Securities, Dec. 31, 1935, *JBP 25-28.*

7. From R. S. Huidekoper, Sept. 30, 1936, *JBP 34-9;* W. T. Edwards, Memorandum to Mrs. duPont on the Two Proposed Methods of Financing the St. Joe Paper Co., undated but in 1936 files, *JBP 35-34;* Almours Securities, Inc., Press Release, Jan. 11, 1937, *JBP 42-4.*

8. Sydney Ferguson, president of St. Joe Paper Co., to Ed Ball, Aug. 12, 1937, and Ed Ball to Ferguson, Aug. 14, 1937, both in *JBP 42-4;* Ed Ball to Huidekoper, Aug. 30, 1937, *JBP 40-27;* to Ethan A. Dennison, Sept. 19, 1937, *JBP 38-35;* from W. T. Edwards, Oct. 16, 20, 30, 1937, in *JBP 39-10.*

9. Adair and Bright to Ed Ball, Jan. 29, 1936, *JBP 242-8;* Charter of the Nemours Corporation, Feb. 25, 1936, and Deed of Assignment, Aug. 21, 1936, both in *JBP 242-10.*

10. From R. G. Huidekoper, Sept. 30, 1936, *JBP 34-9.*

11. To Baker P. Lee, Dec. 8, 1936, *JBP 33-48.*

12. Alfred R. Shands, Jr., "Jessie Ball duPont, Our Great Lady" (manuscript, n.d.), chap. 9, p. 4. Mrs. Shands kindly provided the author with a copy of the manuscript.

13. To Elsie Bowley, Mar. 8, 1937, *JBP 37-53;* to Tom Ball, Mar. 10, 1937, *JBP 37-45.*

14. To Jean Glasgow, June 24, 1937, *JBP 40-10;* to Helen Knox, June 25, 1937, *JBP 41-1.*

15. To Elsie Bowley, Mar. 1, 1937, *JBP 37-53;* to Tom Ball, May 2, 1937, *JBP 37-45.*

16. Gerard Colby, *DuPont Dynasty: Behind the Nylon Curtain* (Secaucus, N.J.: Lyle Stuart, Inc., 1984), pp. 368–69; to Denise duPont, May 2, 1937, *JBP 39-8;* to Julia V. Harding, June 23, 1937, *JBP 40-17.*

17. Interview with Carl and Denise Zapffe, June 12, 1987; to Placidia Edwards, July 6, 1937, *JBP 39-10.*

18. Interview with Mrs. Shands, May 11, 1987, Wilmington, Del.

19. JBP Annual Financial Reports, Dec. 31, 1934, *JBP 22-14;* Dec. 31, 1936, *JBP 33-12.*

20. Compiled from Annual Reports, Dec. 31, for the years indicated. The reports are in *JBP 12-16, JBP 33-12, JBP 39-32, JBP 46-20, JBP 52-26,* and *JBP 58-38.*

21. M. G. Shaw to Olive Byrne, Mar. 18, 1937, *JBP 38-3;* to Sarah W. Pyle, People's Settlement, Dec. 7, 1937, *JBP 41-34;* Shaw to Byrne, Jan. 17, 1938, *JBP 44-27.*

22. To Laura C. Walls, Jan. 31, 1936, *JBP 32-25;* Joseph Frazier Wall, *Alfred I. duPont: The Man and His Family* (New York: Oxford University Press, 1990), pp. 517–18.

23. Charter of the Alfred I. duPont Foundation, Dec. 30, 1936, *JBP Fund;* JBP Annual Financial Report, Dec. 31, 1936, *JBP 33-12;* from J. G. Bright, Oct. 20, 1937, and to Bright, Nov. 8, 1937, both in *JBP 37-56;* Alfred I. duPont Foundation, Cash Report, Jan. 31, 1938, *JBP 45-23.*

24. M. G. Shaw to C. C. Bucci, Jan. 30, 1937, *JBP 37-30;* to W. H. Goodman, Aug. 2, 1937, *JBP 40-9;* to George J. Avent, Apr. 8, 1938, *JBP 44-1;* Shaw to Brinson McGown, July 17, 1939, *JBP 51-1;* Shaw to Frank A. Juhan, Oct. 21, 1939, *JBP 53-26;* Shaw to C. G. McGehee, Oct. 31, 1940, *JBP 57-22.*

25. M. G. Shaw to Ethel Tignor, Nov. 2, 1936, *JBP 36-2;* from Thomas Wheeldon, June 2, 1936, *JBP 36-15;* Shaw to Wheeldon, Apr. 1, 1937, *JBP 42-31.*

26. To Eoline Jesse, March 22, June 17, 1938, both in *JBP 47-18.*

27. To Mrs. A. J. Montague, Feb. 7, 1938, *JBP 48-5;* to Elizabeth L. Neal, Apr. 20, 1937, *JBP 41-18.* Background on the Sheltering Arms Hospital is in *JBP 48-33.* From John G. Pollard, Dec. 23, 1935, *JBP 36-11;* from Thomas C. Colt, Jr., June 21, 1937, *JBP 42-27;* from Corinne L. Melchers, Jan. 18, 1939, *JBP 55-16.*

28. M. G. Shaw to Mountain Mission School, Feb. 1, 1937, *JBP 41-16;* Shaw to Mrs. Graham R. Holly, Feb. 22, 1937, *JBP 40-16;* Shaw to Mrs. J. E. Johnson, Prentiss, Miss., June 19, 1937, *JBP 40-32;* from Doris James,

Piney Woods, Miss., Feb 25, 1938, *JBP 48-23;* to C. F. Penniman, Feb. 23, 1938, *JBP 48-22;* to Arthur Howe, Hampton Institute, Dec. 5, 1938, *JBP 47-1.*

29. Marguerite duPont Lee to Adair, Aug. 11, 1936, as quoted in Wall, *duPont,* p. 616.

30. To John Baker, June 16, 1937, *JBP 37-43;* to Thomas Wright, Apr. 20, 1937, *JBP 42-34;* to W. A. Martin, Apr. 19, 1937, *JBP 41-10.*

31. To Fannie Coles, Mar. 7, 1938, *JBP 45-1.*

32. To Virginia Church, Jan. 15, 1940, *JBP 57-22.*

33. To N. Addison Baker, Jan. 5, 1938, *JBP 44-12;* to J. Shelton Horsley, Aug. 30, 1937, *JBP 40-16.*

34. Wilmington *Delmarva Star,* Apr. 21, 1935, "Ancient River Landing to be Restored," copy in *JBP 189-26;* to Helen Knox May 29, 1936, *JBP 34-14;* from Knox, Nov. 27, 1936, and to Knox, Nov. 30, 1936, both in *JBP 34-19;* to Mrs. Ralph Worthington, Jan. 4, 1937, *JBP 41-1;* to Knox, Jan. 23, 1937, *JBP 41-5,* and Apr. 18, 1939, *JBP 53-36.*

35. M. F. Lanier to Fiske Kimball, July 22, 1936, *JBP 34-16;* to Mrs. Robert W. Bingham, Jan. 7, 1937, *JBP 41-1;* to R. E. Lee Memorial Foundation, Oct. 16, 1937, *JBP 41-2;* Treasurer's Report, Oct. 2, 1938, *JBP 47-25.*

36. New York *World-Telegram,* [April?] 1945, copy in *JBP 187-3;* to Mrs. William L. Clayton, Oct. 24, 1939, *JBP 55-37;* to Janon Fisher, Mar. 5, 1940, *JBP 58-29.*

37. To Hugh Tait, Mar. 22, 1938, *JBP 45-20;* to Tait, Jan. 12, 1940, *JBP 58-1.* Each Ditchley folder for the years after 1936 contains scores of letters similar to these.

38. To James D. Jesse, Apr. 19, 1939, *JBP 53-27;* to Tom Ball, May 11, 1939, *JBP 51-5.*

39. Almours Securities, Inc., Stock Ownership of Subsidiaries and Controlled Companies as of December 31, 1937, *JBP 51-10.*

40. To Isabel Baker, Mar. 11, 1938, *JBP 44-12.*

41. From Huidekoper, Dec. 3, 1936, and reply, Dec. 11, 1936, both in *JBP 34-9;* from Huidekoper, Dec. 22, 1937, *JBP 40-27;* J. G. Bright, Memorandum Covering Trip to See Colonel Reginald S. Huidekoper, Apr. 1, 1939, *JBP 51-18.*

42. To Tom Ball, Feb. 3, 1936, *JBP 31-26.*

43. From Robert N. Miller, Sept. 13, 1938, *JBP 48-3.*

44. To W. T. Edwards, Sept. 7, Oct. 15, 1938, both in *JBP 46-1;* from Edwards, July 9, 1938, *JBP 48-40;* to Dean of Harvard School of Finance, Mar. 16, 1937, and to John G. Baker, July 9, 1937, both in *JBP 38-38.*

45. To Tom Ball, July 8, 1940, *JBP 57-6.*

46. List of Corporations with Names of Officers, undated but in 1940 files, *JBP 57-22*.

47. To Tom Ball, Feb. 28, 1936, *JBP 31-26;* from Adair, Feb. 17, 1937, *JBP 37-34;* Minutes of the Annual Meeting of the Stockholders of Almours Securities, Inc., Feb. 8, 1938, *JBP 44-3*.

48. From Elbert Dent, Apr. 12, 1937, and to Victorine Dent, Apr. 19, 1937, both in *JBP 38-37*.

49. Minutes of the Annual Meeting of the Stockholders of Almours Securities, Inc., Feb. 8, 1938, *JBP 44-3*.

50. From J. G. Bright, Oct. 5, 1938, *JBP 44-25*.

51. H. Adair to Mr. and Mrs. N. Addison Baker, Dec. 28, 1938, *JBP 51-2;* Tampa *Tribune,* Apr. 2, 1939, copy in *JBP 54-34;* to Beverly Tucker, Sept. 20, 1939, *JBP 55-13*.

52. From Maurice duPont Lee, Jan. 9, 1939, *JBP 54-4*.

53. From M. dP. Lee, Feb. 4, 1939, and reply, Feb. 8, 1939; to M. dP. Lee, Mar. 28, 1939, all in *JBP 54-4;* Wall, *duPont,* pp. 620–22.

54. To Tom Ball, May 13, 1939, *JBP 51-5*.

55. To Isabel Baker, May 9, 1938, *JBP 44-12;* to Shands, Apr. 19, 1938, from private collection.

56. To S. Frank Mathewson, Feb. 24, 1939, *JBP 54-7;* to Mrs. Thomas P. Denham, May 26, 1939, *JBP 51-28;* from M. L. Des Barres, July 11, 1939, *JBP 51-23*.

57. To Beverly Tucker, Jan. 28, 1940, *JBP 61-28*.

58. To A. B. Shands, May 8, 1940, from private collection.

59. W. T. Edwards to Employees of the St. Joe Paper Co., May 29, 1940, and T. Mooney to J. G. Bright, July 8, 1940, both in *JBP 61-20;* from Edwards, June 24, 1940, *JBP 58-15;* Notice of Special Meeting of Stockholders of the Florida National Building Co., Nov. 30, 1940, and Ball to the Holders of Common Capital Stock of Florida National Bank Group, Inc., undated, both in *JBP 58-49*.

60. From Frank Gaines, undated but probably June 1938, *JBP 46-34;* to Ed Ball, Aug. 8, 1940, *JBP 59-29*.

61. To Marquis James, Aug. 1, 1941, *JBP 243-1;* from Marquis James, Sept. 27, 1939, and List of files taken from Mr. duPont's file cases in Wilmington office, Jan. 23, 1940, both in *JBP 243-1;* Information Supplied by Mrs. Jessie Ball duPont for Marquis James, undated but in 1939 files, *JBP 52-4;* to D. Laurance Chambers, two letters, July 28, 1941, both in *JBP 243-1;* the following all in *JBP 58-4*: Files Taken to Nemours for Use of Marquis James, Aug. 1, 1940; from James, Mar. 21, Apr. 27, 1940; to James, Nov. 19, May 6, 1940.

62. To Marquis James, Aug. 1, 1941, *JBP 243-1*.

CHAPTER SIX

1. To Victorine Dent, Aug. 12, 1936, *JBP 32-26;* Wilmington *Journal,* Aug. 11, 1936, copy in *JBP 32-32.*

2. Marquis James, *Alfred I. duPont: The Family Rebel* (Indianapolis: Bobbs-Merrill, 1941), p. 515; Joseph Frazier Wall, *Alfred I duPont: The Man and His Family* (New York: Oxford University Press, 1990), pp. 558–59; Leonard Mosley, *Blood Relations: The Rise and Fall of the duPonts of Delaware* (New York: Atheneum, 1980), pp. 212–13; from Bayard Hiebler, Apr. 5, May 21, 1936, both in *JBP 33-21.*

3. Wall, *duPont,* pp. 560–65.

4. Ibid., p. 565; to Madeleine Ruoff, Feb. 20, Apr. 5, 1934; to Bayard Hiebler, Apr. 14, 1934; from Victorine Dent, Mar. 14, 1934, all in *JBP 23-32.*

5. Wilmington *Journal,* Aug. 11, 1936, copy in *JBP 32-32.*

6. To Victorine Dent, Aug. 12, 1936, *JBP 32-26.*

7. From Bayard Hiebler, Nov. 3, 1936, *JBP 33-21;* Mosley, *Blood Relations,* pp. 354–55.

8. From Frank P. Gaines, undated, but probably Sept. 1938, *JBP 46-34.*

9. To Alfred Hiebler, Mar. 25, 1939, *JBP 53-19.*

10. From J. B. Bernardin, Oct. 19, 1939, *JBP 51-12.*

11. To J. B. Bernardin, Oct. 24, 1939, *JBP 51-12.*

12. To Mrs. Donald Darroch, Nov. 26, 1940, *JBP 57-30.*

13. To Tom Ball, Oct. 29, 1938, *JBP 44-14;* to Tom Ball, Mar. 2, 1940, *JBP 57-6.*

14. To John Baker, Jan. 10, 1941, *JBP 63-11;* to Hugh Tait, Feb. 17, 1941, *JBP 64-4.*

15. Rules and Regulations of the Alfred I. duPont Institute, Feb. 26, 1941, *JBP 196-9.*

16. To Frank Juhan, June 3, 30, 1941, both in *JBP 65-26;* from Ellen LaMotte, June 16, 1941, *JBP 64-5.*

17. To Tom Ball, Aug. 22, 1941, *JBP 63-12.*

18. To Captain Jesse Smith, Jr., Nov. 7, 1941, *JBP 67-13;* Adm. E. M. Eller to Robert L. F. Sikes, July 29, 1959, *JBP 156-12.*

19. To Rebecca Harding Adams, Dec. 15, 1941, *JBP 63-6.*

20. To Tom Ball, Mar. 3, 1942, *JBP 68-86.*

21. To Beverly Tucker, Mar. 31, 1942, *JBP 72-33;* to Helen Knox, Mar. 16, 1942, *JBP 71-13.*

22. To J. Bland Dew, June 10, 1942, *JBP 69-31.*

23. To Minnie J. Edwards, Aug. 11, 1942, *JBP 70-4.*

24. To Alfred Shands, Sept. 19, 1942, *JBP 72-22.*

25. To Lewise W. Gregory, Feb. 1, 1943, *JBP 75-32;* to Arthur Gould, Oct. 23, 1943, *JBP 75-31.*

26. To Tom Ball, Oct. 5, 1942, *JBP 68-86.*

27. To Tom Ball, Feb. 3, 1943, *JBP 74-14.*

28. Ibid.

29. To Braxton Dew, Aug. 27, 1932, *JBP 14-22.*

30. For her father's views on organized religion, see chap. 1. For Alfred duPont's views, see James, *The Family Rebel,* pp. 531–32.

31. To British American Ambulance Corps, June 26, 1941, *JBP 63-23;* from Mrs. R. Alger Sawyer, Oct. 21, 1942, and to Aleen Bingham, Nov. 7, 1942, both in *JBP 69-12;* David Leon Chandler with Mary Voelz Chandler, *The Binghams of Louisville: The Dark History Behind One of America's Great Fortunes* (New York: Crown, 1987), pp. 181–82, 245.

32. To Mrs. F. H. Taylor, Jan. 24, 1941, *JBP 67-19;* to Harry H. Saunders, Aug. 31, 1942, *JBP 69-12;* St. Joe Paper Co., *St. Joe at War,* Mar. 1945, *JBP 187-1.*

33. To Shirley Martin, Oct. 27, 1944, *JBP 80-8.*

34. To Arthur R. McKinstry, Dec. 18, 1945, *JBP 84-20.*

35. To N. A. Baker, Mar. 24, 1930, *JBP 9-25.*

36. To Christ Church Restoration Assoc., Aug. 1, 1941, *JBP 63-31;* to Thomas Waterman, June 20, 1944, *JBP 81-27.*

37. *The Living Church Annual: The Year Book of the Episcopal Church* (Milwaukee: Morehouse, 1934), pp. 215–16; interview with Frances Juhan Freeman, Mar. 23, 1987.

38. To Tom Ball, Jan. 29, 1941, *JBP 63-12.*

39. To Frank Juhan, Dec. 1, 1941, *JBP 65-26;* interview with Arthur McKinstry, May 13, 1987; Arthur R. McKinstry, *All I Have Seen: The McKinstry Memoirs by the Fifth Bishop of Delaware, 1939–1954* (Wilmington: Serendipity Press, 1975), pp. 84–88.

40. To F. Bland Mitchell, Apr. 11, 1942, *JBP 71-29;* to Arthur R. McKinstry, Nov. 23, 1942, *JBP 71-28;* to George C. Culleny, Sept. 1, 1943, *JBP 74-25;* from Walter J. Laird, Nov. 22, 1943, *JBP 76-46;* from M. G. Shaw, Jan. 29, 1944, *JBP 78-38;* to McKinstry, Feb. 24, Mar. 16, 1944, both in *JBP 80-12.*

41. To May Field Lanier, Jan. 16, 1942, *JBP 71-20.*

42. To Bror G. Dahlberg, Sept. 11, 1941, *JBP 64-1.*

43. Endowment Fund Principal and Income Accounts, Feb. 28, 1943, *JBP 76-1;* to Tom Ball, Oct. 9, 1943, *JBP 74-14;* Cumulative Statement of Contributions by State and Other Agencies, Aug. 31, 1945, *JBP 84-11.*

44. To Tom Ball, Apr. 8, 1942, *JBP 68-86;* Roger L. Main to M. G. Shaw, May 25, 1942, *JBP 71-22.*

45. To J. L. Sharit, June 30, 1943, *JBP 76-42.*

46. From Sharit, July 25, 1944, to Sharit, Aug. 18, 1944, and to W. T. Edwards, Aug. 18, 1944, all in *JBP 81-6;* from Sharit, July 25, 1945, *JBP 89-38.*

47. To W. T. Edwards, Nov. 23, 1945, *JBP 83-15.*

48. JBP Annual Financial Report, Dec. 31, 1941, *JBP 64-15.*

49. To James Ball, June 26, 1942, *JBP 68-84.*

50. To Ethel Tignor, Jan. 25, 1945, *JBP 85-23.*

51. JBP, Other Contributions, Dec. 31, 1941, *JBP 72-30.*

52. JBP, Contributions to Educational Institutions, Dec. 31, 1941, *JBP 72-30.*

53. From F. D. Goodwin, May 19, 1941, and reply, May 20, 1941, both in *JBP 68-13.*

54. From J. S. Bryan, Aug. 22, 1941, *JBP 67-7;* to Bessie C. Randolph, Nov. 28, 1941, *JBP 67-2;* to M. L. Combs, Dec. 29, 1945; from C. E. Kilbourne, July 9, 1945; and to Alexander Guerry, Dec. 18, 1945, all in *JBP 85-8.* On year-end tax strategies, see Bright to JBP, Dec. 21, 1945, *JBP 82-37.* Neither the will nor the 1942 codicil is in *JBP,* but evidence of her decision appears in form letters of inquiry to nine institutions, June 25, 1942, and a letter to her attorney, A. W. Cockrell, Jr., June 26, 1942, both in *JBP 69-22.*

55. From Julie Targarona, June 9, 1942, and to Targarona, June 10, 1942, both in *JBP 73-53.*

56. Stephen R. Graubard, "Preface to the issue '*Philanthropy, Patronage, Politics*'," *Daedalus* 116 (Winter 1987):v.

57. Resolution of the Florida National Group, undated but probably Jan. 1943, *JBP 72-16.*

58. From W. H. Goodman, Jan. 14, 1943, *JBP 76-34;* to Tom Ball, Feb. 22, 1943, *JBP 74-14.*

59. To Victorine Dent, Mar. 9, 1943, *JBP 74-28.*

60. JBP, trust agreement with Florida National Bank, Aug. 10, 1943, *JBP 76-34;* to Frank Gaines, Mar. 16, 1945, *JBP 83-40;* from W. H. Goodman, June 14, 1945, *JBP 85-3.*

61. Jessie Ball duPont, Last Will and Testament, May 17, 1943, *JBP 251-2.*

62. Ibid.

63. To Mrs. Marquis James, Aug. 17, 1943, *JBP 75-48.*

64. To Frank Juhan, Sept. 14, 1943, *JBP 75-48.*

65. To Mr. and Mrs. Charles Martin, Sept. 14, 1943, *JBP 76-7.*

66. To Tom Ball, Sept. 16, 1943, *JBP 74-14.*

67. To Mrs. Charles Martin, Dec. 17, 1943, *JBP 76-7.*

68. To Charles Hardwicke, June 24, 1943, *JBP 75-36;* to Tom Ball, May 12, 1943, *JBP 74-14.*

69. To General and Mrs. Bowley, Feb. 26, 1943, *JBP 74-12.*
70. To J. Bland Dew, June 24, 1943, *JBP 74-31.*
71. To Rebecca Adams, Feb. 15, 1944, *JBP 77-76;* to Denise Zapffe, Apr. 5, 1944, *JBP 81-35.*
72. To Tom Ball, June 6, 1944, *JBP 78-3.*
73. To Ed Ball, June 6, 1944, *JBP 78-2.*
74. Maureen Honey, *Creating Rosie the Riveter: Class, Gender, and Propaganda During World War II* (Amherst: University of Massachusetts Press, 1964); Karen Anderson, *Wartime Women: Sex Roles, Family Relations, and the Status of Women During World War II* (Westport, Conn.: Greenwood Press, 1981). The Association of Bank Women was founded in 1915 primarily to support women's suffrage rather than professional opportunity. Membership fell rapidly after World War I and all but disappeared during the depression, but it took on new life as a professional association during World War II. See J. Stanley Lemons, *The Woman Citizen: Social Feminism in the 1920s* (Urbana: University of Illinois Press, 1973), pp. 47–48.
75. To Mrs. G. H. Westbrook, Feb. 5, 1947, *JBP 91-43;* to A. J. Bowley, Sept. 28, 1944, *JBP 78-8;* from Helen Knox, Oct. 1, 1946; from Anna Rousse, Apr. 15, 1946; and to Willa Riley, Oct. 8, 1946, all in *JBP 86-32;* "Prominent Bank Women to Arrive for Conference," *Atlanta Constitution,* Apr. 20, 1945, copy in *JBP 187-3.*
76. To Ed Ball, Aug. 15, 1945, *JBP 82-25.*
77. To Ed Ball, Dec. 22, 1945, *JBP 82-25.*

CHAPTER SEVEN

1. Dedication of the Council House, Stratford, Oct. 12, 1951, *JBP 116-10.*
2. *The Hymnal of the Protestant Episcopal Church, 1940* (New York: Church Pension Fund, 1940), Hymn 564.
3. For a description of these changes, see Jack Temple Kirby, *Rural Worlds Lost: The American South, 1920–1960* (Baton Rouge: Louisiana State University Press, 1987), and George B. Tindall, *The Emergence of the New South, 1913–1945* (Baton Rouge: Louisiana State University Press, 1967).
4. To Mrs. Henry Ridgely, undated but in 1946 files, *JBP 88-26.*
5. To Tom Ball, Mar. 12, 1946, *JBP 86-39.*
6. From Hardin Goodman, June 26, 1946, *JBP 89-24*
7. To Carl Zapffe, April 24, 1946, *JBP 90-22;* from Shands, May 2, 1946, private collection; to R. B. Osgood, Oct. 8, 1946, *JBP 89-15.*
8. To W. T. Edwards, June 1, 1946; to H. H. Saunders, Dec. 16, 1946; from J. L Sharit, Dec. 23, 1946, all in *JBP 89-38;* from Sharit, Jan. 7, 1947, *JBP 95-12;* from Edwards, June 24, 1946, *JBP 87-20;* to Saunders, Mar. 18,

1947, *JBP 95-12;* from Edwards, June 7, 1946, *JBP 87-20;* Federal Income Tax Return, Schedule of Donations, Dec. 31, 1946, p. 4, *JBP 90-58.*

9. To Ed Ball, June 30, 1947, *JBP 91-23.*

10. To Ed Ball, Sept. 9, 1947, *JBP 91-23.*

11. Interview with Seabury Stoneburner, Jan. 20, 1989.

12. Freeman Lincoln, "The Terrible-Tempered Mr. Ball," *Fortune,* Nov. 1952, pp. 160–62; Raymond K. Mason and Virginia Harrison, *Confusion to the Enemy: A Biography of Edward Ball* (New York: Dodd, Mead, 1976), pp. 68–72.

13. Alexander R. Stoesen, "Road from Receivership: Claude Pepper, the DuPont Trust, and the Florida East Coast Railway," *Florida Historical Quarterly* 52 (Oct. 1973):135–37; Mason and Harrison, *Confusion,* pp. 73–76.

14. Stoesen, "Road from Receivership," p. 137.

15. Miami *Herald,* Nov. 22, 1945; Palm Beach *Post,* Nov. 22, 1945, copies in *JBP 83-38.* The Pepper quotation is from *An Urgent Plea by Employees of the Florida East Coast Railway to All Citizens of the East Coast of Florida,* undated but in 1945 folder, *JBP 83-38.*

16. Claude Denson Pepper with Hays Gorey, *Pepper: Eyewitness to a Century* (New York: Harcourt Brace Jovanovich, 1987), pp. 1–32; Robert Sherrill, *Gothic Politics in the Deep South: Stars of the New Confederacy* (New York: Grossman Publishers, 1968), p. 138.

17. Pepper and Gorey, *Pepper,* pp. 117–18; Sherrill, p. 139.

18. To Frank Gaines, Sept. 22, 1947, *JBP 93-18.*

19. To Tom Ball, May 27, 1947, *JBP 91-22.*

20. To Sir James Purves-Stewart, Mar. 6, 1947, *JBP 95-1.*

21. To Virginia Church, Sept. 18, 1947, *JBP 92-2.*

22. Federal Income Tax Return, Dec. 31, 1946, Schedule of Donations, p. 2, *JBP 90-58.*

23. Virtually identical letters transmitting the gifts went to Hollins, Washington and Lee, and the University of the South: to Hollins, Sept. 10, 1946, *JBP 88-13,* and to Washington and Lee and University of the South, Sept. 6, 1946, in *JBP 90-1,* and *JBP 90-14,* respectively.

24. To Tom Ball, Oct. 7, 1946, *JBP 86-39.*

25. Ibid.

26. To Winifred Stephenson, Oct. 8, 1946, *JBP 89-35.*

27. Ibid.

28. Ibid.

29. To W. G. Pendleton, Mar. 11, 1947, *JBP 94-33.*

30. To Gwendolyne Holland, Mar. 28, 1947, *JBP 93-17.*

31. To J. Garland Pollard, Jr., Oct. 25, 1947, *JBP 93-8;* to James Ball, Dec. 15, 1947, *JBP 91-20;* from Thomas Gresham, Feb. 10, 1950, *JBP 112-24;*

to Helen Knox, July 10, 1950, *JBP 110-24;* to J. J. Mercer, July 22, 1950, *JBP 111-5.*

32. To Tom Ball, Jan. 9, 1948, *JBP 97-3.* The Supreme Court heard the case, *Sipuel* v. *Board of Regents of the University of Oklahoma* on Jan. 7, 1948, and reversed the decision of the Supreme Court of Oklahoma by denying the applicant's petition. *U.S. Reports* 332: 631–33; Margaret C. Rung, "A Civil Rights Chronology With an Emphasis on the School Integration Issue" (unpublished paper, 1988, *JBP* end note file).

33. To William Gresham, Mar. 10, 1948, *JBP 98-32;* David W. Southern, *Gunnar Myrdal and Black-White Relations: The Use and Abuse of the American Dilemma, 1944–1969* (Baton Rouge: Louisiana State University Press, 1987), pp. 71–125; Gunnar Myrdal, with Richard Sterner and Arnold Rose, *An American Dilemma: The Negro Problem and Modern Democracy* (New York: Harper, 1944).

34. From J. L. McGuigan, Mar. 5, 1946, and reply, May 6, 1946, both in *JBP 90-23.*

35. To Col. and Mrs. Charles F. Martin, Aug. 10, 1946, *JBP 88-32;* to Mrs. William A. Martin, Aug. 10, 1946, *JBP 88-34;* to Mrs. Thomas P. Denham, Aug. 12, 1946, *JBP 87-4.*

36. To Tom Ball, Aug. 3, 1947, *JBP 91-22;* to J. Bland Dew, Aug. 3, 1947, *JBP 92-15;* to Denise Zapffe, Aug. 11, 1947, *JBP 95-31.*

37. To Monica McGinness, Nov. 7, 1947, *JBP 94-14.*

38. M. G. Shaw to Cooperative for American Remittances to Europe, Mar. 1, 1948, *JBP 100-3.*

39. To A. B. Kinsolving, Sept. 24, 1948, *JBP 99-4;* to M. G. Shaw, Aug. 5, 1948, *JBP 97-36;* interview with Arthur McKinstry, May 13, 1987; Arthur R. McKinstry, *All I Have Seen: The McKinstry Memoirs by the Fifth Bishop of Delaware, 1939–1954* (Wilmington: Serendipity Press, 1975), pp. 173–87.

40. To John W. Suter, Jan. 8, 1947, *JBP 95-19;* from Rosemond Fisher, Mar. 22, July 20, 1950, both in *JBP 109-36.*

41. Interview with Mr. and Mrs. Solace Freeman, Mar. 23, 1987.

42. Stoesen, "Road from Receivership," pp. 148–49; to McKinstry, Feb. 15, 1949, *JBP 104-24.*

43. Lincoln, "The Terrible-Tempered Mr. Ball," pp. 157–58; J. F. Byrnes to H. A. Bergson, Mar. 10, 1949; Byrnes to E. A. Jinkinson, Mar. 29, 1949; [J. Ollie Edmunds], Excerpt of telephone conversation, Apr. 18, 1949; Earl W. Shinn, Sworn Affidavit, June 30, 1949, all in *JBP 251-2;* Memorandum for Mrs. duPont, May 16, 1949, *JBP 102-11.*

44. Mason and Harrison, *Confusion,* pp. 136–39.

45. Jacksonville *Journal,* Dec. 20, 1949, copy in *JBP 102-11.*

46. Stoesen, "Road from Receivership," pp. 149–50.

47. Sherrill, *Gothic Politics,* pp. 142–45.

48. Ibid., p. 149; Stoesen, "Road from Receivership," p. 150.

49. George Smathers Papers, in Special Collections, University of Florida Library, contain two cubic feet of campaign materials, newspaper clippings, Smathers's speeches, and correspondence. See especially Smathers's speech in Miami, Feb. 16, 1950; Smathers to Daniel T. Crisp, Crisp and Harrison Agency, Jacksonville, n.d.; and *The Red Record of Senator Claude Pepper: A Documented Case History from Official Government Records and Original Communist Documents,* published in Jacksonville during the campaign. See also Pepper and Gorey, *Pepper,* pp. 197–212.

50. To Thomas R. Brown, May 17, 1950, *JBP 108-16.* For a detailed statistical analysis of the factors in Pepper's defeat, see John L. Moore, Jr., "Good Reason, Bad Reason, and No Reason at All: A Study of Florida Politics with Special Reference to the Pepper–Smathers Primary" (unpublished Senior Honors Thesis, Harvard College, 1951). A microfilm copy is in the University of Florida Library.

51. James C. Merrill, treasurer, Duval County finance committee, to Smathers, June 9, 1950, Smathers Papers, Box 100, University of Florida.

52. To Alfred Shands, May 6, 1948, *JBP 100-16.*

53. From Alfred Shands, May 3, 1948, *JBP 100-16.*

54. Minutes of Joint Meeting of Trustees, Directors, and Board of Managers, Apr. 26, 1949, *JBP 102-10;* interview with Ramona Edwards, Apr. 29, 1987.

55. From Sylvia Carothers, Feb. 11, 1949, *JBP 103-34.*

56. Minutes of Joint Meeting, Apr. 26, 1949, *JBP 102-10.*

57. From Shands, June 17, 1949, *JBP 106-1;* to Maurice duPont Lee, Jan. 30, 1950, *JBP 110-31.*

58. From William B. Mills, Aug. 15, 1949, *JBP 104-25;* interview with Helen Mills, Mar. 19, 1987.

59. Interview with Helen Mills, Mar. 19, 1987; from William B. Mills, July 1 and July 28, 1949, both in *JBP 104-25.*

60. From Adair, Dec. 14, 1949; identical deeds of gift with covering letters to the three institutions, Dec. 16, 1949, all in *JBP 103-2.*

61. From Gaines, Jan. 6, 1950, *JBP 110-5.*

62. To Frank Juhan, Dec. 16, 1949, *JBP 103-2.*

63. Schedule of Beneficiary Proportions in First General Trust, May 27, 1950, *JBP 117-25;* Adair to Juhan, Dec. 22, 1950, and from Adair, Dec. 24, 1950, both in *JBP 107-36; The Sewanee News,* Mar. 31, 1951, copy in *JBP 116-14.*

64. Schedule of Beneficiary Portions in Second General Trust, Dec. 27,

1950; *JBP 117-25;* draft letter to the three institutions, Dec. 29, 1951, *JBP 117-33.*

65. Data from contribution lists for these years, found in *JBP 90-58, JBP 100-23, JBP 106-6,* and *JBP 117-25.*

66. To Arthur B. Kinsolving, Nov. 21, 1946, *JBP 88-17.*

67. To L. Valentine Lee, Apr. 19, 1949, *JBP 104-10;* to Martha B. Lucas, Jan. 14, 1948, *JBP 100-20.*

68. To J. Ollie Edmunds and to Frank Gaines, both dated Apr. 23, 1951, *JBP 190-39.*

69. To Niles Trammel, Apr. 2, 1951, *JBP 117-24;* from W. B. Mills, May 8, 1951, *JBP 116-21;* Jacksonville *Florida Times-Union,* May 6, 1951, p. 22.

70. To M. G. Shaw, Jan. 29, 1951, *JBP 190-36;* from F. D. Goodwin, July 26, 1951, and reply, July 30, 1951, both in *JBP 118-15.*

71. To Tom Ball, June 6, July 26, 1950, both in *JBP 108-7;* to F. Bland Mitchell, July 27, 1950, *JBP 111-5.*

72. To Frank Juhan, Nov. 19, 1951, *JBP 116-1.*

73. To Stanley Brown–Serman, Nov. 23, 1951, *JBP 117-7.*

74. From Stanley Brown–Serman, Nov. 28, 1951, *JBP 117-7.* The black student, whose name never appears in Mrs. duPont's correspondence, was John Thomas Walker, who in 1975 became the bishop of Washington and in 1987 vice-president of the House of Bishops of the Episcopal church.

75. To Brown–Serman, Dec. 17, 1951, *JBP 117-7.*

76. From Fiske Kimball, undated, but probably Sept. 1949, and to Kimball, Oct. 25, 1949, both in *JBP 111-33;* from Eppes Hawes, June 1, 1950, *JBP 110-30;* to Henry P. Adair, June 5, 1950, *JBP 107-36.*

77. To Randolph Williams, June 20, 1947, *JBP 95-34;* to Henry W. Anderson, Apr. 22, 1948, *JBP 101-5;* to William M. Tuck, Sept. 14, 1949, *JBP 106-5;* to Anderson, July 10, 1950, *JBP 112-11.*

78. To Robert Porterfield, Nov. 8, 1948, *JBP 97-1;* from Porterfield, Apr. 5, 1951, *JBP 114-8.*

CHAPTER EIGHT

1. Endowment for Faculty Salaries and Scholarships, enclosure in letter to F. A. Juhan, Aug. 5, 1954, *JBP 134-4.* Similar letters went to Hollins and to Washington and Lee.

2. Warren Weaver, *U. S. Philanthropic Foundations: Their History, Structure, Management, and Record* (New York: Harper & Row, 1967), pp. 25–89; Donald Fisher, "The Role of Philanthropic Foundations in the Reproduction and Production of Hegemony: Rockefeller Foundations and the Social Sciences," *Sociology* 17 (May 1983):206–33; Stephen R. Graubard, "Preface to

the issue 'Philanthropy, Patronage, Politics'," *Daedalus* 116 (Winter 1987):v–xii; Margaret C. Rung, "The Recent Historical Debate on Philanthropy" (unpublished paper, 1988, *JBP* end note file).

3. Barry D. Karl and Stanley N. Katz, "Foundations and Ruling Class Elites," *Daedalus* 116 (Winter 1987):1–40; Martin Bulmer, "Philanthropic Foundations and the Development of the Social Sciences in the Early Twentieth Century: A Reply to Donald Fisher," *Sociology* 18 (Nov. 1984):572–87; Sheila Slaughter and Edward T. Silva, "Looking Backwards: How Foundations Formulated Ideology in the Progressive Period," in *Philanthropy and Cultural Imperialism: The Foundations at Home and Abroad,* ed. Robert F. Arnove (Boston: G. K. Hall, 1980), pp. 55–86.

4. Jessie Ball duPont Financial Report, Aug. 31, 1949, *JBP 106-20.*

5. For later attacks on Mrs. duPont's use of her income, see chap. 9.

6. To L. A. Usina, Mar. 9, 1950, *JBP 112-21;* Ball to Edwards, Apr. 19, 1951, and reply, Apr. 20, 1951, both in *JBP 115-10;* interview with Hazel Williams, Mar. 24, 1987; interview with Mrs. Henry Dew, March 20, 1987.

7. Hazel O. Williams, "My 'Boss' (December 15, 1947–September 26, 1970)," in *Jessie Ball duPont, 1884–1970,* ed. Mary Tyler Freemen Cheek (Stratford, Va.: Robert E. Lee Memorial Association, 1985), pp. 18–23.

8. Interview with Hazel O. Williams, Mar. 24, 1987.

9. From Ed Ball, May 14, 1951, Folder Mrs. A. I. duPont 1951, *EB-STJ.*

10. From W. B. Mills, June 16, 1951, *JBP 116-21.*

11. From L. S. Aspinwall, July 23, 1951, *JBP 116-16;* from Ed Ball, July 21, 1951, and to Ed Ball, Aug 10, 1951, both in *JBP 114-9.*

12. Raymond K. Mason and Virginia Harrison, *Confusion to the Enemy: A Biography of Edward Ball* (New York: Dodd, Mead, 1976), pp. 165–68.

13. To Tom Ball, Sept. 21, 1951, *JBP 114-1;* to Ed Ball, Sept. 21, 1951, Folder Mrs. A. I. duPont, 1951, *EB-STJ;* to Fuller Warren, Sept. 17, 1951, *JBP 114-32.*

14. Statement by Fuller Warren, Sept. 17, 1951, *JBP 114-32;* Fuller Warren, "Women in Government," File C.10, Fuller Warren Papers, Special Collections, Florida State University.

15. For evidence of the close relationship, see J. Hillis Miller to A. R. Shands, Feb. 1, 1951, *JBP 117-33;* to Miller, June 17, 1952, *JBP 118-49.*

16. From Roger L. Main, Sept. 25, 1951, *JBP 116-16;* to Homer G. Lindsay, Oct. 25, 1951, *JBP 113-59.*

17. From Ed Ball, Oct. 5, 1951, Folder Mrs. A. I. duPont 1951, *EB-STJ.*

18. From W. B. Mills, Dec. 17, 1951, with encl., Draft Letter to Company Employees, *JBP 117-16.*

19. To Tom Ball, Feb. 10, 1952, *JBP 118-39.*

20. To Leslie Cheek, Feb. 9, 1952, *JBP 122-23.*

21. Recommendation from Fourth Province Synod, Nov. 10, 1951, *JBP 122-21.*

22. A. R. McKinstry to E. A. Penick, Dec. 4, 1951, *JBP 121-16.*

23. Action by the Board of Trustees, University of the South, June 6, 1952, *JBP 122-21.*

24. To B. R. Lacey, Jr., June 9, 1952, *JBP 122-20.*

25. To F. D. Goodwin, June 2, 1952, *JBP 122-22.*

26. From F. D. Goodwin, June 12, 1952, *JBP 122-22.*

27. Communication from Faculty Members, School of Theology, June 9, 1952; Statement by Bishop Mitchell to the Associated Press, June 10, 1952; and Jacksonville *Florida Times-Union,* June 12, 1952, all in *JBP 122-21.*

28. F. B. Mitchell to the Editor, *Episcopal Churchnews,* June 30, 1952, and JBP to Mitchell, July 1, 1952, both in *JBP 122-21.*

29. To Edward McCrady, July 1, 1952, *JBP 122-21.*

30. Sewanee Newsroom, Press Release, Aug. 1, 1952, *JBP 122-21.* See also letter from Mitchell, July 9, 1952, and Edmund Orgill to Board of Trustees, July 31, 1952, both in *JBP 122-21.*

31. To Mitchell, Aug. 16, 1952, *JBP 122-21.*

32. Ibid.; *New York Times,* Nov. 6, 1952, p. 31.

33. *New York Times,* Jan. 15, Feb. 14, 15, 1953, pp. 35, 23, 10, respectively.

34. To Arthur Chitty, June 15, 1953, *JBP 128-2; New York Times,* June 5, 1953, p. 1.

35. From Peter Day, May 25, 1953, and reply, May 30, 1953, both in *JBP 190-46.*

36. To Peter Day, June 18, 1953, *JBP 190-46;* to J. Garland Pollard, Jr., Sept. 27, 1952, *JBP 121-39.*

37. To Edward McCrady, June 30, 1953, *JBP 128-2.*

38. Gunnar Myrdal, with the assistance of Richard Sterner and Arnold Rose, *An American Dilemma: The Negro Problem and Modern Democracy* (New York: Harper, 1944), p. xlvii.

39. David W. Southern, *Gunnar Myrdal and Black-White Relations: The Use and Abuse of An American Dilemma, 1944–1969* (Baton Rouge: Louisiana State University Press, 1987), p. 59.

40. To Bishop Mitchell, Aug. 16, 1952, *JBP 122-21.*

41. To Governor and Mrs. Byrnes, July 31, 1952, *JBP 119-1.*

42. To Governor and Mrs. Byrnes, Jan. 6, 1954, *JBP 129-38;* to Frank Gaines, June 1, 1954, *JBP 131-11.*

43. To Henry K. Sherrill, Dec. 13, 1955, *JBP 193-78.*

44. Minutes of the Board of Control, 17:185, 285, 453, 482–85; 18:1, 53, 79–81, 108, 156, 196, 253, 258, *FSA.* The minutes contain only formal

motions and votes, no record of discussion. Interview with Eli B. Fink, Mar. 20, 1987.

45. To Helen Knox, Apr. 29, 1953, *JBP 190-9.*

46. To Tom Ball, June 11, 1953, *JBP 124-21.*

47. To Ed Ball, July 7, 1953, *JBP 124-20.*

48. From Ed Ball, July 27, 1953, and reply, July 31, 1953, both in *JBP 187-4.*

49. To Ed Ball, July 31, 1953, *JBP 187-4.*

50. From Isabel Baker, n.d., and reply, Sept. 21, 1953, *JBP 124-19.*

51. To Carl and Denise Zapffe, Oct. 6, 1953, *JBP 128-11.*

52. To Elizabeth Chamberlain, Oct. 26, 1953, *JBP 124-43;* from S. C. Burgess, June 11, 1952, and reply, June 13, 1952, both in *JBP 119-1;* to John Dos Passos, Sept. 1, 1953, *JBP 124-43; Religious Herald,* Nov. 5, 1953, copy in *JBP 126–5;* to Leslie Cheek, Jan. 3, 1953, and to Henry W. Anderson, Oct. 17, 1953, both in *JBP 128-3.*

53. To Eoline Jesse, June 29, 1952, *JBP 120-39.*

54. M. G. Shaw to Annie E. ———, Jan. 20, 1955, *JBP 135-31.*

55. To Mrs. Lucile P. ———, Feb 12, 1955, *JBP 190-67.*

56. M. G. Shaw to Home of Merciful Rest and to Home for Aged Women, both Apr. 6, 1955, both in *JBP 135-45.*

57. To Thurlan Poitevint, Oct. 31, 1952, *JBP 121-39;* to Shands, Jan. 26, 1952, *JBP 204-9.*

58. To Eli Harry Fink, Jr., May 6, 1954, *JBP 131-1;* interview with Eli Fink, Sr., Mar. 20, 1987.

59. To Elizabeth Chamberlain, June 5, 1953, *JBP 124-43.*

60. From Lois Johnson, Jan. 22, 1953, *JBP 127-34;* from H. H. Saunders, Jan 13, 1954, *JBP 132-37.*

61. From Martha S. Lynde, president of the Civic Art Institute, Apr. 3, 1940, *JBP 57-22;* H. O. Williams to Civic Music Association, Feb. 2, 1954, *JBP 130-9;* To L. Valentine Lee, Nov. 21, 1955, *JBP.*

62. From John W. Donahoo, Apr. 13, 1959, *JBP 196-4;* from Donahoo, Oct. 28, 1960, *JBP 160-14;* from H. S. Buckworth, May 8, 1963, *JBP 173-25.*

63. To Clarence C. Nice, Dec. 9, 1955, *JBP 136-1;* H. O. Williams to Jacksonville Symphony, Dec. 30, 1957, *JBP 146-23,* and Dec. 15, 1958, *JBP 150-9;* to Roger L. Main, Feb. 12, 1963, *JBP 173-25.*

64. To Barton Barrs, July 13, 1944, *JBP 79-48;* to Carl B. Swisher, undated but probably March 1950, *JBP 110-21.*

65. To Franklyn A. Johnson, Sept. 7, 1956, *JBP 140-28;* to Johnson, Sept. 8, 1958, *JBP 151-54.*

66. To W. H. Goodman, Mar. 7, 1951, *JBP 115-50;* to B. S. Reid, Jan. 17, 1955, *JBP 114-18;* from W. E. Arnold, July 28, 1955, *JBP 137-4;* to Brewster

Hospital, Dec. 27, 1957, *JBP 144-29;* H. O. Williams to St. Vincent's Hospital, Dec. 15, 1958, *JBP 150-9.*

67. To W. S. Cirswell, Jan. 16, 1953, *JBP 124-27;* Walter R. Sherman to M. G. Shaw, Dec. 29, 1959, *JBP 155-25;* M. G. Shaw to Daniel Memorial Home, Dec. 18, 1964, *JBP 244-8;* from Eartha M. M. White, Jan. 11, 1962, *JBP 244-4;* to Roger L. Main, Dec. 29, 1955, *JBP 136-13;* H. W. Dew and W. B. Mills to M. G. Shaw, Dec. 11, 1963, *JBP 172-35.*

68. From E. M. Tignor, Nov. 19, 1956, and reply, Nov. 23, 1956, both in *JBP 142-9.*

CHAPTER NINE

1. Application for Scholarship, undated but in 1951 files, *JBP 118-14.*

2. For examples of Mrs. duPont's decisions on students' grades: from Shaw, Mar. 4, 1954, and to Shaw, Apr. 24, 1954, both in *JBP 130-23;* to Shaw, Mar. 9, 1955, *JBP 135-1.*

3. M. G. Shaw, Draft letter to those interested in scholarships awarded by Mrs. Alfred I. duPont, undated, but in 1953 files, *JBP 126-9;* to M. G. Shaw, Feb. 26, 1954, *JBP 130-23.*

4. From Shaw, Apr. 7, 1951, *JBP 212-7.*

5. From R. C. Beaty, July 16, 1951, and reply, July 25, 1951, both in *JBP 118-29;* Roger L. Main to Shaw, July 20, 1953, *JBP 126-35.*

6. W. H. Goodman, Research and Recommendations for Revision of Administrative Procedure and Purposes of the Alfred I. duPont Awards Foundation, Aug. 21, 1951, *JBP 117-9;* from Gaines, Dec. 4, 1951, *JBP 131-11;* The Scholarship Plan of the Alfred I. duPont Awards Foundation, undated but in 1952 files, *JBP 121-29;* to O. W. Riegel, May 6, 1955, *JBP 191-40.*

7. JBP Educational Contributions, Form 1040, 1953, *JBP 133-1;* Scholarships Awarded for Academic Year Sept. 1954 to June 1955, undated but in 1954 files, *JBP 133-48.*

8. Estimates of Allowable Contributions and Income Tax for the Year 1955, Oct. 14, 1955, *JBP 142-15.*

9. From Webster, Nov. 22, 1955, *JBP 142-15;* to Tom Ball, Dec. 20, 1955, *JBP 134-13.*

10. From Juhan, Dec. 19, 1955, and reply, Dec. 21, 1955, both in *JBP 136-1.*

11. To Addison Baker, Oct. 24, 1955, *JBP 124-9.*

12. Codicil to Last Will and Testament of May 17, 1943, dated June 11, 1948, *JBP 251-4.*

13. From R. N. Miller, Aug 1, 1955, *JBP 136-19;* to Ed Ball, Oct. 7, 1955,

JBP 134-12; JBP, draft paragraphs for will, undated but in 1955 file, *JBP 137-27.*

14. Interviews with Charles T. Akre, Oct. 21, 1987, and April 20, 1989.

15. The probated will and codicils were later printed by the fund as *In Re the Estate of Jessie Ball duPont Deceased,* County Judge's Court, Duval County Florida, Probate File 35883, Oct. 16, 1970. Copies are available in the fund's office in Jacksonville.

16. Ibid., p. 2.

17. Ibid., pp. 10–11.

18. Ibid,. pp. 4–5, 26–28. When Denise later decided that she did not want Epping Forest, Mrs. duPont changed her will to give the property to the Alfred I. duPont Foundation. She also revised her will to give the Zapffes and their children the use of Ditchley during their lifetimes.

19. To M. G. Shaw, Jan. 23, 1956, and reply, Jan. 25, 1956, both in *JBP 139-24.*

20. To Alfred Shands, Mar. 14, 1956, *JBP 192-39.*

21. To Mrs. Charles Adams, Mar. 30, 1956, *JBP 191-70.*

22. To Lytleton Cockrell, Apr. 10, 1947, *JBP 92-2;* Confirmation Record, St. John's Cathedral, Jan. 20, 1956; to F. A. Juhan, Jan. 28, 1956, *JBP 140-28;* from H. B. Hodgkins, Feb. 20, 1956, and from W. C. Munds, Feb. 11, 1956, both in *JBP 251-2.*

23. To Mrs. Charles Adams, Mar. 30, 1956, *JBP 191-70.*

24. To Mrs. Lemuel C. Stubbs, Apr. 27, 1956, *JBP 191-86;* to Helen Knox, Apr. 16, 1956, *JBP 140-39;* to Helen Knox, May 3, 1956, *JBP 192-6.*

25. To Elsie Bowley, May 17, 1956, *JBP 191-75;* to D. E. Finley, June 26, 1956, *JBP 139-43.*

26. To Elsie Bowley, May 17, 1956, *JBP 191-75;* to Isabel Baker, June 11, 1956, *JBP 138-31.*

27. Shaw to Edwards, Aug. 9, 1956, *JBP 139-29.*

28. To Juhan, July 7, 1956, *JBP 140-28;* to Helen Knox, Nov. 15, 1956, *JBP 140-32;* to F. P. Gaines, Sept. 3, 1956, *JBP 140-13.*

29. To Dr. Pomfret, Dec. 7, 1953, *JBP 127-23;* to Broward Culpepper, May 25, 1954, *JBP 194-12;* interview with Frederick H. Kent, Jr., Mar. 17, 1987; Minutes of the Board of Control, 18:444, 526–27, 548, 563–66, 589, 607, *FSA.*

30. Charlie Johns to LeRoy Collins, Mar. 18, 1955, Record Group 102, Series 776A, Box 16, Folder CON-COU, *FSA;* Ronnie Stark, "McCarthyism in Florida: Charley Johns and the Florida Legislative Investigation Committee, July 1956 to July, 1965" (master's thesis, University of South Florida, 1985).

31. To F. P. Gaines, Sept. 22, 1954, *JBP 131-11;* to W. H. Goodman,

Nov. 23, 1954, *JBP 129-35;* to Members of the Board of Control, Dec. 1, 1954, and to J. Lee Ballard, Dec. 21, 1954, both in *JBP 129-35;* Ballard to Johns, Dec. 15, 1954; Johns to Ballard, Dec. 20, 1954, both in Record Group 102, Series 569, Box 10, Folder: Governor Johns, Board of Control, *FSA;* Ballard to Collins, Feb. 25, 1955; Collins to Ballard, Mar. 2, 1955; Statement by Governor Collins, Mar. 22, 1955; Hollis Rinehart to Collins,. Mar. 18, 1955; Ballard to Collins, Mar. 18, 1955, all in Record Group 102, Series 776A, Box 16, Folder: CON-COU, *FSA;* Minutes of the Board of Control, 19:1, 29, 97, 112–13, *FSA.*

32. Memo of telephone conversation with Governor Collins, July 13, 1955, *JBP 195-44.*

33. Ann Deines and Richard G. Hewlett, "Jessie Ball duPont, Annual Tax-Deductible Cash Contributions to Charitable Institutions, 1957–1970 ($1,000 or over)" (unpublished report, 1988, *JBP* end note file). The figures in this report were compiled from a variety of sources, some of which are contradictory. Some of the blanks in the table probably represent missing data rather than zeros, and the figures reported should be considered only as relative values.

34. To O. N. Torian, Oct. 10, 1955; to E. McCrady, Oct. 21, 1955; to J. A. Woods, Oct. 20, 1955, all in *JBP 137-20;* from F. A. Juhan, May 28, 1957, *JBP 146-23;* Jacksonville *Florida Times-Union,* June 9, 1957, copy in *JBP 148-12.*

35. From J. R. Everett, Mar. 8, 1954, and reply, Mar. 25, 1954, both in *JBP 131-21;* to Everett, Nov. 30, 1955, *JBP 135-45.* A copy of the dedication program is in *JBP 196-30.*

36. To Ed Ball, Dec. 6, 1960, and reply, Dec. 8, 1960, both in Folder 1960 DI-DY, EB-*STJ;* from J. O. Edmunds, Feb. 11, 1959, and reply, Feb 12, 1959, both in *JBP 197-10;* to Edmunds, Nov. 21, 1960, *JBP 162-5.*

37. From F. A. Juhan, Dec. 10, 1963, *JBP 185-25.*

38. To C. T. Chenery, Nov. 22, 1958, *JBP 153-30;* from E. Fink, Nov. 10, 1959, *JBP 156-27;* from M. G. Shaw, Mar. 28, 1960, *JBP 160-16.*

39. Undated resumé, but in 1960 files, *JBP 161-8;* to Rebecca Adams, Feb. 27, 1960, *JBP 160-1;* to W. N. James, July 18, 1960, and to C. F. Cocke, Dec. 8, 1960, both in *JBP 161-8.*

40. Statement of Monies Expended by Ladies Aid Society of White Chapel Church, Feb. 1956, *JBP 140-28;* Ann Deines and Richard Hewlett, "Jessie Ball duPont, Annual Tax-Deductible Contributions to Educational and Charitable Institutions, 1957–1970 (over $1,000)" (unpublished report, 1989). The caveat on validity of the data in note 29 also applies here. JBP, U.S. Individual Income Tax Return, 1957, *JBP 150-20.*

41. JBP, Christmas Gifts, 1957, *JBP 145-4;* JBP, Statement of Financial Report, Year Ended Dec. 31, 1957, *JBP 195-11.*

42. From Mrs. S. J. Campbell, May 20, 1957, *JBP 147-2;* to Mrs. Pratt Thomas, Sept. 24, 1958, *JBP 152-6;* from Mrs. Pratt Thomas, Apr. 9, 1959, *JBP 157-20.*

43. To J. R. Everett, May 13, 1957, *JBP 193-25;* to Dr. and Mrs. Gaines, June 19, 1957, *JBP 146-7;* to Tom Ball, June 20, 1957, *JBP 144-20;* to W. H. Davies, June 13, 1958, *JBP 150-13;* interview with Mrs. Leslie Cheek, Nov. 17, 1987.

44. To Mrs. James Ball, July 10, 1956, *JBP 138-29;* to F. H. Kent, Sept. 5, 1956, *JBP 140-31.*

45. To W. T. Rice, Aug. 2, 1957, *JBP 147-34;* from Rice, June 16, 1958, *JBP 153-19;* to Rice, June 6, 1958, *JBP 151-18;* Gerard Colby, *DuPont Dynasty* (Secaucus, N.J.: Lyle Stuart, Inc., 1984), pp. 528–31.

46. Interview with W. T. Rice, Nov. 18, 1987. On earlier events in the Crummer case, see chap. 6. The suit came to trial again in 1959. See Orlando *Sentinel,* Apr. 1, 1959, copy in *JBP 196-3.*

47. From W. B. Mills, Dec. 27, 1957, *JBP 147-9;* from A. R. Shands, Nov. 25, 1956, and reply, Nov. 26, 1956, both in *JBP 153-13;* Deines and Hewlett, "Charitable Contributions."

48. M. G. Shaw to H. W. Dew, Apr. 25, 1957, *JBP 194-23;* Shaw to Dew, Apr. 15, 1959, *JBP 196-8;* Alfred I. duPont Foundation, List of Monthly Checks, 1957, *JBP 194-23.*

49. From F. A. Juhan, Jan. 6, 1959, and reply, Jan. 9, 1959, both in *JBP 157-11;* to Juhan, Sept. 14, 1959, *JBP Fund.* Allin later served as presiding bishop of the Episcopal church from 1974 until 1986.

50. To Tom Ball, Sept. 16, 1952, *JBP 118-39.*

51. To H. K. Sherrill, July 28, 1954, *JBP 132-39.*

52. To F. B. Sayre, Jr., Dec. 13, 1955, *JBP 137-4.*

53. To J. R. Cunningham, Sept. 19, 1956, *JBP 139-16.*

54. From F. S. Hutchins, Apr. 2, 1956; H. O. Williams to F. S. Hutchins, Apr. 21, 1956; from Hutchins, Apr. 23, 1956, all in *JBP 191-77;* to D. C. Loving, Jan. 2. 1957, *JBP 144-27;* to J. W. Chinn, Dec. 2, 1957, *JBP 145-20.*

55. From R. N. Miller, Nov. 27, 1956 and reply, Nov. 29, 1956, both in *JBP 141-8;* U.S. Supreme Court, Order 769, Apr. 29, 1957, Oct. Term, 1956, attachment, from Miller, May 2, 1957, *JBP 193-44;* Milton M. Gordon, "The Girard College Case: Desegregation and a Municipal Trust," *Annals of the American Academy of Political and Social Science* 304 (Mar. 1956):53–61.

56. From R. N. Miller, May 2, 1957, *JBP 193-44;* to R. N. Miller, May

15, 1957, *JBP 193-44;* to Tom Ball, June 4, 1957, *JBP 144-20;* to M. D. Jones, Dec. 9, 1958, *JBP 151-35.*

CHAPTER TEN

1. To Tom Ball, July 8, 1957, *JBP 192-70.*

2. From Ed Ball, July 20, 1957, and to Ed Ball, Aug. 8, 1957, both in *JBP 144-19.*

3. Raymond K. Mason and Virginia Harrison, *Confusion to the Enemy: A Biography of Edward Ball* (New York: Dodd, Mead, 1976), pp. 147–48; to Rebecca Adams, Mar. 14, 1957, *JBP 192-60.*

4. From Elsie Bowley, June 11, 1963, *JBP 174-27.*

5. To Ed Ball, Dec. 30, 1958, *JBP 149-26;* to Tom Ball, Jan. 2, 1959, *JBP 155-13.*

6. From Laura Bertram, Aug. 17, 1959; to Bertram, Sept. 24, 1959; to Tom Ball, Oct. 15, 1959, all in *JBP 155-13;* M. G. Shaw, Memorandum, June 10, 1961, *JBP 163-8;* from M. B. Corlette, June 2, 1960, Folder 1960, DI-DY, EB-*STJ.*

7. To F. A. Juhan, June 23, 1960, *JBP 161-10;* interview with Hazel O. Williams, March 24, 1987.

8. From Ed Ball, July 11, 1960, *JBP 187-4.*

9. To Ed Ball, July 16, 1959, *JBP 155-14.*

10. To A. R. Shands, Mar. 11, 1958, *JBP 195-16;* to Bishop and Mrs. Juhan, July 22, 1958, *JBP 151-35;* from Ed Ball, Feb. 21, 1959, and from L. R. Crandall, Apr. 8, 1959, both in *JBP 196-9.*

11. To Board of Directors and Board of Managers of the Nemours Foundation, Sept. 1, 1959, *JBP 237-23;* from W. H. Goodman, Dec. 3, 1958, *JBP 197-42;* to Goodman, Nov. 12, 1959, *JBP 156-42.*

12. First Codicil to the Last Will and Testament of Jessie Ball duPont, Oct. 16, 1960, p. 1, *JBP* end note file.

13. To Ed Ball, Dec. 30, 1960, *JBP 187-4.*

14. A. R. Shands to L. R. Geeslin, Feb. 27, 1961, private collection.

15. To Ed Ball, Mar. 24, 1961, *JBP 240-15.*

16. Interview with Hazel O. Williams, January 20, 1989.

17. To M. G. Shaw, Mar. 2, 1960, *JBP 162-2;* draft of letter, Jan. 1961, *JBP 212-9;* to President, Florida State University, June 26, 1961, *JBP 212-7.* Identical letters were sent to twenty other colleges and universities. Copies are in this file.

18. To President, Florida State University, June 26, 1961, *JBP 212-7.*

19. From Gordon W. Blackwell, June 30, 1961, *JBP 212-7.* Letters from other university presidents are also in this file. Ann Deines and Richard G.

Hewlett, "Jessie Ball duPont, Annual Tax-Deductible Contributions to Educational and Charitable Institutions, 1957–1970 (over $1,000)" (unpublished report, 1989).

20. JBP, Resumé of Year End Contributions, 1957, *JBP 150-9;* List of Year End Contributions, Cash, 1960, *JBP 244-1;* Cash Report, Personal Account, for the Week Ending Dec. 31, 1961, *JBP 169-9.*

21. To Isabel Baker, Sept. 19, 1961, *JBP 163-4.*

22. Minutes of the meetings held on July 6 and Oct. 30, 1961, are in *JBP 188-39.*

23. To Dr. and Mrs. Cole, Oct. 12, 1961, *JBP 163-22;* to Ed Ball, Dec. 7, 1961, *JBP 163-6;* to Ed Ball, Dec. 20, 1961, *JBP 187-4;* interview with Irvin P. Golden, Mar. 29, 1989.

24. To Ed Ball, Jan. 9, 1962, Folder Mrs. Alfred I. duPont 1962, EB-*STJ.*

25. Minutes of the two meetings, Feb. 3, 1961, are in *JBP 188-39.* To P. B. Waldrop, Feb. 8, 1962, *JBP 171-32;* H. O. Williams to F. H. Kent, undated but in 1970 files, *JBP 189-15.*

26. M. G. Shaw to J. A. Logan, Mar. 12, 1962, *JBP 170-11.*

27. M. G. Shaw to F. A. Juhan, Apr. 23, 1962, *JBP 170-18;* Shaw to Rebecca Adams, July 16, 1962, *JBP 168-35;* to Helen Mills, Aug. 10, 1962, *WBM;* Shaw to Isabel Baker, Sept. 28, 1962, *JBP 168-41;* Minutes of Meeting of Trustees of the Alfred I. duPont Estate, Sept. 28, 1962, *JBP 188-39.*

28. From L. E. Geeslin, Jan. 15, 1963, *JBP 172-39;* to Ed Ball, Jan. 31, 1964, *JBP 187-4.*

29. Interview with H. O. Williams, Mar. 24, 1987; interview with Mrs. A. R. Shands, May 11, 1987; to M. S. Sheehy, Feb. 20, 1964, *JBP 176-21.*

30. A detailed medical report on Mrs. duPont's physical condition is attached to A. R. Shands to Ed Ball, Jan. 7, 1963, Folder Mrs. Alfred I. duPont 1962, EB-*STJ.* To F. A. Juhan, Jan. 8, 1963, *JBP 170-18;* to Henry Dew, June 18, 1963, *JBP 172-27.* Mrs. duPont's illnesses in 1963 are described in Shands to District Director, Internal Revenue Service, Aug. 2, 1963, *JBP 174-9;* Shaw to Rebecca Adams, Oct. 8, 1963, *JBP 172-1.*

31. O. W. Riegel to T. Catledge, Jan. 16, 1967, W. B. Mills Files, *JBP Fund;* W. H. Goodman to M. G. Shaw, Aug. 6, 1963, and Shaw to Goodman, Sept. 23, 1963, both in *JBP 173-14;* Goodman to Shaw, Mar. 21, Dec. 5, 1963, and Goodman to K. E. Haefele, Dec. 31, 1963, all in *JBP 244-16.*

32. T. Spackman to W. B. Mills, Oct. 27, 1966; F. C. Cole to Mills, Nov. 17, 1966, and reply, Nov. 30, 1966; K. E. Haefele to L. C. Cowan, Dec. 9, 1966, all in *JBP 244-16; Broadcasting* 72 (Jan. 23, 1967):74. Columbia was still administering the award program in 1989.

33. W. H. Goodman to Trustees of the Estate, Nov. 19, 1963, *JBP 172-12;* interview with Mrs. A. R. Shands, May 11, 1987.

34. First Codicil, Oct. 16, 1960, pp. 2–7, *JBP* end note file; A. R. Shands to W. T. Thompson, Nov. 20, 1963, *JBP 174-9*.

35. To Ed Ball, Feb. 25, 1963, *JBP 187-4;* to Elizabeth Chamberlain, Jan. 28, 1964, *JBP 175-4;*

36. Deines and Hewlett, "Contribution Tables."

37. Burton Altman, " 'In the Public Interest?' Ed Ball and the FEC Railway War," *Florida Historical Quarterly* 64 (July 1985):34–37.

38. House Committee on Banking and Currency, *Hearings on H.R. 10688 and H.R. 10872 to Amend the Bank Holding Company Act of 1956,* 88th Cong., 2d sess., Apr.–June 1964, pp. 255–80; Mason and Harrison, *Confusion,* pp. 81–88; Gerard Colby, *DuPont Dynasty* (Secaucus, N.J.: Lyle Stuart, Inc., 1984), pp. 530–31; Altman, "In the Public Interest," pp. 38–40.

39. House Select Subcommittee on Small Business, *Tax-Exempt Foundations and Charitable Trusts: Their Impact on Our Economy,* Third Installment, 88th Cong., 2d sess., Mar. 20, 1964, p. iii.

40. Ibid., p. 12.

41. Hearings on Bank Holding Company Act, pp. 1–55.

42. Ibid., pp. 5–51, 237–39.

43. Ibid., pp. 133–85, 245–80; Mason and Harrison, *Confusion,* pp. 57–67.

44. *Congressional Record,* 88th Cong., 2d sess., Feb. 20, 1964, pp. 3170–72.

45. W. B. Mills, draft statement, Feb. 21, 1964, *WBM.* See also H. F. McKean to W. Morse, Apr. 7, 1964, *JBP 176-19*.

46. A. R. McKinstry to Mrs. L. B. Johnson, Feb. 22, 1964, *JBP 241-16*.

47. W. Morse to C. E. Bennett, Mar. 12, 1964, *JBP 174-45;* interview with Denise duPont Zapffe, June 12, 1987.

48. To C. E. Bennett, Apr. 8, 1964, *JBP 174-45;* St. Petersburg *Times,* Mar. 22, 1964. A copy with Mrs. duPont's comments is in *JBP 176-28*.

49. M. G. Shaw to Mrs. W. T. Edwards, June 10, 1964, *JBP 175-16;* from H. W. Dew, July 7, 1964, *JBP 175-11;* Shaw to Mrs. F. A. Juhan, Aug. 5, 1964, *JBP 175-34;* Shaw to Mrs. A. J. Bowley, Aug. 26, 1964, *JBP 174-46*.

50. To F. A. Juhan, Oct. 28, 1964, *JBP 175-34;* M. G. Shaw to Mrs. N. A. Baker, Jan. 7, 1965, *JBP 174-44;* obituary, M. G. Shaw, Wilmington *Evening Journal,* Mar. 6, 1965.

51. From H. O. Williams, June 22, 1964, *JBP 175-23*.

52. Interview with Hazel Williams, Jan. 20, 1989. For correspondence between Miss Shaw and George Webster, see *JBP 233-1*.

53. Minutes, Meeting of the Trustees of the Alfred I. duPont Estate, May 10, 1965, *JBP 188-39*. The St. Joe officials were Thomas S. Coldewey and A. L. Hargraves.

54. This paragraph and those following are based largely on interviews with C. T. Akre, Oct. 21, 1987, and April 20, 1989.

55. Fifth Codicil to the Last Will and Testament of Jessie Ball duPont, June 23, 1965, p. 4. The second codicil, Aug. 24, 1962, made technical revisions to reflect interpretations of the federal estate tax laws. The third codicil, Apr. 7, 1963, appointed Mills as trustee to replace Seabury Stoneburner. The fourth codicil, Apr. 16, 1964, made certain changes in the designation of successor trustees and the general attorney for the estate. (All codicils in *JBP* end note file.)

56. Akre interviews, Oct. 21, 1987, and Apr. 20, 1989.

57. H. O. Williams to Mrs. W. B. Mills, July 13, 1965, *WBM.*

58. H. O. Williams to F. A. Juhan, Aug. 24, 1965, *JBP 177-36;* Williams to Denise Zapffe, July 18, 1969, *JBP 186-39.*

59. H. O. Williams to Helen Mills, May 22, 1969, *WBM.* Williams, telephone call from Dr. Shands, Dec. 1, 1966, *JBP 178-37.*

60. H. O. Williams to L. Bertram, July 26, 1966, *JBP 78-35;* Williams to F. A. Juhan, Apr. 12, 1967, *JBP 181-17.*

61. To W. H. Ball, Aug. 4, 1965, *JBP 177-3.*

62. Interview with Hazel Williams, Mar. 24, 1987.

63. To Lee Booth, May 23, 1966, *JBP 188-1.*

64. Ed Ball testified at the House hearings in June 1964. House Committee on Banking and Currency, *Hearings on a Bill to Amend the Bank Holding Company Act of 1956—H.R. 10688 and H.R. 10872,* 88th Cong., 2d sess., Apr.–June 1964, pp. 193–237. He repeated much of his testimony in a hearing before the same committee on June 14, 1965 (1965 *Hearings, to Amend the Bank Holding Company Act,* 89th Cong., 2d sess., May–June 1965, pp. 39–76).

65. Meeting with Mrs. duPont and Mr. Mills, Feb. 9, 1966, *JBP 211-29;* H. O. Williams, telephone conversation with Mr. Mills, concerning Mr. Ball's requests, Dec. 2, 1966, *JBP 211-30.*

66. Deines and Hewlett, "Contribution Tables."

67. To Elizabeth Chamberlain, May 16, 1968, *JBP 183-1.*

68. H. O. Williams to Mrs. N. Snydelaar, Dec. 7, 1968, *JBP 189-13.*

69. JBP, Federal Income Tax Returns for these years in *JBP 233-18, JBP 235-18, JBP 236-6,* and *JBP 236-25.*

70. Williams to Juhan, May 18 and Sept. 13, 1967, both in *JBP 181-17.*

71. Williams to Mrs. W. T. Edwards, July 22, 1970, *JBP 188-3.*

72. Williams to Mr. and Mrs. Zapffe, Aug. 21, 1970, *JBP 189-16.*

73. Interview with Arthur R. McKinstry, May 13, 1987.

74. A. R. Shands, Jr., "Jessie Ball duPont: A Great Southern Lady," address at the dedication of the Jessie Ball duPont Library, Sewanee, Apr. 3, 1965, *JBP 167-35.*

CHAPTER ELEVEN

1. Interview with Hazel O. Williams, March 8, 1989.

2. The third codicil, Apr. 7, 1963, replaced Stoneburner with Mills. The fourth codicil, Apr. 16, 1964, appointed A. D. Juhan as successor to his father.

3. Interview with Irvin P. Golden, Mar. 29, 1989.

4. Jacksonville *Florida Times-Union*, Oct. 17, 1970, copy in *JBP 243-2*.

5. Jessie Ball duPont, Balance Sheet, Sept. 26, 1970, *JBP 242-8*.

6. Last Will and Testament of Jessie Ball duPont, Dec. 22, 1955, pp. 2–7, 10–26.

7. First Codicil to the Last Will and Testament of Jessie Ball duPont, Oct. 16, 1960, pp. 7–19.

8. Minutes of First Meeting of the Executors, Nov. 3, 1970, *JBP 242-2*.

9. House Committee on Ways and Means, *Hearings on the Subject of Tax Reform*, 91st Cong., 1st sess., Apr. 24, 1969, pp. 2–20. The bill was printed as passed by the House, Aug. 7, 1969, in Senate Committee on Finance, *Hearings on H. R. 13270*, 91st Cong., 1st sess., pp. 127–494; Waldemar A. Nielsen, *The Golden Donors: A New Anatomy of the Great Foundations* (New York: E. P. Dutton, 1985), pp. 23–27.

10. Employees of the Estate of Alfred I. duPont and Mrs. duPont's Personal Staff, undated but probably prepared by Hazel Williams in Oct. 1970, *JBP 238-3;* I. P. Golden, Nemours Maintenance Account, *JBP 238-9*. See also Report on Progress—From Minutes and Correspondence: First Meeting of the Executors, Nov. 3, 1970; Second Meeting, Nov. 27, 1970; Third Meeting, Dec. 29, 1970; Fourth Meeting, Jan 14, 1971, all in *JBP 242-8*.

11. Minutes, Fifth Meeting, Feb. 2, 1971, *JBP 239-12*.

12. C. T. Akre, Must the Decedent's Will be Reformed, Dec. 1, 1970, *JBP 241-6*. The new tax law added Section 508(e) to the Internal Revenue Code. The new section provided that a private foundation, in order to be exempt from Section 501(a), had to have provisions in its governing instrument that (1) required its income to be distributed and that prohibited it from (2) engaging in self-dealing; (3) retaining any excess business holdings; (4) making investments that under the statute would jeopardize the charitable purpose or function; and (5) making any taxable expenditures.

13. Section 4942.

14. Transcript of Discussions between Mr. Kent, Mr. Akre, and the Executors, Oct. 30, 1974, *JBP 242-2*. Prohibitions on self-dealing had been part of federal tax law since 1950. The provisions of Section 4941 of the tax reform act are complex and cover a wide variety of situations, only one of which is covered in this paragraph. For a concise discussion of the

"self-dealing" provisions of the act, see William H. Smith and Carolyn P. Chiechi, *Private Foundations Before and After the Tax Reform Act of 1969* (Washington: American Enterprise Institute, 1974), pp. 52–58.

15. Akre, Distribution of Income by the Fund, Dec. 2, 1970, *JBP 241-6.* The relevant section of the act is 4942(g).

16. Akre to the Executors, Feb. 19 and Aug. 2, 1971, both in *JBP 241-6.*

17. Akre to Executors, Feb. 19, 1971, *JBP 241-6.*

18. Akre, Memorandum on Payment of Federal Estate Tax, Aug. 19, 1971, *JBP 241-6;* Minutes, Tenth Meeting of the Executors, Jan. 10, 1972, *JBP 242-2.*

19. Akre, Memorandum on Suit in Florida Circuit Court to Reform the Will, Aug. 19, 1971, *JBP 241-6.*

20. Smith and Chiechi, *Private Foundations,* p. 47.

21. In addition to Smith and Chiechi, see John R. Labovitz, *The Impact of the Private Foundation Provisions of the Tax Reform Act of 1969: Early Empirical Measurements* (Washington: American Bar Foundation, 1974), and John H. Watson III, *The Impact of the Tax Reform Act of 1969 on Company Foundations* (New York: The Conference Board, 1973). These books refer to numerous articles in tax journals and other publications.

22. D. Creel, "Problems Posed for Larger Foundations," in *Tax Problems for Larger Foundations,* p. 186, as quoted in Smith and Chiechi, *Private Foundations,* p. 75.

23. *Tampa Tribune-Times,* Nov. 23, 1975, copy in *JBP 242-8;* Ball to Golden, Dec. 5, 1974, *JBP 242-2.*

24. Transcript of Discussions Between Executors and Counsel, Apr. 30, 1975, *JBP 242-1.*

25. Minutes, Executors' Meeting, Aug. 10, 1976, *JBP 242-1.*

26. Minutes, First Meeting of the Trustees, Jan. 19, 1977; Ed Ball, Draft Motion on Fund Organization, Jan. 19, 1977, both in *JBP Fund.*

27. Kent to the Trustees, Mar. 16, 1977, with draft letter attached; Williams to Trustees, May 4, 1977; and Kent to Trustees, May 12, 1977, all in *JBP Fund.*

28. Minutes of Special Meeting of the Trustees, Oct. 13, 1977, *JBP Fund.*

29. Minutes of First Annual Meeting of the Trustees, Jan. 18, 1978, *JBP Fund.*

30. Minutes of Special Meeting of the Trustees and attachments, Apr. 17, 1978, and Williams to the Trustees, Apr. 17, 1978, with 50-page attachment, both in *JBP Fund.*

31. Nielsen, *The Golden Donors,* p. 21.

32. Data constructed from a table in the fund's Five-Year Report, 1976–81, p. 47.

Essay on Sources

The Papers of Jessie Ball duPont constituted the principal source of documentation for this book. Maintained since Mrs. duPont's death in 1970 by the Jessie Ball duPont Religious, Charitable, and Educational Fund in Jacksonville, Florida, the collection (325 cubic feet) contains virtually every document accumulated in Mrs. duPont's Wilmington and Jacksonville files from 1925 until 1970. The bulk of the collection consists of correspondence files containing for the most part copies of letters dictated by Mrs. duPont or written by her secretaries, Mary Shaw and later Hazel Williams. They started a new file at the beginning of each calendar year and labeled folders with the names of correspondents. Because Mrs. duPont dictated almost all of her personal as well as her business correspondence, the collection provides a rich insight into her private opinions and concerns. Only occasionally, however, did she keep incoming personal correspondence for her files. Personal letters from her brothers and sisters she often passed on to other members of the family or destroyed. Thus the collection contains few letters of interest to biographers of Mrs. duPont's friends or associates.

Incoming correspondence, however, does include an extraordinary collection of business letters, brokers' and bank statements, tax returns, auditors' reports, quarterly and annual financial statements, bills for purchases of household and personal items, and applications for scholarships and grants. For historians of philanthropy, these records provide an excellent opportunity for further in-depth study of the financial resources available to Mrs. duPont and how she chose to use them for charitable purposes. For social historians these records reflect in great detail the domestic life of a wealthy matron in the middle years of the twentieth century.

In addition to preserving the correspondence files intact, Hazel Williams was also careful to collect all of Mrs. duPont's personal effects, including occasional personal diaries, family letters going back to her childhood, family photographs, Christmas and birthday cards, a few love letters to and from Alfred, newspaper clippings, handwritten notes and scraps of poetry, and the contents of her desk drawers. Because she tried to screen her private life from public view, these records are indispensable for understanding who Mrs. duPont really was.

The Papers of Alfred I. duPont, like those of his third wife, have been preserved by the fund in Jacksonville. Most of Alfred's personal papers that still survive and some business correspondence for the years before his marriage to Jessie Ball were maintained until 1989 in the mansion house at Nemours. The art curator at Nemours processed these papers, which include a valuable collection of photographs, and designed a finding aid that describes the records. In 1989 the entire collection (24 cubic feet) was transferred to the fund's offices in Jacksonville, where the files could be combined with a large collection of Alfred duPont's business correspondence, which was maintained in Jacksonville from the time of his move to Florida in 1925 until his death in 1935. These records (76 cubic feet) relate solely to routine business affairs and contain little or nothing about Alfred duPont's personal life. The collection also includes some routine business files of Edward Ball and Jessie Ball duPont during the same years. In 1988 the fund transferred the latter collection to Mrs. duPont's files.

By the terms of Mrs. duPont's will, Alfred's papers were to become the property of Washington and Lee University in Lexington, Virginia. The trustees of the Jessie Ball duPont Fund decided likewise to give her papers to Washington and Lee. Both collections were delivered to the university in the fall of 1990, and they will be open for scholarly research in Lexington when archival processing is completed.

The Edward Ball Papers, held by the St. Joe Paper Company in Jacksonville, contain extensive files relating to Ball's business career as well as a few papers relating to Mrs. duPont. Jacob C. Belin, president of the company, generously made some of the papers available for this book.

The records of the Alfred I. duPont Institute in Wilmington, Delaware, contain a large number of files relating to the formation and early years of the institute and the Nemours Foundation. However, strict limitations imposed by the institute on access to and citation of these records greatly reduced the value of this collection in research for this book.

Record Group 205, National Archives, Washington, D.C., provided valuable information on the career of Mrs. duPont's father, Captain Thomas Ball, as a federal official during the 1880s. The records of the Department of the Interior relating to claims against Indian depredations made it possible to trace the movements of the Ball family during Jessie's childhood.

Congressional reports, including Edward Ball's lengthy testimony before congressional committees, provide the best insight into his personality and the financial empire that he built in Florida: House Committee on Banking and Currency, *Hearings on a Bill to Amend the Bank Holding Company Act of 1956—H.R. 10688 and H.R. 10872,* 88th Cong., 2d sess. (Washington, 1964); House Committee on Ways and Means, *Hearings on the Subject of Tax Reform* 91st Cong., 1st sess. (Washington, 1969); and House Select Subcommittee on Small Business, *Tax-Exempt Foundations and Charitable Trusts: Their Impact on Our Economy,* 3d installment, 88th Cong. 2d sess. (Washington, 1964).

The archives of the Texas State Library, Austin, Texas, contains tax rolls of Jacks County, 1872–78, which identify the property held by Thomas Ball during the years when the Ball family lived there.

The archives of the Virginia Historical Society and the Virginia State Library in Richmond hold many collections relating to Virginia history and Virginia families, but they have no significant documents relating to Mrs. duPont or to the Ball family. The state library, however, does have some important documents on the beginnings of the public school system in Virginia.

The Florida State Archives in Tallahassee has the official minutes of the State Board of Control, on which Mrs. duPont served from 1951 until 1955. The voluminous minutes contain copies of all papers coming before the board and a record of all formal actions, but no record of discussions. It was still possible, however, to determine the kinds of issues in which Mrs. duPont took an interest and how she voted on each issue. The records of Governor Dan McCarty and Acting Governor Charley E. Johns (R.G. 102, Series 569, Box 10) contain correspondence relating to the appointment of the new president of the University of Florida, the principal issue in which Mrs. duPont was involved as a member of the board. Also important on this issue are the papers of Governor T. LeRoy Collins (R.G. 102, Series 776A, Box 16).

The Fuller Warren Papers, in Special Collections at the Florida State University Library, Tallahassee, provided some background on Mrs. duPont's appointment to the Board of Control.

The Claude Pepper Papers in the Maude and Claude Pepper Library at Florida State University contain extensive materials on Pepper's early life and political career. Most useful for this book was Pepper's correspondence (R.G. 300, Series 301, Box 38, and Series 302B, Box 3) that relates to the bank holding company legislation and his continuing battle as a member of the House Banking Committee with Edward Ball.

SECONDARY SOURCES

The Ball Family

There are few published accounts of Jessie Ball's forbears. Robert O. Norris ("Mary Ball Washington and Her Family," *Northern Neck of Virginia*

Historical Society 3 [1953]: 190–97) describes the Balls' relationship to George Washington's mother. Jessie's mother, Lalla Gresham Ball, described her childhood in "Reminiscences of Plantation Life in Virginia" (*Northern Neck Historical Quarterly* 12 [1962]: 1060–67).

Mrs. duPont was the subject of many magazine and newspaper articles during her later years, but only two accounts of her career have appeared in book-length publications. In 1985 the Robert E. Lee Memorial Foundation published a collection of recollections by Mrs. duPont's friends and associates, principally those who had served with her on the Stratford board. The collection (*Jessie Ball duPont 1884–1970*, ed. Mary Tyler Freeman Cheek, Stratford, Va.: Robert E. Lee Memorial Association, 1985) presents an intimate portrayal of Mrs. duPont's personality. Helen Knox wrote a brief biography of her friend, "Jessie Ball duPont: Banker, Financier and Doctor of Humanities" (*The Woman Banker*, Aug.–Sept. 1948, pp. 4–8). Arthur R. McKinstry painted an admiring and appreciative portrait of Mrs. duPont in his autobiography, *All I have Seen: The McKinstry Memoirs by the Fifth Bishop of Delaware, 1939–1954* (Wilmington, Del.: Serendipity Press, 1975).

Congressman Charles E. Bennett, who first met Mrs. duPont as a young man, included a chapter on the duPonts and Edward Ball in *Twelve on the River St. Johns* (Jacksonville: University of North Florida Press, 1989). Bennett's account of his experiences with Ball adds to the growing collection of colorful stories about Mrs. duPont's legendary brother. Two books with similar titles have been published on Edward Ball. Raymond K. Mason, a close friend and protégé, and Virginia Harrison, a free-lance writer, wrote *Confusion to the Enemy: A Biography of Edward Ball* (New York: Dodd, Mead, 1976). Although journalistic in style and undocumented, I believe the biography is on the whole accurate and presents information not available elsewhere. Leon Odell Griffith, in *Ed Ball: Confusion to the Enemy* (Miami: Trend House, 1975), relates many of the same stories. An excellent article by Freeman Lincoln, "The Terrible-Tempered Mr. Ball," appeared in *Fortune* (Nov. 1952, pp. 160–62).

The Dupont Family

Over the past decade many books and magazine articles have been written about the generations of duPonts who followed Pierre Samuel in building the company that bears their name. Alfred D. Chandler and Stephen Salisbury (*Pierre S. DuPont and the Making of the Modern Corporation*, New York: Harper & Row, 1971) and David A. Hounshell and John Kenly Smith, Jr. (*Science and Corporate Strategy: DuPont R & D, 1902–1980*, Cambridge: Cambridge University Press, 1989), are among the most reliable, although they focus more on the company than on individuals. More relevant to Mrs. duPont than these books is the bulky volume by Gerard Colby, *DuPont Dynasty: Behind the Nylon Curtain* (Secaucus, N.J.: Lyle Stuart, 1984), which grew out of congressional investigations of the company over the last twenty years. Exhaustive in detail and lacking in perspective, the book resembles a congressional report more than a history. Leonard Mosely's *Blood Relations: The Rise and Fall of the duPonts of Delaware* (New York: Atheneum, 1980) is a casual compendium of human interest stories about the family. In its details the book only begins to approximate the truth and thus it cannot serve as a reliable source of information.

That only two books have been published on Alfred I. duPont and his branch of the family is not surprising in light of Alfred's almost complete alienation from most of the Wilmington duPonts after his second marriage and certainly after he pulled up stakes in Wilmington and moved to Florida in 1925. Soon after Alfred's death in 1935, as described in chapter 4, Mrs. duPont commissioned Marquis James to write a biography of her late husband. James, a Pulitzer prize winner with two popular biographies to his credit, received full cooperation from Mrs. duPont, who made available all of Alfred's papers at Nemours as well as some, but far from all, of her personal papers. She granted James two long interviews and asked many of Alfred's former associates to meet with the author. In the course of his research and writing, James and his wife developed a personal friendship with Mrs. duPont. In the end, James wrote the biography the way he wanted it, and Mrs. duPont suggested only a few minor changes, many of which James did not accept. James certainly believed that his book, published as *Alfred I. duPont: The Family Rebel* (Indianapolis: Bobbs-Merrill, 1941) represented his unvarnished opinions, free of any coercion from Mrs. duPont or members of the family. A reading of the book today, however, suggests either that she did in fact assert her influence in subtle ways or that James, at the very least, pulled his punches out of concern for the feelings of his new friend. James's biography is sympathetic if not overly laudatory. It leaves many important questions unanswered and now shows its age. Because James had access to some documents that no longer exist and to individuals long since dead, the book continues to be an indispensable if dated source on the life of its subject.

When James published his book, Mrs. duPont wrote to him that she was "deeply appreciative and delighted with the results of your work. It is a masterpiece." Whether this statement was a true expression of her feelings or whether she changed her mind with the passing years, she evidently concluded that James's book was not a sufficient monument to her husband. In her will, she directed that her trustees provide funds from her estate to commission a new biography. The result is Joseph Frazier Wall's book, *Alfred I. duPont: The Man and His Family* (New York: Oxford University Press, 1990).

In his biography Wall expanded on and refined James's treatment of Alfred duPont's business and political career. He also dug deep into the history of the duPont family, going back to the early career of Pierre Samuel duPont in France before the American Revolution. Wall brought to life the more than eighty family members in three generations who had an impact on Alfred. The book centers on Alfred's tumultuous career in the DuPont Company, his monumental struggles with his cousins, Pierre S. and T. Coleman duPont, for control of the company, and the tangle of relationships generated by his three marriages. Of the three wives, the author gives the least space to Jessie Ball duPont.

History of Philanthropy

In recent decades historians have written more about the giants of philanthropy than about the impact of philanthropy on American society. A promising framework for a general history of philanthropy appeared in a scholarly debate presented in two articles (*Sociology* 17 [May 1983]: 206–33, and 18 [Nov. 1984]: 572–87). The debate between two sociologists, Donald Fisher and Martin Bulmer, centered on the question of hegemony: whether the Rockefeller Foundation had used its enormous financial resources to influence the direction of social science research. Three years later two historians, Barry D. Karl and Stanley Katz, explored the hegemony theme in their article "Foundations and Ruling Class Elites," which appeared in *Daedalus* (116 [Winter 1987]: 1–40), titled "Philanthropy, Patronage, and Politics." These articles provided a useful bench mark against which to analyze Mrs. duPont's charitable activities.

Most books on the history of philanthropy have been written by practitioners in the field rather than by historians. Again, most of these address the great U.S. foundations, but they proved useful in placing Mrs. duPont's work in context: Robert F. Arnove, ed., *Philanthropy and Cultural Imperialism: The Foundations at Home and Abroad* (Boston: G. K. Hall, 1980); Robert H. Bremmer, *American Philanthropy* (Chicago: University of Chicago Press, 1960); Kathleen D. McCarthy, *Noblesse Oblige: Charity and Cultural Philanthropy in Chicago, 1849–1929* (Chicago, University of Chicago Press, 1960): Brian O'Connell, ed., *America's Voluntary Spirit* (New York: Foundation Center, 1983); and Warren Weaver, *U. S. Philanthropic Foundations: Their Structure, Management, and Record* (New York: Harper & Row, 1967). An excellent guide to other books on philanthropy is Daphne Niobe Layton,

Philanthropy and Voluntarism: An Annotated Bibliography (New York: Foundation Center, 1987).

Three useful studies have appeared on the Tax Reform Act of 1969, which had a direct impact on the terms of Mrs. duPont's will: William H. Smith and Carolyn P. Chiechi, *Private Foundations and the Tax Reform Act of 1969* (Washington, D.C.: American Enterprise Institute, 1974); John R. Labovitz, *The Impact of the Private Foundation Provisions of the Tax Reform Act of 1969: Early Empirical Measurements* (Washington, D.C.: American Bar Association, 1974); and John H. Watson III, *The Impact of the Tax Reform Act of 1969 on Company Foundations* (New York: Conference Board, 1973).

Particularly helpful in describing the evolution of the Jessie Ball duPont Fund in its early years was Waldemar A. Nielsen, *The Golden Donors: A New Anatomy of the Great Foundations* (New York: E. P. Dutton, 1985).

Southern History

For a general background in southern history during Mrs. duPont's lifetime, I found the following books helpful: Orville B. Burton and Robert C. McMath, Jr., *Towards a New South?: Studies in Post Civil-War Southern Communities* (Westport, Conn.: Greenwood Press, 1982); Clement Eaton, *The Waning of the Old South Civilization* (Athens, Ga.: University of Georgia Press, 1968); Jack Temple Kirby, *Rural Worlds Lost: The American South, 1920–1960* (Baton Rouge, La.: Louisiana State University Press, 1987); George B. Tindall, *The Emergence of the New South, 1913–1945* (Baton Rouge, La.: Louisiana State University Press, 1967); C. Vann Woodward, *Origins of the New South, 1877–1913* (Baton Rouge, La.: Louisiana State University Press, 1971), especially the revised bibliography; and Bertram Wyatt-Brown, *Southern Honor: Ethics and Behavior in the Old South* (New York: Oxford University Press, 1982).

Two classic studies provided the foundation for my analysis of Mrs. duPont's position on racial segregation: Wilbur J. Cash, *The Mind of the South* (New York: Alfred A. Knopf, 1941), and Gunnar Myrdal, with the assistance of Richard Sterner and Arnold Rose, *An American Dilemma: The Negro Problem and Modern Democracy* (New York: Harper, 1944). The following were of great help in interpreting these works in the larger dimensions of southern history: Kenneth K. Baily, "Southern White Protestantism at the Turn of the Century" (*American Historical Review* 68 [Apr. 1963]: 619–20); David W. Southern, *Gunnar Myrdal and Black-White Relations: The Use and Abuse of An American Dilemma* (Baton Rouge, La.: Louisiana State University Press, 1987); and Joel Williamson, *The Crucible of Race: Black-White Relations in the American South Since Emancipation* (New York: Oxford University Press, 1984).

Florida History

The *Florida Historical Quarterly* contains numerous articles relating to the history of the state during Mrs. duPont's lifetime. On the history of Jacksonville the best sources are James B. Crooks, "Changing Face of Jacksonville, Florida, 1900–1910" (62 [Apr. 1984]: 439–40) and "Jacksonville in the Progressive Era: Responses to Urban Growth," 65 [July 1986]: 58–59); and Herbert J. Doherty, Jr., "Jacksonville as a Nineteenth-Century Railroad Center" (58 [Oct. 1977]: 373–86). These articles largely supersede the book by T. Fredrick Davis, *History of Jacksonville, Florida* (St. Augustine: Florida Historical Society, 1925). Two helpful articles on the Florida East Coast Railway dispute are Burton Altman, " 'In the Public Interest?' Ed Ball and the FEC Railway War" (64 [July 1985]: 34–37), and Alexander R. Stoesen, "Road to Receivership: Claude Pepper, the duPont Trust, and the Florida East Coast Railway" (52 [Oct. 1973]: 135–37).

No scholarly history of the state as a whole exists, but Charlton W. Tebeau's *A History of Florida* (Coral Gables: University of Miami Press, 1971) provides a popular survey of the subject. The best general collection of secondary works on the history of the state is in the Florida History Room of the state library in Tallahassee. The Special Collections Division of the University of Florida Library in Gainesville has on microfilm a number of dissertations and theses relating to Florida history. Two studies I used are John L. Moore, Jr.'s "Good Reason, Bad Reason, and No Reason at All: A Study of Florida Politics with Special Reference to the Pepper-Smathers Primary" (senior honors thesis, Harvard College, 1951) and Ronnie Stark's "McCarthyism in Florida: Charley Johns and the Florida State Legislative Investigation Committee, July 1956 to July 1965" (master's thesis, University of South Florida, 1985).

Although Mrs. duPont took little interest in Florida politics, her brother Edward did. His longstanding controversy with Claude Pepper is described at length in two books: Claude Denson Pepper with Hays Gorey, *Pepper: Eyewitness to a Century* (New York: Harcourt Brace Jovanovich, 1987), and Robert Sherrill, *Gothic Politics in the Deep South: Stars of the New Confederacy* (New York: Grossman Publishers, 1968).

Women's History

Although most historians have focused on women in the Northeast and in the period before the Civil War, some of their studies apply in important respects to southern women. A classic source still useful is Sophonisba P. Breckinridge, *Women in the Twentieth Century: A Study of Their Political, Social, and Economic Activities* (New York: McGraw-Hill, 1933). More recent studies include: Karen Anderson, *Wartime Women: Sex Roles, Family Relations, and the Status of Women During World War II* (Westport, Conn.: Greenwood Press, 1981); Sondra R. Herman, "Loving Courtship or the Marriage Market?: The Ideal and Its Critics, 1871–1911" (*American Quarterly* 25 [May 1973]: 360); Maureen Honey, *Creating Rosie the Riveter: Class, Gender, and Propaganda During World War II* (Amherst, Mass.: University of Massachusetss Press, 1964); J. Stanley Lemons, *The Woman Citizen: Social Feminism in the 1920s* (Urbana: University of Illinois Press, 1973); James R. McGovern, "The American Woman's Pre-World War I Freedom in Manners and Morals" (*Journal of American History* 55 [Sept. 1968]: 320); Sheila M. Rothman, *Women's Proper Place: A History of Changing Ideals and Practices, 1870 to the Present* (New York: Basic Books, 1978); and Leila J. Rupp, "Reflections on Twentieth-Century American Women's History" (*Reviews in American History* 9 [June 1981]: 279–81). An important work focusing directly on the South is Anne Firor Scott's *The Southern Lady from Pedestal to Politics, 1830–1930* (Chicago: University of Chicago Press, 1970).

Barbara J. Howe describes the origins of women's interests in preserving historic structures in "Women in Historic Preservation: The Legacy of Ann Pamela Cunningham" (*The Public Historian* 12 [Winter 1990]: 31–39).

History of Education

Teaching provided an escape route for many women, including Jessie Ball, in their quest for professional status and economic independence during the early decades of the twentieth century. Hence the history of education in this period is closely related to women's history. Especially relevant to Jessie Ball's career as a teacher is J. L. Blair Buck, *The Development of Public Schools in Virginia, 1607–1952* (Richmond: Virginia State Board of Education, 1952). More general but still useful studies are: Charles A. Harper, *A Century of Public Teacher Education* (Westport, Conn.: Greenwood Press, 1970); Jessie M. Pangburn, *The Evolution of the American Teachers College* (New York: Teachers College, Columbia University, 1932); and Thomas Woody, *A History of Women's Education in the United States* (New York: Octagon Books, 1966). Anne Firor Scott's "The Ever-Widening Circle: The Diffusion of Feminist Values for the Troy Female Seminary, 1822–1872" (*History of Education Quarterly* 10 [Spring 1970]: 3–25) cites characteristics closely resembling Jessie Ball's education.

INTERVIEWS

Most of Mrs. duPont's close friends and associates had died before research for this book began. With the help of Hazel Williams, I was able to find most of the survivors. All of the following provided human insights that never could have been extracted from the documents.

Mr. and Mrs. Charles C. Adams
Jean Adams (Mrs. Kennard)
Charles T. Akre
Robert Carter Ball
Jacob C. Belin
Charles E. Bennett
Mary Tyler Freeman Cheek
Sarah Dew (Mrs. Henry W.)
Ramona Edwards (Mrs. William T.)
Eli B. Fink
Frances Juhan Freeman
Sollace Freeman
Irvin P. Golden
Frederick H. Kent, Sr.
Arthur R. McKinstry
Elwyn Major
Minerva Mason (Mrs. Raymond K.)
Helen Mills (Mrs. William B.)
W. Thomas Rice
Polly Shands (Mrs. Alfred)
Seabury D. Stoneburner
Jessie Gresham Baker Thompson
William Taliaferro Thompson
Hazel O. Williams
Carl A. Zapffe
Denise duPont Zapffe

PHYSICAL SURVIVALS

The birthplace of Jessie Ball at Cressfield on Ball's Neck was destroyed by fire in 1907. Today the property is deserted except for the Ball family burial ground just east of where the house stood. A short distance up the road is the dilapidated shell of the Shiloh school, which the Ball children attended. Up the same dirt road some of the great homes where Jessie and her sisters enjoyed dances and parties are still standing in a rural setting perhaps much like that which the Ball family knew.

Across Dividing Creek from Ball's Neck is Ditchley, the historic Lee home that Mrs. duPont purchased in 1933. Ditchley is still furnished as it was in Mrs. DuPont's lifetime. Under the terms of her will, the house is maintained by the Alfred I. duPont Foundation as a residence for occasional visits by members of her family. Robert Carter Ball, Mrs. duPont's distant cousin, who lives in Wicomico Church, Virginia, conducts tours of the house by appointment.

Nemours, the 300-acre estate and mansion that Alfred built for his second wife, still stands in the northern suburbs of Wilmington. During her lifetime Mrs. duPont maintained the house essentially as it was when Alfred was living, and since her death the Nemours Foundation has done the same under the terms of Alfred's will. Thus the mansion has the character of a home although it still holds the many art treasures and furnishings that the duPonts collected and installed. The mansion and the gardens are open to visitors by appointment except during the winter months.

Also on the grounds of Nemours is the Alfred I. duPont Institute, the children's hospital, which is still in operation. The original building, completed under Mrs. duPont's direction in 1940, has been expanded with a large addition built since her death. Nearby is the carillon, once the tallest structure in Delaware, which is the tomb for Alfred, Jessie, and Ed Ball. The garage behind the mansion contains the automobiles that Mrs. duPont owned at the time of her death. The residence that she built for the Shandses is still in use by the institute.

The Delaware Trust Building, where Alfred and Jessie had their offices, is still standing in downtown Wilmington, but recent renovation of the eighth floor has obliterated any evidence of the offices as they looked before 1970.

Stratford Plantation in Virginia, the birthplace of Robert E. Lee, was the scene of Mrs. duPont's many pleasant meetings with the state directors and officers of the Memorial Foundation. The rustic Delaware cabin that Mrs. duPont had constructed at Stratford is still standing. Nearby is the Council House, which she helped to design and largely financed. The Jessie Ball duPont Library at Stratford was built after her death with a grant from her Fund.

In Jacksonville the only surviving structure related directly to Mrs. duPont is Epping Forest, the winter estate that she and Alfred built between San Jose Boulevard and the St. Johns River in South Jacksonville. Before her death Mrs. duPont transferred Epping Forest to the Alfred I. duPont Foundation, which later sold the property. A real estate development corporation purchased the mansion and the property in the 1980s and converted it into a residential community. The mansion has been extensively remodeled as the Epping Forest Yacht Club, but several rooms on the ground floor retain their original architectural detail. The gardens on the river front are maintained essentially as Alfred designed them.

To this list of survivals could be added the scores of buildings constructed, remodeled, or expanded with funds provided by Mrs. duPont or the fund. These structures, however, are the products of her philanthropy rather than reflections of her personality and life. For that reason, they are not included here.

Index

Library of Congress Cataloging-in-Publication Data

Hewlett, Richard Greening.
    Jessie Ball duPont / Richard Greening Hewlett.
      p.   cm.
    Includes bibliographical references and index.
    ISBN 0-8130-1134-5 (alk. paper)
    1. duPont, Jessie Ball, 1884–1970.   2. duPont, Alfred I., 1864–1935.
    3. Philanthropists—United States—Biography.   I. Title.
    HV28.D86H48   1992
    361.7'4'092—dc20
    [B]   92-3780
                                               CIP